The New Classical
Macroeconomics

The New Classical Macroeconomics

A Sceptical Inquiry

Kevin D. Hoover

Basil Blackwell

Copyright © Kevin D. Hoover 1988

First published 1988
Reprinted 1989
First published in paperback 1990

Reprinted in paperback 1991

Basil Blackwell Ltd
108 Cowley Road, Oxford OX4 1JF, UK

Basil Blackwell Inc.
3 Cambridge Center
Cambridge, Massachusetts 02142, USA

British Library Cataloguing in Publication Data
A CIP catalogue record for this book is available from the British Library.

Library of Congress Cataloging in Publication Data
Hoover, Kevin D.,
   The new classical macroeconomics: a sceptical inquiry
   Bibliography: p.
   Includes index.
   1. Macroeconomics. 2. Neoclassical school of
economics. I. Title.
HB172.5H66   1988   339   88–6056
ISBN 0–631–14605–9
ISBN 0–631–17263–7 (pbk.)

Typeset in 10 on 12pt Times
by Times Graphics, Singapore
Printed and Bound in Great Britain
T.J. Press (Padstow) Ltd, Padstow, Cornwall.

To Catherine, my wife

In this world things are beautiful only because they are not quite seen, or not perfectly understood.

Anthony Trollope, *Can You Forgive Her?*

Contents

List of Figures

Preface

The genesis of this book was two questions. The first was put to me at the beginning of my graduate studies by my supervisor, Peter Oppenheimer: why is Milton Friedman not a rational expectationist? At the time, the early new classical models of Lucas, Sargent and Wallace appeared to most observers to be a kind of radical monetarism; yet Friedman demurred. I discovered on close examination that there are important methodological differences between Friedman and the new classicals. This resulted in my article, 'Two Types of Monetarism' (*Journal of Economic Literature*, March 1984), which is largely reproduced as chapter 9, although I now believe that the title should be followed by a question mark.

The second question was put to me by Sue Corbett, then a commissioning editor for Basil Blackwell, publishers, who had recently read my article in the *Journal of Economic Literature*: would I be interested in writing a book on *conservative* macroeconomics? My immediate answer was, no! I did not then, and do not now, believe, whatever the political views of the principals, that monetarism or the new classical economics should be thought of as political ideologies. In Britain, particularly, 'monetarism' and 'monetarist' had become terms of abuse to be hurled at any policy or platform advocated by Mrs Thatcher's government or in any way, however vaguely, associated with Milton Friedman. This is unfortunate. Rational economic arguments, which I in fact found flawed, were dismissed because of their party label – the worst of possible reasons. I am reminded of a line from Sidney Hook: '*Before* impugning an opponent's motives, even when they may be legitimately impugned, answer his arguments' ('The Ethics of Controversy'). To dismiss Milton Friedman's monetary theories because one dislikes Mrs Thatcher's industrial policy or her union bashing, which stand on foundations completely unrelated – unless one digs very deep and very wide indeed – or to dismiss new classical economics because Patrick Minford sometimes gives advice to Her Majesty's Government struck me as the antithesis of reasonable debate.

In place of a book on conservative economics, I proposed a more extended examination of the new classical economics than I had managed in 'Two Types of Monetarism'. The principal concession to the idea of an ideologically classifiable book was my proposal to look at the relationship between the new classicals and the Austrian school (see chapter 10) as well as between the new classicals and the monetarists, while offering no comparable examination of Keynesian thought or any other more leftish school. Miss Corbett and Basil Blackwell approved the project.

The book is the beginning of an attempt to answer new classical arguments. It is not an answer; relatively more weight is given to understanding just what the new classical arguments are and, to some extent, exposing flaws in them than to offering worked-out alternatives. The book is subtitled, 'A Sceptical Inquiry', because that best expresses my attitude – not a true believer, but willing to learn and to understand.

In the absence of a worked-out alternative position to new classical thinking, my scepticism appears to some readers as sniping: 'A leaky roof is better than no roof at all.' But that is not quite the point: in order to know how to repair a roof or whether to construct a replacement, one must ascertain where it leaks and why. Diagnosis precedes cure.

From the beginning of my research, the identification of the new classical economics with the rational expectations hypothesis seemed wrong-headed. The rational expectations hypothesis is an essential, but derivative, new classical doctrine, and is used by many who are not new classical. Besides, the rational expectations hypothesis has been thoroughly examined in many books and articles over many years; another book devoted to the subject would be useless. Thus, while rational expectations are discussed in chapter 1 and in passing elsewhere, this book is devoted to other issues. New classical analyses of the labour market and business cycles are examined in part II (chapters 2 and 3). Monetary and fiscal policy – particularly, well-known and less well-known new classical policy-invariance propositions and their microfoundations – are considered in part III (chapters 4–6). The application of new classical principles to the econometric analysis of macroeconomic policy is investigated in part IV (chapter 8). Finally, the methodological foundations of new classicism are compared with those of monetarism and the Austrian school, with both of which it is often confused (chapters 9 and 10).

Much of the new classical literature is highly technical and, as is widely true in the economics profession, poorly written and obscured by unnecessary formalism. I have tried throughout to restate the main arguments in words or diagrams. Where I have used mathematics, it is little more advanced than elementary algebra. Statistics are employed in chapters 2 and 8, but only of the simplest kind. For all this simplification, my goal was not to sacrifice any necessary rigour. Others will have to judge how successful I have been. In any case, while derivations are occasionally long, and chains of verbal logic may require some attention, any reader having reached university should have no essential difficulty in following the argument.

I am indebted to a number of people for help at various stages of the writing. I have already mentioned Sue Corbett, to whom I should add Romesh Vaitilingam, who took over from her at Basil Blackwell when she moved on to new duties. Peter Oppenheimer not only asked the original question, but was my spur and number one critic for 'Two Types of Monetarism' as well as for other parts of the book in their earliest incarnations. Seth Masters, Milton Friedman and David Laidler provided useful criticism of that article. I would especially like to thank Moses Abramovitz, then editor of the *Journal of Economic Literature*, who ranks with Peter Oppenheimer as the midwife of 'Two Types of Monetarism'. My thanks to him were deleted – whether out of modesty or as a matter of editorial policy I cannot say – when it was originally published.

I am particularly grateful to my colleagues Thomas Mayer and Steven Sheffrin, to my student Jeffrey Bond, to Michael Artis and to an anonymous reader, who have carefully read and commented on the whole first draft. I thank Lawrence White, Peter Sinclair, Charles Goodhart, Jeroen Kremers, Wing Woo, Carl Galopin, Stephen LeRoy, Andrzej Brzeski and Gianluigi Pelloni, all of whom provided helpful comments on parts of earlier drafts, sometimes without knowing that they would eventually form parts of this book. Having received so much advice, I was obviously pulled in many ways. Many of the comments led to revisions; some of them were ignored; but even those which I found least congenial to my way of thinking and writing helped to clarify and sharpen the final product.

I thank Kailash Khandke, who has assiduously performed the necessary, but unenviable tasks, of checking my cross-references, reading the final draft and compiling the index. Thanks also to Petrina Ho, Kathleen Miner, Donna Raymond, Nicholas Ramsing and Dean MacKinnon for expert wordprocessing.

I acknowledge with thanks the permission of the American

Economic Association to use 'Two Types of Monetarism' (*Journal of Economic Literature*, Vol. 22, No. 1), most of which appears in an edited form in chapter 9 and a small part of which appears in chapter 1. I also acknowledge the permission of Oxford University Press to use 'Money, Prices and Finance in the New Monetary Economics' (*Oxford Economic Papers*, new series, Vol. 40, No. 1), which forms the basis of chapter 5.

Kevin D. Hoover

Part I   Introduction

1 The Varieties of Macroeconomics

1.1 The End of Orthodoxy

For about three decades after the end of the Second World War, Keynesian macroeconomics – particularly as interpreted in Sir John Hicks's celebrated essay 'Mr Keynes and the Classics' (1937) as the IS–LM model – was the orthodox view. It dominated the textbooks and formed the basis for most professional discussions of macro-economics, as well as the foundation for large-scale macroeconometric models which were increasingly relied upon to give advice on policy. But in the early 1970s this orthodoxy was shattered. Keynesian economics did, and still does, have its advocates, but several compet-ing schools of thought appeared (or reappeared). While none has overwhelmed the others with its unquestioned theoretical and empiri-cal success, the undisputed reign of Keynesian economics is over.

Keynesian dominance of macroeconomics ended because of the confluence of two factors – one theoretical and the other practical. The theoretical factor was the unhappiness – widespread among pro-fessional economists – with the absence of microfoundations for macroeconomics.

The desire for microfoundations was expressed indirectly in the work of some of Keynes's early critics. Leontief (1936), for example, argued on the basis of microeconomic theory that involuntary unemployment in Keynes's model was inconsistent with rational behaviour on the part of workers. It must be the result of 'money illusion'.[1] Earlier Hicks had argued that the main obstacle to progress in monetary theory was the failure to provide a basis for it in microeconomic value theory.[2] His *Value and Capital* (1939) attempts to apply microeconomic theory to a number of Keynesian and macroeconomic topics.

After the Second World War, at the same time that Keynesian macroeconomics began to dominate the profession, a number of economists began to search more earnestly for microfoundations for aggregate economic relationships. The most famous examples are the life-cycle and permanent-income theories of the consumption function, which sought to derive observed consumption–income relationships from rational individual behaviour.[3] On a different tack, Don Patinkin attempted to answer Hicks's call for an integration of monetary and value theories by incorporating real money balances into a general equilibrium model.[4] Macroeconomic models based on this microeconomic framework invariably result in labour markets clearing in equilibrium, i.e. there is no involuntary unemployment in equilibrium. Patinkin concluded, therefore, that Keynesian economics was the economics of disequilibrium.

Robert Clower reached similar conclusions for the consumption function.[5] The Keynesian consumption function, which relates consumption to current income, is not, he argues, compatible with general equilibrium. In general equilibrium, individual demand functions should be functions of prices only, not of current income, as income is derived endogenously from factor prices and available endowments. Once again, Keynesian economics appears to be the economics of disequilibrium. Clower's paper spawned an extensive research programme in disequilibrium or fixed-price models.[6]

The disequilibrium approach seeks to tease Keynesian notions out of microeconomic models by making limited adjustments to their underlying assumptions. An alternative approach saw the problem somewhat differently. Instead of altering the standard assumptions of microeconomics, it would be better to recognize that Keynesian constructs such as the consumption function or involuntary unemployment are not features of reality but theoretical interpretations of reality and may very well be dispensed with. The alternative is to embrace market-clearing microeconomics fully and to explain variations in consumption and employment as the optimal decisions of rational economic agents. Lucas and Rapping first suggested such an approach to unemployment and consciously or unconsciously began a revival of pre-Keynesian or classical economic analysis.[7] The strength and appeal of this market-clearing approach is the major theoretical factor in the demise of Keynesian orthodoxy.

The second factor was more practical. Keynes himself had relatively little to say about inflation. Keynesian economists nevertheless incorporated the inverse empirical relationship between inflation and unemployment, uncovered by A. W. Phillips, into their analysis. The 'Phillips curve' was taken to indicate that unemployment could be lowered simply by allowing a somewhat higher rate of inflation.

Economists offered advice to policy makers on the basis of estimated Phillips curves. Unfortunately, in the early 1970s both the rate of inflation and the rate of unemployment rose to new heights. The Phillips curve no longer appeared to be stable.

Milton Friedman and Edmund Phelps had independently anticipated this problem.[8] They argued that there is no *permanent* trade-off between inflation and unemployment. Instead, unemployment tends to its market-clearing rate (*pace* Keynes, it is not involuntary). Increased inflation can lower the unemployment rate only for as long as people mistake higher absolute prices for higher relative prices for the goods or labour which they wish to sell. Friedman and Phelps assumed that in the long run people would not mistake absolute and relative prices, and that they would come to anticipate correctly the effects of inflation. The long run might, however, be fairly far in the future, so that there might still be substantial room for temporarily lowering unemployment at the expense of higher inflation.

Expectations are critical to Friedman's and Phelps's argument that there is no long-run trade-off between inflation and unemployment. They both assume that people form their expectations of future inflation on the basis of past inflation in such a manner that their expectations only gradually converge on the true value. Because people are fooled about inflation until their expectations do finally converge, there remains a short-run trade-off between unemployment and inflation. Lucas, and later Sargent, argued that if people's expectations were persistently and systematically mistaken – as they would be on Friedman's or Phelps's hypotheses about their formation – they could not be considered rational.[9] A rational agent would learn from his mistakes, and would not repeat the same mistake again and again.

In order to integrate this idea into formal economic models, Lucas and Sargent adopt John Muth's technique of 'rational expectations'.[10] Expectations are 'rational' within a model if they are the same as the model's own predictions. Incorporation of rational expectations into the analysis of the Phillips curve led to a startling result. While an unexpected rise in inflation would still be associated with a fall in unemployment, expected rises would not, and any systematic attempt to generate inflation would produce only expected inflation so that intentional manipulation of macroeconomic policy could not be expected to lower unemployment.[11] Macroeconomic policy was declared to be ineffective.

Keynesian economics had largely been directed at giving policy advice. Thus the analysis of stagflation, which eventually led to the incorporation of rational expectations into macroeconomic models, was the second important factor in the demise of Keynesian orthodoxy.

Although it came to be widely used even in otherwise Keynesian models, many economists saw the rational expectations hypothesis as closely related to the idea of market-clearing economics. Both were considered to be implications of the assumption of optimization on the part of rational economic agents. Joined together, these two assumptions formed the foundation of what came to be called the *new classical macroeconomics*. The exact origin of this term is obscure.[12] While recognizable new classical analysis was prominent throughout the 1970s, its advocates were then generally referred to as 'rational expectationists'. Unfortunately, this term fails to distinguish Keynesian and eclectic economists who use rational expectations as a convenient technique for modelling from those who use it because they believe that macroeconomic models are legitimate only if they possess market-clearing microfoundations grounded in individual rationality. The term 'new classical' used to refer to this latter group gained currency only in the 1980s.

1.2 Schools of Macroeconomic Thought

Keynes remarked that, in referring to such disparate economists as Ricardo, Mill and Marshall by the single term 'classical', he was perhaps perpetrating a solecism.[13] To apply the term 'new classical' to the advocates of market-clearing macroeconomics may simply be to compound the error a stage further. Although in this and later chapters we shall investigate the relationship between the new classical school and some other schools, a full inquiry along those lines would take us too deeply into the history of economic thought and well beyond the purposes of this book. It is nevertheless appropriate to ask exactly what is *new* and what is *classical* about the new classical economics.

To answer this question it is useful to survey the competing schools of macroeconomic thought in order to discern better how the new classical macroeconomics is distinguished from them. Any attempt to assign economists to particular well-defined schools is bound to be a Procrustean enterprise. Any economist is described most fully by a vector of characteristics. A definition emphasizes some elements of this vector, while playing down related ones. Another definition might take the related elements to be more important. The borders of such categories are bound to be poorly defined. Definitions may necessarily be arbitrary to some degree. Still, the attempts to formulate them need not be sterile. The members of a school may bear only a family resemblance to each other; nevertheless, the attempt to classify them yields clarification of the nature of alternative views of the economic process as a by-product. That being said, let us now try to place the new classicals among the principal schools of macroeconomic thought.

Keynes and the Classics

Many debates between Keynesians and anti-Keynesians from the 1930s to the 1970s hinged upon the slopes of one or other of the curves from which the IS and LM curves are derived. Debates about whether or not the investment function or the demand-for-money function were interest elastic obscured the fact that the fundamental difference between Keynesian and classical economics was to be found in the analysis of aggregate supply and not of aggregate demand.

The simplest way to think about the difference between Keynes and the classics is to concentrate on the labour market. For the classics all prices, including wages, were perfectly flexible in the absence of interference such as government regulation, unions, cartels or monopolies. In the face of incipient unemployment, money wages could be expected to fall until all those who wished to work at the going wage rate would be employed. The implications for aggregate supply are straightforward. Figure 1.1 shows a classical aggregate supply curve. It plots real output against nominal prices. It is a vertical line at the level of output corresponding to full employment or a clearing labour market. If prices rise, the real wage will fall and employers will wish to hire more labour. But since workers are supplying all the labour they wish to supply at the old real wage, some of them will choose not to work at a lower real wage and, in any case, no additional labour will be forthcoming. The demand for labour will exceed supply, and this situation will continue until the nominal wage is bid up by the same proportion as prices. At this point, the old real wage is restored, the labour market is again in equilibrium and full-employment output remains at its old level.

Keynes argued that, while wages and prices were not inflexible, they

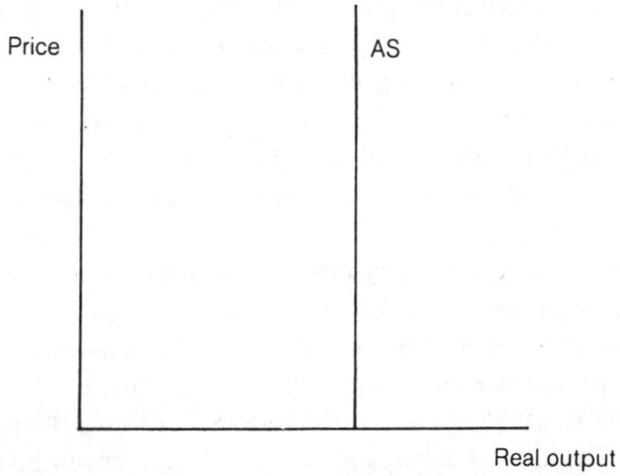

[Marginal handwritten notes:]

Classic

at full employment, if P↑ no workers available to hire.

$\frac{w_0}{P_0}$

if · P↑ to P_1

⇒ $\frac{w_0}{P_0}$ ↓ to $\frac{w_0}{P_1}$

⇒ $L^D > L^S$

⇒ w↑ to w_1

⇒ $\frac{w_0}{P_1}$ ↑ to $\frac{w_1}{P_1}$

$\frac{w_1}{P_1} = \frac{w_0}{P_0}$

Keynes

Figure 1.1   The classical aggregate supply curve

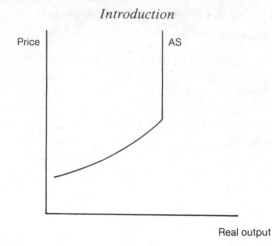

Figure 1.2   The Keynesian aggregate supply curve

did not move in such a manner as to clear the labour market. Although
he believed that there were reasons why this was so which were
consistent with rationality, he ultimately took it to be simply a fact
that workers were sometimes involuntarily unemployed. In such cases
employers would be able to hire more workers without offering a
higher wage – indeed they may well be able to hire more workers at a
real wage lower than its current level. This too has straightforward
implications for the aggregate supply curve. Figure 1.2 shows a
Keynesian aggregate supply curve. The upward-sloping segment
corresponds to less than full employment. In this range, if prices rise,
the real wage falls and employers find it desirable to hire more
workers. Because there is unemployment, workers are forthcoming
and generate additional output. If prices were to continue to rise, the
real wage would ultimately fall to its market-clearing level. At this
point workers would no longer be forthcoming at lower real wages and
the classical analysis would apply. This explains the vertical segment
in the aggregate supply curve in figure 1.2. It is precisely because his
analysis of aggregate supply embraced both the case of unemployment
and the classical case of full employment that Keynes referred to his
theory as *general*.

The vertical aggregate supply curve provides an adequate capsuliz-
ation of the classical view. Yet it is unlikely to have appealed to
classical economists as an analytical tool. The reason is that they did
not typically think of *aggregate* output, but rather of the output of
individual firms. Although they did use the construct of an aggregate
price level, it was almost always in the context of monetary theory, e.g.
in Fisher's quantity equation $MV = PT$. The fundamental division for

the classicals was between value theory (the theory of the consumer or of the firm at a disaggregated level) and aggregate monetary theory. The vertical aggregate supply curve reflects the limited connection between the real side of the economy (the province of value theory) and the monetary side. Changes in the level of the stock of money would change the general level of prices, but, because money was thought to be neutral over some time-horizon, relative prices and the levels of employment and output would not be affected.

Keynes sought to alter the topography of economic theory in two ways. First, he wished to replace the distinction between value theory and monetary theory by a distinction between the theory of output as a whole and the theory of the individual consumer or firm. Although he did not invent the terms, Keynes was the first to introduce the commonplace division of the discipline into microeconomics and macroeconomics. Second, he wished to provide a theory in which the monetary and real sides of the economy were directly linked, so that the stock of money mattered for more than just the general level of prices.

The Neoclassical Synthesis

Keynes's new macroeconomic theory was welcome because it seemed to fill the yawning gap between economic analysis and the real-world problem of the Great Depression. It offered a plausible explanation and a feasible course of action. The profession, wedded to pre-Keynesian value theory, was nevertheless unhappy, and soon launched what Clower somewhat oddly calls the 'Keynesian counter-revolution'.[14] The early shots in the counter-revolution were fired by Leontief, who saw Keynes's theory as the special case in which workers suffered from 'money illusion', and Hicks, who saw it as the special case in which the economy was caught in a liquidity trap. For Hicks, '. . . the General Theory of Employment is the Economics of Depression'.[15] Both Leontief and Hicks thought that a truly general theory would be a general equilibrium theory. For Leontief this clearly meant a disaggregated Walrasian theory, while Hicks seemed willing to admit a more aggregated general equilibrium.

The counter-revolution culminated in the so-called 'neoclassical synthesis', which in turn became the standard textbook approach to macroeconomics.[16] The idea behind the neoclassical synthesis was that the Keynesian analysis explains unemployment and suggests remedies. Once full employment is established, however (i.e. once we are back to the vertical segment of the aggregate supply curve), the classical analysis of resource allocation, income distribution and welfare economics, all of which are grounded in microeconomics, becomes relevant. The neoclassical synthesis was a schizophrenic approach to economics – a way of subscribing to both Keynesian and classical analysis.

As the dominant view, the neoclassical synthesis faced its own analytical problems and followed its own logic of development. Its most famous addition to the 'tool kit' of economic analysis was the Phillips curve, already mentioned in section 1.1. The Phillips curve was a 'Keynesian' construct only in the sense that some people who called themselves Keynesian thought it necessary to incorporate it into their analysis.[17]

Monetarism

The Keynesian analysis and the neoclassical synthesis repudiate the quantity theory of money and monetary neutrality, at least in states of unemployment (i.e. the upward-sloping portion of the aggregate supply curve). Not every economist was willing to join in this attack on classical analysis. The quantity theory was kept alive throughout the 1950s and 1960s by Milton Friedman and his colleagues at the University of Chicago.[18] With the apparent breakdown of the Phillips curve in the early 1970s, the quantity theory now associated with a school of economic thought called 'monetarism' once again enjoyed wider currency.

Defining 'monetarism' and deciding who was and who was not a monetarist became for a time a kind of intellectual parlour game.[19] Despite the multiplication of criteria for inclusion in the category 'monetarist', just two will adequately identify the monetarist for most purposes. First, a monetarist believes that in the long run markets clear, i.e. the long-run aggregate supply curve is vertical. Monetarists are thus a subspecies of classical economists. Second, monetarists believe that money causally dominates prices and nominal income. Inflation for Friedman, the prototypical monetarist, is always and everywhere a monetary phenomenon.[20] Unlike many other classicals, but like Keynes, most monetarists are relatively at ease working at a high level of aggregation.

The distinction between the long run and the short run is extremely important for monetarist analysis. In the long run, the real side of the economy is independent of the monetary side, as it typically is for other classicals: the level of the stock of money is of no importance. In the short run, however, monetarists typically believe that money has powerful effects. Figure 1.3 clarifies their position. The long-run aggregate supply curve is shown as a vertical line. The short-run aggregate supply curve is shown sloping upwards as a result of incorrect expectations ('money illusion') on the part of workers.

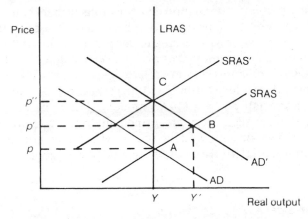

Figure 1.3   The monetarist analysis of aggregate supply and demand

Suppose that the economy was in equilibrium at point A in figure 1.3. An increase in aggregate demand because of an increase in the supply of money would shift the aggregate demand curve from AD to AD', and would raise output from Y to Y' and prices from p to p' as the equilibrium moved out along the short-run aggregate supply curve (SRAS) to point B. As workers' expectations came to coincide with the actual level of prices, the short-run aggregate supply curve would gradually shift upwards until long-run equilibrium was reached at point C, with output again at its old level Y and prices even higher at p''.

This analysis of the short-run and long-run aggregate supply is what lies at the heart of the monetarist argument that the Phillips curve will not remain invariant to changes in the underlying rate of inflation. The estimated Phillips curve can be thought of as a short-run aggregate supply curve translated in a fairly obvious way into inflation–unemployment space rather than price–output space.

Some important monetarists place a premium on the practical applicability of their economic analysis. Consequently, they are unsympathetic to disaggregated general equilibrium analysis, preferring to take a Marshallian partial equilibrium approach. While this is perhaps the critical methodological issue between the monetarists and the new classicals, it will be dealt with in detail in chapter 9 and need not concern us further here.

Monetarism and the Neoclassical Synthesis

The monetarists and the Keynesians have reached a theoretical accord. The dominant view in both schools is that the differences between them revolve around empirical questions rather than matters of theoretical principle.[21] This is perhaps best exemplified, on the one side, by the willingness of Keynesians to adopt the monetarist notions of the natural rate of unemployment and the vertical long-run Phillips curve as ways of making their models relevant to periods of stagflation. On the other side, Milton Friedman's 'theoretical framework' is essentially a specialized IS–LM–AS model.[22] The remaining theoretical differences between them are principally questions about how self-correcting the economic system is and whether or not money is sufficiently differentiated from other assets to be singled out for special treatment.

The New Classical Macroeconomics

When the rational expectations hypothesis was first applied to the analysis of the Phillips curve, the new classical macroeconomics was seen simply as a sort of radical monetarism. The plausibility of this interpretation can be made clear with the new classical analysis of aggregate supply shown in figure 1.4. Figure 1.4 is similar to figure 1.3 except that the short-run aggregate supply curves have been replaced by virtual aggregate supply (VAS) curves (broken curves). Movements along the virtual aggregate supply curve are the result of 'money illusion'. They are *virtual* because the hypothesis of rational expectations rules out movements along such curves lasting for more than the time that it takes to correct inadvertent random errors. They might then be thought of as *very short-run* aggregate supply curves. If we start in equilibrium at A, and an increase in the money supply moves the

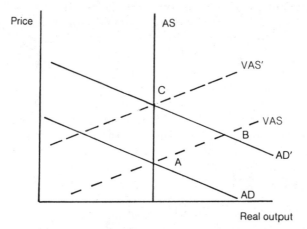

Real output

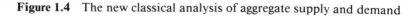

Figure 1.4   The new classical analysis of aggregate supply and demand

aggregate demand curve from AD to AD', there are two possibilities. If the shift in aggregate demand is correctly anticipated, equilibrium moves immediately to C. If it is unexpected, equilibrium moves to B and then to C as the error is uncovered, just as it does for the monetarist. The difference between the new classical analysis and the monetarist analysis, however, is that equilibrium remains only fleetingly at B and moves quickly to C when the error is discovered. Rational expectations is the hypothesis that such errors are discovered with almost no delay.

The analysis of aggregate supply and aggregate demand gives the approximate flavour of the new classical economics and reveals its kindred spirit with other subspecies of classical economics. It does not, however, do justice to what most distinguishes the new classicals from other related schools – namely the relentless drive for microfoundations. Aggregate curves, the new classicals believe, are crude heuristic devices that do not reveal the underlying behaviour of optimizing individuals. As a result, such curves should not be treated as stable invariant relations and must not form the foundations of any fundamental economic analysis.[23]

It would be a mistake to conclude, however, that the new classicals are simply monetarists with microfoundations. There is a range of views within the new classical school. Monetarists generally believe that money is neutral in the long run and that it has direct causal effects on the economy in the short run. Such a position is endorsed by such a prominent new classical as Lucas.[24] Sargent and Wallace, however, in their work on the foundations of monetary theory, advocate models in which neutrality often fails to hold.[25] New classical advocates of real business cycle models relegate the relationship between money and prices to the status of a non-causal epiphenomenon.[26] Sorting out the varieties of new classical economics is a principal aim of this book.

1.3   The New Classical Economics Defined

The Tenets of New Classicism

So far we have sketched how the new classical economics arose as a reaction to the Keynesian orthodoxy and to economic events. We have also tried to place the new classical economics into its proper relationship with other current schools of economic thought. It would be useful now to state more positively what features mark an economist out as an adherent to the new classical school.

Three tenets are keys to the new classical doctrine. First, agents' real economic decisions – for example, about savings, consumption or investment – are based solely on real, not nominal or monetary, factors. Second, agents are, to the limits of their information, consistent and successful optimizers, i.e. they are continuously in equilibrium. Third, agents make no *systematic* errors in evaluating the economic environment, i.e. they hold rational expectations.

Many economists would accept the first of these tenets. It simply marks the new classicals out as classical. The apparent radicalism of the new classicals derives from the second tenet. Most classical economists treat equilibrium as a limiting case; new classical economists treat it as always obtaining. Some interpret the Austrian doctrine of Mises, Hayek, Lachmann and others to be compatible with this tenet. The new classicals are then seen as neo-Austrians. Whether this attribution is apt is a central question addressed in chapter 10.

The Role of Rational Expectations

The rational expectations hypothesis is perhaps the most striking feature of the new classical doctrine. It is not, however, the principal topic of this book, and it has been thoroughly discussed elsewhere.[27] Yet the hypothesis plays such an important role in many of the arguments which will concern us in later chapters that it is useful to say more about it here.

The universally accepted formulation is due to John Muth: 'Expectations . . . tend to be distributed, for the same information set, about the prediction of the theory (or the "objective" probability distribution of outcomes).'[28] Muth claims that this hypothesis involves three assertions: first, information is scarce and the economic system does not waste it; second, expectations are formed from the specific structure of the relevant system describing the economy; and third, public predictions can have no substantial effects unless there is 'inside' information, i.e. a (true) economic forecast does not give anyone a special opportunity to profit from it if it is known to everyone.

Muth's notion of an information set can be taken broadly, but if taken too broadly it is of little use. Typically the information set is defined to include all the exogenous variables, all past values of the endogenous variables and, crucially, the structure of the model (i.e. Muth's 'relevant system'). This amounts to claiming that the model adequately captures those features of the world relevant to the formation of expectations, and that agents act *as if* they know the model when forming their expectations.

A serious question arises about how we are to understand rational expectations as statements about economic reality. There are at least two interpretations of the hypothesis. A weak form is that people do the best they can with the information that they have. Lucas calls this interpretation 'vacuous'.[29] Vacuous or not, this interpretation can be restated as people learn from their mistakes and do not persist in them, and in such a form it is the most plausible version of the rational expectations hypothesis. It is not clear, however, that this weak form actually implies the mathematical properties of Muth's hypothesis. In any case, in this version, specifying the exact process by which people learn from their mistakes is obviously important and is usually omitted.

A strong form of the rational expectations hypothesis would be that people actually know the structure of the model that truly describes the world and use it to form their expectations. This is a 'strong' form because it seems to imply that the man in the street performs calculations in his head that economists find conceptually difficult and often mathematically intractable.

Lucas, however, describes this form as 'silly'. 'The term "rational expectations", as Muth used it,' he writes, 'refers to a consistency axiom for economic models, so it can be given precise meaning only in the context of specific models.'[30] This view leaves open the question of how models relate to the real world, for a model is useful precisely to the degree that it isolates certain important features of the world in a way that accurately describes their behaviour. If rational expectations is just a consistency criterion for modellers which makes no claim to capture how people in the real world act, it is difficult to see why new classicals believe that any acceptable model *must* incorporate rational expectations. The usual fallback position is Friedman's line that the truth of a hypothesis does not matter as long as it generates true predictions.[31] What is important is that people act as if they had rational expectations, and not that they actually use a model to generate their expectations. Friedman's thesis is philosophically suspect.[32] What is more, it undercuts the new classical belief that any acceptable model must incorporate rational expectations, because a model with a good predictive record without rational expectations would meet Friedman's criterion.

It is sometimes said that the case for rational expectations is precisely the same as the case for the assumption of utility maximization in economics: rationality requires both. The persuasive use of the adjective 'rational' is no doubt intended to reinforce this connection. Of course, the assumption of utility maximization is not itself unquestioned. But even if it were, it is not at all clear that the hypothesis of rational expectations is derivable from general assumptions of rationality. Frank Hahn points out that to jump from '. . . the respectable proposition that an agent will not persist in expectations which are systematically disappointed . . .' to the proposition that '. . . agents have expectations which are not systematically disappointed [is a] non sequitur of a rather obvious kind'.[33] Furthermore, there are alternative hypotheses about expectations which are consistent and which, in some instances, seem to have better support than rational expectations.[34]

While the rational expectations hypothesis is a fundamental part of the new classical economics, it is nevertheless independent of the other tenets. A new classical economist necessarily believes in rational expectations, but a belief in rational expectations by itself is not sufficient for one to be a new classical. In his survey of the new classical macroeconomics, Sargent characterizes it as going beyond *ad hoc* supply and demand curves.[35] He argues that, in order to explain the behaviour of macroeconomic aggregates, we must go back to the underlying objective functions and the constraints that agents face. In a static framework, this requires the first two tenets of the new classical doctrine – that only real phenomena count, and that agents are consistent and successful optimizers.

The importance of the rational expectations hypothesis is to carry these features over to the dynamic problem. If agents are to optimize over their future behaviour, their expectations of the future are bound to be important. Rational expectations implies that what they *do* expect is (within a serially uncorrelated error) what the true model says they *should* expect. This guarantees that they will be consistent and successful.

Not everyone who uses the rational expectations hypothesis should be classified as new classical. The principle of rational expectations can be employed by anyone seeking a convenient and, in some sense, neutral way of introducing endogenous expectations into an economic model. One may adhere to the rational expectations hypothesis, yet violate the other tenets by, for example, holding that prices are not flexible or that agents do not optimize.[36] Fischer, for example, constructs a model in which long-term wage contracts produce nominal wage rigidity, which in turn permits monetary policy to have real effects since real wages then depend on price movements.[37] This violates the first tenet of the new classical economics. Lucas criticizes Fischer's model for supposing wage rigidity, rather than explaining it as the outcome of an optimizing decision consistent with the second tenet.[38]

1.4 Where Do We Go from Here?

Having laid out a bare description of the most important tenets of new classical thought, most of the remainder of the book will be devoted to elaborating on and examining the application of this doctrine to particular issues in macroeconomics. The book is divided into five parts consisting of nine additional chapters.

The labour market and business cycles are discussed in part II. The earliest application of new classical principles – the analysis of the Phillips curve – is presented in detail in chapter 2. The influential idea that economic fluctuations may be attributable to the difficulties that people have in processing the information conveyed by nominal prices (i.e. that noise in the monetary system explains output fluctuations) was first stated in this context. It is but a small step from this idea to the hope that complete models of the business cycle can be built around monetary misinformation. Therefore both new classical *monetary* models of the business cycle and some recent, albeit equally new classical, alternative *real* models are examined in chapter 3, which ends with an examination of how both sorts of new classical models have assumed away the important problem of unemployment.

The original new classical work on the Phillips curve was extended in two directions: to the analysis of business cycles and to the analysis of monetary and fiscal policy. Monetary theory and policy are considered in part III.

The new classical economics first became prominent with its claim that monetary policy could not systematically improve the performance of the economy. That claim, as well as several other limitations on the conduct of macroeconomic policy that new classical economists believe a correct analysis imposes, is examined in chapter 4.

The monetary theory underlying new classical business cycle models and claims for the ineffectiveness of macroeconomic policy are usually not specified in great detail. Yet a fundamental new classical belief is that no theory is secure until it is reduced to its microfoundations. One aspect of the so-called new monetary economics, as we shall call new classical approaches to the integration of monetary and value theory, is considered in chapter 5. Eugene Fama and others have attempted to apply modern theories of finance to monetary theory. These stress that money is a transactions medium, but because there are other transactions media (say current accounts or demand deposits at banks), it is feasible to have economies without money and therefore without inflation. Since the price of money is simply the inverse of the price of goods, control of the narrow money supply (cash base) should yield control of the price level. Other assets are not important for control of the price level unless government restrictions give them a significance that they would not otherwise have. Even cash turns out to be valuable only because of government intervention. This argument is explained in detail in chapter 5 and is shown to be deeply flawed.

Fama's model is informal. Varieties of the new monetary economics that employ more formal models are examined in chapter 6. Two models are considered in some detail. The first is the overlapping-generations model. Here money acts as a store of value, and is used to overcome the 'friction' that some trades between generations would be infeasible without money. A major conclusion of this literature is that non-interest-bearing money is held in preference to other assets with a higher rate of return only because of government regulation. It is therefore similar to Fama's model as providing a basis for a 'legal-restrictions' theory of the demand for money. The second variety of model examined in chapter 6 models money's function as a trans-actions medium as well as a store of value by explicitly imposing the requirement that purchases must be financed by cash held prior to the purchase. Within this context it is possible to provide more formal models of money and finance. Such finance-constrained models generate conclusions strikingly different from those of the other approaches.

The models of chapters 5 and 6 provide the theoretical under-pinning for new classical monetary theory. These models as well as models of fiscal policy are used in chapter 7 in order to investigate the basis of new classical policy advice. New classical claims for the correctness of Ricardian equivalence (i.e. the irrelevance of govern-ment financing), of the irrelevance of open-market operations and for the real bills doctrine are examined and assessed.

From early on, new classical economists have argued that their principles have strong implications for the conduct of empirical economics. New classical econometrics is investigated in part IV which consists of chapter 8 only. A non-technical explication of two distinct threads in new classical econometrics – pure time-series modelling and structural modelling – is presented, beginning with a critical appraisal of the concept of Granger-causality, which is not itself an exclusively new classical technique but which is widely applied by new classical economists. Some important early econo-metric work which highlights a number of issues for new classical econometrics is then considered. Among these issues is the problem of observational equivalence, i.e. the fact that very different underlying theories (say, theories with and without rational expectations) have the same empirical implications. Another related issue, policy non-invariance or the Lucas critique, is examined in detail and various new classical strategies for dealing with it are discussed and criticized.

Parts II–IV are a presentation and assessment of the bulk of the substance of the new classical macroeconomics. The final part, part V, is a critical examination of the underlying presuppositions of new classical methodology. This is partly a further exercise in locating the new classicals in the landscape of rival schools of thought. More importantly, it is an attempt to discover the implicit methodological principles of the new classical school by isolating those features that distinguish the new classicals from other schools which, on the surface at least, appear to be closely related. In chapter 9 the methodology of the new classicals is compared with that of the monetarists with whom they are sometimes confused. Here it is argued that the new classicals are Walrasian in the sense that only a comprehensive economic analysis can ever be taken as acceptable, while the monetarists are Marshallian. Some commentators have taken the methodological individualism and the emphasis on rationality of the new classicals as evidence that they are a variety of neo-Austrian. This interpretation is explored and rejected in the final chapter, chapter 10, principally on the grounds that the new classicals' understanding of rationality is radically different from that of the Austrians and that their commitment to methodological individualism is partly illusory.

Part II   The Labour Market and Business Cycles

2 Clearing Labour Markets

2.1 The Phillips Curve and the Natural Rate Hypothesis

Keynesian macroeconomics was born into the Great Depression, a period of falling prices. While Keynes and his followers were aware that stimulation of aggregate demand in the face of full employment could lead to inflation, they were generally unconcerned with inflation because full employment seemed so far away.[1] After the Second World War, however, when developed economies were by and large fully employed, the absence of a well-developed theory of inflation became an acute problem for Keynesian economics. The Phillips curve, which related the rate of wage inflation to the level of unemployment, was widely, though wrongly, seen as filling this gap.

A. W. Phillips undertook an empirical investigation (1958) of the relationship between the level of unemployment and the rate of change of nominal wages in the United Kingdom over the period 1861–1957.[2] Phillips hypothesized that the tighter the labour market the more rapidly employers would have to raise wages in order to attract new employees and retain the old ones. He guessed that the relationship was non-linear, as well as different in the short run than in the long run. In order to capture these features, he fitted a hyperbola to data averaged over individual trade cycles, and he discovered that the relationship was remarkably stable over this period of nearly 100 years.

Phillips's original curve is most accurately understood as the long-run relationship between the rate of change of wages and the level of the unemployment rate given that the *rate of change* of the unemployment rate is zero. By averaging his data over the trade cycle, Phillips generated data for which periods of rising and falling unemployment rates more or less cancelled. The systematic deviations of the annual data from the curve fit through the cycle averages confirm that the

Phillips curve is an abstraction from short-run behaviour.[3] Further-more, Phillips carefully excluded periods of high inflation from his estimates and analysis on the ground that the wage-setting process would incorporate price inflation above a certain moderate level.[4] An estimated Phillips curve would not then be expected to remain stable during episodes of high inflation.

Because the curve represents exactly those combinations of unemployment and wage inflation for which the rate of unemployment does not change, movement along the Phillips curve from, say, a higher to a lower rate of unemployment is not an option on this interpretation. Nonetheless, after Samuelson and Solow's paper 'Analytical Aspects of Anti-inflation Policy' (1960), the standard interpretation of the Phillips curve represented it as an exploitable trade-off between unemployment and inflation – a menu of choices for the policy maker. Samuelson and Solow also began the tradition of relating the rate of change of prices rather than wages to unemployment, arguing that prices are connected to wages through a simple mark-up relation. Once their interpretation of the Phillips curve became standard, empirical estimates were made for virtually every country for which data were available. The inverse relationship between inflation and unemployment was reproduced in almost every case. Phillips's caveats about the instability of the relationship in the face of high inflation were virtually forgotten.

During the 1960s and 1970s Phillips curves were integrated into macroeconometric models and widely used in the analysis of government macroeconomic policy. Before the end of the 1960s, however, their usefulness for these tasks was called into question. In his presidential address to the American Economic Association, Milton Friedman (1968a) argued that the possibility of securing lower unemployment in exchange for higher inflation, which the standard interpretation of the Phillips curve implied, was chimerical in all but the short run.[5] Friedman's argument was based upon the application of general principles of neoclassical economics, rather than upon a particular model of the economy.

Friedman argued that rational workers do not suffer from money illusion, i.e. relative (real) rather than absolute prices should matter to them. Furthermore, the fundamental relationship is between the level of real wages and the levels of employment and participation in the labour force and therefore unemployment. Phillips thus stands convicted in Friedman's eyes of making two elementary errors in economic analysis. First, the Phillips curve should relate the rate of unemployment to changes in the *real* not the nominal wage rate, and second the long-run relationship should be between the level of the wage rate and the rate of unemployment and not between *changes* in the wage rate and the rate of unemployment.[6] If the Phillips curve were plotted with the rate of change of nominal wages on the vertical axis and the rate of unemployment on the horizontal axis, then economic theory demands, according to Friedman, that it be a vertical line at the equilibrium or *natural rate of unemployment*.

Friedman defines the natural rate of unemployment as

> ... the level that would be ground out by the Walrasian system of general equilibrium equations, provided there is imbedded in them the actual characteristics of the labour and commodity markets, including market imperfections, stochastic variability in demands and supplies, the cost of gathering information about job vacancies and labour availabilities, the costs of mobility, and so on.[7]

The natural rate therefore is the equilibrium rate of unemployment to which the stable private economy tends to return once disruptive influences, such as attempts of governments to manipulate aggregate demand, are removed. Friedman believes that the economy is usually reasonably close to the natural rate and, when displaced from it, tends to return to it.

Estimated downward-sloping Phillips curves, Friedman maintains, are short-run phenomena – disequilibrium deviations from the natural rate of unemployment. Friedman's explanation relies on workers mistaking changes in their nominal wages for changes in real wages. Such mistakes, he believes, are bound to be temporary. Suppose that after a period of full employment with zero inflation (or any other constant rate of inflation) government policy stimulates aggregate demand. At first, output and the price of output both rise somewhat. Firms are then willing to hire more workers and to offer them higher nominal wages. As long as prices rise faster than wages, firms perceive that the real wage that they must pay to workers has fallen, which is what makes them willing to produce more and employ more workers. Unlike firms, the workers in Friedman's view will not at first notice that the prices have risen, and so will judge their real wage to have risen, which makes them willing to supply more labour. The rate of unemployment therefore falls. But workers cannot be fooled indefinitely. Once they begin to perceive that prices have risen and that the underlying rate of inflation is higher, they will revise their estimate of their real wage and will notice that it is actually lower than before. This encourages them to withdraw labour and to push for higher nominal wages in order to compensate for the inflation. The excess demand for labour then leads firms to offer higher wages, and higher wages encourage them to reduce output and employment back to their natural rates.

For any constant, and therefore correctly anticipated, rate of inflation, the natural rate hypothesis implies that there is no trade-off between unemployment and inflation. Any short-run trade-off requires mistakes about the future course of inflation. Such mistakes, Friedman believes, may persist for some time, but gradually workers adjust their expectations and the downward-sloping Phillips curve converges to the long-run Phillips curve, which is vertical at the natural rate of unemployment.

Friedman's analysis seemed remarkably prescient. Phillips curves estimated in the early 1960s continued to fit well until the early 1970s – a few years after Friedman's address. But this was a period of moderate inflation and so in line with his prediction. When inflation accelerated in the early 1970s, the Phillips curves broke down, just as Friedman said they would.[8] This experience convinced many economists – including many Keynesians – to adopt some form of Friedman's natural rate hypothesis.

2.2   The Birth of the New Classical Economics

The Equilibrium Phillips Curve

Friedman's criticisms of the standard interpretation of the Phillips curve were widely accepted within a few years of his presidential address. This was as much a consequence of the embarrassing failure of the empirically estimated Phillips curves of the 1960s to chart the relation of inflation to unemployment in the period of stagflation of the early 1970s as it was of a commitment to the economic principles upon which Friedman had based his analysis. To many Keynesians the notion of a *natural* rate of unemployment suggested an impotence of economic policy that they were loth to accept.[9]

A few economists, however, took Friedman's analysis to be incomplete but suggestive of a deeper reformulation of macroeconomics. For Friedman, the natural rate of unemployment represented frictional unemployment, which he took to be voluntary in the sense that it was the outcome of the utility- or profit-maximizing choices of individual workers and firms. It might not be desirable, in that some other rate of unemployment under other circumstances might lead to higher utility and profits, but it was the best that could be done given the existing set of constraints on economic choices. Furthermore, deviations from the natural rate were seen as essentially voluntary. Unemployment was a disequilibrium phenomenon, but the source of the disequilibrium was the failure of individual workers (and perhaps firms) to form accurate expectations of the future course of inflation. Given their expectations, their choices were optimal.

Keynesians who adopted the Friedmanian expectations-augmented

Phillips curve underplayed the voluntary or equilibrium nature of unemployment implicit in Friedman's analysis. Lucas and Rapping (1969a), in what is surely the first paper to deserve to be called 'new classical', made it the centre-piece of their analysis. Friedman's analysis was fairly informal. Its basis was the simple proposition from static neoclassical economic theory that the higher the real wage, the more labour would be supplied. Since such a static analysis treats any change in the wage rate as if it were maintained indefinitely, Friedman's explanation of the Phillips curve implicity assumed that the supply of labour was elastic in the long run. In contrast, the neoclassical theory of economic growth treated labour supply as depending exogenously on the growth of population and long-term demographic changes and therefore as inelastic with respect to the real wage in the long run. Casual observation suggested to Lucas and Rapping that this might in fact be true and that labour supply was rather more elastic in the short run.

Lucas and Rapping attempted to unite the short-run elasticity/long-run inelasticity of the labour supply with Friedman's essentially equilibrium approach to unemployment. They posited a utility function for workers in which current leisure and future leisure were close substitutes. Thus when the real wage rises in the current period, yet is expected to fall back to its 'normal' level in the future, the price of current leisure has risen relative to future leisure, and more labour will be willingly supplied (i.e. workers economize on expensive current leisure). In contrast, when the real wage rises permanently, both the current and the future price of leisure are the same, and there is no shift in relative prices and hence no change in the current supply of labour owing to substitution of leisure between periods. Of course, the higher real wage could cause workers to substitute consumption for leisure in every period, but Lucas and Rapping treated this elasticity as small. Similarly they treated the income effects of a change of wages as small and of uncertain sign. Lucas and Rapping presented empirical evidence that lent some support to their theoretical analysis.

Lucas and Rapping provide a coherent account of how transient fluctuations in the real wage could generate fluctuations in total employment (or at least in man-hours worked, if workers have some discretion over their hours). Its implications for the Phillips curve are not, however, completely straightforward, since the Phillips curve relates changes in wages to unemployment and not employment.[10] Lucas and Rapping argue that workers judge themselves to be unemployed not when they are unable to find work at the current wage, but when they are unable to find work at what they regard as their normal wage. Measured unemployment thus fluctuates inversely with fluctuations in total employment caused by transient movements in real wages.[11] The inverse relation between changes in nominal wages and the rate of unemployment captured by the Phillips curve would be observed, then, whenever nominal wages and prices diverged, even if they did so only for a very short time and were expected with certainty to revert to their former relationship in the future. Given the process by which people form their expectations of the future course of wages and prices and of their own normal wage rate, the Phillips curve represents a dynamic equilibrium in the labour market, and not disequilibrium as many economists believe.

Rational Expectations

What actually happens to unemployment seems to depend critically on the process by which economic agents form their expectations of future wages and prices and determine what the normal wage rate is. Friedman employed the hypothesis of adaptive expectations in many contexts.[12] One example of adaptive expectations would be

$$_tW_{t+1}^e = {}_{t-1}W_t^e + \lambda(W_t - {}_{t-1}W_t^e).\tag{2.1}$$

Equation (2.1) says that expectations formed in period t of wages in period $t + 1$ are equal to the expectations formed in period $t - 1$ of wages in period t plus a proportion λ $(0 \leq \lambda \leq 1)$ of the difference between the actual level of wages in time t and what they were expected to be at time $t - 1$. Expectations *adapt* to past mistakes.

For the lack of any more plausible hypothesis, Lucas and Rapping used an adaptive expectations scheme in their model of the labour market. Lucas was not, however, content with this formulation. The problem was obvious. A formula, such as equation (2.1), does not in general ever generate correct expectations. Say, for example, that wages had been constant into the indefinite past at a level of 100, and then at time 0 they rose to a new constant level of 200. If the adaptation coefficient λ were, say, 1/2, the expected wage would be 150 for time 1, 175 for time 2, 187.5 for time 3 and so on – approaching ever closer to 200, but never quite reaching it. Workers' expectational errors are systematic, and, in general, any mechanical scheme of forming expectations generates systematic errors. Lucas (1972a, b) argued that rational economic agents would not persist in a systematic mistake, because from its very nature it was easily and profitably correctable. What was worse in his view was that the intuitive insight of Friedman's natural rate hypothesis, that there was no permanent gain to output or employment from inflation, was wrong if workers had adaptive expectations.[13] An unexpected rise in actual inflation would encourage workers to offer more labour, lowering measured unemployment and boosting output. Their expectations would begin to adapt, and gradually they would withdraw their labour. But, since expectations would never adapt fully to the new actual wage rate but would always lag behind it, they would continue over any finite horizon to perceive incorrectly that their real wage was higher than normal and so would never adjust their labour supply back to its initial level. The gain to output and employment, although diminishing over time, would nevertheless be permanent.[14] In Lucas's view adaptive or other mechanical expectations hypotheses are not compatible with the natural rate hypothesis.

The great appeal of Lucas and Rapping's analysis of the labour market was that, rather than relying on unspecified notions of disequilibrium, it explained fluctuations in employment as the product of the utility-maximizing choices of rational economic agents. Similarly, Lucas (1972a, b, 1973) adopted Muth's 'rational expectations' hypothesis as an extension of the methodological precept: seek optimizing solutions to economic problems.[15] On this hypothesis, expectations may be incorrect but not systematically incorrect: expectations are correct up to a serially uncorrelated error.

To return to the earlier example, it is easy to see that with rational expectations there are no permanent gains to inflation. If wages had been at 100 up through time −1 and then were unexpectedly raised to 200 at time 0, employment and output would rise at time 0 only. The rational expectation of wages at time 1 and later would be 200, the same as actual wages, so that no further gains to output and employment would be possible. Once the rational expectations hypothesis is embedded in Lucas and Rapping's analysis of the labour market, deviations from the natural rate are strictly temporary.[16] For Friedman, the natural rate is a level of unemployment to which the actual rate gravitated only in the long (infinite) run. For Lucas, the natural rate is re-established as soon as unavoidable expectational errors are corrected.

Neutrality and the Slope of the Phillips Curve

Long before his attack on the standard interpretation of the Phillips curve, Friedman was famous as an indefatigable advocate of the quantity theory of money. The quantity theory implies that money is neutral, i.e. that changes in the stock of money generate proportional changes in the level of prices – at least in the long run. The existence of a Phillips curve, however, calls the neutrality of money into question. Money is not neutral if an increase in its supply is dissipated partly in higher inflation and partly in higher output, which lowers unemployment and generates the inverse relationship between inflation and unemployment captured in the Phillips curve.

In order to reconcile the neutrality of money with the observed inverse relation between inflation and unemployment, Friedman claims that money is neutral only in the long run. The picture is one of disequilibrium in which the short-run negatively sloped Phillips curve gradually converges on the long-run vertically sloped Phillips curve. Once the natural rate of unemployment (and output) is re-established, all the increase in the stock of money must be reflected in the level of prices.

Clearly, Lucas's analysis would not allow such gradual convergence to the natural rate. As soon as workers discover their mistake they reduce their labour supply to its equilibrium level. The distinction between the long run and the short run is not very useful in this analysis. The real distinction is between the expected and the unexpected. In effect, rational expectations collapses the short run into the long run. The puzzle remains, nonetheless, for Lucas as for Friedman: why do econometric estimates invariably show an inverse relationship between inflation and unemployment?

In order to solve this puzzle, Lucas (1972a) sets up a model in which money is held as a means of transferring value from one period to the next, in which consumption and labour-supply decisions are taken on the basis of utility maximization and in which all agents have rational expectations. In this model Lucas is able to show that, if people have perfect information, money is neutral and there are never any deviations from the natural rate, i.e. there is no Phillips curve.

An inverse relation between inflation and unemployment will be generated nonetheless if the assumption of perfect information is relaxed in the following way. Let individual agents have expectations of the general level of prices and of the prices of the goods they sell (labour, other factors of production or produced goods). Rational expectations implies that these expectations are correct on average. Now assume that agents are able to observe the current (nominal or absolute) price of their own goods, but that they observe the general level of prices only with a delay of one period.[17] When the price of their own good rises, agents are faced with the problem of deciding whether the price rise represents a change in relative prices in their favour, which would suggest an increase in their output, or merely a rise in the general level of prices, which would leave relative prices unchanged and suggest no change in their output. Experience will undoubtedly have taught them that part of most price rises is a change in relative prices and part is a change in the general level of prices. Hence they will react to any surprise increase in the general level of prices as if it were, at least in part, a rise in relative prices: they will increase their output (or labour supply) for any surprise increase in the rate of inflation and decrease it for any surprise decrease in the rate of inflation.

When the inflation rate has been zero on average over a long period, any rate above or below zero will be unexpected. Output will rise and unemployment will fall when the rate is above zero, and output will fall and unemployment will rise when it is below zero. If unemployment is plotted against inflation and a curve is fitted to the points, the relationship will obviously be inverse – a Phillips curve. The existence of such a Phillips curve depends on two things: the reaction of output and employment to relative price changes, and the mistaken belief that changes in the general level of prices are really changes in relative prices. As soon as the agents' confusion on this point is corrected – by assumption after a lag of one period – when they observe the actual general level of prices, output and employment fall back to their original levels.

Such an ephemeral Phillips curve is an epiphenomenon. It cannot be exploited by the authorities. Any attempt to generate consistently surprising higher levels of inflation in order to reduce unemployment will fail. One cannot *systematically* do the unexpected. Agents will simply raise their expectations of what the average level of inflation is, from zero or any other constant level to the new higher level. Just as Friedman and Phillips maintained, the Phillips curve will not be stable in environments in which the rate of inflation is not on average stable.[18] Lucas's analysis is more radical than that of either Friedman or Phillips: deviations from the natural rate of unemployment are purely transitory; there is no trade-off between inflation and unemployment even in the short run. Expected changes in the stock of money are neutral in the long and short runs, but unexpected changes are not neutral.

Signal Extraction

The existence of an empirically observed downward-sloping Phillips curve in Lucas's analysis depends crucially on the confusion by economic agents of absolute changes in the general level of prices with changes in relative prices. Clearly, for agents with rational expectations, such confusion can result in random mistakes only. Mistakes can still be random, yet on average large or small. A rational agent would attempt to reduce the average size of his mistakes as much as possible. This means that he would attempt as best he could to discern what fraction of any change in his own price was actually a relative shift in his favour rather than pure inflation. In the language of engineering, he would try to extract the signal from the surrounding noise as efficiently as possible. The more background noise there is (in this case the greater the variability of inflation), the less easy it will be to extract an accurate signal (i.e. an accurate assessment of relative prices) and the smaller will be his response to any given observed increase in prices. Highly variable inflation therefore implies steeply sloping Phillips curves.

This point can be explained somewhat more formally.[19] Let agent z's output (i.e. labour supplied for a worker, goods produced for a firm) be

$$y_z = \bar{y}_z + \gamma(p_z - p_z^e), \qquad (2.2)$$

where y_z is the output supplied by the zth agent, $\bar{y}_z$ is the average level supplied, p_z is the current price and p_z^e is the expected future price of z's output (all lower-case variables in the rest of this section are in logarithms). Equation (2.2) captures in a single equation the results of Lucas and Rapping's analysis of factor supplies: when current and expected future prices are equal, output is supplied at its long-run level (here taken to be a constant, but generally determined by tastes, productivity and resources), while when current prices exceed expected future prices, output is supplied above its long-run level by the factor γ.

Assume further that agent z's price can be expressed as a deviation from the general level of prices:

$$p_z = p + \varepsilon_z, \qquad (2.3)$$

where p is the general level of prices and ε_z is the factor by which p_z deviates from p. Let p be a normal variable with mean $\bar{p}$ and variance σ^2, and let ε_z be a normal variable with mean zero and variance τ^2. Let p and ε_z be independent of each other, i.e. $\text{cov}(p, \varepsilon_z) = 0$. The mean of p_z is then also $\bar{p}$ and its variance is $\sigma^2 + \tau^2$.

Let each agent have rational expectations:

$$p_z^e = E(p_z | I), \qquad (2.4)$$

where I is all the information available up to time t (by assumption not including the value of p). In the light of equation (2.3), equation (2.4) can be rewritten

$$p_z^e = E(p | I). \qquad (2.4')$$

On our earlier assumptions, the most prominent piece of information available to agents is their own current price. Equation (2.4') can thus be rewritten once more:

$$p_z^e = E(p | p_z). \qquad (2.4'')$$

Equation (2.4'') is a classic signal-extraction problem. It poses the question: what is the best guess of the value of the currently

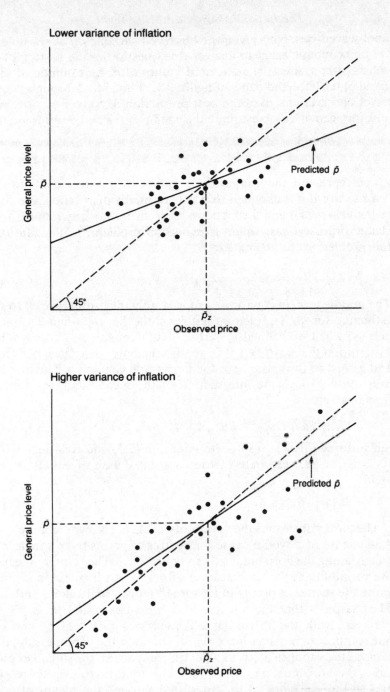

Figure 2.1 Signal extraction: an increase in the variance of inflation increases the amount of any observed price increase attributed to the general price level

unobserved variable p given the observed variable p_z? A sensible way for an economic agent to answer this question would be to plot past values of p_z against the associated values of p. An example of this is given in the left-hand panel of figure 2.1. A line fitted through the scatter of observations gives the best prediction of p given p_z. Algebraically, the agent needs to estimate the coefficients a and β in the equation

$$p = \alpha + \beta p_z + w, \qquad (2.5)$$

which represents the line on the graph (w is the irreducible random error term). If it is assumed that w is normally distributed, the choice of the values of a and β which are 'best' or most likely reduces to the classic ordinary least squares regression problem.[20] The solution to this problem is the estimate of β:

$$\hat{\beta} = \frac{\text{cov}(p_z, p)}{\text{var}(p_z)} = \frac{\sigma^2}{\sigma^2 + \tau^2}. \qquad (2.6)$$

The middle term in equation (2.6) is simply the ordinary least squares estimator for $\hat{\beta}$. The denominator of the far right-hand term was derived when we defined p_z earlier. The numerator follows from the assumption that $\text{cov}(p, \varepsilon_z) = 0$, so that the only covariance between p_z and p must be the variance of their common element p. The fitted line must pass through the intersection of the mean values of p and p_z; therefore

$$\hat{\alpha} = \bar{p} - \hat{\beta}\bar{p}_z = (1 - \hat{\beta})\bar{p}. \qquad (2.7)$$

Substituting this last result into equation (2.5) and treating equation (2.5) as the best estimate of the right-hand side of equation (2.4″) yields

$$p^e = (1 - \hat{\beta})\bar{p} + \hat{\beta}p_z. \qquad (2.8)$$

The term τ^2 measures the variability of agent z's own (relative) price. An increase in τ^2 would cause the scatter of points to be spread more widely along the horizontal axis in figure 2.1.[21] The term σ^2 measures the variability of the general level of prices. An increase in σ^2 would cause the scatter of points to be spread more widely along both axes. The reason is that the vertical axis measures p and σ^2 is p's own variance, while the horizontal axis measures p_z ($= p + \varepsilon_z$) and σ^2 is one component of its variance ($\sigma^2 + \tau^2$). Since the variance of p_z is the same as the variance of p plus an extra component, the spread of points along the horizontal axis must be wider than that along the vertical axis so that the slope of the line fitted through the scatter of points must be less than 45°. If τ^2 is held constant, an increase in the variability of the general price level would increase the spread of points along the horizontal axis proportionally less than that along the vertical axis. As a result, the greater the variability of inflation, the closer the scatter of points and the fitted line come to lying along a 45° line. The lower panel of figure 2.1 shows the consequence of a greater variability of p.

The economic significance of this bit of geometry is to confirm our earlier intuition that, the higher the variability of the general level of prices, the less likely a rational agent is to interpret an observed increase in his own price as a favourable shift in relative prices. Were inflation to be held at any constant level (say, zero), σ^2 and $\hat{\beta}$ would fall to zero. Any change in p_z would then be interpreted as a shift in relative prices. Were σ^2 to approach infinity as inflation became more and more variable, $\hat{\beta}$ would approach unity and any change in p_z would be interpreted merely as more inflation. Noise would completely overwhelm the signal.

In order to see the implication of this signal-extraction process on the aggregate supply curve, substitute equation (2.8) into (2.2) to yield

$$y_z = \bar{y}_z + \gamma[p_z - (1 - \hat{\beta})\bar{p} - \hat{\beta}p_z]$$
$$= \bar{y}_z + \gamma(1 - \hat{\beta})(p_z - \bar{p}). \tag{2.9}$$

Equation (2.9) refers to a single market. If it is assumed that all agents are identical, the *per capita* aggregate supply function can be obtained by averaging (2.9) over all markets to yield

$$y = \bar{y} + \gamma(1 - \hat{\beta})(p - \bar{p}). \tag{2.10}$$

Equation (2.10) states that the higher is $\hat{\beta}$ (i.e. the more variable is inflation), the more steeply upward the aggregate supply function will slope. In the limit, as inflation becomes infinitely variable ($\hat{\beta}$ approaches unity), the function becomes vertical. Unemployment is inversely related to output, so that equation (2.10) can also be interpreted as saying that, the more variable is inflation, the more steeply downward sloping is the empirically observed Phillips curve. In the limit, it also becomes vertical: variations in the rate of inflation cease to affect unemployment.[22]

The Change of Agenda

The work of Lucas (as well as his work with Rapping) in the early 1970s altered many economists' perspective on two central problems in macroeconomics – unemployment and the neutrality of money – in subtle but remarkable ways. Before 1970 most work on the possible non-neutrality of money centred around the interaction of money with other assets – physical capital or financial assets. An increase in the stock of money would not only increase the total stock of financial assets but would also raise money as a proportion of the total. In order to make these new shares desirable to participants in financial markets, interest rates would adjust, affecting the demand for money. This would affect the equilibrium level of prices beyond any direct effect from the change in the stock of money. Proportionality between money and prices would no longer be expected. Similarly, substitution into capital would encourage real investment and expand aggregate supply and so somewhat dissipate inflation. Although there were some models which displayed *superneutrality* (i.e. real variables were unaffected by either the *rate* of inflation or the level of prices), the general conclusion of this research was that money was not neutral in any realistic model of the economy.[23]

In contrast with the theoretical work of the time, the empirical investigations of Friedman and other monetarists seemed to support the thesis of the neutrality of money. Lucas's early models are monetarist in the sense that the one-for-one proportionality between expected changes in the stock of money and changes in the level of prices is maintained. This is achieved through the use of simple models in which money is the only asset, so that questions of portfolio balance are simply set to one side. Non-neutrality is no longer a question of substitution between assets, but purely and simply one of monetary confusion, of the difficulties economic agents face in extracting information about relative prices from noisy prices.[24]

This exclusive attention to monetary confusion as a source of non-neutrality is not a necessary feature of the new classical economics. The overlapping-generations models of money discussed in chapters 6 and 7 are new classical models in which money's substitution with other assets is critical. Nevertheless, the most important empirical tests of new classical models have been based exclusively on the analysis of monetary confusion.[25]

The second area in which Lucas's new classical analysis has altered the focus of macroeconomics is the analysis of unemployment. Before Lucas and Rapping (1969a, b) most economists saw unemployment as a disequilibrium phenomenon. Most accepted Keynes's distinction between involuntary unemployment, on the one hand, and voluntary and frictional unemployment, on the other.[26] Even Friedman, who with his natural rate hypothesis asserted the dominance of frictional unemployment interpreted as a consequence of voluntary actions, did not deny that involuntary unemployment was real. Rather, he asserted that it was transitory and not effectively meliorated by macroeconomic policy. Lucas, however, denies that involuntary unemployment is even a meaningful concept. This is already implicit in Lucas and Rapping (1969a), which seeks a purely equilibrium explanation for measured unemployment and which, as discussed earlier, questions the unusual interpretation of reported unemployment. Later Lucas argues more directly that Keynes's distinction was merely a misdirected attempt to distinguish between trend and cyclical unemployment, both of which should ideally be explained by means of an equilibrium model.[27] While many economists would be loth to dismiss Keynes's distinctions between the types of unemployment as conceptually wrong-headed, much of the work on the macroeconomics of unemployment – even among non-new classical economists – now seeks some sort of equilibrium explanation.[28]

3 Market-clearing Models of the Business Cycle

Keynesians believe that the labour market is often in disequilibrium. Involuntary unemployment is excess supply of labour. An excess demand for labour causes wages and prices to rise. Keynesians quickly adopted the standard interpretation of the Phillips curve because it fitted neatly into this framework. The rate of inflation appeared to be a well-defined function of excess demand for labour as measured by the reported rate of unemployment. The principal challenge facing the early new classicals was to show that the Phillips curve could be reinterpreted to be consistent with equilibrium in the labour market. New classical efforts to meet this challenge were simply the first example of their general commitment to equilibrium analysis. Disequilibria, they believe, are only apparent; equilibrium models are adequate to explain observed phenomena.

Of all the apparent disequilibria in the economy, business cycles – the fluctuation of output, employment, and related aggregates about their trend levels – are perhaps the most important. Providing an equilibrium explanation of business cycles is a major goal of new classical research. In this chapter we consider the general problem of formulating an equilibrium explanation of business cycles, and we examine several prominent new classical models.

The new classicals were forced to confront the problem of business cycles as soon as they attempted to apply the Lucas aggregate supply function to actual data. That function – as derived in the last chapter (equation (2.10)) – can be written

$$y = \bar{y} + a(p - \bar{p}) \tag{3.1}$$

or equivalently, given rational expectations, as

$$y = \bar{y} + a(p - p^c), \tag{3.2}$$

where $a = \gamma(1 - \beta)$ or, in terms of the variances of the general price level and relative prices, a $= \gamma\tau^2/(\sigma^2 + \tau^2)$.

Empirical investigations using these particular forms of the Lucas aggregate supply function have met with little success. The problem is that these forms predict that the actual output y will vary randomly about its mean $\bar{y}$, whereas in fact there is a great deal of serial correlation in output: periods in which output is above its (trend-adjusted) mean tend to follow periods in which output is also above its mean. Unemployment and many other economic aggregates behave similarly. This poses for new classical theorists the *problem of persistence*: how are serially correlated movements in economic aggregates to be explained?

Early new classical empirical work (e.g. Lucas 1973, Sargent 1976a) dealt with serial correlation in output simply through a modification of the aggregate supply function:

$$y = \bar{y} + a(p - \bar{p}) + b(y_{-1} - \bar{y}).\tag{3.3}$$

Equation (3.3) is (3.1) with an additional term representing deviations of past output y_{-1} from the mean.[1] The coefficient b ($0 \leqslant b \leqslant 1$) determines the speed with which output returns to its mean level after a one-time disturbance.

Equations of the same general form as (3.3) fit the data for output and unemployment far better than their serially uncorrelated cousins. Such adjustments were, however, rather uneasy compromises with the real world, for nothing in the new classical theory of the early 1970s provided a deep justification for the appearance of lagged output in aggregate supply functions or lagged unemployment in Phillips curves. The necessity of including them in any reasonably successful empirical studies raised their justification and, equivalently, the explanation of business cycles as the central unsolved problem for new classical theory.

All definitions of the term 'business cycle' aim to capture the fact that many macroeconomic variables seem to fluctuate around their trend levels or growth paths with a sort of rough regularity. Furthermore, the fluctuations of different series seem to be related to each other.[2] Lucas defines the business cycle fairly narrowly as the fact that '... real output undergoes serially correlated movements about trend which are not explainable by movements in the availability of factors of production.'[3] Other economic variables are bound to be related to output: consumption, investment, employment, interest rates, nominal prices and wages generally move procyclically with output, unemployment moves counter-cyclically and real wages show no clear cycle at all.

To explain the related movements of macroeconomic aggregates and prices without recourse to the notion of disequilibrium is the desideratum of new classical research on the theory of business cycles.

3.1 Equilibrium Business Cycles

New classical economists do not agree on the appropriate model of the business cycle. Some see monetary mismanagement, while others see real shocks, as the original source of fluctuations. Within each of these camps, any number of models, differing in detail, compete for adherents. All new classical models of the business cycle, however, have one thing in common: fluctuations are described as competitive equilibria. Lucas's (1975) model of the business cycle belongs to the 'monetary' camp. Still, it is the paradigm for all new classical models of the business cycle – real and monetary. It clearly shows the general strategy as well as many of the pitfalls of equilibrium models of the business cycle.

Lucas's model is closely related to his earlier analysis of the Phillips curve in that the structure and processing of information in the economy is critical to the translation of monetary shocks into fluctuations in output. At its heart, the model is a species of neoclassical growth model. When such models are in their *steady states*, the labour force, capital and other inputs to the production process (measured in units adjusted for changes in productivity) as well as output all grow at the same rate, so that the ratios of any aggregate to any other (e.g. the capital–output ratio or the capital–labour ratio) remain constant. Wage rates and rental rates for other factors of production also remain constant.

As in the analysis of the Phillips curve, the economy in Lucas's model consists of a large number of separate consumers/producers who can observe the current price of their own output. They must, however, use that known price plus information on past prices and rates of return to infer the current general level of prices as well as all future prices and rates of return, i.e. they face a signal-extraction problem.

Aggregate demand in this economy consists of consumption (financed out of wages and holdings of real balances) and government spending (financed out of increments to the stock of money). Again, as in the earlier analysis, money enters in such a way that anticipated changes in the stock of money are neutral; only unanticipated changes can have real effects.[4]

By hypothesis, the source of fluctuations in this model is noise in the money supply process. Government expenditure is financed completely through monetary expansion. The amount of sales of any one producer to the government and hence the amount of money in that producer's portfolio is a random process. Lucas assumes that it is serially correlated. Thus, if a producer finds that demand and his receipt of money balances are above average in one period, he can expect them to be diminished but still above average in the next period as well. This is one of the ultimate sources of persistence in this model. The existence of a long-lived capital stock is the other.

Obviously, if information is perfect, there is no confusion of relative prices with the general price level and even serially correlated random fluctuations in the stock of money do not induce persistent deviations from the natural rates of output and unemployment. But information is assumed not to be perfect. Consider first the case in which investment is insensitive to changes in rates of return, so that capital simply grows along its steady state path. An unexpected increase in the stock of money in particular markets generates an apparent increase in demand in those markets. Producers must determine how much of this increased demand is a favourable shift in demand for their product and how much is simply an inflationary increase in the aggregate stock of money. Using the same signal-extraction method as in the earlier analysis of the Phillips curve, they are bound to assign part of the increase to each cause. They will therefore underestimate the actual increase in the stock of money; that is, they will at first underpredict prices. Since actual prices are higher than expected prices, they produce more. Now, if there were no serial correlation in the stock of money, this scenario would be precisely the same as the original analysis of the Phillips curve: random shocks to the money supply produce at most serially uncorrelated fluctuations of output about the trend. Since it is assumed, however, that the shocks to the money supply are themselves serially correlated, the current shock carries information about the future path of the stock of money. Producers use this knowledge to separate the signal more accurately from the noise in future periods. Consequently, in each period after a positive shock, more and more of the apparent increase in demand is attributed to the aggregate increase in the stock of money rather than to a favourable shift in demand for the individual producer. Expectations and actual prices gradually converge, so that output and employment return to their trend paths.

The paths of output and employment after a shock look rather like the paths that adaptive expectations would generate. It is important to recognize, however, that expectations in this model are rational, and that the gradual adaptation of expectations to actual values arises not from failure to use information but from a gradual improvement in the ability of producers to separate signal from noise. Because signal extraction improves over time, the biggest mistake from any monetary shock must be made in the first period. Hence output rises most in the first period, and gradually approaches its trend in future periods. Deviations from the natural rate cannot cumulate.

If the assumption that investment is unresponsive to rates of return is relaxed, a wider range of cyclical patterns becomes possible. An unexpected increase in the stock of money, as before, stimulates current output. Since producers expect future demand to be above trend whenever current demand is above trend, they also expect future rates of return on real capital to rise. This increased return encourages increased investment, raising the capital stock and slowing down the rise in actual prices. With prices rising more slowly, it also takes longer for producers to learn that the increase in the money supply is not a favourable shift in demand, so that the effect of the shock on output and employment persists longer than it otherwise would. Furthermore, in some cases, rather than expectations in each period becoming closer to actual prices and rates of return, they may actually diverge for some time. Deviations from the natural rate may therefore cumulate for a period. Eventually, however, producers learn that the increase in the money supply was simply noise. The capital stock by this time is above its steady state level. The optimal path back to the steady state, even with no further shocks, may require investment and output below the steady state level, and may therefore require unemployment actually to rise before returning to the natural rate.

3.2 Monetary versus Real Business Cycles

Lucas's model is simply one example of how a standard economic model can be modified to produce cyclical behaviour. Its details, therefore, are far less important than the general principles that guided its construction. Foremost among these is that it is an equilibrium model: self-interested economic agents successfully maximize their utility or profits subject to constraints on their budgets and, crucially, on available information. Expectations are rational and relative prices clear all markets.

Lucas's model displays a structure common, although not unique, to all new classical models of the business cycle. There is first a clearly identified *original source* of fluctuations: in his model, random variations in the stock of money. Second, there is a *propagation mechanism*: in his model, serial correlation in the shocks to the money supply combined with the interaction of the inability of agents to process information perfectly with a long-lived stock of capital.

The broad division of the new classical school between advocates of monetary models and real models of the business cycle is founded on differences over the original sources of fluctuations. Although many propagation mechanisms have been suggested, commitments to one mechanism over another do not distinguish distinct camps. Real business cycle models have been defined to be those models that rule out the influence of money on output and related aggregates.[6] Advocates of real business cycle models are nonetheless at pains to point out that they do not rule out the influence of money on output in principle.[7] A fairer and more accurate characterization of the difference between monetary and real models of the cycle would be that monetary models predict that a benign monetary policy would eliminate the source of cyclical fluctuations, while real models predict that cycles are endemic and would continue even if the money stock was held to a constant rate of growth.[8]

While the advocates of real business cycle models do not rule out the effects of money on output in principle, they do believe that the actual influence of money on output in the United States since the Second World War has been relatively small. The evidence adduced in support of models of real business cycles is mainly evidence for the unimportance of money as an influence on output. At least four types of evidence have been offered in support of real models as an alternative explanation of business cycles.

First, nearly every advocate of real business cycles claims that his model fairly closely mimics the actual variances and covariances of output, employment, consumption and other important aggregates. We shall consider this claim as a factual matter for some of the particular models discussed in section 3.3. In the meantime, it is important to note that it is not logically compelling evidence in favour of real models of the business cycle. A true model would necessarily mimic the behaviour of the actual economy, but a model that mimics the behaviour of the economy may not, in fact, be true, for there may be many other incompatible models that do so as well. Correctly mimicking the economy is a necessary but not sufficient condition for the correctness of a model.[9] Stronger evidence, which the advocates of real models of the business cycle do not offer, would be to show that rival models do not successfully imitate the behaviour of important economic aggregates.

The second type of evidence offered in support of real models of the business cycle comes from tests of Granger-causality and the analysis of vector autoregressions. Since the basis and limitations of both techniques are discussed in detail in chapter 8, a brief description will suffice here. Money Granger-causes output if current output is predicted better from previous values of money as well as previous values of output than from previous values of output alone. That is to say, money Granger-causes output if it has some incremental power to improve the prediction of output. Early studies by Sims and others discovered that money in fact Granger-causes output.[10] Later studies contradicted this finding. If output is related to interest rates as well as to money and its own past, money no longer has incremental predictive power over output; the interest rates seem to carry all the information.[11]

Vector autoregressions consider a group of variables. Each is estimated as a function of its own past values and the past values of the other variables. Then, using techniques described in chapter 8, the predictive power of each variable for each of the others is determined. Again, recent research indicates that money has little predictive power over output when interest rates are included among the variables in the estimated system.[12]

The failure of money to contribute significantly to the explanation of output on either the tests of Granger-causality or the analysis of vector autoregressions has been taken to be evidence against monetary models of the business cycle and in favour of real models. It is not clear that it is actually evidence one way or another. First, both methods are subject to ambiguities of interpretation, as explained in detail in chapter 8. In particular, if money is used optimally to reduce the variance of output, it will not appear in the tests to have explanatory power, and this just at the time when it has the greatest actual influence. Second, for most of the period after the Second World War in the United States and the other countries studied, central banks targeted interest rates.[13] If money were adjusted to keep interest rates at particular levels, then interest rates would carry information about the conduct of monetary policy. Interest rates would then have explanatory power over output just when money is influential. Interest rates could push money out of a significant place in tests of Granger-causality or in vector autoregressions, or both could be significant. Only if both were shown to be without influence could the behaviour of money be treated as unimportant for output. Third, even if money is shown to be unimportant, that is evidence against monetary models; it is not strong evidence in favour of new classical *market-clearing* real models of the business cycle. Non-market-clearing Keynesian models, e.g. multiplier–accelerator models, would also be supported.

The third type of evidence offered is again evidence against market-clearing monetary models and is again subject to the reservation that it supports alternative models as well as or better than real market-clearing models of the business cycle. New classical monetary models such as that of Lucas described in section 3.1 are based on misperceptions of the current stance of monetary policy. If the stock of money were increased above the level agents had expected, then actual prices would be higher than expected prices and output would rise above its natural rate. This story implicitly assumes that agents cannot observe the current stock of money (i.e. they misperceive it in the current period as well as fail to anticipate it in the previous period), for if they knew the current stock of money they would be able to infer the current actual level of prices and would not be duped into supplying more output. One objection to Lucas's monetary model and its cousins is that people in most countries need not be ignorant of the stock of money: money supply figures are published regularly. Of course, they are also revised regularly, so that people acting on the published data would nonetheless make some mistakes. If the basic structure of the Lucas model is correct, each revision of the money supply would affect output, for each revision would change people's perceptions of the true level of the stock of money and therefore of prices.

Barro and Hercowitz (1980) test the theory that misperceptions of the money supply affect output. They look for a relationship between revisions in the United States money supply data and changes in output. They find no relationship, which suggests that the theory based on misperceptions is incorrect. Advocates of real models of the business cycle take this as support for their view against market-clearing monetary models.

Once again the evidence is not compelling. Typical non-market-clearing monetary models posit prices or wages which are set in earlier periods to agree with the rationally expected prices or wages for the current period but which cannot fully adjust to clear the market in the current period.[14] If money is higher than expected, output is increased because prices and wages cannot adjust until later periods. It is the actual level of the stock of money, not its perceived level, that is important. In non-market-clearing monetary models, one would not therefore expect revisions of the reported data on the money supply to affect output. Clearly, Barro and Hercowitz's results are compatible with real models of the business cycle, which are market-clearing models, but they are also compatible with monetary models of the business cycle as long as the market-clearing hypothesis is rejected.[15]

The fourth type of evidence offered in support of real models of the business cycle is purely statistical. Many economists conceive of output and other aggregates as growing along steady underlying trends with business cycle fluctuations superimposed. An equation such as

$$y_t = \alpha t + \beta y_{t-1} + \varepsilon_t, \tag{3.4}$$

where t is time, α and β are constants and ε_t is a random error, might adequately describe the behaviour of output. The deterministic trend αt in (3.4), and not its exact form, is what is important. If there is a shock to ε_t, output rises above trend. Since y_t depends on y_{t-1}, the shock is transmitted to future periods as well, generating the serial correlation typical of business cycles. But if $|\beta| < 1$, the effect of a shock to ε_t on future output gradually diminishes and output reverts to trend.

Equations of the general form of (3.4) are not the only way in which output data might be described. Output could also follow a random walk. A simple example of a random walk is

$$y_t = \alpha t + y_{t-1} + \varepsilon_t. \tag{3.5}$$

Equation (3.5) is a random walk with a drift (the term αt). It differs from (3.4) only in that β is set to unity. But this is a critical difference. Consider a shock to ε_t. Output rises in the current period and, because $\beta = 1$, *this rise persists in every future period*. There is no reversion to trend. Nelson and Plosser test statistical specifications similar to equation (3.4) against specifications similar to (3.5) for output, employment, industrial production and many other important aggregates.[16] They conclude that most aggregates are better described as random walks than as fluctuations about deterministic trends.

Advocates of real models of business cycles interpret these results as evidence for real models and against monetary models. They summarize the results as saying that business cycles do not appear to be fluctuations around a steady underlying trend but are, to a large degree, fluctuations in the trend itself. In fact fluctuations around the fluctuating trend appear to be fairly small. They assume that monetary policy could not cause the fluctuations in the underlying trend, because that would allow monetary policy to have permanent effects in violation of the natural rate hypothesis. Consequently, monetary policy is at best a secondary cause of fluctuations. Real models are the natural candidate to supplant monetary models as the premier new classical explanation of business cycles.

Once again, the evidence is not unequivocal. First, it is not clear that the data are in fact best described as a random walk. Say that the data were actually generated as

$$y_t = \alpha t + 0.999 y_{t-1} + \varepsilon_t. \tag{3.6}$$

This is close to a random walk, but it is not a random walk. A shock to ε is transmitted to current and future output. Its effect diminishes *very slowly*, but it does diminish and eventually output reverts to trend. Because equation (3.6) is so close to a random walk, if (3.4) were estimated on data generated by (3.6), it would fit very well but it would suggest completely false long-run properties for output. A statistical test based on the fit of equation (3.5) would have low power, i.e. it would often suggest accepting the random walk hypothesis when it is in fact false.[17]

Even if the random walk hypothesis is accepted, the evidence offered in support of real models is really evidence only against *market-clearing* monetary models, and not against the whole range of monetary models.

So far we have considered the evidence offered in favour of real models of the business cycle and have been content to question whether or not it is really compelling. Monetary models and non-market-clearing models were clearly on the defensive. Non-market-clearing models violate the essential tenets of the new classical school. And evidence in their favour is evidence against the whole enterprise of formulating equilibrium models of the business cycle. Criticism of the new classical school along these lines is entertained in section 3.4. One may remain, however, within the confines of the new classical school and observe that at least two types of evidence support market-clearing monetary models and, in turn, place real models on the defensive.

The first real models of the business cycle were formulated before formal tests of their validity were conducted and before evidence was marshalled in their support. Similarly, monetary models of the business cycle, which are natural outgrowths of the new classical analysis of the Phillips curve, were formulated ahead of any serious consideration of the evidence. Nevertheless the first type of evidence in favour of monetary models is long established. It is that there is a consistent long-run correlation between the stock of money and the levels of nominal income and prices in virtually every country for which there are data. Monetary models explain this quite naturally because the quantity theory of money is embedded in their structure. An unexpected and unperceived increase in money causes an increase in output and nominal income. Once people learn what has happened, output returns to its old level and prices rise, while nominal income remains permanently higher. Lacking a monetary sector, most real models of business cycles can give no explanation for the relationship between money, prices and nominal income.

One possible line of defence for real models would be to incorporate a monetary sector. If the models are to retain their real character, however, this monetary sector must be passive, with little or no causal influence over real variables. The model of King and Plosser described in section 3.3 incorporates money in just such a manner.

The second type of evidence in favour of monetary models is that empirical studies indicate that money does affect real output. Barro's original study of the effects of monetary 'surprises' on output is discussed in chapter 8, section 8.2. Later work indicated that it is not only surprises but anticipated changes in the money supply that affect output.[18] Each case supports a monetary model of the business cycle.

Advocates of real models might reply that their own empirical studies using a wide set of variables reject the influence of money on output. We have already observed that this evidence is not compelling, since interest rates, which seem to eliminate the influence of money in vector autoregressions and tests of Granger-causality, may themselves reflect the behaviour of money and the stance of monetary policy. The advocates of monetary models can, at least, point to the concrete source of fluctuations in their models. Advocates of real models have yet to provide independent evidence of the existence and size of the real shocks that are supposed to be the original source of fluctuations in their models. We shall return to this point in the next section.

3.3   Alternative Real Models of the Business Cycle

A Paradigm

Real business cycle models are distinguished from monetary models in that they find the original source of cyclical fluctuations in shocks to the real economy, e.g. autonomous shifts in technology or factor availability. Particular real business cycle models are usually offered as partial explanations of actual cycles. Their advocates believe that a complete model would integrate the features of a number of models. No integration is yet available.[19]

Kydland and Prescott's time-to-build model is the paradigm for almost all other new classical real business cycle models.[20] We shall therefore consider it in some detail. Other real business cycle models will then be considered as addressing particular omissions and weaknesses in Kydland and Prescott's paradigm.

Like Lucas's model, Kydland and Prescott's model is essentially a variation on the single-sector neoclassical growth model. Kydland and Prescott exclude monetary policy as the original source of business cycle fluctuations. Instead they consider only real shocks, modelled as random variations in technology. While the original source of fluctuations in Lucas's model is monetary shocks and in Kydland and Prescott's model it is technological shocks, the two models nonetheless share the common feature that information about these shocks is assumed to be incomplete: in each case agents must somehow extract the signal from the noise, and their inability to do so perfectly is what initiates cyclical fluctuations. Similarly, just as Lucas found part of the persistence in fluctuations of output in serial correlation of the monetary shocks, Kydland and Prescott assume that shocks to technology are serially correlated in a manner unknown to economic agents.

Kydland and Prescott stress the importance of the technical structure of production, particularly the fact that production of any good takes some finite time. In their model, production of capital goods requires inputs over several periods. This differs sharply from Lucas's model, in which investment adds to the stock of productive capital immediately.

Kydland and Prescott borrow another important feature of their model, not from Lucas's business cycle model, but from Lucas and Rapping's (1969a) work on the supply of labour (see chapter 2, section 2.2) – namely a utility function for workers that possesses a high degree of intertemporal substitutability, so that transient shocks have large effects.

Cycles are generated in Kydland and Prescott's model in the following manner. Let there be a favourable shock to technology. Such a shock increases production, the demand for labour and the current real wage. Individual agents (workers/producers) must decide how much of this shock is transitory and how much is permanent, which depends of course on the amount of (unobserved) serial correlation of the technological shocks. Agents face a signal-extraction problem. To the degree that workers estimate the shock to be transitory, the real wage seems high *relative* to future real wages. Because leisure tomorrow is a good substitute for leisure today, workers then supply more labour in the current period in order to take advantage of their passing good fortune: current output rises. To the degree that they estimate the shock to be permanent, producers initiate the construction of new capital in order to provide for increased production in the future. The fact that technological shocks are serially correlated in itself generates some persistence in output fluctuations, and it encourages producers to begin constructing new capital, not only in the current period but also in periods following the initial shock. Such capital takes a definite time to build, so that output increases some time after the initial shock and continues to increase for some time after the series of serially correlated shocks dwindles away. Were there no further shocks to technology, producers might find themselves with too much capital compared with what is needed to maintain steady state growth. In that case, the optimal plan would be to slow investment down until capital depreciation brought the economy back to its steady state path. Output and employment would of course fluctuate along with capital.

Let us now consider six criticisms of the Kydland and Prescott model, three of which are essentially unanswered in the new classical literature and three of which are addressed by some of the alternative real business cycle models described later in this section.

1   The Kydland and Prescott model does not adequately describe the data. In order to provide some test of their model, Kydland and Prescott assign values to its parameters. Some of these are taken from

other economists' research (e.g. on investment or consumption), while others are estimated econometrically. A key parameter is the variance of capital productivity, which gives an indication of the size of original technological shocks to the economy. This parameter is simply assigned a value large enough for the variance in output generated by the model to be the same as the variance in output actually found in the American economy after the Second World War. Once the parameters of the model have been assigned actual values, Kydland and Prescott simulate its performance and find that it generates cycles in various aggregates that are, for the most part, roughly similar to those in the actual American economy.

Kydland and Prescott take the ability to mimic the behaviour of key aggregates as empirical support for their model. We have already observed in section 3.2 that positive confirmation is logically weak evidence for the truth of a model. The situation here is even worse: formal econometric tests of Kydland and Prescott's model reject it as an adequate description of the data.[21] The only sense in which this criticism is addressed in the new classical literature is that extensions and elaborations of Kydland and Prescott's model which promise to be more realistic have been and are being developed. Greater realism, it is hoped, will bring greater agreement between the model and the data.[22]

2   Kydland and Prescott present no independent evidence on the size of the parameter that governs technological shocks in their model. They merely choose it to be as large as necessary to obtain their desired result. If it turned out that it were, say, half or twice the size they chose, the model would generate output fluctuations much too small or much too large to be realistic.[23]

In later work, Prescott estimates a Cobb–Douglas production function in which capital and labour are the inputs. Changes in output not explained by changes in capital and labour inputs are assumed to be attributable to shocks to technology.[24] The reliability of this method obviously depends on the correct specification of the production function and the accuracy of the measurements of capital and labour, both of which are questionable.[25] In any case, it is often objected that plausible technological shocks are too small to account for the observed variability of output. Prescott responds, however, that, given the dynamic structure of the model, small *frequent* shocks are sufficient.[26]

Unless technological shocks are tiny, one might expect Kydland and Prescott to be able to point to particular instances of shocks and their effects on output. They never do. Furthermore, it is hard to believe that technology actually regresses to any significant degree, yet total factor productivity does regularly fall, not only cyclically but, in some industries, on trend.[27] Independent evidence on the source and nature of the technological shocks, including an explanation of falling productivity, is needed to make the case for equilibrium real business cycles compelling. Summers, for example, argues that labour hoarding causes observed cyclical falls in productivity.[28] Such an explanation suggests that business cycles are disequilibrium phenomena.

3   Kydland and Prescott justify their assumption that capital requires a definite time to be built with the commonsense observation: '. . . wine is not made in a day . . . neither are ships nor factories built in a day'.[29] In their actual simulations they choose the average construction time for factories reported in empirical studies.[30] While it is true that no capital can be produced instantly, an unanswered criticism of their theory is simply that the time it does take is an economic variable and not a technological constant. Much of the delay in building equipment, for example, arises because the fabricators keep outstanding order books. When a sufficiently unusual opportunity arises, it may be profitable to pay extra to jump the queue. Similarly, faster construction is at the margin typically more expensive construction. The investor must balance the added returns from producing output sooner against the added expense of early completion. This calculation implies that there is an optimal time to build that varies with changing prices and demands. Equally, there should be optimal order queues, and time to build should vary endogenously with the cycle.

4   In Kydland and Prescott's simulations the number of hours worked is not variable enough relative to the variability of productivity to be realistic, and productivity is not a leading indicator of output as it is in the actual economy. They suggest that the very simplicity of the model may account for some of these discrepancies. More constructively, they suggest that the assumption of a homogeneous labour force may prevent the relationship between hours worked and productivity from being accurately modelled. Kydland (1984) extends the model to consider the case of heterogeneous workers, and claims some success in improving its performance. Hansen's extension of their model (discussed below) better captures the relationship between the variabilities of hours and productivity than does Kydland and Prescott's model itself.

5   Kydland and Prescott's model, like a number of other new classical models, places a great deal of emphasis on a high degree of intertemporal substitutability of leisure in order to derive large labour supply and output responses from relatively weak price signals. This hypothesis has some formal econometric support.[31] But much of its support is simply anecdotal: for example, people will rearrange their vacations or work overtime for fairly small premiums over the usual

wage. Recent empirical studies by Ashenfelter (1984) and Mankiw et al. (1985) however, cast serious doubt on the belief that the elasticity of current leisure with respect to future leisure is very high. If their results are true, models built around this premise do not account for enough of the actual fluctuations in output to be plausible. We consider below two models of real business cycles that address this issue: Hansen's model with indivisible labour and Long and Plosser's model with heterogeneous goods.

6   Kydland and Prescott's model, like most real business cycle models, ignores money. Yet the empirical evidence for correlations between money and output and prices is overwhelming. A model by King and Plosser, considered below, addresses this omission. Money in that model reacts passively to the business cycle.

Indivisible Labour

The question of whether the intertemporal substitutability of leisure is high or low turns out to be moot in Hansen's (1985) extension of Kydland and Prescott's model. In their model, in common with most other equilibrium business cycle models, workers are free to supply as many or few hours of work as they wish. Hansen explores the opposite case of complete inflexibility: workers either supply the standard number of hours (say, eight) or they supply none at all. Hansen further assumes that employers do not offer simply to hire workers; rather, they offer a range of contracts, each with particular probabilities of working and not working, and all offering the same wage whether the luck of the draw puts an individual worker in or out of work. Such a contract seems extremely peculiar at first glance. It is in effect, however, the equivalent of workers taking out insurance that fully replaces their lost earnings when out of work. The insurance companies would have to estimate the probability of a worker's being laid off in order to price the insurance contract. While Hansen's assumptions constitute an extreme case, both the relative inability of the typical worker to choose his own hours and the existence of state-run unemployment insurance in most developed countries at least roughly conform to these assumptions. Of course, the limitations and restrictions on state-run insurance mean that insurance is not complete as Hansen's model assumes. With complete insurance, workers in Hansen's model *prefer* to be unemployed: leisure is a good, so that if the wage is the same while leisure is greater when one is out of work, unemployment must be a preferred state.[32]

Hansen's model generates a surprising result that seems to answer one of the strongest objections to Kydland and Prescott's model. No matter what the underlying tastes of workers for leisure in different periods, the intertemporal rate of substitution between leisure in different periods turns out to be infinite. Microeconomic studies that show a low intertemporal rate of substitution based on attempts to characterize the underlying utility functions of workers may not then be relevant to the question of whether the supply of labour is highly sensitive to small changes in relative (intertemporal) wage rates.

This result is easily grasped intuitively. If the working day is fixed at eight hours – no more, no less – then substitution of leisure for any other good is not possible. The expected utility of leisure is an average:

[utility from work × probability of work] +
[utility from not working × (1 − probability of work)].

The utility from working and the utility from not working are constants. Therefore the expected utility of leisure is a linear function of the probability of work. This means that the gain to utility from any small increase in the probability of work is constant. For any given wage rate the probability of work is itself a linear function of the demand for labour. If at some wage the demand for labour is half the labour force then the probability of work is ½, if it is three-quarters of the labour force the probability is ¾ and so on. The expected utility of leisure is then in turn a linear function of labour demanded (or leisure supplied). The marginal utility of leisure (or disutility of labour), like the marginal utility of the probability of work, is then constant. This is true for each period. But, if the marginal utility of leisure is constant in each period irrespective of prices, the marginal benefits of working in each period cannot be brought into equality by adjusting labour supplied smoothly between periods. If, for example, the marginal utility of leisure is the same in every period, then a rational worker would work as much as possible when the wage rate is high (i.e. when leisure is expensive) and as little as possible when the wage rate is low (i.e. when leisure is cheap). Consequently, the elasticity of substitution between leisure in different periods must be infinite – no matter what the underlying preferences of workers are like, and no matter what the elasticity would be if workers were able to choose the number of hours of work at will. If Hansen's model describes the world better than those models which permit continuous adjustment of hours worked, the question of how close a substitute leisure in one period is for leisure in another in the underlying preferences of workers is simply irrelevant.

Hansen's model generates cycles in the same general manner as Kydland and Prescott's model. He assigns values to its parameters in the same way as they do and conducts simulations in order to reveal its properties. He finds that it performs similarly to theirs in most respects. Given its structure, it is not surprising that, unlike theirs, it predicts that some people will be out of work in some stages of the cycle. In Kydland and Prescott's model, when the total number of hours of work demanded in the economy falls, every worker works fewer hours. In Hansen's model, since workers must work the standard number of hours if they work at all, some workers are laid off. Simulations of Hansen's model also show, in contrast with Kydland and Prescott's model, that the total number of hours worked is much more variable than productivity. In fact, it generates a greater variability in hours worked relative to productivity than actual American data support. Hansen believes that this results from his extreme assumption that there is *no* choice in the hours worked. Because there is some choice, the actual data, he argues, fall somewhere between his results and those of Kydland and Prescott.

Models with Heterogeneous Goods

Hansen's model was formulated particularly to overcome a perceived flaw in Kydland and Prescott's model. While not explicitly directed at this problem, Long and Plosser (1983) explore a model in which cycles are generated with no special assumptions about the intertemporal substitutability of leisure. Indeed, Long and Plosser take pains to eliminate most of the usual sources of serial correlation of output from their model. Their model is like other new classical models of the business cycle in that it is an equilibrium model with rational expectations and fixed tastes. It differs sharply from Lucas's model in that agents possess complete current information, there is no government and no money. By construction, monetary misperceptions cannot then be the source of cyclical fluctuations. Lucas's model derives some of the persistence of output fluctuations from the assumption that monetary shocks are themselves serially correlated. Similarly, Kydland and Prescott's model and related models assume that real shocks are serially correlated. Long and Plosser's model permits real shocks, but does not assume that they are serially correlated. The only friction in Kydland and Prescott's model is the fixed time needed to build new capital. Long and Plosser's model has a similar friction: the time needed to build new capital is set at one period. But in contrast with both Lucas's and Kydland and Prescott's model, capital is not long lived but depreciates completely each period.

These assumptions eliminate the usual sources of persistence at the outset. The point is not that they are realistic, but that they help isolate two other features of the economy as likely sources of cyclical fluctuations. The first feature is that output consists of a wide variety of different goods. This is hardly a debatable point. Most formal models, however, treat aggregate output as a single variable, while

Long and Plosser maintain that it is important to pay attention to the separate goods that constitute aggregate output. In particular, they assume that the production of any good requires inputs of labour *and* all other produced goods. The second feature is that a real shock that raises the supply of any good raises the demand for all goods now and in all future periods. Technically, this amounts to the assumption that all (dated) goods are normal goods. While these assumptions are no doubt not strictly correct, they are likely to be good first approximations.

The source of real shocks in this model is random fluctuations in output of particular goods. To take a concrete example: inputs into the production of wheat might be exactly the same in two different years, and yet one year the harvest is high and another year it is low.

Cycles are generated in the model in the following manner. Suppose that the output of, say, wheat is unusually high in the current period. Demand for wheat and all other commodities rises both now and in the future. The new demand for wheat can be satisfied immediately, but since production levels of other commodities are determined by the amount of inputs inherited from the previous period, they cannot be increased in this period to meet the new demand; prices must rise to clear the markets for these commodities. Since demand has also risen for commodities in the future and since extra resources are available in the form of wheat to be used as an input in the production of other commodities, production of all other commodities will increase in the next period. Some of this production will be consumed, but some of it will become increased inputs into production in the third period. The initial shock is thus diffused across various commodities as each serves as an input into the next until its effect finally dwindles away.

This model clearly mimics a key feature of business cycles: various sectors of the economy tend to fluctuate similarly, although typically with some lag between them. It is not obvious from this informal description, but Long and Plosser demonstrate mathematically that their model can imitate the other key feature of business cycles as well: once perturbed, the output of individual goods can oscillate without any further shocks as the model returns to its steady state.[33] Long and Plosser simulate the model using parameters derived from the actual (simplified) input–output table for the United States, and find that it does generate cycles similar to actual business cycles in the United States.

A Model with Money

Most real business cycle models are silent on the relationship of money to output and prices, even though these relationships are among the best documented in economics. To fill this obvious gap, King and

Plosser (1984) explore a model in which money responds passively to the business cycle. King and Plosser's model abstracts from many of the complications addressed by other real business cycle models in order to focus narrowly on the behaviour of money.

Banks in King and Plosser's model use real inputs (capital and labour) to produce real monetary (transactions and accounting) services. These real services are in turn one of the inputs used to produce final output. As in Long and Plosser's model, inputs today produce outputs tomorrow, i.e. there is a fixed period of production of one period. The demand for real monetary services is thus derived from the demand for final output.

Demand deposits (current accounts), sometimes called 'inside money', are the debt of banks to the public.[34] King and Plosser assume that monetary services received are proportional to deposits held. When production of final output is set to increase, the demand for monetary services increases and so do deposits. Production actually increases only after the increase in inputs to the production process. The stock of deposits is, therefore, well correlated with and a leading indication of output. This corresponds to Friedman and Schwartz's evidence on timing of correlated movements of money and output.[35] Yet it is planned movements in output that induce movements in deposits rather than autonomous movements in deposits causing movements in output as Friedman and Schwartz would have it.

Up to this point, King and Plosser ignore any connection between money and prices. This is justified by an appeal to the argument of Fama (1980) that the general price level is the inverse price of *currency* and *central bank reserves* (monetary base or high-powered money) and unrelated to the volume and composition of bank deposits.[36] An extended version of King and Plosser's model includes the monetary base. Currency is assumed to have a comparative advantage over deposits in some transactions. Central bank reserves are held because of reserve requirements. The demand for each component of the monetary base is then well defined and depends on real output and the nominal rate of interest.

A positive shock to output, which also tends to lower interest rates, raises the demand for the monetary base. If its supply is fixed, prices must fall to equilibrate supply and demand. Prices then appear to be counter-cyclical. Actual prices appear to be pro-cyclical. King and Plosser suggest two modifications that would account for pro-cyclical prices. If technological shocks lead to sufficiently large permanent increases in the returns to capital, interest rates would rise enough for the demand for the monetary base to fall, raising prices. Alternatively, if the supply of the monetary base is itself pro-cyclical as the authorities accommodate demand, prices would rise.

One objection to King and Plosser's model is that, given the institutional structure of banking in most countries, deposits cannot respond passively to output. If banks are subject to binding reserve requirements, then deposits cannot be expanded to meet demand in the face of a fixed stock of reserves. It is argued, for example, that, since American banks hold few excess reserves, they could not supply additional deposits to meet increases in demand.[37] This argument overlooks two points. First, central banks generally permit free exchange of currency for bank reserves, so that, even if the monetary base is held constant, its reserve component may expand to meet demand. Second, most central banks do not hold the monetary base constant but allow borrowing, so that a rising demand for reserves is met by an increased supply. The real objection to King and Plosser's model is not the impossibility of money's responding passively to economic activity but the overdifferentiation of the monetary base from deposits (see chapter 5) and the assumption of constantly clearing markets, which is an objection to all new classical models of the business cycle (and is taken up in the next section).

King and Plosser offer some empirical evidence that mildly supports their hypothesis. It is that deposits (inside money) correlate better with output than does the monetary base (outside money), while the monetary base correlates better with prices than do deposits. Both are predictions of their model.

3.4 The Persistence of the Keynesian Problem

The debate between advocates of monetary and real equilibrium models of the business cycle is a domestic dispute. Fundamental methodological commitments are not at stake. The issue is only which sort of model best captures the actual sources of cyclical fluctuations. Neither camp questions the belief that models of business cycles should conform to the fundamental tenets of new classicism. If models such as King and Plosser's challenge the monetarist presumption that money causally dominates prices and output, it shows only that the new classical school was never as close a cousin to monetarism as many at first believed.

Criticism of equilibrium models of the business cycle also comes from outside the new classical family. While much of this criticism is like the domestic disputes (i.e. it is criticism of the details of the construction of particular models), the most important criticism challenges the fundamental new classical belief that markets clear continuously throughout the cycle. Modern macroeconomics began with Keynes's *General Theory*, which is primarily an attempt to diagnose the causes and to suggest cures for involuntary unemployment. Equilibrium business cycle models – both the models based on misperceptions of monetary policy and real business cycle models – banish the whole notion of involuntary unemployment.

For Keynes, a worker is involuntarily unemployed when he is willing and able to work at the same wage received by workers like him in every relevant respect, yet the employer will not hire him.[38] The maximum economically efficient output produced in an economy occurs when there is no involuntary unemployment, i.e. when the labour market clears. In Keynes's view, variations in aggregate demand cause fluctuations in output below this maximum, and total involuntary unemployment varies in step with output. Business cycles are thought of as disequilibrium departures from market clearing, the result of some sort of market failure which stands in need of correction. States of involuntary unemployment are not Pareto efficient in that an intervention (say, stimulation of aggregate demand) can make everyone richer and no one poorer.

In contrast, unemployment in equilibrium business cycle models is voluntary. Workers choose to supply varying amounts of labour because that is what allows them to achieve their most desirable mixture of leisure and consumption in the current and future periods. (Even in Hansen's model, the unemployed have freely chosen a contract that gives them some probability of being out of work.) Similarly, producers choose to produce varying amounts of output because, given their information and the constraints they face, this helps them to maximize profits. Business cycles, then, are not deviations from equilibrium but transitory fluctuations of the equilibrium itself. As equilibrium phenomena, they are also Pareto efficient: they do not represent a flaw in the economy that a rearrangement of resources could correct at no cost to anyone.[39]

Lucas argues that the differences between the Keynesian approach to fluctuations in employment and output and the new classical equilibrium business cycle models arise because new classical economists draw a sounder distinction in defining unemployment than Keynes did. The actual patterns of output and employment over time seem to be well characterized as long-term (slowly changing) trends with rather more rapid cycles about these trends. Faced with such patterns, Lucas claims that Keynes's distinction is meant to assign different theoretical explanations to the cycle (the theory of involuntary unemployment) and to the trend (the classical theory of long-run equilibrium, which involves only voluntary unemployment).[40] This distinction is flawed, Lucas believes, because it distinguishes between *types* of unemployment, each requiring a separate theoretical explanation, rather than between *sources* of unemployment within a single theoretical explanation. Lucas writes:

Nor is there any evident reason why one would *want* to draw this distinction. Certainly the more one thinks about the decision problem facing individual workers and firms the less sense this distinction makes. The worker who loses a good job in prosperous times does not *volunteer* to be in this situation: he has suffered a capital loss. Similarly, the firm which loses an experienced employee in depressed times suffers an undesired capital loss. Nevertheless the unemployed worker at any time can always find *some* job at once, and a firm can always fill a vacancy instantaneously. That neither typically does so *by choice* is not difficult to understand given the quality of the jobs and the employees which are easiest to find. Thus there is an involuntary element in *all* unemployment, in the sense that no one chooses bad luck over good; there is also a voluntary element in all unemployment, in the sense that however miserable one's current work options, one can always choose to accept them.[41]

Lucas goes on to accuse Keynes of indulging in mere word-play in his definition of unemployment. The phrase 'the existing money wage', he argues, is completely ambiguous. Unless it is defined '. . . as the price someone else is willing to pay him for his labor. . . , what *is* it?' And, if it is defined in this way, there is no such thing as involuntary unemployment, for there is always some wage available to any worker and, if they do not accept it, they are voluntarily unemployed.

The unemployed in new classical equilibrium models have chosen leisure over work. Lucas suggests that people dislike saying that the unemployed in a recession are enjoying leisure because this might be taken to imply that they like depressions. He writes: 'Of course, the hypothesis of a cleared labour market carries with it no such suggestion, any more than the observation that people go hungry in cleared food markets suggests that people enjoy hunger.'[42] Lucas's observation is really no more than the elementary point that a Pareto-efficient allocation may be a perfectly frightful one. Still, it is beside the point. The real objection to equilibrium business cycles is more fundamental and correct.

The point at issue between the new classicals and those opponents who endorse Keynes's notion of involuntary unemployment is not the happiness of the worker, but rather whether the concept of involuntary unemployment actually delineates circumstances of economic importance. According to new classicals, a worker sets his real reservation wage equal to the value of his marginal disutility of labour. A firm sets its offer wage equal to the worker's expected marginal product. If the worker's reservation wage is higher than all offer wages, then he is unemployed. This is his preference given his options. For the new classicals, the unemployed have placed and lost a bet. It is sad perhaps, but optimal.

Keynes agrees that a worker sets his real reservation wage to the value of the marginal disutility of labour. But he calls a worker unemployed not when wages offered to him directly fall short of his reservation wage, but when wages received by objectively similar workers *exceed* his reservation wage as well as their own. In such a situation the unemployed do not prefer to be out of work, nor are they even indifferent between working and not working: instead, they positively wish to work, and most of those in work would be willing to work for less than they actually receive.

It is relatively easy to formulate models that exhibit such Keynesian unemployment. One model that appeals to many modern Keynesians rests on the notion of 'efficiency wages'.[43] If productivity is a function of the wage rate, because wages influence morale or shirking behaviour or for other reasons, rather than take the wage rate as given and choose only the amount of labour demanded, a firm will choose both the amount of labour demanded *and* the wage rate in order to maximize profits. In general, less labour will be demanded at the efficiency wage than would be willingly supplied. The wage may not be cut because the loss to the firm from lower productivity counteracts the gain from lower wages. Those people who would work and could work at the current wage but receive no offers are involuntarily unemployed.

The problem for Keynesians is not that there is any ambiguity about the concept of involuntary unemployment. Rather, it is that the reason why wages do not adjust to clear the market needs to be spelled out. Keynes's own attempts to do so were not overwhelming successes, and the issue remains live. Still, involuntary unemployment is not, as the new classicals would have it, unreal just because we do not fully understand it. If that were true we would all be able to fly because physicists do not fully understand gravity.

Involuntary unemployment for Keynes is rightly not measured against the standard of offers of employment that are actually forthcoming. A steelworker is not involuntarily unemployed because he refuses a job as a street-sweeper at £2 an hour. He is involuntarily unemployed because other men with the same abilities are employed as steelworkers at £5 an hour, and he would take the same job were it offered to him. Lucas is correct to observe that the question usually asked to determine measured unemployment, 'Are you actively seeking work?', does not correspond precisely to Keynes's concept of involuntary unemployment, but who could doubt that many who respond 'yes' to this question could also honestly and accurately say that there are jobs for which they are perfectly well qualified that they would accept at the current rate if those jobs were offered to them?

Of course Lucas's argument suggests the possible saving move of saying that the unemployed steelworker does not really possess the same abilities and qualifications as his employed fellow, otherwise it would be one of the others and not him who was out of work. But this would be to make Lucas's view empty and his definition of voluntary unemployment tautological. To take one example, the fact that workers are often laid off according to seniority, which in many cases bears little relation to productivity, and later rehired to the same job shows that, during their period out of work, they were qualified and willing to work at the wage other workers received, yet were not employed, i.e. they were involuntarily unemployed on Keynes's definition.

Lucas acknowledges that there are models in which workers are constrained from supplying all the hours they might like, and that the voluntary/involuntary distinction makes some sense in them.[44] Such models are often meant to explain involuntary unemployment. But, says Lucas,

> [t]his misses the point: involuntary unemployment is not a fact or a phenomenon which it is the task of theorists to explain. It is, on the contrary, a theoretical construct which Keynes introduced in the hope that it would be helpful in discovering a correct explanation for a genuine phenomenon: large-scale fluctuations in measured, total unemployment. Is it the task of modern theoretical economics to 'explain' the theoretical constructs of our predecessors, whether or not they have proved fruitful?[45]

While it is easy to agree with Lucas that it is not our task as economists to explain the theoretical constructs of our predecessors, it is wrong to dismiss involuntary unemployment as simply an ill-defined term that fails to isolate a genuine phenomenon. It is not Keynes who has engaged in word-play, but Lucas who, from having paid insufficient attention to Keynes's words, has misconstrued their clear meaning. It is not Keynes's theoretical construct that economists need to explain, but the real phenomenon of there sometimes being a pool of qualified workers who are not employed in jobs that currently pay wages at rates that they would in fact accept *and* at the same time those wage rates showing no tendency to fall.

Part III Monetary Theory and Policy

4 The Limits of Monetary Policy: Macroeconomic Models

An oft-told tale in the mythology surrounding Keynesian macroeconomics holds that it claimed to provide both the intellectual justification and the analytical tools needed delicately to manipulate (to 'fine tune') the performance of the economy. As with many myths, this one contains a kernel of truth. Yet, as is usually the case, the debunkers of the myth exaggerated the credulity of its supposed adherents. Milton Friedman is the most prominent of the early debunkers. The message of his famous presidential address to the American Economic Association (1968a) was twofold: first, monetary policy has the power in the long run to control the rate of inflation, but not the level of real output or employment; second, in the short run it will often have pernicious effects on real variables if badly executed, and only temporary favourable effects even if well executed.

The best-known proposition to emerge from the new classical economics asserts that Friedman was too generous in ascribing power to monetary policy over real output: monetary policy cannot *systematically* affect real output (or employment) even in the short run. The notion that the new classical economics is a kind of radical monetarism originates principally in this so-called *policy-ineffectiveness proposition*. The fact that the same new classical models that generate the policy-ineffectiveness proposition also demonstrate a quantity-theoretic relationship between money and prices seems to confirm the aptness of the title 'radical monetarism'.

The policy-ineffectiveness proposition is derived from the application of the essential principles of new classicism – market clearing, rational expectations and only real variables matter – to fairly standard macromodels. For some new classicals the application of these principles was too tentative and of too limited a scope. Sargent and Wallace, for example, observe that policy in the standard policy-ineffectiveness models is too unfettered. In real life an intertemporal budget constraint binds the government's hands. The choice of a particular fiscal policy rules out certain monetary policies. The new classical tenets must then be applied to coordinated policy strategies and not to independent policy actions. From their analysis, Sargent and Wallace reach a yet more radical conclusion: monetarist policy prescriptions may not be capable of achieving monetarist ends; inflation may sometimes be beyond the control of monetary policy.

Some new classicals see even this application of new classical principles as too limited. Policy makers are still seen as freely choosing among alternative strategies. Yet as economic agents, if new classical principles hold, they should make optimal choices given their preferences and the constraints they face. Such an analysis emasculates the positive/normative distinction in economics, for if policy makers already choose optimally they have no need for normative advice. The best the economist can do is to describe their behaviour.

In this chapter we examine the progressive widening of the scope of application of the principles of new classicism. Each step imposes more stringent limitations on the usefulness of policy and carries the new classical analysis further from its monetarist roots.

4.1 Policy Ineffectiveness

Radical Monetarism?

The policy-ineffectiveness proposition is easily understood with a simple model. The first of two essential elements is that output is determined by a Lucas aggregate supply function (see chapter 2 section 2.2):

$$y_t = \bar{y} + \alpha(p_t - {}_{t-1}p_t^e) + \varepsilon_t, \tag{4.1}$$

Where y_t is the level of output in period t, $\bar{y}$ is a constant natural rate of output determined by technology and resources, p_t is the actual level of prices in period t; ${}_{t-1}p_t^e$ is the level of prices that economic agents in period $t - 1$ expect to hold in period t, ε_t is a serially uncorrelated random error with a mean of zero and α is a constant. (Throughout section 4.1 lower-case letters indicate the natural logarithms of variables.) The Lucas supply function states that deviations of output around its natural rate depend on deviations of actual from expected prices.

The simplest way to model aggregate demand is as a quantity equation: $MV = PY$. Choosing units so that the income velocity V of money is unity and taking logarithms, this can be written

$$p_t = m_t - y_t + u_t, \tag{4.2}$$

where u_t is a random error term added to reflect velocity shocks[1]

Systematic monetary policy can be described as the choice of a fixed rate of growth λ for the money stock. A policy rule would then be $M_t = (1 + \lambda)M_{t-1}$ or, written in logarithms,[2]

$$m_t = \lambda + m_{t-1} + e_t, \tag{4.3}$$

where e_t is a serially uncorrelated random error term with mean zero added to reflect mistakes in targeting the growth of the money stock.

Finally, the second essential element of the model is the hypothesis that expectations of prices are formed rationally:

$$_{t-1}p_t^e = E(p_t \mid I_{t-1}), \tag{4.4}$$

where I_{t-1} represents all information available at time $t - 1$. The question of whether or not monetary policy can systematically affect output (and employment) is simply a question of whether or not the policy parameter λ is part of the solution of the model for output y_t. In order to answer this question, apply expression (4.4) to expression (4.2) by taking the mathematical expectation of both sides given the information available at time $t - 1$. The best predictor of m_t is given by the non-random part of equation (4.3). The best prediction of y_t is its average value $\bar{y}$. Since u_t is random and not serially correlated, its best predicted value is its mean $\bar{u} = 0$. Therefore

$$_{t-1}p_t^e = E\left(p_t \mid I_{t-1}\right) - \lambda + m_{t-1} - \bar{y}. \tag{4.5}$$

Substitute equation (4.3) into equation (4.2) to give

$$p_t = \lambda + m_{t-1} + e_t - y_t + u_t \tag{4.6}$$

Subtract equation (4.5) from equation (4.6) to yield

$$\begin{aligned} p_t - {}_{t-1}p_t^e &= \lambda + m_{t-1} + e_t - y_t + u_t - \lambda - m_{t-1} + \bar{y} \\ &= \bar{y} - y_t + e_t + u_t \end{aligned} \tag{4.7}$$

Substitute this into equation (4.1) and rearrange to yield

$$y_t = \bar{y} + (1 + \alpha)^{-1}[\alpha(u_t + e_t) + \varepsilon_t]. \tag{4.8}$$

The important message of equation (4.8) is that the rate of growth λ of the supply of money does not enter into the determination of output y_t. Systematic monetary policy is ineffective.

Although the algebra behind this result is simple, the underlying intuition is even simpler. According to Lucas's view of aggregate supply, deviations of output from its natural level occur because of expectational errors: actual prices that are higher or lower than expected prices lead people to believe that relative prices have altered, so that it is desirable to adjust their output. If people have rational expectations, then they use their knowledge of the monetary authority's policy rule to form their expectations of future prices. Consequently, no matter what rate of growth of the money stock the authority chooses, it cannot trick economic agents into incorrectly forecasting prices. Because prices are assumed to clear the market quickly and because there are no systematic expectational errors, there is no systematic effect on output.

All this is not to say that economic agents do not make expectational errors. The term in square brackets in equation (4.8) represents the errors. Equation (4.8) shows that output varies randomly about the natural rate. The monetary authorities could affect output by randomly varying the stock of money. This would show up as a rise in the variance of e_t in equations (4.3) and (4.8). This would merely cause output to become more variable – probably an undesirable result. The authorities could not cause y_t to become systematically greater by forcing the shocks to e_t to be positive on average, for any *systematic* departure of e_t from zero would by definition be more correctly represented as a change in λ, which we have already seen does not affect output.

Monetarism holds that, in the long run, monetary policy cannot control real variables while it can completely control the level of prices. From the standpoint of the policy-ineffectiveness proposition, the new classical economics appears to be *radical* monetarism because it confirms not only the monetarist belief in the limits of monetary policy, but also claims that the long run is in fact very short. Monetary policy, they maintain, operates essentially by inducing expectational errors. Friedman suggested that such errors might persist for some time, while Lucas, Sargent and Wallace, Barro and others argue that rational expectations require that they not persist beyond an initial surprise. Were the authorities to attempt to surprise the public with a series of positive shocks to the supply of money, the public would very quickly come to anticipate their policy and the resulting level of prices, rendering it ineffective.

Without offering any argument, Sargent and Wallace assert:

> There is no longer any serious debate about whether monetary policy should be conducted according to rules or discretion. Quite appropriately, it is widely agreed that monetary policy should obey a rule, that is, a schedule expressing the setting of the monetary authority's instrument (e.g. the money supply) as a function of all the information it has received up through the current moment.[3]

The issue of rules versus discretion simply does not arise for the new classicals. On this they are at one with the monetarists, although their reasons are different. Monetarists such as Friedman believe that rules are best because the difficulties of obtaining accurate and timely information about the state of the economy and the inability of the government to adjust policy quickly and accurately mean that discretionary policy is at best useless and at worst maladjusted and destabilizing. The new classical case, in contrast, rests not on the inefficiency of the government but on the efficiency of the private sector in ascertaining the true nature of policy and taking countervailing steps.

Given that both the monetarists and the new classicals advocate rules, the question remains: what kind of rule is best? Friedman's rule of constant growth of the supply of money is a *fixed* (or 'no-feedback') rule to be followed no matter what the current state of the economy. Another possibility, however, is a *contingent* (or 'feedback') rule, which adjusts the instruments of monetary policy in a predetermined way contingent upon the current state of the economy.

It seems plausible that contingent rules are superior to fixed rules as policy is allowed to adjust to changing circumstances. Yet the policy-ineffectiveness proposition suggests that this is not so. In the model (equations (4.1)–(4.4)) a contingent rule would make λ a function of the shocks to the economy ε_t and u_t. Thus the rises in world oil prices in 1973 and 1979 would be represented as large positive values for ε_t, and might suggest a larger value for the growth of money λ in order to accommodate the shock. But clearly, if there are rational expectations and the public can observe the shock and understands the rule, they will correctly anticipate the effect of the monetary accommodation on prices and output will not be affected. Whether λ is a constant or a known function, it does not appear in equation (4.8).

The policy-ineffectiveness proposition, then, gives only weak support to a fixed rule such as Friedman's. No rule has any effect on average output.[4] Of course this result depends on the assumption of rational expectations and perfectly clearing markets, which is meant to be only an approximation of actual behaviour. A simple fixed rule might then be preferred because the public has more difficulty working out the implications of a contingent rule, and consequently makes more frequent, even if unsystematic, mistakes, raising the variance of output. Similarly, the monetary authority might have difficulty in applying a contingent rule, raising e_t in equation (4.3) and again raising the variance of output.

Even if a fixed rule seems preferable to a contingent rule, Friedman's preference for a *low* rate of growth of the money supply finds no special support in the new classical analysis. Only if perfectly anticipated inflation can be shown to be bad would such support follow.[5]

Using a model related to equations (4.1)–(4.4), Sargent and Wallace

(1975) do find support for the monetarist's preference for targeting the stock of money rather than an interest rate. Their model replaces equation (4.2) with IS and LM curves in which the demand for money depends on the nominal rate of interest and real aggregate demand depends on the real rate of interest. The monetary authority now has a choice of using money or the interest rate as a target. If it targets money, the policy-ineffectiveness proposition is derived as before, and the rate of inflation is determined by the rate of growth of the stock of money.

$R = r + \dot{p}^e$

If instead it targets the rate of interest, policy ineffectiveness is again established but the rate of inflation is indeterminate. The indeterminacy arises because the public knows that, whatever rate of inflation it expects, the monetary authority must adjust the stock of money in order to accommodate it. To see this, suppose that the public expects a high rate of inflation; this would raise the nominal rate of interest above its targeted level unless the monetary authority expands the supply of money, but the increased supply of money simply increases the actual rate of inflation. Whatever rate of inflation the public expects it gets. If perfectly anticipated inflation is bad, then there seems to be a case for adopting a money supply rule rather than an interest rate rule.

How Robust is the Policy-ineffectiveness Proposition?

The policy-ineffectiveness proposition rests on two essential planks of the new classical platform: the hypothesis of rational expectations (and a subsidiary assumption that information is equally well known to the public and to the monetary authorities) and the Lucas aggregate supply function. Obviously, the proposition fails if expectations are not rational. For example, if people eventually, but only slowly, learn what the authority's rule for the growth of the supply of money is, as Friedman assumes, then, when the authority chooses a higher rate of growth, the public's expectation of prices will lag behind actual prices and output will be higher on average. Once the public catches on to the current rule, the authority chooses an even higher rate, and again reaps the benefit.

Rational expectations is not, however, itself enough to ensure that the proposition holds. For suppose that the monetary authorities have better information about the state of the economy than the public. For example, suppose that they learn about shocks to aggregate demand before the public does. In terms of our model, they know the actual value of u_t. They could then adopt a policy rule:

$$m_t = \lambda + m_{t-1} - u_t + e_t. \tag{4.3'}$$

The rule says that the authorities reduce the money stock whenever there is a positive shock to aggregate demand and increase it for negative shocks: they 'lean against the wind'. The analogous expression to equation (4.8) can be derived using equation (4.3').

$$y_t = \bar{y} + (1 + \alpha)^{-1}(\alpha e_t + \varepsilon_t). \tag{4.8'}$$

This shows that, although a systematic monetary policy still cannot raise the mean level of output above its natural rate (i.e. λ does not appear), it can stabilize output in the sense of reducing its variability around the natural rate (this follows, since the random error u_t has been eliminated from equation (4.8') so that it must have a lower variance than equation (4.8) as long as e_t and ε_t are independent of u_t).

Systematic monetary policy can be effective, even under new classical rules, as long as the monetary authorities have an informational advantage over the public. Some new classicals question whether or not such an advantage exists. Others point out that, even if it does exist, sharing the information with the public would achieve the same end of stabilizing output.[6] Whether information should be shared or the policy rule should exploit the authority's informational advantage depends on which is the less costly procedure.

The Lucas aggregate supply function is the second essential plank supporting the policy-ineffectiveness proposition, and it is the one challenged in the most formidable attacks on the proposition. The Lucas aggregate supply function is derived on the assumption that all prices are perfectly flexible and move rapidly to clear the market. Several authors have pointed out, however, that because of contractual arrangements, costs of adjustment or other sources of inertia many prices are sticky. The implications of this fact are well illustrated in Fischer's (1977) model of staggered two-period wage contracts.

Fischer adopts a modified version of the model in equations (4.1)–(4.4). He concentrates on wage contracts as a likely source of inertia. Suppose that workers and firms negotiate two year contracts aimed at keeping the real wage constant: $W_t/P_t = $ constant. Choosing units so that the constant is unity and taking logarithms, this can be rewritten as $w_t = p_t$. Assume that half the firms make contracts in even-numbered years and the other half in odd-numbered years. Equation (4.1) can then be rewritten:

$$y_t = \bar{y} + \tfrac{1}{2}\alpha(p_t - {}_{t-2}w_t^e) + \tfrac{1}{2}\alpha(p_t - {}_{t-1}w_t^e) + \varepsilon_t. \tag{4.1'}$$

This says that output exceeds its natural rate whenever prices are higher (so that real wages are lower) than had been expected when the wage contract was drawn up. The expectations for half the firms were formed at time $t - 2$ (i.e. they are in the second period of their contract), while expectations for the other half were formed at time $t - 1$. We continue to assume that expectations are formed rationally.

In order to give a sensible role to policy, assume that in equation (4.2) $u_t = \rho u_{t-1} + z_t$, where ρ is a constant and z_t is a serially uncorrelated random variable with mean zero. This expression simply means that u_t is serially correlated. If, for example, an unexpected slump in foreign trade generates a negative shock to aggregate demand, it can be expected to have negative effects in subsequent periods as well (as long as $\rho > 0$).

Now suppose that the monetary authority follows a modified form of the contingent rule (4.3'):

$$m_t = \lambda + m_{t-1} - \gamma u_{t-1} + e_t, \qquad (4.3'')$$

where γ is a constant. This says that they react to shocks to aggregate demand in the last period by estimating their effects on the current period (i.e. ρu_{t-1}) and 'leaning against the wind'. We do not assume that the authorities have any informational advantage over the public – in particular, they do not know z_t, the new shock to current aggregate demand.

We have already seen that when contracts are for one period, the policy-ineffectiveness proposition goes through. It is nevertheless easy to see that with two-period staggered contracts it does not.

Consider the case of the unexpected slump in trade ($z_0 < 0$) that reduces aggregate demand in period 0. Since it was unexpected, prices in period 0 fall (equation (4.2)), real wages rise and therefore output falls below its natural rate (equation (4.1')). Even if there are no new shocks in period 1 (i.e. $z_1 = 0$), the slump will continue in period 1 (by the amount ρu_{t-1}). Those firms negotiating new contracts in period 0 for period 1 can account for the continuing slump and lower their nominal wage offers for the contract covering periods 1 and 2. But those firms that negotiated contracts in period 1 for periods 0 and 1 are stuck with a real wage that is too high, so that output is depressed below the natural rate.

Now suppose that the monetary authority 'leans against the wind' i.e. it expands the stock of money by γu_{t-1}. (γ can be chosen optimally to minimize the variance in y_t.) This tends to raise demand and prices. Firms which are able to negotiate new contracts for period 1 rationally anticipate this action and set their nominal wages in order to offset any effect of the authority's action. Although they rationally anticipate the authority's actions as well, firms which are contractually obligated to a fixed nominal wage nevertheless benefit from it. The higher price level lowers their real wage and boosts their output above its natural rate.

Therefore the policy-ineffectiveness proposition fails, not because of a failure of expectations to be rational or an informational advantage of the monetary authority over the public, but rather because of an institutionalized inability of some firms to make full use of available information. Because of their binding contracts, firms cannot obtain desirable real wages by adjusting nominal wages. The monetary authority, in contrast, can make a favourable adjustment to real wages by adjusting prices.

4.2 Monetarist Arithmetic

Strategies versus Actions

The policy-ineffectiveness proposition was developed in fairly standard macroeconomic models. The new classicals used such models more as a means of demonstrating the importance of the hypothesis of rational expectations than for their intrinsic merits as models of the economy. Since the rational expectations hypothesis is now widely used even by non-new classical economists, criticism is usually directed to other features of the models, such as the Lucas aggregate supply function. Two criticisms of the models originate within the new classical camp itself. First, the models are *ad hoc;* they are not derived from the behaviour of individual optimizing agents.[8] This issue is taken up in chapters 6 and 7. Second, the models do not adequately characterize the nature of policy making. We take up this criticism here and in the next section.

Up to this point, policy has been characterized simply as a matter of choosing parameters (λ or γ in equation (4.3″)) and choosing fixed or contingent rules. Changing policy appears to be simply a matter of choosing new parameters. If, for example, $\lambda = 10$ per cent in the model (equations (4.1)–(4.4)) the stock of money would grow at 10 per cent, as would prices. If a monetarist were to object that inflation were too high, lowering inflation would merely require choosing a lower λ. The new classicals make at least three related objections to characterizing policy in this simple manner.

First, the model's asset structure is too simple – money is the only financial asset – so that it is not possible to address important questions about government finance or open-market operations. A more realistic model must at least include government bonds. Second, once government bonds are included, it is clear that the choice of the level of the money stock is not unfettered but is related to the choice of policy with respect to deficits and the stock of bonds. But, third, once it is recognized that the *stocks* of money and bonds are related to deficits, which are *flows* of income per unit time, it becomes clear that one should address the dynamic problem of policy *strategies* rather than individual independent policy *actions*.[9]

Sargent and Wallace (1981) offer an analysis of monetary and fiscal policy which meets these objections and, strikingly, generates very non-monetarist conclusions about the conduct of monetary policy from apparently monetarist assumptions. The starting point for the analysis is the simple observation that the government deficit (defined as expenditure on goods and services less tax revenue) must be financed through some combination of additions to the monetary base (currency plus bank reserves at the central bank) or additions to the stock of government bonds. Furthermore, interest payments on outstanding government debt must be financed similarly. Governments are therefore bound by a budget constraint:[10]

$$D_t + r_{t-1}B_{t-1} = (B_t - B_{t-1}) + (M_t - M_{t-1}), \tag{4.9}$$

where D is the deficit excluding interest payments, B is the stock of bonds, M is the monetary base and r is the rate of interest. (Bonds are here all assumed to be one-period bonds.)

The government budget constraint reminds us that fiscal policy may dictate monetary policy and vice versa. Furthermore, because past decisions to issue or retire bonds affect the current amount of interest paid, a complete analysis of policy must examine the expected paths of future policy as well as current policy.

Sargent and Wallace examine the possible conflict between monetary policy and fiscal policy. They consider two polar cases. First, monetary policy dominates: the monetary authority refuses to allow rapid monetary growth, and so the government reins in its deficit. Second, fiscal policy dominates: deficit policy is determined independently of monetary policy; monetary policy must conform. Sargent and Wallace believe that the second case is the most relevant – especially in the United States.

In the case in which fiscal policy dominates, the monetary authority still appears to have a choice between a loose or tight monetary policy. A monetary policy might be called tight if the bond stock grows faster than national income, i.e. the monetary base grows more slowly than national income. Sargent and Wallace attempt to demonstrate that the apparent choice of a tight or loose monetary policy is sometimes illusory: tight money today may necessarily imply loose money tomorrow.

The critical assumption in their argument is that there is some definite limit to the amount of government debt that the public will hold as a proportion of national income. In the face of a continuing deficit, a tight monetary policy implies that the ratio of debt to national income is rising. Eventually it must reach the limit, and monetary policy must then be loosened, with inflation the result.

Tight Money and Inflation

Sargent and Wallace consider two versions of the analysis. The details of each version are easily illustrated.

Version I: tight money now implies inflation later Assume that the economy is monetarist in that the quantity theory holds so that prices are directly proportional to the stock of money: $P = MV/Y$. Assume that national income Y grows at a constant rate g. Assume that the public will hold government debt as a proportion of national income only below some definite limit: $b = B/Y < \bar{b}$. Finally assume that the real rate of interest is constant at a rate greater than the rate of growth of national income: $r > g$.

Now consider the following policy illustrated in figure 4.1. The deficit is assumed to be a constant fraction of national income: $D_t/Y_t = $ constant. Therefore both D and Y grow at a rate g. The path of national income is shown by the line Y_0Y with a slope g. Monetary policy is tight: the deficit and the interest payments on goverment debt are financed entirely through the sale of government bonds. The stock of money is therefore constant along the horizontal line M_0M_1. Total government debt grows along the path B_0B_1.[11] The ratio of the debt to national income is found by subtracting Y_0Y from B_0B and is shown as b_0b_1. Since $r > g$, the gap between Y_0Y and B_0B must close and then reverse, so that b_0b_1 is upward sloping with a gradient r-g. That is, since the rate of interest exceeds the rate of growth of national income, the ratio of debt to national income must rise steadily under a tight monetary policy.

Figure 4.1 shows b steadily growing, surpassing $\bar{b}$ at time T. But that is infeasible by assumption: the public simply will not hold debt at an ever-increasing ratio to national income. Once we arrive at time T, debt cannot grow faster than national income. Consequently, the actual path of the bond stock must be given by $B_0B_TB_2$, where the segment B_TB_2 is parallel to Y_0Y with a slope g. But once on this more slowly growing path for debt, acceptable increases in the bond stock are not sufficient to cover the faster increases of the interest payments on the existing debt. The monetary base must therefore be allowed to grow if the government budget constraint is to be respected. Its path is shown by $M_0M_TM_2$, where the segment M_TM_2 increases, but at a diminishing rate, as the ratio of government's unfunded liability to the debt itself diminishes.

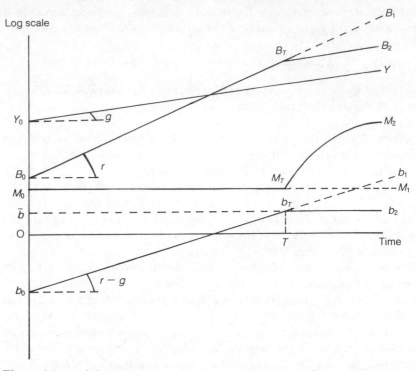

Figure 4.1 A tight monetary policy eventually causes inflation of the money stock (the rate of interest exceeds the rate of growth of national income)

Since the quantity theory with a constant velocity holds by assumption, the increase in the monetary base at a rate greater than national income after time T immediately translates into inflation. Tight money eventually generates inflation. The conclusion is not restricted to the example chosen: as long as the stock of bonds is positive, the interest rate is greater than the rate of growth of the economy and the government does not adjust its real expenditures or taxes to offset rising interest payments, if there is a limit to the volume of bonds that the public will hold, the deficit must eventually be monetized. Tight monetary policy (i.e. any policy in which the monetary base grows less quickly than $r - g$ resulting in a rising b) ensures more rapid monetary growth later. A perfectly accommodating monetary policy (i.e. the monetary base growing at $r - g$) may not generate any inflation at all (as long as $r - g < g$).

Version 2: tight money now implies inflation now Sargent and Wallace also consider a case in which the inflationary consequences of tight money are immediate. In this version they replace the simple quantity equation with a demand-for-money function that relates the quantity of real balances that people desire to hold inversely to the expected rate of inflation. Expected inflation raises the opportunity cost of holding real balances (i.e. it lowers their real return) so that people prefer to hold fewer real balances and to consume more now and less later. This demand-for-money function has a long history in monetarist analyses of hyperinflation.[12]

If people wish to hold fewer real balances and nominal balances are held constant, prices must rise. Therefore a tight monetary policy that implies future inflation, as in version 1, can also imply current inflation through an expectational mechanism. Again, a looser monetary policy may eliminate the need for such a sharp rise in monetary growth in the future and, if it raises *current prices*, may reduce the otherwise unfavourable trade-off between current and future consumption, mitigating the effect of future inflation on the current demand for real balances.

Arithmetical Errors?

Both versions of Sargent and Wallace's analysis suggest that in some circumstances monetarist prescriptions for the conduct of monetary policy are unable to achieve the monetarist end of control over the rate of inflation. Their analysis has been challenged on two grounds. First, Nissan Liviatan (1984) suggests that Sargent and Wallace may have wrongly defined a constant fiscal policy to be one in which the government sticks to a definite set of plans for taxation and expenditures on real goods and services but *excludes* interest payments from these plans. It is more reasonable, he argues, to suppose that a constant fiscal policy is a definite set of plans for taxation and total expenditure *including* interest payments.[13] In this case, bonds could not grow without limit because real expenditures and taxes would be adjusted to compensate for any unplanned interest payments in order to hold total outlays to planned levels.

This alternative definition of the budget of course seems reasonable: political discussions of balanced budgets implicitly include interest payments.[14] The usual inability of politicians, however, actually to agree to cut real expenditures in the face of deficits suggests that Sargent and Wallace are right to exclude interest payments. In the clash of monetary and fiscal policy – as we observed earlier – fiscal policy seems to dominate in practice.

Michael Darby (1984) challenges the anti-monetarist conclusion on another ground. He observes that the rate of interest is more likely to

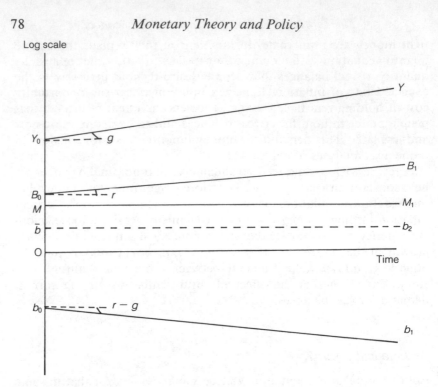

Figure 4.2 A tight monetary policy is sustainable (the rate of growth of national income exceeds the rate of interest)

be less than the rate of growth of national income than to be greater as Sargent and Wallace assume. Consider figure 4.2. Suppose that $r < g$. Then the line B_0B_1 in figure 4.2 is shallower than its analogue in figure 4.1. The gap between Y_0Y and B_0B_1 widens rather than narrows, so that b becomes smaller rather than larger over time, as shown by b_0b_1 which never crosses $\bar{b}b_2$. The ratio of debt to national income declines in this case; it becomes easier and not harder to sell the public more debt. Tight money in such a case does not imply future monetary expansion, so that, in a world governed by the quantity theory, it does not imply future or current inflation. Monetarist policies achieve monetarist ends.

Darby's case for the assumption $r < g$ is based on the fact that the average real rate of interest in the past in the United States was well below the rate of growth of national income. Sargent and Miller (1984) respond to Darby in two parts. First, past history does not restrict the future. Darby's data refer to earlier policy regimes, and when regimes change, the behaviour of observed variables such as interest rates usually changes.[15] Real interest rates in 1981, when Sargent and

Wallace's paper was written, were in fact greater than the rate of growth of national income. The Reagan administration, they believe, represented a change in policy regime.

Second, even if real rates were not yet higher than the expected future rate of growth of national income, rising budget deficits, as under the Reagan regime, would tend to drive real rates up in order to persuade people to hold more debt.[16]

Whether or not monetarist policies can achieve monetarist ends would, then, appear to be a question of whether the real rate of interest will remain below the rate of growth of national income, to be judged on the basis of empirical facts and the supposition of a correct understanding of the workings of the economy. Sargent and Miller's own argument, however, suggests a deeper objection to their analysis. If interest rates are positively related to the level of bond sales, is there any reason to believe that there is some volume of bonds that the public would refuse to hold at *any* rate of interest? That is, is there any reason to believe that a limit such as $\bar{b}$ exists? If not, Sargent and Wallace's argument fails because perpetual bond finance is never ruled out; the debt need never be monetized.[17]

Sargent and Wallace derive the limit $\bar{b}$ in an overlapping-generations model with legal restrictions in which the rich hold only bonds and the poor only money. The limit follows from the assumption of particular restrictions on the utility functions and the endowments of the rich and the poor. It fails to hold when reasonable alterations are made to these assumptions.[18] Their strategy of showing that *some* model implies the assumptions needed to demonstrate the infeasibility of monetarist policies shows, at best, that their demonstration is not vacuous: there exists a possible world in which it it true. It does not show that the possible world is our world. Few would find the legal-restrictions model with Sargent and Wallace's special restrictions to be sufficiently like our world to be a robust source of information about the feasibility of actual policy.

Underlying models to one side, there is a general feeling that there must be *some* limit to the ratio of debt to national income.[19] That limit is not unity: government debt in the United States in the Second World War exceeded annual GNP.[20] Nor does logic imply that a limit is reached when debt service exceeds national income, for the real consumption possibilities of the private sector are not impaired by purchasing vast amounts of bonds if the funds are immediately returned to them as interest payments. A limit is more likely to arise from the crowding out of private investment by higher rates of interest. Sargent and Miller suggest this possibility. Such a limit arises, however, not from the *infeasibility* of a particular combination of monetary and fiscal policies, but from its *undesirability*. Governments could stick to tight money policies, but, in the face of higher interest rates and crowding out, they are unlikely to do so.

4.3   The Impossibility of Policy

Both the policy-ineffectiveness proposition and Sargent and Wallace's analysis of monetarist arithmetic aim to apply new classical principles to the formulation of monetary policy. Both suggest limitations on the ability of policy makers to manipulate real or nominal quantities. Both are implicitly criticized by another train of new classical thinking which, at its extreme, suggests that the whole notion of making policy is flawed.

In both models there is an asymmetry: the public is assumed to hold rational expectations because it consists of optimizing agents, yet policy makers are seen to have a range of options – discretion and various fixed or contingent rules – rather than a unique optimal choice. Some new classicals regard this asymmetry as invidious. Policy makers as policy makers, they believe, have goals and preferences and face constraints on their resources and freedom to manoeuvre just as private individuals do. In keeping with essential new classical tenets, they should then be modelled as maximizing an objective function subject to these constraints.

The Inconsistency of Optimal Plans

New classicals typically work with models of perfect competition. One of their distinguishing features is that each agent is so small a player that he can simply take the actions of other players as given. The game-theoretical problems that arise for oligopolists or bilateral bargainers can be neglected. When the government is one of the players, this is no longer true. The actions of the government affect all players and there is considerable potential profit in correctly guessing what those actions will be.

An early example of the application of game theory to macroeconomic policy is Kydland and Prescott's (1977) analysis of the old problem of rules versus discretion. Discretion, as they define it, is a policy that is chosen optimally each period anew in order to best achieve the policy maker's goals. They then show that such a policy may be *dynamically inconsistent* in the sense that a policy chosen today as optimal for tomorrow will no longer be optimal when tomorrow comes. Agents with rational expectations may use this fact to thwart the policy.

The point is most easily made using Kydland and Prescott's own non-economic example. Suppose that the government believes that it is undesirable to build houses in the flood plain of a river. In order to discourage such building, its optimal policy is to announce that no disaster relief will be available to those who build close to the river. Once the river actually floods, however, most governments would wish to aid the victims, regardless of its previous announcement. People who expect the government to behave in this way will not be discouraged from building in the flood plain no matter what the government declares its policy to be.

Kydland and Prescott see this problem of the dynamic inconsistency of optimal plans as favouring rules over discretion. If the government were able to bind its own action with a rule forbidding it ever to give relief to the victims of the flood, the problem would be solved. Such a policy would seem suboptimal and hard-hearted after a flood, but, if people foresaw that a suboptimal policy would be followed according to the rule, they would not build in the flood plain at the start. The rule therefore achieves a better policy than discretion could.

Monetary Policy

Although Kydland and Prescott apply their analysis to monetary and fiscal policy, in this section we restrict our attention to Barro and Gordon's (1983a, b) more recent work.

Barro and Gordon assume that the authorities are able to use their monetary instruments to select any desired rate of inflation. Furthermore, according to a Lucas aggregate supply function, they can lower the rate of unemployment if they raise the inflation rate above the rate that the public expects. Without providing any deeper justification, they assume that inflation is a bad which imposes costs on society. Deviations of unemployment from some target rate are also assumed to be bad.[21] The monetary authority therefore seeks to minimize social costs, which can be represented as

$$Z = f(\pi, U^* - U), \tag{4.10}$$

where π is the rate of inflation, U is the rate of unemployment and U^* is the target rate of unemployment. Given a Lucas aggregate supply function, equation (4.10) could be rewritten as

$$Z = f\{\pi, [U^* - \alpha(\pi - \pi^e)]\}, \tag{4.10'}$$

where π^e is the public's expected rate of inflation and α is a constant.

The problem for the monetary authority would seem to be to choose the rate of inflation π in order to minimize social costs Z. The actual rate of inflation must exceed a given expected rate in order for the actual rate of unemployment to be reduced in the direction of the

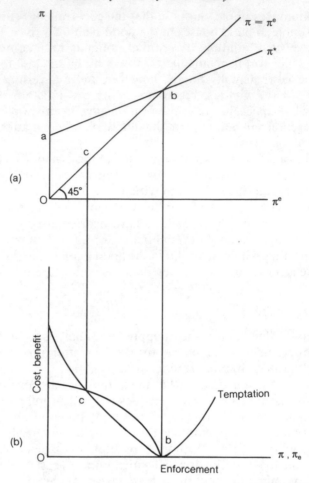

Figure 4.3 The equilibrium inflation rate in a monetary policy game

target rate. Thus the higher π^e is, the higher π must be in order to minimize costs. Of course, inflation is itself costly, so that an arbitrarily
high π would increase rather than reduce costs. Figure 4.3(a) plots π^*,
the levels of π which minimize costs for each level of π^e.[22]
    When the public has rational expectations, it is not possible to trick
it systematically into lowering the rate of unemployment below the
natural rate. It might seem obvious then that the optimal policy is
simply to set the rate of inflation to zero, accepting the cost of
unemployment as inevitable, while eliminating the cost of inflation.
Such a policy is not, however, sustainable. It is represented in figure
4.3 as the origin. If the authorities believed that people expected the

rate of inflation to be zero ($\pi^e = 0$), then costs could be lowered by raising the rate of inflation to point a, trading-off some higher costs of inflation against a greater reduction in costs of unemployment. In the face of higher actual inflation, expectations of inflation would be revised upwards. The authority would then choose a still higher rate of inflation in order to reduce costs. Only when a point such as b is reached, where the optimal and the expected rates of inflation are equal, does the incentive to trick the public disappear.

Any policy that does not lie on the π^* line is not optimal: the monetary authority will always be tempted to alter it. Any policy that does not lie on the $\pi = \pi^e$ line is dynamically inconsistent: it depends on a mismatch between the actual and the expected rates of inflation that cannot be sustained under rational expectations. The $\pi = \pi^e$ line might then be called the *consistency line*.

The policy game has been analysed as if it were played just once: the policy makers are then always tempted to announce a rule and then inflate further, while the public is always ready to second-guess their announced intention so that an equilibrium such as that at b is inevitable. In reality, however, the policy game is played many times. Barro and Gordon (1983b) investigate whether the desire to maintain a reputation would be enough to permit the authority to announce and maintain a *sustainable* rule, better than discretionary equilibrium (point b).

They assume the following behaviour of the public. The public believes that inflation will actually be at the rate the monetary authority announces until it is tricked by an actual higher rate. If the authority breaks the rule, the public assumes that the inflation rate in the next period will be given by the discretionary equilibrium at b. In the period after that they again believe the authority's announcement. Thus, the public 'punishes' the authority for its indiscretions by not believing its announcements, but then forgives and forgets those indiscretions. The authority must then balance the temptation to cheat on its announced rule against the cost of the discretionary equilibrium in the next period.

Figure 4.3(b) plots both the benefit or *temptation* to cheat and its cost or the *public's enforcement* of the rule against the rate (expected rate) of inflation.[23] Any sustainable rule must lie on the consistency line in figure 4.3(a). The temptation to break the rule is then related to the absolute difference between the consistency line and the optimality line. The benefit of cheating is therefore greatest when π is low, declines as π approaches b and rises again thereafter. The enforcement cost imposed when the authority breaks the rule is the discounted value of the difference in cost between discretion and the rule. This cost is discounted because it is incurred in the period after the rule is

broken. The enforcement cost is greatest when π is low and falls
monotonically to zero as π approaches b. Since enforcement behaviour for π greater than b would actually help reduce social costs, it becomes negative to the right of b. An enforceable rule is any point
between c and b at which the costs imposed on the authority, were it to
cheat, outweigh the temptation to cheat. The best enforceable rule is
then the point c, the lowest rate of inflation for which the enforcement
costs just balance the temptation to cheat.

The actual best enforceable rule obviously depends on the actual
form of the cost function (equation 4.10′) and on the monetary
authority's rate of discount. It also depends critically on the game
being played. Barro and Gordon's one-period enforcement interval
and implicit assumption that both the public and the monetary
authority know the pay-off of the game with certainty are arbitrary.
Many plausible alternative assumptions about the public's and monetary authority's behaviour might be made with very different results.
Futhermore, game theory provides a number of different equilibrium
concepts; detailed consideration of these would take us too far afield.[24]
It is important to observe that not all who would apply game theory to
the analysis of monetary and fiscal policy are new classicals. It is just
that new classical principles, when pushed far enough, seem to lead
naturally to game-theoretical analysis.

The End of the Positive–Normative Distinction

A striking result of Barro and Gordon's model is that it makes positive
predictions about the behaviour of policy makers. Suppose, for
example, that a supply shock (such as the 1973 oil-price shock) raises
structural unemployment further above the desired target level. At
every level of expectations of the rate of inflation, a higher rate of
actual inflation will minimize costs since the benefits of reducing
unemployment are now higher. The optimal inflation line in figure
4.3(a) will then shift up and both curves in figure 4.3(b) will shift to the
right, while their vertical intercepts rise. Both the discretionary rate
and the best enforceable rule for inflation will be higher.

Consider another example. Suppose that widespread indexation is
introduced, which reduces the costs of inflation. The benefits of higher
inflation – temporarily lower unemployment – now become higher in
relation to its costs. The optimal inflation line in figure 4.3(a) thus
becomes steeper, the curves in figure 4.3(b) shift to the right, and both
the discretionary rate and the best enforceable rule are again higher.

Finally, consider an outside institution that imposes an effective
discipline on the monetary authority. Barro and Gordon consider the
gold standard, but IMF lending rules may act similarly for some

countries.[25] Effective enforcement makes the monetary authority's announcement of a rule credible, so that a rule of zero inflation (the origin in figure 4.3) is sustainable. The theory then predicts that the end of effective enforcement – say, the abandonment of the gold standard – leads to higher inflation. Barro and Gordon see the recent history of developed economies as confirmation of these predictions.

Analyses along the lines of Barro and Gordon treat both the policy maker and the public as optimizing agents, and so seem to be the natural extensions of new classical principles. But in reducing the behaviour of policy makers to the predictions of a well-specified model, they also eliminate the policy maker's options. The distinction between normative and positive economics becomes irrelevant. Taken to its logical extreme the argument removes the need for the economist to give advice of the form, 'If you wish to achieve X, then do Y', or criticism of the forms, 'Given its goals, the policy was badly chosen.' Instead the economist stands as a spectator who simply seeks to understand in what way policies are optimal.[26]

Barro and Gordon, for example, state: 'In our model the economist has no useful day-to-day advice to offer to the monetary authority. If monetary institutions were set optimally, then the economist's counsel would also not enter at this level.'[27] They go on to argue that the useful function of the economist is to identify and design improvements to existing institutions: 'We would like to know which mechanisms – such as commodity standards and legal restrictions on the behavior of paper money – would effectively (and cheaply) restrict the course of future money and prices.'[28] As well as nearly contradicting themselves – one might suppose that such institutions are chosen optimally – Barro and Gordon have chosen an essentially arbitrary stopping place in an argument which of its very nature is an infinite regress.[29] The limiting case is that, as Dr Pangloss claims, 'All is for the best in the best of all possible worlds' – a silly view, as Candide eventually came to see.

Recognition of this line of argument in new classical models goes back at least to Sargent and Wallace (1976). They treat policy making as choosing among different possible rules (see section 4.1). They consider the case of a new rule adopted in secret and ask how it will affect the economy. They observe that if the public knew that such a rule was possible and assigned a probability to its being adopted, then the standard policy-ineffectiveness argument would go through. In effect, a policy is a set of rules each with a probability of being adopted, and individuals simply follow the standard rules of choice under uncertainty.

> But invoking this kind of completely rational expectation seems to rule
> out normative economics completely by, in effect, ruling out freedom

for the policymaker. For in a model with completely rational expectations, including a rich enough description of policy, it seems impossible to define a sense in which there is any scope for discussing the optimal design of policy rules. That is because equilibrium values of the endogenous variables already reflect, in the proper way, the parameters describing the authorities' prospective subsequent behaviour, including the probability that this or that proposal for reforming policy will be adopted.[30]

The problem arises because of the strong form of the rational expectations hypothesis that is invoked. It is not simply that agents muddle their way by trial and error to solutions that are approximately optimal. Rather, they understand the structure of the economy completely. If they are ignorant, it is only of the actual realizations of future random processes; it is not of the nature of their own ignorance or of the structure of the constraints which they face.

Such a strong form of rational expectations seems natural in simple formal models. But the fact that as economists we generally use *simple* models should warn us against pushing them too far. Modelling complex phenomena is difficult, and it is wrong to suppose that untutored individuals do what experts are often unable to do. Barro and Gordon's analysis is very revealing in this regard because it relies on game theory. Within game theory, and with respect to their particular problem, there are a number of possible solution concepts. Each will generate different solutions for different assumptions about underlying behaviour, e.g. the length of the enforcement period. This lack of uniqueness is not simply a problem for the economist, but rather reflects the problem that economic agents themselves face.

Our understanding of economic phenomena is imperfect. The role of the economist will always be to improve it. Improvements will always be the basis for policy advice at some level.

5 The New Monetary Economics

The ultimate goal of the new classical economics is the euthanasia of macroeconomics. Early new classical work simply modified existing aggregate macroeconomic models, but the point was not to endorse those models. Rather, it was to demonstrate the power of the fundamental assumptions of market clearing and rational expectations to overturn accepted conclusions about the conduct of policy. New classicals believe that only when macroeconomic aggregates are explicable as consequences of well-formulated optimization problems for individuals, i.e. only when complete microfoundations are worked out, will macroeconomic reasoning be secure. The new classicals, therefore, stigmatize monetarism, Keynesian monetary theory and even early new classical work itself for 'starting with curves' rather than deriving the position and shape of those curves (e.g. money supply and demand) from more fundamental individual optimization problems.[1]

A formidable obstacle to the new classical goal of providing adequate microfoundations for macroeconomics is to provide adequate microfoundations for monetary theory. Before the publication of Keynes's *General Theory* (1936) the distinction between *microeconomics* and *macroeconomics* was unknown.[2] Instead *monetary theory*, which largely concerned the general level of prices, was customarily taken to be one of the two main branches of economic theory, while *value theory*, the theory of relative prices, was the other. The new classical problem of providing microfoundations for monetary theory was already mirrored in the uneasy relation between monetary theory and value theory. The new classicals in fact self-consciously revive the programme suggested by John Hicks in 'A Suggestion for Simplifying the Theory of Money' (1935) to ground monetary theory in value theory.[3] Hicks's article was written before Keynes's *General*

Theory (1936) and was principally a response to the quantity equations of Keynes's earlier *Treatise on Money* ([1930] 1971) and to the quantity theory in general. Hicks's article remains remarkably fresh, suggesting all the main issues that dominate the debate even today. Characteristic of his anticipations, he writes: 'But merely to call [the] marginal utility [of money] X, and then to proceed to draw curves, would not be very helpful.'[4]

The chief difficulty in providing a theory of the demand for money, in Hicks's view, is in explaining why non-interest-bearing money is held when interest- or profit-yielding securities or investments are available. Hicks writes:

> This, as I see it, is really the central issue in the theory of money. Either we have to give an explanation of the fact that people do hold money when rates of interest are positive, or we have to evade the difficulty somehow. It is the great traditional evasions which have led to Velocities of Circulation, Natural Rates of Interest, *et id genus omne*.[5]

Hicks's suggestion for a non-evasive approach to this difficulty is to show that optimizing individuals will hold money, even when it bears no interest, provided that there are 'frictions' which money helps to overcome.[6] The successful monetary theory will carefully specify these frictions – transactions costs, risk etc. – and derive the demand for money from the principles of utility and profit maximization under the constraints that they impose. It is this suggestion that the new classicals adopt.

In this chapter and the next we shall examine new classical approaches to the microfoundations of monetary theory, what is called the new monetary economics.[7] In order to set the stage for a discussion of the new monetary economics it is useful to review some history.

5.1 The Integration of Monetary Theory and Value Theory: A Historical Sketch

The Quantity Theory

The modern theory of the determination of relative prices was first given a reasonably complete formulation by Leon Walras and finally made mathematically rigorous by Gerard Debreu. Their formulations are systems of exchange, or of production and exchange, with given tastes, technology and initial endowments. Supply and demand functions that depend on all relative prices are derived on the assumption that each consumer or firm takes prices as given from outside the model – by an auctioneer in Walras's interpretation – and indicates his supplies and demands at those prices. The role of the auctioneer is to note where supplies differ from demands and to adjust the price vector accordingly until all markets clear. Since no trading is permitted out of equilibrium, demanders can take all supplies and suppliers can take all demands as perfectly elastic at the auctioneer's vector.

Something like this system was believed to lie behind the determination of relative prices long before Walras.[8] But what of absolute prices, the actual prices attached to and paid for goods? The crude quantity theory of money went back to Locke and Hume, at least, and was somewhat refined by the Cambridge school and by Irving Fisher. The theory held that, with correction for the velocity of circulation, the general price level was determined by the quantity of money in circulation. An increase (decrease) in money produced an increase (decrease) in the general price level. Relative prices, determined by the Walrasian system, were scaled up (down) proportionately without their relationship one to the other being affected. The problem here is that the determination of the general level of prices does not seem, at least in the formalism of the Walrasian model, to have anything to do with the choices of individuals which determine every other price and quantity.

The modern quantity theory of Friedman (1956b) and other monetarists does little to alter this schema. Money is seen to be one among many assets, and so velocity is allowed to vary with the changing patterns of rates of return on real and financial assets. Also, the possibility of a short-term effect of money on output is admitted so that the theory is one of nominal income rather than of prices. Only in the long term is there a necessary relationship between the level of the money supply and the level of prices. Only in the long term is real output independent of the money supply.

The distinction between real and nominal quantities is central to any presentation of the quantity theory of money. Monetarists argue that agents do not care how much money they hold, but only how much it will buy. If money is to fit into a Walrasian system, it will have to be in the guise of real cash balances. They argue that it is the attempt to spend excess cash balances which connects disturbances in the money supply to disturbances in income and ultimately in prices. Inflation is a very simple phenomenon: the money supply somehow increases by more than money demanded; people with excess cash balances bid up prices; since the demand for money depends directly on the general level of prices, the process stops when the quantity of money demanded has risen to equal the quantity of money supplied. An increase in the money supply above the amount currently demanded is a necessary and sufficient condition for inflation.

Patinkin

Friedman bows to Walras, but does not present us with the integration of money into the Walrasian system that he takes for granted. For this we must look past the monetarists to Patinkin, a quantity theorist of a different sort, who explicitly attempts such an integration (Patinkin 1956, 1965). Patinkin observes that the problem is that the same economic activity can be carried on at any level of absolute prices and with any supply of money. Yet money is not without value; rather, its value depends on what it will buy and, therefore, on the price level. So in order to turn money and other financial assets denominated in money into well-defined goods with a place in the Walrasian system, he divides them by the price level and thus enters their real purchasing power directly into utility functions.

This schema, Patinkin believes, represents an integration of monetary and value theory for two reasons. First, the demand for real money balances is now governed by the same considerations of utility as the demand for every other good in the system. Second, the level of absolute prices is determined jointly with all relative prices: we simply need to choose a standard by setting the price of some real good (say gold) or of fiat money to a constant. Furthermore, Patinkin believes that he has a microeconomic foundation for macroeconomics – particularly, for real balance effects. For if there is an exogenous increase in the supply of money or a fall in the level of prices, there will be an excess supply of real money balances and an excess demand for commodities. If the equilibrium is stable, prices will respond by rising to a new level in the one case or returning to their old level in the other.

Frank Hahn (1965) makes two important criticisms of Patinkin's schema. The first is of its formalization. The value of money depends in Patinkin's formal system on what it will buy, and not on what it can itself do. His formalization does not actually distinguish between a barter economy and a monetary economy, i.e. it does not model money in such a way that having it is an indispensable precondition for consuming goods. Hahn shows that, as long as money is not indispensable for consumption, then, if there exists a monetary equilibrium (i.e. one in which money has a positive value), there also exists a non-monetary (or barter) equilibrium (i.e. one in which money is worthless) which still fulfils the equilibrium conditions of the Walrasian system.

Hahn's criticism serves to remind us that a Walrasian system with an auctioneer does not need money. The criticism applies nonetheless only to Patinkin's formalization. Patinkin argues that money serves a necessary function, and although he imagines an economy of Hicksian weeks with perfectly foreseen prices set at the beginning of each week, he also imagines that the pattern of sales and purchases and, therefore, of receipts and payments during the week is not known with certainty. Furthermore, he supposes that there is some disutility associated with insufficient funds for a necessary purchase or repayment of debt; the disutility, a product of uncertainty, generates a demand for real cash balances. Patinkin asserts that this demand is always positive because he assumes that goods cannot be bought without money. A weakness of Patinkin's formalization is that his assumption of the interconnection between holding money and being able to purchase goods, and therefore the dependence of goods and money on each other for their ability to yield utility is not reflected in the utility function.

Hahn's second criticism is that, even if it is allowed that money cannot be without value in equilibrium, it is not possible to prove in *general* that an equilibrium exists. Imagine a Walrasian auction. The real quantities of most goods are independent of their prices. But the real quantities of money and financial assets change with every new price vector that the auctioneer calls out. A series of price vectors which in a barter model would converge on equilibrium may in a monetary model cause arbitrary redistributions of wealth that force supplies and demands apart rather than closer together.

In a sense, the problem of the non-existence of equilibrium does not arise for Patinkin, because he supposes in order to simplify his exposition that there are no distribution effects – i.e. that a rearrangement in the endowments of cash balances or other goods does not affect the price and output solution to the Walrasian system. This requirement is extremely strong: it implies that all agents have identical tastes and that they consume the same proportions of each good no matter how rich or poor.[9] This rules out distribution effects: if an agent receives more cash balances, he simply increases his supplies and demands proportionately to the increase in his cash balances; relative proportions remain unchanged. That each agent is alike of course means that it makes no difference which one receives the increase.

The assumption of no distribution effects is *sufficient* to prove the existence of an equilibrium price vector in an otherwise well-behaved Walrasian system with money. Relative prices cannot change as the result of redistributions of endowments. Without arbitrary redistributions, real balances are a well-defined good.

Patinkin introduces the assumption of no distribution effects for analytical convenience, and he recognizes some of its restrictive implications. He notes for example that claims for the neutrality of money will not withstand relaxing it. For if agents have different tastes, the prices of goods preferred by those agents who receive the most additional cash balances will rise by more than goods preferred by others. Unfortunately, the equilibrium of his system depends crucially on this economically adventitious assumption.

The 'New View'

The upshot of Hahn's criticisms is that a satisfactory integration of monetary and value theory must specify formally in what way money is indispensable to the exchange or enjoyment of those commodities that are, unlike money itself, direct sources of utility. It must meet Hicks's challenge to specify what frictions money overcomes and exactly how it does it.

Patinkin's book stands at the centre of modern monetary theory. Nearly everything written on *pure* monetary theory since the Second World War is a direct or indirect response to it. Patinkin's project is to integrate monetary and value theory in the sense that nominal prices as well as relative prices should be determined by the optimizing choices of economic agents. He writes:

> ... in order for the absolute price level to be determined by market equilibrating forces, changes in it must impinge on aggregate *real* behaviour in *some* market – i.e. must create excess demands in some market.[10]

Money in Patinkin's model impinges on the markets for real goods through the wealth or real balance effect, i.e. through the appearance of real money balances in utility and (excess) demand functions.

Unfortunately, Patinkin's attempt at integration is at best partial and it leaves the (at least) twofold distinction between money's functions (store of value, means of exchange) unclear. Reactions to Patinkin can be divided according to the emphasis they give to one or the other function. Economists such as Hahn and Robert Clower (see chapter 6, section 6.3) emphasize the transaction function, believing that only if the value of money can be explained by its mechanism will monetary theory make any real progress.

Hahn and Clower offer direct criticisms of the microfoundations of Patinkin's system. The so-called new view in monetary economics, however, represents an indirect attack on its adequacy. The classic statement of the new view is Gurley and Shaw's *Money in a Theory of Finance* (1960).[11] Gurley and Shaw argue that an analysis of fiat money alone is inadequate. The whole process of finance is important.

Gurley and Shaw's analysis is aggregative. It is, nevertheless, based implicitly on a microeconomic foundation quite close to that of Patinkin. Gurley and Shaw operate under 'neoclassical rules': ' ...

absence of money illusion, freedom from distribution effects of change in the price level and bond rate, perfect competition and flexibility of prices. . . '.[12] Money is defined to be the medium of transactions, and its demand is assumed to arise from uncertainty about the timing of receipts and payments. So far, so like Patinkin.

Gurley and Shaw set the new view off from Patinkin by defining all money to be debt. Cash or central bank reserves are the debt of the government. If they are issued in payment for real goods they are 'outside' money – outside with respect to the private sector. If they are issued in exchange for private sector debt they are 'inside' – they are an asset whose value is balanced out against debt inside the private sector. Bank deposits too are a means of exchange and therefore money. They must correspond to private sector debts and are thus also inside money. If private sector balance sheets are consolidated, inside money vanishes – one person's asset exactly cancels the other's debt. Gurley and Shaw call the belief that it is appropriate to conduct monetary analysis with consolidated balance sheets the 'net money doctrine', and the belief that it is inappropriate the 'gross money doctrine'.

Patinkin is accused by implication of adopting the net money doctrine, because in his aggregative analysis he follows his microeconomic analysis by considering only fiat money and government bonds, i.e. outside assets.[13] In contrast, Gurley and Shaw believe that monetary analysis must adopt the gross money doctrine. They argue that, while private debtors may be indifferent as to who holds their bonds (other private agents or the monetary system), private creditors are not indifferent to the division of their portfolio between bonds and money – either of which can be inside or outside assets. In an economy with both inside and outside money, money affects portfolio balance differently depending on whether it was created against private debt or not. This portfolio distribution effect can produce non-neutralities despite the fact that the neoclassical rules are followed so that no distribution effects related to changes in the relative prices of goods are allowed.

The new view pays lip service to money's function as a means of exchange, but it emphasizes its function as a store of value. Money, according to Gurley and Shaw, earns an implicit rate of return. It does so because of its usefulness in transactions, given uncertainty. Portfolio choice is, nevertheless, largely a matter of comparing rates of return on money and other assets. Where Patinkin attends most closely to income or wealth effects, Gurley and Shaw concern themselves with substitution effects. The new view recognizes that money has some unique characteristics; nevertheless, it stresses not money's uniqueness but its similarity to other financial assets.

The New Monetary Economics

The new monetary economics (i.e. the new classical analysis of monetary theory, not to be confused with the new view) attempts to offer solutions to the long-standing problem of integrating monetary theory and value theory. In this chapter and the next we consider three distinct new classical approaches to this problem. Eugene Fama's well-known paper, 'Banking in the Theory of Finance' (1980), which attempts to wed monetary theory to modern theories of finance, is investigated in this chapter. More formal monetary models – the overlapping-generations models of Sargent, Wallace and Bryant and the models with finance constraints, largely associated with Lucas – are considered in the next chapter.

Fama's analysis directly addresses the points at issue between Patinkin and Gurley and Shaw. On the one hand, he argues that money is not unique either as a store of value or as a transaction medium – a wide range of financial assets could perform both functions. On the other hand, he agrees with Patinkin's micro-economic analysis that outside money uniquely determines the price level. He goes on to argue that the uniqueness of money is the product of government regulation. Without such regulation he believes that the theory of finance and the theory of Walrasian barter would be sufficient; monetary theory need not exist, much less need be integrated with value theory.

The more formal models of Sargent, Wallace, Bryant and Lucas considered in chapter 6 are not such direct extensions of the debates of the 1950s and 1960s. They are instead the product of the internal logic of the new classical programme which seeks to reduce *all* aspects of macroeconomics to microeconomics. Rather than directly confronting the analyses of Patinkin or of Gurley and Shaw, they refer back to a much earlier stage – to Hicks and the idea that money can be integrated into Walrasian value theory only if economists are explicit in specifying the frictions it serves to reduce.

5.2 Money and Finance

Any complete account of the new monetary economics must consider Fama's paper. For while the roots of the effort to apply modern theories of finance to monetary economics go back at least to Fischer Black's paper, 'Banking and Interest Rates in a World Without Money' (1970), it is Fama's paper which has been called '. . . perhaps the most influential statement of the new monetary economics . . .'[14] Fama's paper is particularly important because it concludes that money exists and is important only because of government-imposed legal restrictions on other financial assets and because it attempts to apply the Modigliani–Miller theorem from the theory of corporate finance to the analysis of monetary policy. Both ideas are part of mainstream new classical analysis (see chapters 6 and 7). Finally, Fama's paper is important as an intellectual precursor to particular new classical models such as King and Plosser's real business cycle model discussed in chapter 3, section 3.3.[15]

Fama might not be seen as a mainstream new classical. He is certainly better known as a specialist in finance than as a macroeconomist. Yet it is clear that his general outlook is greatly sympathetic to the new classical school. The idea that financial markets are *efficient* is closely related to rational expectations. Similarly, the main thrust of his monetary theory is that the analysis of money must be consistent with the general principles of rationality embodied in neoclassical microeconomics – a very new classical sentiment.

Fama's analysis of the monetary economy reaches some striking conclusions: in principle the economic system could function perfectly well without fiat money; fiat money could be introduced through government intervention; if it were introduced, control of inflation would be a simple matter of controlling the stock of fiat money (cash and central bank reserves); most striking of all, the price level would be independent of the composition of private portfolios – in particular, independent of the stock of bank deposits, which constitute by far the largest component of the money stock as reported by central banks. The policy implications of this view are that monetary control should focus on the monetary base and that the regulation of banks and related financial intermediaries is no more or less necessary than the regulation of any other industry.

Fama's attack on the problem of integrating monetary theory and value theory is radical: he simply abolishes monetary theory. The crucial step in his argument is what might be called 'the separation theorem', i.e. the belief that the real services of banks are independent of the compositions of their portfolios.[16] We shall argue that the separation theorem is false.

A Parable

In order to acquire a sense of the main lines of Fama's argument consider the story he tells at the end of his paper. He asks us to imagine a future in which computerized banking and exchange is so well developed that cash has ceased to exist altogether. In the absence of coins and bank-notes, accounts have come to be denominated in units of a real good – in particular, in steel ingots. The steel ingots are a pure *numéraire*. They are not used as an intermediary in exchange; they merely serve as a convenient unit for expressing the value of a good when bargaining, setting a price or keeping the (fully computerized) books. In such a world, if I buy a spaceship from you for, say, 6000 ingots, I merely key in the transfer of 6000 ingots worth of my financial assets to you and the computer at my 'bank' ('broker' or 'financial intermediary'), which is linked to other banks' computers and presumably to the various stock and bond exchanges, registers the transfer.

Obviously, in such a world the supply and demand for steel ingots and other real goods determines the price of steel ingots. The fact that steel ingots are used as the *numéraire* has no effect on their price and hence on the general level of prices at all. Financial assets are merely claims to the yields of real assets. As such their prices are derived from the current and expected future prices of those real assets and do not affect them.

Given the advanced technology of the spaceship age, the only loser from the withering of the currency system is the government, which can no longer gain seigniorage from currency creation. But Fama observes that the government could itself start supplying a sort of abstract currency, which he calls 'units', by entering them into the accounts of various people – most likely in payment for the goods and services it uses. If the government then placed a tax on spaceships payable in units, the demand for spaceships would be depressed somewhat, but at the same time a demand for units and an opportunity for seigniorage would be created. Units could replace steel ingots as the *numéraire*, and the level of prices in terms of units would then depend on the supply of units (controlled by the government) and the supplies of and demands for spaceships and other goods, but not of financial assets.

This tale is seductive because it is easy to imagine projecting the current trend in transactions technology until cash is no longer used. The central flaw in the tale is the implication that the essential real service provided by cash is that of an efficient surrogate for a bookkeeping system. If that were so, then a highly developed computerized bookkeeping system, which may someday eliminate cash from hand-to-hand transactions, would be an efficient substitute for cash in all its uses. But in fact it is not so. In stressing the possibility that the use of cash can relieve us from the need to keep complex accounts, Fama ignores its role as a preferred good for settling many outstanding debts.

Whenever we purchase a real good – except in direct barter – we create an incipient debt. Cash settles such a debt. In Fama's spaceship economy these debts are settled by transfers of assets of equal value. Unfortunately this ignores the fact that we usually have preferences over what sort of assets we wish to accept in exchange. The only situation in which such preferences can be dismissed as irrelevant is when there is an economy-wide Walrasian auction, for then no matter what combination of assets I choose to sell in order to transfer 6000 ingots (or units) worth of value to you, you may purchase *any* combination of 6000 ingots worth of assets you choose. With such an auction it is always the case that it is only the *value* of one's endowment and not its actual composition that limits one's choice of consumption goods or acquisition of assets.

The spaceship economy works by sleight of hand. The fact that computerization may allow us to dispense with notes and coins does not transform our economy from one in which transactions are made in a higgledy-piggledy uncontrolled manner into one in which they are coordinated by a central auction. Without the auction, cash serves in a middleman role, severing my obligations to the seller of goods I buy and allowing him to buy other goods without incurring obligations. It is clear that cash can replace the bookkeeping system. It is not clear, however, that anything in the spaceship economy's bookkeeping system adequately replaces money's role as a middleman in transactions.

The story seems plausible only because the natures of financial assets and exchange have not been sufficiently analysed. Fama's argument for the fundamental unimportance of money does not, however, rest simply on a plausible tale, but on a more formal analysis, to which we now turn.

A Modigliani-Miller Theorem for Banks

The key to Fama's analysis of the monetary system is that banks are just like other firms in that they sell a real service (transactions service) in order to maximize their profits. Since they are ordinary corporations, the standard propositions of corporate finance should apply to banks as to other firms.

A cornerstone of the modern theory of finance is the Modigliani–Miller theorem. There are many versions of the Modigliani–Miller theorem, but they have in common that, under a set of more or less reasonable assumptions, how a firm finances its real activities has no effect on its own market value or on the production and consumption decisions of other economic agents.[17] (Readers who are unfamiliar with the Modigliani–Miller theorem should consult the appendix to this chapter.)

One set of assumptions that Fama uses for the 'strong' form of the theorem is as follows.[18] First, there are perfect capital markets, i.e. no taxes, transactions costs or danger of bankruptcy. Second, there is informational efficiency or rational expectations. Third, agents are concerned only about the pattern of returns of their financial assets under different states of the world, i.e. risk and return matter only inasmuch as they affect wealth. Fourth, firms' investment decisions are made independently of how the investment is financed and according to fixed rules. Fifth, agents have equal access to capital markets – in particular, if a firm can issue a liability, an individual can issue one on his own account with the same pattern of returns under various states of the world.

The assumption of equal access to capital markets can be replaced by two other assumptions to yield a 'weak' form of the theorem. The first is that no firm produces any security monopolistically, i.e. there are always perfect substitutes for any financial asset. Second, the firm's goal is always to maximize profits at prevailing prices. These imply that, even if an individual is barred from full participation in the capital market, some firm will provide him any asset or liability he chooses, giving him effectively equal access.

In either its strong or weak form, the intuition behind the Modigliani–Miller theorem is the same. Agents' tastes for risk and return are derived from their tastes for real goods in different states of the world. If a firm alters the composition of its finance (say, its debt–equity ratio or the type of debt or shares it issues) this may *ceteris paribus* adversely affect the real opportunities of other agents (say, shareholders). The *status quo ante* in the real economy can always be restored, however, under either set of assumptions if agents make compensating changes in their own portfolios. Arbitrage guarantees – and this is the importance of the assumption of equal access or of perfect substitutes – that neither the real opportunities of agents nor the market value of the firm is altered by the firm's portfolio decision.

With the Modigliani–Miller theorem in hand, we can now take up the main thread of Fama's argument. Fama's major contention is that the banking system plays no special role in the establishment of the price level. He begins by imagining a world with banks and financial intermediaries but no money. The unique function of banks is that they maintain a system of accounts for the transfer of wealth. Banks constitute a transactions industry and so provide a real service to the community. They are competitive profit-seeking firms with a different product, but are not otherwise distinct from other firms.[19] They are also financial intermediaries, selling deposits and buying portfolios of (riskier) assets. Intermediation is a real but secondary service, for clearly banks need not hold the assets just in order to provide accounting services.

Banks in such a world might offer various sorts of deposits – some risk free, and others with varying degrees and types of risk. For example, there might be ordinary demand deposits or deposits whose values were tied to a stock market index or deposits which were claims on a money market mutual fund. In any case, deposits would be heterogeneous and thus not suitable as the *numéraire* or unit of account. Efficiency demands, however, that accounts be maintained in some common *numéraire*. Fama suggests choosing one of the real goods of the system and does not agonize over which. He does observe, however, that it need not be portable or storable – crude oil or sides of beef would do quite well. The *numéraire* is just an accounting device; it need not be transferred.[20]

The last part of the argument is simple. Fama applies the Modigliani–Miller theorem to banks in order to show that the amount and composition of their liabilities do not affect the level of prices. Banks, Fama argues, provide real services just as other firms do, and their deposits finance their real activities just as other firms' liabilities finance their real activities. Hence the Modigliani–Miller theorem can be applied to a competitive banking system without currency, and the conclusion can be drawn that the composition of bank portfolios does not affect the details of the general equilibrium with respect to real goods. Furthermore, the price level in terms of the *numéraire* is not affected.[21]

Since deposits, even of the sort we are in the habit of calling money, do not affect the price level, the problem of determining the price level in an accounting system of exchange reduces to the question of whether there exists a stable solution to the general equilibrium system without money. Fama's use of the term 'price level' is somewhat misleading. The barrel-of-oil price of each good is a *relative* price, while the price level is usually taken to refer to *absolute* or *nominal* prices. What Fama claims is that, since the activities of banks can be split between real (accounting, exchange and intermediation) services on one side and finance on the other and because finance is irrelevant, there are only relative prices. The distinction between absolute and relative prices, then, is itself misleading. The term 'absolute prices' has no other meaning than the relative prices of goods in terms of money (currency). In a system in which currency does not exist and deposits are, by virtue of the Modigliani–Miller theorem, irrelevant to the relative prices of any real goods, there are no absolute prices.[22]

Regulating the sort of portfolios banks may hold against deposits or the interest rates they may pay on certain types of assets which they offer may affect bank behaviour, but, Fama believes, it does not alter the banks' essentially passive nature with respect to the real economy and the price level. Imposing reserve requirements is the equivalent of imposing a tax on certain types of assets. Again, this does not alter the fundamental conclusion: taxes of course have real effects, but the banks as deposit creators are nonetheless passive.

Fama next considers a second case in which his moneyless world is complicated through the introduction of currency supplied by the government. Currency may be more efficient than the accounting system in some sorts of transactions. The demand for currency will depend on the opportunity cost of holding it (interest foregone), the real transactions in which it has a comparative advantage and the minimum real cost of executing those transactions through other means. With a well-defined demand, if supply is also well defined, then, Fama believes, this complication again leaves intact his main conclusion that non-money financial assets do not affect the price level. Indeed, if the currency unit is the *numéraire*, the price level, which for Fama in the system without currency was the various relative prices of goods in units of barrels of oil, is now the various relative prices in units of currency. The government need only fix the supply of currency and its demand will determine the price level, no matter what the composition of financial portfolios.

Fama's position is that Patinkin and others err in their analysis of the financial system by assuming that certain heterogeneous financial assets are on a par with hand-to-hand currency – that both are money.[23] The mistake arises from the fact that both can be used in the exchange process and both are denominated in the same units. The similarity, Fama argues, is an illusion. At each point that currency changes hands a transaction is complete; currency acts as an intermediate store of value (a temporary abode of purchasing power). Currency is thus a good. This is clear in the case of gold coin or other commodity money, but is equally true for fiat paper (a point we shall return to in due course). In contrast, exchange through banks, Fama believes, is very different. There are no intermediate stores of value, and transactions involve only entries in the bank's books or computer. Most important is that the transactions services of a bank (i.e. bookkeeping) do not require that the bank hold the assets exchanged: portfolio management is a separate activity from providing transactions services. Only government regulation distinguishes banks from other intermediaries. There is, therefore, nothing special about the services provided by banks as economic goods. Along with currency they can enter into the list of goods in a Walrasian general equilibrium system. The problem of a determinate price level is, he argues once again, simply the problem of the existence of a stable equilibrium.[24] If currency is the *numéraire* and its relative price is fixed along with the prices of all other goods, the price level is fixed.

Fama's strategy is to separate the transactions–intermediation complex into three well-defined real economic goods (currency, accounting exchange services and intermediation services) on the one side and the financial system on the other, and then to use the Modigliani–Miller theorem to assert the independence of all real goods from the financial system, thus leaving relative prices to be established in a Walrasian system in which the composition of agents' portfolios is irrelevant.

The conclusion of Fama's analysis is what we have called the 'separation theorem'. It is the claim that in any economy relative prices, including the relative prices of the real services provided by financial assets, are independent of the volume and composition of financial portfolios. It follows from this that, if an economy has a real good (commodity or fiat money) which is used in transactions, absolute prices are simply relative prices expressed in terms of this good, and these absolute prices (and therefore inflation) are themselves independent of financial assets including bank deposits.

5.3 Is Money Unique?

The Nature of Money and Financial Assets

The argument that the price level is independent of the volume and composition of bank deposits depends crucially on the assumption that it is sensible to consider a financial system without money. The fundamental flaw in Fama's account is that such a system is not a practical possibility.[25] The mistake arises from a failure to analyse the nature and function of financial assets properly. In this section we argue that a financial system cannot function without money, and that the value of money cannot therefore be separated from the volume and composition of financial portfolios.

As we observed of the parable of the spaceship economy, Fama implicitly assumes that prices are set in a Walrasian auction. Obviously, such an assumption is meant to be taken not as an accurate representation, but as a good approximation.[26] Unfortunately, it is not even that. A fictitious auction serves to eliminate two distinct problems from real-life trading. The first is the establishment of market-clearing relative prices. In Fama's account, as with other accounts, this function holds centrestage. Still, even if market-clearing prices are set, a second problem remains – namely, actually to execute the trades that are needed to establish the equilibrium. An auction hall where traders all meet is one way of imagining this second problem's being solved. Other institutions, such as trading posts, might also work equally well. Once we look past any of these fictitious systems, however, the problem of guaranteeing that desired trades can in fact be executed looms larger than that of establishing relative prices. In practice matching buyers and sellers is a fairly haphazard business, and generally there will be only a coincidence of wants and not the vaunted double-coincidence of pure barter. Traders are, then, constantly faced with a balance of payments problem in which one has made a desired purchase while the other must hold some sort of debt – at least temporarily – until he in turn is able to find a seller.

In a Walrasian system with a once-and-for-all auction, financial assets are simply claims to goods which may be exercised given well-defined contingencies.[27] They serve as devices to alter the risk characteristics of one's endowments, and are priced derivatively in relation to the underlying real goods which stand behind them. Actual economies are sequential in the sense that trade occurs continuously and no institutions guarantee a match between buyers and sellers. In sequential economies, financial assets serve the additional function of permitting unbalanced trade and of redistributing purchasing power through time.

A developed financial system in a sequential economy is practically possible only if there is money. This follows from two critical characteristics of financial assets. The first is convertibility: all financial assets represent a claim on something else – a good or another asset. The claim may be on an infinite stream of payments alone, as with a consol, or on a fixed amount on demand, as with a current account, or on a definite stream, as with any bond or short-term note, or on an indefinite stream, as with common stock, or on another financial asset, as with stock options. Whatever a financial asset is a claim on, it is on something besides itself. It is inconceivable, for example, that the *only* right a consol-holder had to interest was payable in consols. It might be that such an option existed, but there must be the other option to receive cash as well. Similarly, while corporate shares that do not pay dividends are conceivable and even desirable in order to avoid taxes, it is hardly possible that they would be valuable if they were legally restricted from *ever* paying dividends.[28]

A financial asset may be directly convertible only into another financial asset. Ultimately, however, there must be a chain of conversions that ends in a valuable good which carries no further right of conversion. This is not a logical but a practical necessity. Hicks, for example, imagines a banking system in which deposits at one bank are convertible into those at another but not by right into anything else.[29] But he goes on to the case in which there is one dominant asset or competing dominant assets. Such dominant assets or *ultimate goods of conversion* are needed in this sytem: first, because chain-letter valuations of financial assets are more fragile the longer the chain – without an ultimate good of conversion all chains are circular (effectively infinite); second, because the banks are subject to the same problem of settling payments imbalances that arise in a non-Walrasian barter economy – an ultimate good of conversion serves as an ultimate good of settlement of interbank claims. Hicks's banking system is very like Fama's accounting system of exchange, yet Fama does not discuss the necessity of an ultimate good of conversion. He does, however, provide evidence elsewhere that bank-notes produced privately in the United States before the Civil War were successful only when they maintained convertibility at par with dominant Federal coin.[30] Money is typically *the* ultimate good of conversion in developed financial systems in that most financial assets are convertible by right into money through some chain of conversions. Even assets which are convertible into some other real good – say, a future contract into wheat – may generally be settled in money either as a convenience or because of default. This feature of money is so important that 'money' might well be defined as the ultimate good (possibly goods) of conversion or settlement in a developed financial system.

The second characteristic of financial assets in a non-Walrasian economy is the absence of direct connection between the claims represented by the asset and the underlying goods against which it is a claim. This is clearest in the case of current accounts convertible on demand into cash at a bank. When too many attempt to convert the asset, the bank is forced to default (unless it is itself able to borrow enough cash from another source). The same is true of other financial assets as well. Default is sometimes prevented simply because people are willing to hold new financial assets in the place of old ones falling due. This lack of necessary connection between financial assets and their goods of conversion opens up the *possibility* of default. It also reinforces the importance of any single good which is generally accepted as settling accounts (money), since such a good will be more readily obtainable than other goods because of its special role, thus diminishing the chance of *actual* default. Wheat can be had usually only from a farmer or a grain factor, while money can be had in exchange for almost any good including new financial assets.

Money is, then, practically necessary to any developed financial system. First because there must be some ultimate good (or goods) of conversion for all financial assets, and second because the lack of necessary connection between the amount of outstanding claims to goods of conversion and the amount of those goods available enhances the importance of some possible goods of conversion over others. If there exists one good that no one much objects to being stuck with – gold, beaver pelts, cowrie shells or currency – it tends to become the good in which accounts are settled and into which financial assets are ultimately convertible.

The Invalidity of the Separation Theorem

Once it is accepted that a developed financial system requires means of settlement and ultimate goods of conversion and that some goods are likely to become specialized in this role and so become money, there still remain two central questions about money's role. First, what determines its value? Second, can its value really be divorced from the structure of financial portfolios? In answer to the first question, Fama's response is unexceptionable: the value of any good depends on its demand, which is a function of its real services, and on its supply, which is a function of the cost of production for a commodity and of government fiat for an unbacked currency. Notice that Fama's is a narrow definition of money – a commodity or inconvertible paper (currency or central bank reserves) used in exchange. According to our earlier analysis this definition implies that money is not a financial asset because it is not convertible by right into anything else. Money, even fiat money, is a real good.[31]

The real problem is not to observe that money's value derives from its real services, but to say what those services are. This Fama fails to do. Instead he simply notes that the cost of production governs the value of commodity money in the long run.[32] Similarly in the first version of the spaceship economy it is the supply and demand for steel ingots and other goods that determines their value. Since ingots are a pure *numéraire*, the volume and composition of financial assets can have no effect on their price. In the second version, abstract units are introduced, and their value derives from their fixed supply and the supply of and demand for spaceships. Since finance does not affect the value of spaceships, it does not affect the value of abstract units.

Fama means us to see a clear analogy between his abstract units and currency as we know it in actual economies. Unfortunately, the analogy is imperfect because currency is not simply a clever revenue-raising device but also a means for conducting transactions, and Fama gives no satisfactory account of how it functions in this latter role. Yet it is clear how currency works. Currency is a real good and exchange using currency is a form of non-Walrasian barter. I accept currency in exchange generally not because I want to hold it in equilibrium, but because it is a preferred means of settling the payments imbalances that arise as I seek to acquire a desired combination of consumption goods and assets. Any real good (gold, steel ingots or units) which is used in transactions becomes monetized. Once a commodity is monetized, its value is largely governed by its monetary uses. In basing the value of fiat money on the taxing authority of the government Fama exaggerates the difference between fiat money and commodity money, which is itself valued to a great degree because it is money and not for its non-monetary uses.[33] It ignores, furthermore, the 'autocatalytic' character of any money – it is valuable because it is already valued:[34] 'A mere casual patriotism, or familiarity, or force of habit may be sufficient to prevent a shift to other currencies, even in the absence of legal sanctions, provided that the immediate incentive for such a shift is not too great.'[35] Imagine that taxes were abolished or that people were permitted to pay their taxes in gold bars, wheat or some other commodity; there is no reason to suppose that bank-notes would suddenly be treated as valueless. Although taxes and reserve requirements are reminders that currency and central bank reserves have value, their value is more fundamentally derived from their transactions services.[36]

The very existence of currency – an ultimate good of conversion used in transactions and, therefore, monetized – creates a role for financial assets that they could not have in a Walrasian system in which payments imbalances could not arise. Financial assets ('deposits') can now provide access to an accounting (clearing) system. In such a system, the mutually cancelling debt of different financial intermediaries is written off, so that only the uncleared balances need be settled with a mutually acceptable good of settlement – usually central-bank reserves. The assets of these intermediaries may provide brokerage or bookkeeping or even risk-spreading services, but, more essentially, they provide *settlement* services. When you deposit my cheque, my part of the transaction is discharged, while you are holding a financial asset that is ultimately a claim on some ultimate good of conversion.

The ultimate good of conversion may be Fama's units. Now, however, they have been monetized and are no longer valued only because one needs units to own spaceships but also because they are money. Monetized units are fatal to Fama's conclusions about the price level. As long as agents are content to hold claims to units rather than units themselves, a restricted supply of units restricts transactions only to the degree that some units must be reserved to maintain convertibility. Financial assets backed in units cannot be issued in infinite amounts. Yet if convertibility is maintained, such financial assets serve as well as units, and any effect of units on the economy can be reproduced by such assets.

Despite being monetized, units remain abstract rather than concrete goods; they are money, but not currency. Nonetheless, currency may serve instead of units as the ultimate good of conversion, and so may gold or oil. Even with concrete goods such as gold or oil which have alternative real uses inflation is not ruled out because they have become monetized. Inflation of the issue of a fractionally backed paper bank-note convertible into gold, for instance, would depreciate the gold in storage as well as the paper. Only the *actual* insistence of holders on conversion would limit the issue.

The clear consequence of our analysis of the relation of money to financial assets is that Fama's separation theorem – namely, that the price level is independent of the volume and composition of financial assets – is false for any system in which there exists an ultimate good of conversion, i.e. where some good or claims to it serve as a means of settlement, and the good is therefore monetized. Such systems are in practice the only interesting ones, since even with a computerized system of exchange we do not expect to have a Walrasian auction to settle our transactions once and for all future time. The Modigliani–Miller theorem is not appropriate to an economy in which financial assets serve as surrogate money in settling accounts. The theorem requires that the value of real services provided by financial assets be separated from the manner in which they are financed. Bookkeeping, brokerage and such services can be split off, e.g. cheque charges are often independent of the amount of the cheque. But settlement services cannot be split off. Their nominal value is the nominal value of the account; their real value depends on the other prices in the system.

One way to see this is to consider a case close to practical experience in the light of the assumptions needed to prove the Modigliani–Miller theorem. The fourth assumption was that firms' investment decisions are made independently of how the investment is financed and according to fixed rules. Fama would like to think of banks as unit trusts or mutual funds with a transactions service attached – much like money market mutual funds. If such banks wish to earn more money from their transactions business, they of course must invest in more computers, clerks, telephones and so forth, but in order to attract the use of their real services they must also choose a portfolio that attracts additional business. Banks and money market mutual funds understand this well, as their heavy advertising of funds and accounts differentiated by the nature of their asset portfolios attests. The present value of such firms – even if they are merely brokers profiting by management fees and cheque charges – is not unrelated to the portfolios they choose. This violates the fourth assumption needed to prove the Modigliani–Miller theorem. Any agents' real decisions affected by the bank's present value will also be affected by the volume and composition of its portfolio. Relative prices, including the relative price of money, are not then independent of finance.

Appendix: The Modigliani–Miller Theorem

The logic behind the Modigliani–Miller theorem can be brought out using an example.[37] Consider a firm at a given time: it has a certain stock of real capital (plant and machinery, buildings, inventories and its particular organization), certain markets, a set of plans for future investment and expectations of future sales. Let z be the firm's rate of return on its real capital given its future plans and expectations. z may be a random number which is different in each possible state of the world (e.g. z_1 if oil prices drop, z_2 if they do not *and* there is a war in the Middle East etc.), where each state is assigned a probability of coming to pass.

The net market value of the firm is given by the value V of its real capital (in the eyes of the stock market) less its debt B (to banks and bondholders). Thus if a firm has N shares outstanding, each valued at a price s:

$$sN = V - B$$

or

$$V = sN + B. \tag{5A.1}$$

The difference between debt (bonds) and equity (shares) is simply that debtholders are entitled to a *definite* rate of return r, while shareholders receive an *indefinite* residual which varies as z varies in different states of the world. The total return to capital is

$$zV = z(sN + B). \tag{5A.2}$$

The total return to bondholders is rB – here the assumption of perfect capital markets is invoked: the market rate of interest r is treated as independent of the amount of debt B.[38] The return to shareholders is what is left after the interest is paid on the firm's debt: $z(B + sN) - rB$. The return per pound (or dollar) invested in shares is then

$$\rho = \frac{z(B+sN) - rB}{sN} = \left(z - r\frac{B}{B+sN}\right)\left(\frac{B+sN}{sN}\right). \tag{5A.3}$$

The total cost of financial capital to the firm is, then, the sum of the cost of shares and the cost of bonds:

$$C = \rho sN + rB. \tag{5A.4}$$

The average cost is

$$AC = \rho\frac{sN}{B+sN} + r\frac{B}{B+sN}. \tag{5A.5}$$

Using the definition of ρ, this can be rewritten as

$$AC = \left(z - r\frac{B}{B+sN}\right)\left(\frac{B+sN}{sN}\right)\left(\frac{sN}{B+sN}\right) + r\frac{B}{B+sN} = z. \tag{5A.6}$$

This says that the average cost of financial capital to the firm is equal to the rate of return on the firm's real capital, and that the cost is not affected by the composition of a firm's finance – the average cost is the same no matter what combination of bonds and shares are issued – as long as the fourth assumption holds, implying that z itself is independent of the means of finance.

As long as capital markets are perfect, the firm can acquire as much finance as it needs at the going rate. Its average and marginal costs of finance are the same. Since firms are profit maximizers by the third assumption, this analysis shows that their real output and investment decisions are independent of the composition of their liabilities since the marginal cost of financial capital z is itself independent of this composition.

A related argument shows that the real choices of the individuals who own the firm are also not affected in equilibrium by changes in the firm's financial portfolio. Suppose that an individual owns n shares in the firm. His wealth is

$$W = \alpha sN - b, \tag{5A.7}$$

where $\alpha = sn/sN = n/N$ is the proportion of the total number of outstanding shares that the individual owns and b is the amount of his borrowing (bonds or loans). If he is a net lender b is negative.

Substituting equation (5A.1) into equation (5A.7) yields

$$W = \alpha(V - B) - b = \alpha V - (b + \alpha B). \tag{5A.8}$$

The term αB on the right-hand side of this expression shows the effect of the firm's debt issue on the individual. Let $\gamma = (-b - \alpha B)/\alpha V$ be the ratio of the risk-free to risky components of the individual's portfolio. Notice that if wealth is held constant an individual can choose any value of γ he likes. To lower γ, for instance, he can borrow money (raising b) and use that to buy more shares. Perfect capital markets imply that he can do this to any degree he likes. Since individuals have tastes for various degrees of risk relative to total return, a utility-maximizing individual will choose an optimal γ. A change in his portfolio will not produce any change in his choice of γ unless it provides opportunities not previously available.

Consider a firm of value $V = sN + B$, and suppose that the firm decides to raise its equity-to-debt ratio: it issues $\triangle N$ shares and retires $s\triangle N$ pounds (or dollars) worth of debt. Its value is then

$$V = s(N + \triangle N) + (B - s\triangle N) = sN + B = V. \tag{5A.9}$$

Although V remains constant, the individual's preferred combination of risk-free to risky wealth would be upset by this action unless he took countervailing action himself: γ would rise as his share of the firm's debt fell while his personal debt was held constant. But the individual can always undo the firm's effect on his portfolio: in this case he must borrow $\alpha s \triangle N$ more on his own account and use it to buy more shares. Then consider the ratio

$$\gamma = \frac{-(b + \alpha s \triangle N) - \alpha(B - s \triangle N)}{\alpha V} = \frac{-b - \alpha B}{\alpha V}. \tag{5A.10}$$

The term $\alpha s \wedge N$ in the left-hand parentheses of the numerator of the centre term shows the increase in the individual's debt, while the right-hand term shows the decrease in his share of the firm's debt. The far right-hand expression shows that these terms cancel, so that γ remains unaltered. It is clearly within the individual's power, then, to counteract any effect on the riskiness of his own portfolio imposed by the portfolio choices of firms. Since we already saw that the individual could have initially chosen any level of γ he liked, there is no reason for him to accept any change imposed on him by the firm. Optimally, he will undo any action the firm takes and, since his opportunity sets for consumption choices and factor supplies will themselves be unchanged, he will not alter any economic choice as a result of the firm's actions.

It is important to understand the role of the five initial assumptions in supporting the Modigliani–Miller theorem. The first assumption rules out bankruptcy. A firm goes bankrupt when its commitments to debt outweigh its return on real capital, i.e. $rB > zV$, in which case the shares become worthless. Normally, a firm lowers the value of its equity only by supplying more debt. It is by purchasing such debt and selling equity that the individual restores his preferred debt-to-equity ratio. In the case of bankruptcy, the value of the firm's equity falls without a corresponding increase in the supply of debt, so that the individual cannot make the necessary compensating adjustment. The likelihood of bankruptcy increases with the level of debt issued by the firm. Hence, contrary to the Modigliani–Miller theorem, if bankruptcy is possible, the shareholder may have reason to prefer lower over higher debt–equity ratios in the firms in which he holds shares.

The first assumption also rules out taxes and transactions costs. If dividends are taxed, but interest payments are not, a higher debt–equity ratio may be rationally preferred. If individuals face transactions costs in making their countervailing adjustments to firms' actions, they prefer that the firms simply choose the 'right' portfolio in the first place.

The second assumption states that there must be informational efficiency or rational expectations, i.e. individuals and firms must see through their own and each other's actions in order to make adjustments that are correct up to a serially uncorrelated random error. If, for example, the individual failed to observe correctly the effect of the firm's increasing debt on his own portfolio, he would be moved away from his optimum even though it remained in his power to recover it.

The third assumption rules out a taste for particular portfolio combinations independently of their effects on risk and return. Say that an individual thought it a moral evil to be in debt, even when his net worth was positive; he would then be reluctant to undo a firm's portfolio decision if he had to acquire debt in the process. He would, therefore, have a rational perference that the firm not issue equity in order to lend money (i.e. retire debt).[39]

The fourth assumption states that real investment decisions are based on calculations of present value and are independent of the source of finance. To see its importance, consider a counter-example. Suppose that the government would permit a prime location for a factory only if it were financed through the sale of shares (i.e. without debt). Then the expected present value would no longer be independent of the composition of the firm's portfolio, and shareholders would have rational preferences for a lower debt–equity ratio.

Finally, the fifth assumption states that firms do not enjoy any special advantage over individuals in financial markets. If they did and if, say, firms could borrow at a lower rate of interest than individuals, then the individual's own net worth would not be independent of the amount he borrows. He would not, therefore, be able costlessly to undo a change in a firm's portfolio composition if this involved borrowing on his own account and he would prefer the firm to do the borrowing at a preferred rate. Contrary to the Modigliani–Miller theorem, he would prefer a higher to a lower debt–equity ratio in firms in which he held shares.

6 Formal Models of Monetary Economies

Important as it is, Fama's analysis of the monetary economy is not a typical example of the new classical style of argument. The central problem for new classical monetary theory is to provide microfoundations for the theory of money consistent with general equilibrium and individual optimization. The extreme solution to this problem requires the preferences of and constraints on each and every individual to be precisely specified. Fama's method of short-circuiting the difficulties of such an impracticable task is to rely only on arguments which can be applied to rational agents irrespective of their specific preferences. This method, which relies on arbitrage, i.e. the idea that if a profitable opportunity exists it will be competed away, is familiar in corporate finance. The Modigliani–Miller theorem is a classic arbitrage argument. It assumes general properties about individuals and firms, while ignoring their specific preferences or budget constraints, and reaches conclusions that should hold as long as all profit opportunities have been eliminated.

A more common new classical solution to the problem of specifying every individual's preferences and constraints is to choose one individual as representative of the whole lot, or at least several as representative of a number of types of individuals, and specify the preferences and constraints of that one or few completely. In this chapter we consider two different new classical monetary models (the overlapping-generations model and the finance-constrained models) that adopt this alternative solution.

6.1 The Overlapping-generations Model

Pure Consumption Loans

Probably the best known new classical model of money is the overlapping-generations model. This model has its roots in the 'pure consumption loan' model of Samuelson (1958). It has been developed and refined for a number of purposes by several economists.[1]

Samuelson's pure consumption loan model was aimed at elucidating one of the reasons why the rate of interest is positive. Samuelson wished to analyse the roles of thrift and of economic growth separately from other possible causes of positive rates of interest such as productive durable capital. In order to isolate these elements, he supposed that there was one perishable good in the economy – 'chocolate bars', which must either be eaten or wasted, as they melt away and cannot be stored for future use.[2] Samuelson assumed that individuals lived for two periods (three in some versions of the model) and that they were endowed with a certain number of chocolate bars in each period (appearing like manna to the Israelites or, indeed, like chocolate bars to Pacific islanders in the Second World War). Individuals may wish to consume more or less than their endowments in either period. If they wish to consume more in their old age (second period), they would be willing to lend part of their endowment in their youth (first period) against it being returned with interest in their old age. Such lending is used to support consumption only, as there is no capital in the model, hence the title 'pure consumption loans'.

Clearly, if any individual were able to lend, there must be another who desires to borrow, i.e. who wishes to consume more than his current endowment. If everyone were young and if, as Samuelson supposes, everyone wished to shift consumption to his old age, i.e. everyone wished to lend, there would be no one to whom to lend. Fortunately, everyone is not young. Samuelson assumes that a new generation is born each period. At any time, therefore, there are both young and old consumers. The old will die at the end of the current period and so will want to consume as much as possible immediately. They would be willing borrowers. But the young would not be ready to lend to the old, because the old will die before the young enter the second period and so would not be able to repay any loans.

Samuelson introduces money as a way out of the impasse. Suppose that at the beginning of time the old were endowed with a certain number of pieces of paper called 'money'. If the young were willing to accept this money in exchange for those chocolate bars surplus to their current wants, the old would be better off. When the young in turn become old, if the new young generation were willing to accept the money, the current young would have succeeded in their effort to shift consumption forward to the second period. This is a Pareto-improvement since every generation is now better off in its own estimation. The 'social contrivance of money' (to use Samuelson's own term) permits a desirable redistribution of endowments, as long as each generation trusts the next to accept the money earned from sales of chocolates to the old.

Of course, if youth today believed that youth tomorrow would not accept the money, they would be unwilling to exchange chocolates with the old for money today. In this case, money would be worthless. If the old today had foreseen in their own youth this collapse in the value of money, they would not have accepted the money either, and it would have been valueless even then, and so on back to the creation of money. Money is valuable only if everyone expects it to be valuable.[3] This is a general property of money, although it is a slightly embarrassing one here as there is no mechanism such as taxes levied in money or contracts legally enforced in money that serves to reinforce people's faith in its value even sporadically (see chapter 5, section 5.3).

Once money has been introduced, it is possible to address Samuelson's original concern: what determines the rate of interest? The nominal rate of interest on money is zero – a dollar or pound today is a dollar or pound tomorrow. The real value of money, however, changes with every change in the level of prices. The real rate of return on money is, then, the negative of the rate of inflation, i.e. if prices rise at 10 per cent per year, the real rate of return is -10 per cent per year, and if they fall at 5 per cent per year, it is $+5$ per cent per year. The price level clearly depends on how much chocolate the young exchange with the old and for how much money. If the stock of money is constant and each generation is just like the others in numbers and tastes, the price level will be constant and the real rate of interest will be zero.[4] If, instead, each successive generation is larger than the one before it by a constant proportion N per cent (constant rate of population growth), then the price level will steadily fall at N per cent per period, as the same stock of money buys more and more chocolate. The real rate of interest will then be N per cent per period.

Stationary Equilibrium

Wallace and his colleagues find Samuelson's pure consumption loans model (or 'overlapping-generations model', as we shall call it, since once capital is introduced loans could be made for other purposes than consumption) an attractive starting place for monetary theory, since the demand for money arises endogenously as the result of the optimizing decisions of rational individuals.

Let us now examine the new classical development of the overlapping-generations model in more detail.

Imagine an economy in which there is a constant number of individuals in each of two generations. At the beginning of any period, one generation is old and will die at the end of the period, the other generation is young and will become old, and a new generation will be born. The assumptions of a constant population and of each life consisting of only two periods simplify the analysis and are easily relaxed. Let each generation be endowed when young with Y_1 units of the only consumption good and with Y_2 units when old. Assume that there is no capital or production.

The young of generation t consume $C_1(t)$ units of the consumption good in their youth and $C_2(t)$ units in their old age. The utility of this consumption is given by

$$U = U[C_1(t), C_2(t)], \tag{6.1}$$

which is represented by indifference curves such as U_1, U_2 and U_3 in figure 6.1(a). These indifference curves are assumed to have the usual shape – smooth, continuous and convex to the origin – and to approach each axis asymptotically, ruling out corner solutions.

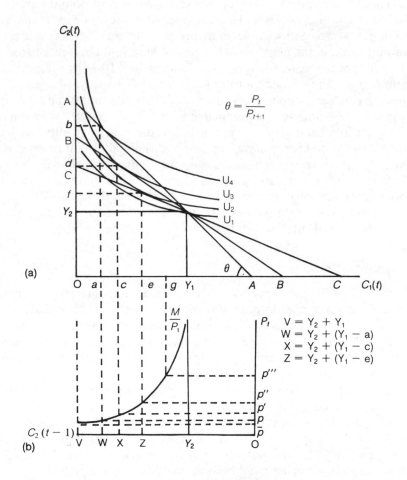

Figure 6.1 A simple overlapping-generations model

The old at time t (who belong to generation $t - 1$) consume $C_2(t - 1)$. They wish to consume as much as possible. Figure 6.1(b) measures consumption by the old from its origin leftwards.

If there were no money, the old would consume Y_2; the young would choose to consume their endowment (Y_1, Y_2) and would reach the level of utility given by U_1. If we assume that a fixed sum of money M had been given to the old in some previous generation, then it would have been traded to the young in successive generations until the old at time t would stand ready to trade it to the current young. Clearly the old wish to trade all their money for whatever it will fetch, and how much it will fetch depends on the price level p_t. The rectangular hyperbola in figure 6.1(b) traces out how much a given M will buy at different levels of p_t $(C_2(t - 1) = Y_2 + M/P_t)$. It approaches the vertical line at Y_2 asymptotically, since no matter how high the price level, the old will always be able to consume their endowment Y_2. It stops at the broken line directly beneath the origin of figure 6.1(a) because at that price level the old could afford to buy the whole endowment Y_1 of the young. How much the old buy and therefore what the price level is depend on how much consumption the young wish to shift to their old age.

The young maximize utility (expression (6.1)) by choosing C_1 and C_2 subject to two budget constraints:

$$C_1(t) = Y_1 - \frac{M}{P_t} \tag{6.2}$$

and

$$C_2(t) = Y_2 + \frac{M}{P_{t+1}}, \tag{6.3}$$

Expression (6.2) says that consumption in their youth must equal their endowment less the real value of the goods that they give to the old (M/P_t). Expression (6.3) says that consumption in their old age equals their endowment plus what their money balances will buy from the young of the next generation (M/P_{t+1}).

The young's maximization problem is shown in figure 6.1(a). The lines AA, BB and CC represent possible budget constraints. Each passes through the point (Y_1, Y_2) because it is always possible for the young to consume their endowment in each period by not trading with the old at all. The optimum is naturally where the highest indifference curve is just tangent to the budget constraint, i.e. where the marginal rate of substitution between consumption in youth and in old age equals the marginal rate of transformation of period t goods into period $t + 1$ goods. Money serves as the means for transforming goods between periods. Thus the amount of goods purchased in period $t + 1$ is M/P_{t+1}, and the amount given up to obtain the money was M/P_t.

Therefore the marginal rate of transformation is

$$\frac{M/P_{t+1}}{M/P_t} = \frac{P_t}{P_{t+1}},$$

which is the slope θ of the budget constraint.

Obviously θ depends on the young's expectation of current and future prices. It is usual to assume that the young have rational expectations or, in simple models with no uncertainty, perfect foresight about prices. Let $t = 1$ and assume that the young believe that prices will be constant at $p_t = p$ for all t; then $\theta = 1$ and the budget constraint is given by AA, which is a 45° line. They then maximize their utility where U_4 is tangent to this line – consuming a in period 1 and planning to consume b in period 2. They trade $Y_1 - a$ to the old for M units of money, so that the price level $p_1 = p$. The old consume $Y_2 + (Y_1 - a)$. In period 2 the young have become old. Since the price level is the same, they also consume $Y_2 + (Y_1 - a)$. This is exactly what they had planned, for observe that, since AA is a 45° line, $Y_1 - a = b - Y_2$ and therefore $Y_2 + (Y_1 - a) = Y_2 + (b - Y_2) = b$ (actual period 2 consumption equals planned period 2 consumption). The young of generation 2 find themselves in precisely the same position as the young of generation 1. Consequently, if they continue to expect p_t to be constant, their equilibrium consumption pattern, the price level and their demand for money will repeat those of generation 1. The equilibrium is *stationary*.

The welfare gain from the social contrivance of money is easily seen to be just as Samuelson described it. Without money, the old consume Y_2; with money, they consume $Y_2 + (Y_1 - a)$, which is a gain in utility. Without money, the young can reach the indifference curve U_1; with money, they reach the higher indifference curve U_4. Since the utilities of both the old and the young are higher, the introduction of money is a Pareto-improvement. Money does not alter the available resources in the economy, but it permits them to be more efficiently distributed.

Non-stationary Equilibria

In order to find the equilibrium in our simple model, we imposed the restriction that the price level was constant. What happens if we relax that restriction?

Suppose that the young in period 1 expect prices in period 2 to be higher than in period 1; then $\theta = p_1/p_2 < 1$ and the budget constraint in figure 6.1 would be flatter than AA. Let BB be the budget constraint; then the young maximize their utility where U_3 is tangent to BB, consuming c in their youth and planning to consume d in their old age. Notice that $c > a$; expected inflation, which produces a less favourable marginal rate of transformation, causes current consumption to be favoured over future consumption (i.e. over savings). The young sell $Y_1 - c$ units of goods to the old for M units of money; therefore the price level is p'.

Now consider what happens in period 2. Generation 1, when young, anticipated that prices would be higher in period 2, say at p'' so that $\theta = p'/p''$. Consequently, the money that they received from the old will purchase $Y_1 - e$ units of goods. (Since their foresight was perfect $Y_2 + (Y_1 - e)$ must equal f in figure 6.1(a).) But if the old receive $Y_1 - e$ from the young, the young of generation 2 must consume e. For this to be optimal, the young of generation 2 must be encouraged to consume more in their youth than did generation 1 ($e > c$). Inspection of the diagram shows that the budget constraint for generation 2 must become flatter, moving from BB to CC where it is tangent at U_2, if this is to be an optimal choice. A flatter budget constraint implies a higher rate of inflation ($p'''/p'' > p''/p'$).

The analysis of period 3 repeats that of period 2. In order to reconcile a further shrinking of the desired transfer of goods from young to old (now $Y_1 - g$), a further increase in inflation and a further flattening of the budget constraint is required, and so on into the fourth, fifth and higher periods. Inflation continues to accelerate. Consumption by the young approaches Y_1 and consumption by the old approaches Y_2 – or exactly the levels they would be in the absence of money. The limit in which each generation simply consumes its endowment is called *portfolio autarky* – the absence of intergenerational trade.

Several features of the inflationary process should be observed. First, there are no disappointed expectations in the model. Individuals correctly predict the precise rate of inflation and their own consumption patterns. These paths of accelerating inflation are just as much equilibria as the stationary equilibrium already identified: call them *non-stationary equilibria*.

Second, the non-stationary equilibria are not unique. Had generation 1 predicted a higher rate of inflation and therefore started with a flatter budget constraint (say CC rather than BB), inflation would have been higher in every period; portfolio autarky would have been approached more quickly. Non-uniqueness of equilibrium is a very common result in models with rational expectations.

Third, inflation has in no way depended on growth in the stock of money. A higher level of M would raise the entire curve M/p_t, giving a higher price level for every level of consumption for the old. An increase in the stock of money is sufficient *ceteris paribus* for inflation but not, it seems, necessary, for the money stock was held constant throughout our thought experiments. Inflation was simply a matter of self-fulfilling expectations.[5]

So far it has been assumed that non-stationary equilibria arise from consumers anticipating higher prices in their old age than in their youth. It might seem that they could also be generated by consumers who anticipate lower prices in their old age. This turns out to be incorrect. There is a lower limit beyond which prices cannot fall. This limit is given when all the young's endowment is sold to the old: $\bar{p} = M/Y_1$ (see figure 6.1(b)). If prices were to fall further than this, the old would be entitled to consume more than the total endowment $Y_1 + Y_2$ for the economy, which is clearly not feasible. Since the non-stationary equilibria would require perfectly foreseen *accelerating* disinflation, and once $\bar{p}$ were reached further acceleration would be impossible, either disinflationary paths would, contrary to assumption, not be perfectly foreseen or consumers would not embark upon them at all.

It has been argued that parallel reasoning could be applied to inflationary equilibria as well.[6] Notice that, as the price level rises, the real amount of the good transferred from the young to the old becomes smaller and smaller. Suppose that the good is indivisible, so that there is a smallest transferable unit $\bar{G}$. Then the highest that prices can rise is to $\bar{p} = M/\bar{G}$. Inflation must stop accelerating once $\bar{p}$ is reached; therefore it would be impossible to embark on a perfectly foreseen equilibrium path which required inflation to accelerate in every period.

How seriously should we take these arguments that non-stationary equilibria are inadmissible? The answer depends upon how strictly we take the assumption of rational expectations. The young obviously cannot know the price level that will prevail in their old age as the model assumes that they do. This assumption is usually taken as a simplified version of the assumption that the young hold rational expectations, i.e. that they do not make *systematic* errors, so that their expectations of prices are correct on average over time. The usual justification of this assumption is that economic agents learn from their mistakes. This, it is often held, obviates the need for agents to know the true model of the economy; instead they act as if they knew the model, although without recourse to any guide beyond their own experience. Unfortunately, the arguments that non-stationary equilibria with either accelerating or decelerating inflation can be ruled out require not only that the young correctly foresee future prices, but that they are also able to deduce from the infeasibility of the optimal choices of some future generations that their own choices should not be optimal. They cannot themselves experience this infeasibility directly; they will be dead, and so they cannot learn from their mistakes. Such deductions, therefore, require an understanding of the true underlying model – an unlikely state for the man in the street.

Non-stationary equilibria are similar in nature to so-called 'bubbles', such as the tulip mania in the seventeenth century and the South Sea Bubble in the eighteenth century as well as some apparently inexplicable booms or slumps in gold and share prices in recent times. The existence of such phenomena, even though they are ultimately infeasible, should warn us against too facile an elimination of non-stationary paths from our simple formal models.

McCallum offers another suggestion for ruling out non-stationary equilibria.[7] He argues that such equilibria are possible only if expectations are formed by conditioning on irrelevant information. In the model above, if the young's expectations of p_{t+1} were formed only from the objective data in the model (Y_1, Y_2 and M) the stationary equilibrium would always result; these data do not change from one period to the next, and so expectations of p_{t+1} should not change either. It is only because of the *arbitrary* assumption of $p_{t+1} > p_t$ that the model ever sets off on a non-stationary path.

McCallum's argument is not meant to rule out the use of expectations of prices conditioned on arbitrary information when one desires to study bubbles. Rather he wants to exonerate models with rational expectations from the charge that they are peculiarly and fatally flawed because they possess non-stationary equilibrium. He observes that the addition of arbitrary information to other schemes for forming expectations may result in non-stationary solutions.

McCallum's argument is not, however, completely convincing. Suppose that expectations are formed adaptively rather than rationally. McCallum's point is that if certain sorts of irrelevant information are added to the adaptive formula then models using it may exhibit non-stationary equilibria just as models with rational expectations do when such irrelevant information is included. But this is not a satisfactory justification for McCallum's procedure of excluding certain information in models with rational expectations. Adaptive expectations is represented by some particular functional form, say

$$p_{t+1}^e = \alpha p_t + (1 - \alpha) p_t^e. \tag{6.4}$$

To add information to this formula, to add extra terms, changes one well-defined hypothesis into a different one. That this second hypothesis exhibits non-stationary equilibria says nothing at all about the adequacy of the first hypothesis. The truth or falsehood of each hypothesis must be judged independently of alternatives, no matter how similar.

Rational expectations, in contrast, cannot be represented as a single well-defined functional form. An expectation is rational if it uses *all* the available information efficiently, so that the expectation is correct up to a serially uncorrelated error. It is a consistency criterion. If the set of available information is enlarged, expectations may become more accurate, but the consistency criterion remains unchanged. Unlike the adaptive expectations (or any mechanical scheme for forming expectations), limiting the information actually used to form rational expectations does not change the structure of the hypothesis. The consistency criterion remains intact. Instead, it arbitrarily violates the spirit of the hypothesis, which is that all information is used. McCallum's procedure for ruling out non-stationary equilibrium, then, is itself arbitrary.

The Problem of Existence

A *monetary equilibrium* is one in which money has a positive value (i.e. $1/p_t > 0$) and is therefore in demand. We have seen that the simple overlapping-generations model has a unique stationary monetary equilibrium and an infinite number of non-stationary monetary equilibria, in which the value of money falls asymptotically towards zero as inflation accelerates. It can also be shown that monetary equilibrium may not exist at all for at least three reasons.

First, consider figure 6.2, which is similar to figure 6.1(a). Assume that the generation t is endowed with (Y_1, Y_2) units of goods in each of the periods of their lives. Assume also that no inflation is expected so that we can consider only stationary equilibria. The young's budget constraint is then the 45° line AA, and their optimal consumption point (C_1, C_2) is given by the tangency of the highest indifference curve

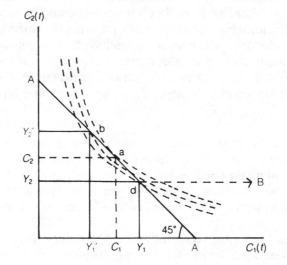

Figure 6.2   Non-monetary equilibrium in an overlapping-generations model

at a. The young sell $Y_1 - C_1$ units of goods to the old for money in order to consume $C_2 - Y_2$ more than their endowment in their old age.

Consider what happens if the young were endowed with (Y_1', Y_2') instead of (Y_1, Y_2). They remain on the same budget constraint and still wish to consume at a. Unhappily a is no longer feasible since it now implies consuming $C_1 - Y_1'$ units of goods *more* than their endowment. This is impossible because the old cannot gain utility from transferring goods to the young, and, even if they could, they would be dead before such a loan could be repaid. No trade then takes place between generations, and money is worthless. The equilibrium for the young is portfolio autarky (at point b), which in this context is sometimes called *barter*, *commodity* or *non-monetary* equilibrium because money is worthless.

Note that monetary equilibrium fails to exist in this example for quite reasonable specifications of the young's preferences (indifference curves) and endowments. It is in no way an aberrant case.

A second way in which monetary equilibrium may fail to exist is that if money is expected to be worthless in the future it will be worthless in the present. Again, consider figure 6.2 with the endowments (Y_1, Y_2). As already observed, if prices are expected to rise, the budget constraint AA becomes flatter and the optimal consumption point shifts to the right. Suppose that the young expect money to be worthless in their old age (i.e. $1/P_{t+1} = 0$); equivalently the price level becomes infinite and then the budget line flattens as far as possible to the infinite horizontal line Y_2B. In this case there is no equilibrium, for at a point of tangency an indifference curve must have the same slope as Y_2B, but since the indifference curves approach the C_1 axis asymptotically, they become horizontal only infinitely far to the right and *below* the budget constraint. Even if there were a point of tangency, it would be to the right of point d and therefore infeasible. Consequently, if money is expected to be worthless in the future, it will be worthless in the present. There will be no monetary equilibrium and the optimal consumption pattern will be portfolio autarky (point d).

Both of the reasons advanced so far for the failure of monetary equilibrium to exist illustrate the more basic problem first noted by Hahn in 1965.[8] It is not in general possible to prove that a monetary equilibrium exists, and it is usually possible to show that a non-monetary equilibrium exists for any general equilibrium model in which money is valued only because it is valuable. The typical response to Hahn's demonstration was to insist that any acceptable model of money should specify what *indispensable* function money performs. The new monetary economics has largely ignored Hahn's warning. Simple overlapping-generations models give money a role, but not an indispensable role: consumption patterns are Pareto-inferior without money, but consumption nonetheless can continue in its absence. They are then an inadequate foundation for monetary theory.

This inadequacy is further heightened by the third manner in which monetary equilibria may fail to exist. Suppose that there is a durable productive capital good in the economy. Let us modify Samuelson's illustration, so that the consumption good is cocoa, rather than chocolate bars, and the young now have the choice of consuming their endowment of cocoa beans or planting them in order to consume more in their old age.

The gross rate of return on capital ϕ (i.e. from planting cocoa) equals the number of beans harvested divided by the number planted and is surely greater than unity. The young now have two means of transferring consumption between their youth and old age. These are illustrated in figure 6.3. The 45° budget line AA again shows the options open to the young when money is held, while the steeper budget line BB, with a slope equal to the rate of return on capital ϕ, shows the options when cocoa trees are planted. Clearly BB dominates

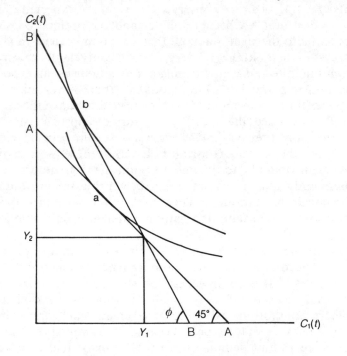

Figure 6.3 Money dominated in rate of return by productive capital in an overlapping-generations model

AA in the sense that it allows the young to reach a higher indifference curve (at b rather than a). The diagram merely states the obvious truth, that in the absence of uncertainty rational agents should prefer to hold the asset which yields the highest rate of return. Once again, since money performs no indispensable service, it will not be held, i.e. there exists no monetary equilibrium, when money is dominated in rate of return by a sufficiently productive capital asset. Since it is patently obvious that the real world contains many sufficiently productive assets, modifying the simple overlapping-generations model in order that money will still be held in it, even when dominated in rate of return, is a critical goal of the new monetary economics.

6.2   The Coexistence of Money and Interest-bearing Assets

Indivisibility

Two methods of explaining the coexistence of money, which bears no interest, with other assets, which bear some positive rate of interest, have been offered by Bryant and Wallace.

The first is suggested in response to the puzzle: why is it that the United States government can issue non-interest-bearing bank-notes (dollar bills) and interest-bearing Treasury bills at the same time?[9] After all both are liabilities of the same government, and should therefore have the same risk of default, and as Treasury bills approach maturity their risk of capital gain or loss from changes in market rates of interest must approach the zero capital risk of money. Given the choice, therefore, why would anyone choose to hold money rather than Treasury bills?

A first step in Bryant and Wallace's suggested solution to this puzzle is to observe that Treasury bills are issued in $10,000 denominations. People, especially poorer people, who wish to hold assets in smaller denominations could not hold Treasury bills. This fact might generate segmentation of the market so that the rate of interest was determined by the supply and demand for Treasury bills with no spillovers into the market for money.

The argument is not, however, watertight. Suppose that banks or other financial intermediaries bought Treasury bills and sold low denomination private bank-notes or, more typically, issued variable-denomination current accounts (checking accounts). They would in effect act as retailers who repackage goods bought in bulk from wholesalers into more convenient sizes. Competition would force banks to offer interest on their notes or accounts. Following the usual rule for profit maximization – set output where marginal cost (i.e. interest paid to account holders plus the marginal costs of maintaining the accounts and facilities for brokerage) is equal to marginal revenue (i.e. the interest earned on holdings of Treasury bills) – obviously implies that the difference between the interest paid on Treasury bills and on bank-notes or accounts equals the marginal costs of brokerage. Since bank accounts are near-perfect substitutes for dollar bills, they must bear nearly the same rate of zero interest. It should be true, therefore, that the rate of interest on Treasury bills would be bid down to a rate equal to the marginal cost of brokerage. The average cost of brokerage in real-world money market mutual funds (unit trusts in the United States that buy short-term assets and issue current accounts) is about 1 per cent of asset value. In long-run equilibrium the marginal cost of brokerage should equal the average cost. Brokerage costs would therefore explain interest rates on Treasury bills of about 1 per cent, but not rates of 7–15 per cent as observed in recent years.

Legal Restrictions

Given the inadequacy of this explanation of the coexistence of money and interest-bearing assets, Bryant and Wallace offer a second related explanation.[10] The existence of banks which broker wholesale Treasury bills into retail notes or deposits is the essential mechanism that forces the rate paid on Treasury bills down to the level of brokerage costs. Bryant and Wallace therefore propose a model in which government regulation rules out such brokerage except for large denominations and retains the monopoly on the issue for small denomination notes for itself. Banks cannot then create a close substitute for small denomination notes based on portfolios of secure Treasury bills. This drives a wedge between the rates of return on money and Treasury bills, allowing a differential greater than the marginal cost of brokerage.

To illustrate the model, consider figure 6.4. As in figure 6.3, AA is the budget line when money is the available asset ($\theta = 45°$) and BB is the budget line when an interest-bearing asset, say a Treasury bill, is available ($\phi = 1 +$ rate of interest $=$ gross rate of return). Let S_{min} be the real value of the smallest denomination of private interest-bearing assets permitted by the government. To the left of $Y_1 - S_{min}$ the young would save enough to be able to afford interest-bearing assets, so that their budget constraint is BB. To the right, their saving falls short of S_{min}; they cannot afford interest-bearing assets, they must hold money instead and their budget constraint is AA. As before, all points to the right of the point (Y_1, Y_2) are not feasible on either budget constraint. The young's operative budget constraint is then the solid portions of BB and AA.

As usual tastes are represented by a set of indifference curves of

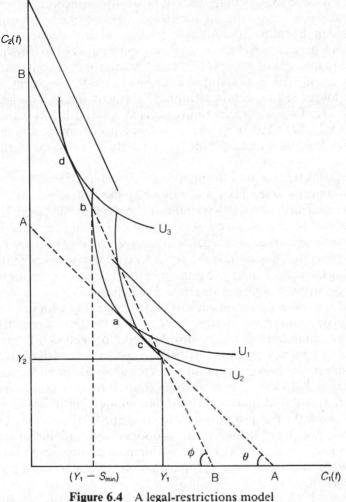

Figure 6.4 A legal-restrictions model

which U_1 may be an example. It is drawn tangent to AA at point a and intersecting BB at the corner b. This shows that it is *possible* that the young may be indifferent between holding money and Treasury bills. But this is a special case. More usual cases are represented by U_2 (one of a different set of indifference curves) tangent to AA at c, where the young are too poor given their tastes to hold Treasury bills, or by U_3 (one of yet a third set of indifference curves) tangent to BB at d, where they are rich enough given different tastes not to hold any money.

In general, richer people will wish to save more than poorer people, so that the restriction against intermediation of Treasury bills into small denominations is less likely to bind for them. This can be seen in figure 6.4. Since S_{min} is independent of wealth or income (i.e. it is the same for rich or poor), an increase in endowments produces an increase in the ratio of the BB portion of the broken budget constraint to the AA portion. An example of this is shown by the full lines parallel to and to the right of AA and BB, which are the budget constraint for a richer agent. The upper (interesting-bearing asset) segment is relatively longer than the lower (money) segment for this budget constraint than for the corresponding parts of AA and BB. It is therefore more likely that a richer consumer will find his optimum on the upper portion, holding Treasury bills, than on the lower portion, holding money.

A legal restriction on intermediation in conjunction with a variety of consumers – some poor and bound by the restriction, and others rich and unaffected by it – is sufficient to explain the coexistence of money and interest-bearing assets. Bryant and Wallace go on to use the analysis to argue that such legal restrictions, which are similar to price discrimination, may permit the government to raise revenue through inflating the money supply in a manner that is Pareto-superior to such inflation without legal restrictions. Here, however, we are not concerned with the policy implications of the model, but with its virtues as a positive account of a monetary economy. On that score, it suffers from the same failings as the simple model of section 6.1, except of course that money and interest-bearing assets do coexist in it. That coexistence is, however, peculiar. The analysis implies that rich consumers hold *only* Treasury bills (optimum at a point like d in figure 6.4) and that poor ones hold *only* money (optimum at a point like c), while the real puzzle is why the same people hold *both*. The fact that it is just possible that agents are sometimes indifferent between money and Treasury bills (double optimum at points a and b) is such a special, fortuitous and unlikely case that it cannot serve as a general explanation.

A further objection to the legal-restrictions version of the overlapping-generations model is that it is not clear that such restrictions are imposed in reality. While it is true that most governments monopolize the production of legal-tender currency, travellers cheques frequently act as a near-perfect substitute for legal tender. That travellers cheques do not bear interest arises from the brokerage costs and the technical difficulties of setting up a manageable arrangement for payment of interest rather than from legal prohibitions.

Furthermore, the poor in the United States and most other countries are not prohibited from holding small-denomination interest-bearing bank accounts (savings accounts and small-denomination time deposits). True, the Federal Reserve's regulation Q prohibited such accounts in the United States from paying market-determined rates of interest between 1966 and 1986, and yet the removal of regulation Q (gradually over the period 1980–6) has not led to any wholesale flight from cash or any tendency of market rates of interest to fall close to the marginal costs of brokerage. All this suggests that the legal-restrictions theory of money is not a sound basis for monetary theory.

6.3   The Finance Constraint

Transactions-constrained Overlapping-generations Model

The root of the failure of Fama's analysis to sustain his conclusions (chapter 5, sections 5.2 and 5.3) can be traced to the absence of any explicit account of how money functions as a medium of exchange. Unlike the advocates of overlapping-generations models, Fama's intention is clearly not to slight the exchange function. He is, nonetheless, misled by leaving it implicit. A third line of development of the new monetary economics concentrates its attention on money's role in exchange with an explicit model, thus remedying Fama's failure. This approach is most closely associated with Lucas.[11]

Lucas's models are technically formidable, but their essential characteristics arise from the incorporation of a device popularized by Robert Clower – the finance or cash-in-advance constraint.[12] Clower argues that what makes a good money is simply the fact that it is involved in almost every exchange: 'Money buys goods and goods buy money; but goods do not buy goods.'[13] Models employing finance constraints are, like the overlapping-generations model, typically divided into discrete periods. The finance constraint then merely states that purchases within the period are limited by the amount of money available at the beginning of the period. Money earned from selling labour or goods within the period cannot be spent before the next period. Money is essential in simple models with a finance constraint, since no transactions can take place without it. In more complicated models the finance constraint is binding only on certain classes of goods.[14]

Lucas justifies the finance constraint with the following story.[15] Imagine households consisting of a wage earner and a shopper, and imagine an economy of spatially dispersed producers and stores. Each store sells one good and each family consumes every type of good. Each worker is involved in the production of just one of these goods. Each day, the worker goes to his place of work and the shopper visits all the stores. For given prices, the amount of money the worker earned before the shopping day begins sets the upper limit to the amount the shopper can purchase. Money is then modelled realistically as the device that allows production and consumption decisions to be made independently without a central coordinating auctioneer.

Lucas's models are set up somewhat differently from the overlapping-generations model of section 6.1 above. Instead of overlapping finite lives, he treats agents with rational expectations as having infinite lives and making consistent plans over infinite time-horizons. Such an assumption, though clearly unrealistic, is convenient for many purposes. The essential insights of such models are not lost, however, if we continue to use an overlapping-generations model but embed the finance constraint in it.

Adopting the assumptions of section 6.1, the young still seek to maximize utility

$$U = U[C_1(t), C_2(t)], \tag{6.5}$$

subject to a new set of budget constraints

$$\frac{M_1(t)}{P_t} + w_t L(t) = C_1(t) + K(t) + \frac{M_2(t)}{P_t} \tag{6.6}$$

$$\frac{M_1(t)}{P_t} \geq C_1(t) + K(t) \tag{6.7}$$

$$\frac{M_2(t)}{P_{t+1}} + (1 + r_t)K(t) = C_2(t) + T(t), \tag{6.8}$$

where M_1 is the amount of money given to the young at the beginning of their youth, L is the young's endowment of labour, which they sell for the real wage rate w_t, M_2 is the amount of money carried over from youth to old age, r_t is the real rate of return on capital K and T is the lump sum taxes payable by the old in money.

Equations (6.6) and (6.8) are the ordinary budget constraints corresponding to equations (6.2) and (6.3) in the earlier model. Their form is somewhat different because we are now modelling money's role as a transactions medium. In the earlier model the young were simply endowed with an amount Y of the consumption good, which they could sell to the old or consume. Here the term $w_t L(t)$ reflects the assumption that they must work for money in order to consume any goods. We further assume, however, that their wages are paid at the end of the period, so that, by the finance constraint, they would be unable to consume anything in their youth unless they began the period with some money $M_1(t)$. This is not an unrealistic assumption at all, since in real life someone must support the young until they have worked long enough to set up independently. Since we abstract here from family relations, we simply assume that the young receive an initial endowment of money. As a whole, equation (6.6) says that the young allocate their resources $M(t)/P_t + w_t L(t)$ between consumption

$C_1(t)$, real savings $K(t)$ and money balances to be carried over to their old age $M_2(t)$.

We assume that individuals are endowed with the ability to work in both their youth and their old age. Nonetheless, since the finance constraint prevents them from spending their wages until the period after they are received, the old will not choose to work.[16] Thus equation (6.8) says that the old are able to spend the money $M_2(t)$ they carried over from their youth and any real savings made in their youth plus the real rate of return $(1 + r_t)K_t$ on those savings. These resources are allocated between consumption $C_2(t)$ and taxes $T(t)$. The tax term is included in order that we can consider cases in which the money supply is constant. If $T(t) = 0$ for all t, then the money supply would grow continuously as each new generation added $M_1(t)$ units of money. If $T(t) = M_1(t)$ for all t, then the money supply will not grow. We can assume that at the beginning of time the generation then old was endowed with $M_2(0) - T(0)$ units of money, which was then passed on from generation to generation.

Expression (6.7) is the finance constraint. It simply says that no matter what total resources the young have, their expenditure in their youth cannot exceed the real value of their initial money balances.

Existence and Stationarity

What difference does it make to add a finance constraint to the overlapping-generations model? First, it means that the existence of a monetary equilibrium is not quite as fragile as it was with the earlier model. Recall that in the simple overlapping-generations model, the existence of an asset with a higher rate of return than money would cause the young to choose not to hold money. In this model, such a case would occur if $(1 + r_t) > P_t/P_{t+1}$. The young still prefer not to hold money and so will spend as much as they can in their youth. Thus expression (6.7) will hold at equality. But subtract (6.7) from (6.6) and rearrange to yield

$$M_2(t) = w_t P_t L(t). \tag{6.9}$$

This simply reminds us that even though the young do not wish to carry any money into their old age they nevertheless will do so (i.e. $M_2(t) > 0$) because the finance constraint prevents them from spending their wages – paid in money – until their old age. Thus an asset with a higher rate of return simply cannot drive money completely out of use.

Similarly, even if the young so strongly preferred present to future consumption that they wished to consume their entire resources in the current period, money would not be rendered worthless as it was in the simple overlapping-generations model for two reasons. First, unlike in the earlier model, the young are not given an endowment of goods, but must work to earn money to buy goods. Money is used to support exchange within as well as between generations. Therefore it does not become worthless simply because the young do not wish to trade with the old. Second, even if the young wish to consume all their resources $M_1(t)/P_t + w_t L(t)$ in their youth, the finance constraint prevents consumption greater than $M_1(t)/P_t$ so that $w_t L(t)$ units of money are carried over into old age. Just as in the case when money is dominated in rate of return by other assets, it cannot be driven out of use with a binding finance constraint.

Monetary equilibrium could fail to exist in the earlier model for a third reason: if money was expected to be worthless in the future, it would also be worthless today as no one would choose to hold it from youth to old age. Again, the finance constraint eliminates this problem. Money cannot be worthless in any period since it is needed to support intragenerational trade. Since this is true in every period, there would never be any justification for the belief that its value would fall to zero in a future period. Even if such a belief was held without justification, the fact that wages are paid at the end of the period in money forces the young to hold money into their old age.

Similarly, non-stationary (accelerating) inflationary equilibria are not possible with a finance constraint. A non-stationary inflation requires an ever greater shift of consumption towards youth. This could occur only if the finance constraint was not binding, since when it binds it completely determines how much an agent may spend irrespective of his preferences. But if the economy were to embark on an inflationary path (provided that M_1 grew less quickly than the price level), the value of real money balances $M_1(t)/P_t$ would fall until eventually the finance constraint would bind. Expenditure could not then be shifted any further towards youth. Anticipating this impasse, individuals with rational expectations would not embark on such an infeasible path. Accelerating deflationary equilibria are also not feasible, for precisely the same reasons as noted in section 6.1 above.

The Quantity Theory

A further important way that the two models differ is that the standard propositions of the quantity theory of money *may not* hold in the simple model, but will hold in the finance-constrained model provided that the finance constraint binds.[17] The quantity theory implies, among other things, that, for constant income (or output), changes in the level of the stock of money should be associated with proportional changes in the level of prices irrespective of the distribution of money balances. It turns out that this proposition does hold in the simple overlapping-generations model of section 6.1. But consider a model like the one in this section except that there is no finance constraint. In order to simplify the exposition, assume that there are no capital assets (i.e. $K(t) = 0$ for all t) and that labour is supplied inelastically at a constant real wage, so that $w_t L(t) = Y_t$ for all t, where Y_t is the total output for the economy in period t. The choice problem for the young is shown in the figure 6.5(a). Consider the budget constraints AA, BB and DD. The young's total resources in period t are given by $Y_t + M_1/P_t$. They may either consume their resources or save them by holding money. Suppose that each generation is alike and the money supply is constant (which requires $T(t) = M_1(t)$ for all t); prices will then be the same in each period and the budget constraint will be a 45° line. Consider first a price level p' which yields the budget constraint DD. At a higher price level p'' real balances held by the young are lower, yielding the budget constraint BB which is closer to the origin. Each price level and the corresponding first-period consumption for the young, given by the tangency with the highest indifference curve, is plotted as the curve PC^Y in figure 6.5(b). As prices rise indefinitely, the value of real balances falls to zero. This limit is shown by the budget constraint AA, which touches the $C_1(t)$ axis at Y. The tangency of AA with the indifference curve shows the young's consumption when real balances have become worthless; call this $\bar{C}_1$. The curve PC^Y approaches $\bar{C}_1$ asymptotically. If M_1 is increased, the whole curve PC^Y shifts up.

The curve PC^O is the same as the old's consumption curve in figure 6.1; it plots out $[M_2(t - 1) - T(t - 1)]/P_t$. Unlike in the earlier model, the old have no endowment of goods. Therefore they consume only what they can buy from the young. Their consumption obviously depends on the price level and is read from right to left in figure 6.5(b). An increase in M_2 raises the curve PC^O. The actual price level is determined where PC^O crosses PC^Y at p'. Here real balances for the young are such that their budget constraint is DD and they consume C_1'. The old consume $Y_t - C_1'$.

Using figure 6.5 it is possible to answer the question: is money neutral, i.e. does a change in total money balances produce a proportional change in the price level? The answer is: only in special cases. Suppose that M_1 were increased; then PC^Y would shift up proportionately and prices would increase, but, because PC^O is not vertical, they would increase less than proportionately to the increase in M_1. Similarly, an increase in M_2 would lead to a proportionate upward shift of PC^O, but to a less than proportionate increase in prices, since PC^Y is not vertical. Only an equiproportionate increase in both

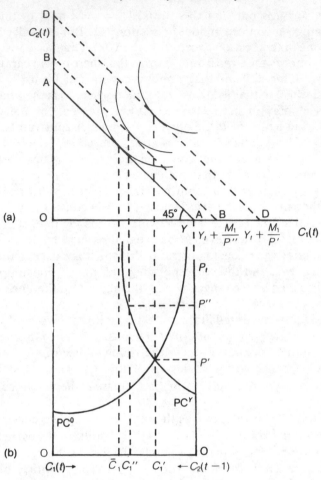

Figure 6.5 Non-neutrality in an overlapping-generations model

M_1 and M_2 would lead to an exactly proportional increase in prices; both curves could rise vertically and would cross at a proportionally higher price level directly above C_1'. Thus the *distribution* of any increase in the money stock and not just its *level* is important in determining the price level in this model with no finance constraint: money is not neutral, except in special cases.

In contrast, money is neutral in the model when there is a binding finance constraint. If the same simplifying assumptions are retained, the finance constraint (6.7) can be written as

$$\frac{M_1(t)}{P_t} = C_1(t). \tag{6.10}$$

Thus the young simply consume their entire real balances. The old consume whatever the young do not, paying with the money held over from their youth. Hence

$$C_2(t - 1) = Y_t - C_1(t) = \frac{M_2(t - 1) - T(t - 1)}{P_t}. \tag{6.11}$$

Substituting (6.10) into (6.11) to eliminate $C_1(t)$ and rearranging yields

$$P_t = \frac{M_2(t - 1) - T(t - 1) + M_1(t)}{Y_t} = \frac{M_t}{Y_t}, \tag{6.12}$$

where $M_t = M_2(t - 1) - T(t - 1) + M_1(t)$ is the total stock of money at time t. Equation (6.12) is a simple quantity equation ($MV = PY$) with velocity set to unity because of the implicit assumption that money turns over once a period. Any change in M_t, no matter how it is distributed between M_1 and M_2, is associated with a proportionate change in P_t: money is neutral.

The absence of neutrality in overlapping-generations models without finance constraints is one reason not to interpret them as monetarist models.[18]

6.4   The Theory of Finance

In an early paper, Lucas (1980a) uses a simple model with a finance constraint (although a model more complex than the one in the last section) to show that it is possible to characterize a stochastic equilibrium when there are many commodities (C_1 and C_2 would be considered vectors of commodities). He assumes that relative prices are constant and that demand for the commodities is subject to random shocks, and then shows that it is possible to derive, among other results, the stochastic analogue to the quantity equation (6.12).

In a more recent paper Lucas (1984) introduces money by means of a finance constraint into a finance model in which not only many goods, but also many types of assets with various risks and returns, are traded. Among the results derived there are that the so-called Ricardian equivalence between taxation and bond finance does not hold in a monetary economy (this result will be considered in chapter 7 section 7.1) and that the Modigliani–Miller theorem – originally derived in a model abstracting from money – remains robust in a monetary economy. The details of Lucas's papers are too complex to be considered in detail. This last result, however, seems to relate to the issues raised in chapter 5 and warrants at least some further consideration here.

Lucas's conclusion that the Modigliani–Miller theorem is robust in a monetary economy results in part from the fact that only money (i.e. cash) can relax the finance constraint in his model. But we need not be so restrictive. The finance constraint aims to capture the need for some medium to settle payments imbalances. Cash is obviously one medium. An individual can borrow cash in order to relax his own finance constraint. Such borrowing merely redistributes cash and therefore leaves prices in the quantity equation (6.12) unaffected. However, an individual can also borrow from a bank in the form of a demand deposit. Because banks need cash or reserves only to settle uncleared balances, i.e. they need only a fraction of their deposits, this borrowing is not simply a redistribution of cash and the quantity equation must be rewritten

$$P_t = \frac{M_t + D_t}{Y_t}, \tag{6.13}$$

where D_t is deposits. Contrary to Fama's claim, the volume of bank liabilities (deposits) is related to the price level.

Fama argues that, since deposits are heterogeneous and different in kind from currency, different deposits should not be added together and certainly not added to currency. We were all taught, of course, not to add apples and oranges, but it can be perfectly correct to add pieces of fruit even if some are apples and others are oranges. Deposits and currency can be properly added together when the question is to what degree they relax the finance constraint, i.e. to what degree they settle payments imbalances, which is properly measured by their nominal value and hence is related to the price level.

6.5   An Assessment

The Overlapping-generations Model and Finance

Formal new classical models of money are held to be superior to any models that 'start from curves' because individual economic agents are separately identified (at least in principle). Their first advantage is that they are supposed to be immune from the so-called Lucas critique (see chapter 8, section 8.3). Lucas argues that estimated macroeconomic relations will break down when government economic policies change. Macroeconomic relations are simply the aggregation of individual optimal responses to policies and the economic environment. Any change in policy (e.g. a change in the rule governing the rate of growth of the stock of money) leads to different optimal responses and therefore to different observed aggregate relations. A model based on individuals allows us to derive their responses and thus to predict the shift of the aggregate relation.

The second advantage of these formal models is held to be that they permit standard Paretian welfare analysis. Since each individual is separately identified, the effect of any policy can be judged with respect to individuals' utility.[19]

While both the advantages claimed for formal new monetary models are correct in principle, their practical importance must be qualified. First, Paretian welfare analysis is less important for economics in general and for the theory of money in particular than is sometimes claimed. Distributional questions overwhelm questions of Pareto-efficiency in judging individual welfare. Furthermore, markets are so far from perfect and our detailed knowledge of the imperfections is so conspiciously absent that we are not in a position to make feasible second-best judgements.

Second, no tractable version of the overlapping-generations model is sufficiently realistic to justify its use in the derivation of believable macroeconomic relations. Obviously, the model must be extended to many periods and must incorporate uncertainty about endowments and length of lives. Neither extension seems to alter the general character of the model radically. But in order to derive actual (econometrically observable) macroeconomic relations or to make fine judgements about welfare, some account must be taken of the fact that the economy consists of millions of individuals, differing in tastes and endowments. The model is hard pressed by what is called in chapter 9 the 'Cournot problem': there are too many individuals (firms and consumers) and too many goods to be handled by direct modelling.

A possible route out of this difficulty is to rely only on arguments that are robust across all types of individuals or, at least, that allow individuals to be reduced to a few types. An example of such an argument is Fama's model of money discussed in chapter 5. Individual tastes are not explicitly specified in that model. Instead all people are treated as members of a single class – the class of rational agents. The Modigliani–Miller theorem says that, under certain general assumptions, if people are rational, then the composition of financial portfolios will not affect their real decisions irrespective of their tastes. Fama tries to apply the Modigliani–Miller theorem to a monetary economy. His strategy of argument is in principle powerful, for, if it were correct, useful conclusions could be drawn about the economy without identifying any particular people.

Similarly, some of the conclusions from models with finance constraints are of the same type. In particular, quantity equations and the neutrality of money hold whenever money is dominated in rate of return in the model of section 6.3 irrespective of any individual's tastes.

Unfortunately, the distribution of consumption and the actual utilities of individuals needed to make Paretian welfare judgements in any overlapping-generations model and even the price level in the model without a finance constraint (section 6.1) depends critically on the actual utility functions of the agents modelled. It is therefore difficult to see why conclusions reached in any tractable version of the model should be robust in economies with millions of diverse people.

The third reason for qualifying the practical importance of overlapping-generations models is that it is no advantage for a theory or model to permit us to derive observable macroeconomic relations or do welfare economics if that theory or model is false in any *relevant* sense. As we have seen already the simple overlapping-generations model is in fact false in some important respects.

A primary respect in which the overlapping-generations model presents a false theory of money is in treating money as primarily a store of value, slighting its other critical function as a transactions medium. Samuelson, to be sure, called the 'social contrivance' used to make mutually beneficial trade possible when generations overlap 'money', but as he himself recognized it might just as well have been called 'social security'. Any institution that permits the young to have faith that consumption foregone today will be repaid tomorrow serves as well as any other – call it 'money', 'bonds', 'social security' or what you will.

Two specious arguments are sometimes raised to support the concentration on the store-of-value function. First, this function is held to be somehow primary over money's other functions; if money did not store value, at least between transactions, how could it ever serve as a means of exchange?[20] But this argument is fully reversible: if money were not acceptable in exchange, why would anyone treat it as being able to store value? The relationship between these functions is symbiotic; neither has primacy over the other.

The second argument is that, since money is used to exchange goods between generations, the means of exchange function is in fact modelled.[21] This misses the point entirely. Suppose that tastes were such that the young never wished to move consumption forward to old age. They would not then wish to trade with the old and money would be worthless. Money is not *essential* to the economy, since the young or the old do not need it simply to consume their own endowments. But when we say that money is a means of exchange, we mean that it serves a critical role in our obtaining goods. A monetary economy is one in which the real opportunities available to consumers as a whole are greater with money than without it; in this sense, the overlapping-generations model fails to capture the means of exchange function of money.[22]

A Note on ad hocness

The dispute over whether money is mainly a store of value or a means of exchange highlights the fact that there is no one new classical monetary theory but a number of alternative approaches all meant to be consistent with the tenets of new classicism. Which approach is adopted in the end makes a considerable difference to the conclusions reached. Whether one approaches money from its aspect of a store of value or a means of exchange largely determines whether or not traditional quantity theory results follow and whether it is a major theoretical hurdle to introduce assets which dominate money in rate of return or simply a minor extension.

Advocates of the overlapping-generations model usually view the finance constraint as *ad hoc* – an arbitrary unexplained assumption – and consequently as an evasion of the central problem of monetary theory.[23] Why, they ask, does this constraint arise? If it truly exists, it should be the outcome of the model, not assumed by it. They argue, furthermore, that money's role as a store of value is primary. But as we have already seen, the relation between these two functions of money is clearly symbiotic.

An emotionally satisfying response to the charge that the finance constraint is arbitrary is the fallacious *tu quoque*: assuming that money and unbacked bonds are the only ways of storing wealth, as simple overlapping-generations models do, is itself arbitrary and unexplained. A response that is not fallacious, but related to this one nonetheless, is that every theory must assume some things and explain others. It may perhaps be desirable to have a theory which explains the function of money as a means of exchange from deeper more fundamental assumptions. In the meantime, in the absence of such a theory, it is appropriate to use an assumption of a cash-in-advance constraint that accords so well with our experience of the uses of money, especially given the light it casts on the consequences of arbitrarily assuming that money's only function is as a store of value.

7 The Limits of Policy: Micromodels

A constant theme in the new classical economics is that policy operates under more severe restraints than casual analysis might at first suggest. The macroeconomic models examined in chapter 4 develop this theme. On the one hand, the policy-ineffectiveness model seems to provide radical confirmation of the monetarist belief that in the long run monetary policy can affect only the price level. On the other hand, the analysis of monetarist arithmetic suggests that control of the price level may itself be beyond the scope of policy. The conflict between these two conclusions arises from the fact that the policy-ineffectiveness model ignores the relationship between monetary policy and fiscal policy. The conflict may, then, really be only apparent – a partial conclusion generated in a partial model. That fiscal policy is in fact relatively unimportant is, however, a recurring monetarist claim. The two models, then, may yet reflect a fundamental issue for policy analysis.

The analysis of both models is conducted at a high level of aggregation. The fundamental tenets of new classicism suggest, however, that sound economic conclusions can be derived only in well-specified models of individual optimization. In this chapter, therefore, we continue the investigation of the limits of policy by examining microeconomic models of policy – both for their intrinsic interest and for the light they shed on the conflicting models of chapter 4. The three models to be considered are all based on overlapping-generations models.

The analyses of policy are of course no better than the underlying models, which were criticized in chapter 6. We do not stop there, however, because these analyses also reveal a very general theme in new classical thinking. Each model generates a notion of policy ineffectiveness that is closely related to the Modigliani–Miller theorem.[1] The theorem concludes that rational people ignore changes in the compositions of corporate portfolios that change the pattern of their lifetime income streams as long as these changes leave the present value of the income streams intact. New classical economists have derived analogues to the Modigliani–Miller theorem for the government: Ricardian equivalence holds that the mixture of tax and debt finance is irrelevant; Wallace's Modigliani–Miller theorem for open-market operations asserts that the composition of central bank portfolios is irrelevant; Sargent and Wallace's rehabilitation of the 'real bills' doctrine asserts that the mixture of public and private debt in private portfolios is irrelevant.

One way to interpret the Modigliani–Miller theorem is as a benchmark to show exactly which assumptions must be relaxed in order to explain theoretically the observed relevance of the composition of corporate portfolios. Clearly, the new classical Modigliani–Miller theorems for public policy might also be interpreted in this way. Sargent and Wallace, for example, attempt to show that government interference in private credit markets can make the stock of money the central factor in controlling the price level. Their analysis could then be seen as a formal development of Fama's idea in chapter 5 that money and its influence on prices are the result of government regulation. Without such regulation policy would be ineffective.

There is nonetheless a tension in new classical thinking between interpreting these results as benchmarks and taking them to be reasonable approximations to the truth.

Let us now consider the models.

7.1 Ricardian Equivalence

In the early nineteenth century David Ricardo observed that under some circumstances taxation and debt finance (issuing bonds) are equivalent means of financing government expenditure.[2] Ricardo's idea was very simple. If the government levies a tax, it reduces one's wealth. If instead it sells bonds to the same value as the tax, to be paid off with interest in, say, a year, wealth apparently remains intact. But this is only apparent because the government will have to raise taxes later in order to pay off the bonds with interest. The taxpayer who foresees this fact must therefore set aside a portion of his wealth equal to the tax. His *disposable* wealth is exactly the same as it would have been had the tax been levied on him at first: in theory, tax and bond finance are equivalent.

Ricardo himself suggested two reasons why this theoretical proposition would not apply in practice. First, bond finance would be genuinely advantageous if the owner of the bonds were to emigrate before taxes were levied to pay off the bond issue. Second, bond owners would act as if bond finance were genuinely advantageous, if, as he thought likely, they did not understand that it implied higher future taxes.

Infinite Lives

Robert Barro (1974) resurrected Ricardo's theoretical argument.[3] Barro uses two distinct models. In the first, individuals are assumed to have infinitely long lives. The point of this is to ensure that the same individuals who buy bonds will be taxed later to pay them off. The key assumption is that perpetual bond finance is ruled out: the debt must be paid off sometime.

Barro's point can be made in a much simpler model. Instead of infinite lives, assume that both the individual and the economy exist for just two periods and that any debt incurred in the first period must be repaid with interest in the second. The intertemporal choice problem for a representative individual is shown in figure 7.1. Let each individual be endowed with Y_1 units of a homogeneous consump-

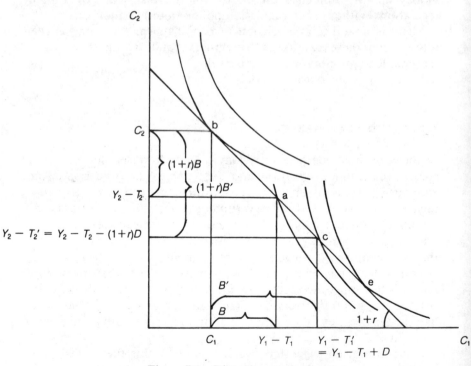

Figure 7.1   Ricardian equivalence

tion good in their youth and Y_2 units in their old age. Let each be subject to lump sum taxes of T_1 and T_2 in each period. The initial disposable income is shown at point a. The individual can borrow or lend at a constant real rate of interest r, and so can consume at any point along the budget constraint through point a. The individual's optimum is at point b where he plans to consume C_1 in period 1 and C_2 in period 2.

Now consider a decrease D in taxes and an equal increase in the sale of bonds. Total government expenditure is not affected. The individual's first-period disposable income is increased from $Y_1 - T_1$ to $Y_1 - T_1' = Y_1 - T_1 + D$. Since the new debt must be repaid with interest, taxes in period 2 must be raised so that second-period disposable income falls from $Y_2 - T_2$ to $Y_2 - T_2' = Y_2 - T_2 - (1 + r)D$. Since the ratio of the changes of disposable income $(1 + r)D/D = 1 + r$, the new point of disposable income, c, must lie on the *same* budget constraint as point a. The individual's optimum remains at b. Tax and bond finance are equivalent as far his consumption decisions are concerned, or, to put it into jargon, the discounted value of the increased taxes in period 2 just offsets the reduced taxes in period 1,

$$\frac{\Delta T_2}{1+r} = \frac{T_2' - T_2}{1+r} = \frac{(1+r)D}{1+r} = D = -(T_1 - T_1') = -\Delta T_1,$$

leaving his opportunity set unaffected.

Overlapping Generations

Barro's first model assumes that people live for an infinitely long time in order that no one might use a convenient death to avoid future taxes. In the simple model here we achieve the same result by compressing all time into two periods and insisting that debt issued in the first period be paid off in the second. The fact that people do not live forever appears to undermine Ricardian equivalence. A tax cut today augments the wealth of those alive today. If the bonds which are issued to replace tax revenues are not repaid until far into the future, then the current generation will be dead and gone and will not be taxed to pay them off; its wealth will be higher.

To demonstrate that taxes may not be escaped through death, Barro recasts the argument into an overlapping-generations model without money.[4] People live for two periods, overlapping one period with their children. When young, they plan how much to consume in each period of their lives and how much to leave to their children as a bequest. Since they have rational expectations (perfect foresight in this con-

Barro's 1st model infinite live

2nd model 2 period overlapping generations model

text), these plans turn out to coincide with their (and their children's) actual choices.

The critical assumption in Barro's second model is not the fact that generations overlap, but that the utility of the children is of some concern to the parents. We shall therefore examine Barro's analysis in a simpler model than his. Assume that each generation lives for only one period, dying just as the next generation is born. Assume that each generation, nevertheless, cares for the welfare of its offspring.[5] Its utility function could be described as

$$U = U(C_1, U^*), \tag{7.1}$$

Where C_1 is its own consumption and U^* is the level of its children's utility, which of course depends on the children's consumption and the children's utility.

This utility function implies that, although the parents care *directly* only about their own children's utility and not that of any future generation, they must care *indirectly* about every future generation, for anything that affects the consumption of their grandchildren affects the utility of their children and therefore affects their own utility. Similar chains of concern can be constructed back from any future generation, however distant.

The chain-linked nature of the utility function means that without loss of generality we can consider only the case in which the children are taxed to pay off debt issued in place of taxes to the parents. Figure 7.1 can be reinterpreted to refer to two generations instead of one. The parent's initial after-tax income is $Y_1 - T_1$, and they perfectly foresee (rationally expect) the children's initial after-tax income to be $Y_2 - T_2$. The budget constraint through point a represents the possible trade-offs between the parents' and the children's consumption, given the real rate of interest r. The indifference curves represent the parents' utility function and take account of the children's and future generations' utility functions and budget constraints.[6] Initially the parents choose to consume C_1 and to leave a bequest of B to their children, whom they correctly expect to consume C_2. Just as in the case of the single generation with two-period lives, substitution of debt for taxes increases the after-tax income of the parents but is exactly offset by increased taxes on the children, leaving the budget constraint and consumption plans unaltered. The parents therefore increase their bequest from B to B' to offset the increased taxes on the children.

Notice that Barro's result does not depend on parents' giving their children's utility equal absolute weight to their own. It merely requires that they give it some weight, equal only at the margin, and treat it consistently. The demonstration of Ricardian equivalence in both Barro's models belongs to the same class of results as the Modigliani–Miller theorem. Both follow the same general plan: there is a general equilibrium over real goods. Not being real goods, financial assets (and taxes) do not figure in utility functions. They do, however, enter into budget constraints. Then if an autonomous change in one element of an agents' portfolio can be shown to be equal but of opposite sign to the discounted value of a related change elsewhere in the portfolio *and* if there is a mechanism through which the agent can make appropriate portfolio adjustments, then neither the value of the agent's portfolio nor the opportunity set for his real choices has changed, and so his equilibrium choices will remain the same. This result is not trivial as it depends upon the existence of a mechanism through which portfolio adjustments can be made. In Barro's models, the fact that income can be saved at a fixed real rate of interest provides the mechanism for appropriate intertemporal portfolio adjustments. Without it the Ricardian equivalence result would not go through.

How Robust is the Argument?

There are two strong related objections to Barro's analysis. It might at first glance seem that Barro's assumption of rational expectations is hard to justify in this particular context. After all, the most persuasive case for the rational expectations hypothesis is that people do not make systematic mistakes, not because they actually know the true model of the economy but because they adjust their behaviour to obvious errors until they act *as if* they knew the true model. Here any mistakes they make in judging the consumption choices of future generations will be made after they are dead, so how could they possibly learn from their mistakes?

This reasoning is incorrect; it does, however, suggest the first strong objection. It is incorrect because Ricardian equivalence does not require knowledge of the actual choices of future generations. Instead it requires that parents take *some* (perhaps incorrect) view of their children's choices and opportunity sets and consistently use that view in determining their bequests. As long as the parents completely offset any losses that increases in the debt impose on future generations, they may be completely wrong in their conjectures about the actual preferences of future generations and incomes and still changes in the composition of government finance will not affect their own consumption decisions. The requirement that parents take a fixed view of the choice of future generations and consistently use it to calculate appropriate bequests is, however, extremely strong. It implies that people in fact understand the true model and use it to calculate consistent adjustments to their bequests. It is not likely that ordinary people implicitly develop an analysis that has only recently been accurately formulated by professional economists, and it is not plausible to suppose that they acquire this skill through a process of trial and error since the necessary experiments generally extend beyond their deaths.

The rule for bequests (or for that matter saving between youth and old age) that comes out of the analysis of Ricardian equivalence is simple: save all windfall gains from tax cuts, and never treat government bonds as net wealth. Although the rule itself is simple, adequate justification for it requires economic sophistication well beyond the commonplace. Because it is too much to assume that most people perform sophisticated economic analysis in order to adjust their bequests consistently, it seems unlikely that they attempt to integrate future generations' utility functions into their own. Barro's argument seems plausible because parents generally care about their children and wish to leave them bequests. While this is no doubt true, they probably do not compare their children's consumption or utility with their own; rather, they compare the actual size of the bequest with their own consumption.

The second strong objection, then, is that Barro has set up the problem incorrectly. A more likely situation is represented in figure 7.2. The horizontal axis measures the parents' consumption and income, and the vertical axis measures the parents' bequest and not the children's consumption and income. If the parents have an after-tax income of $Y_1 - T_1$, they may either consume it all or trade off consumption for bequests at a rate determined by the real rate of interest. They actually choose point a with a bequest B and consumption C_1. Now consider a substitution of debt for taxes that increases their after-tax income to $Y_1 - T_1'$. Since they do not account for their children's income or consumption choices, this shifts their budget constraint out to the right. The new equilibrium is at b. As shown, both current consumption and the level of the bequest rise. Clearly, since the opportunity set has changed, the parents' real choices will change, and any changes in the level of the bequest will only accidentally offset the implied future taxes: Ricardian equivalence fails.[7]

The objection that parents choose absolute bequests and not levels of consumption or utility for their children gains its strength from the supposed critical importance of the possibility of postponing taxes until after the initial beneficiaries of tax cuts are dead. Poterba and Summers (1986) argue that this issue is less important than Barro or his opponents seem to believe. Actual past additions to the stock of government debt have been largely repaid (either directly or through inflation running down their real value) within a short period – much shorter than the average person's lifespan. The problem is, therefore, more like Barro's model with infinite lives than like the model with

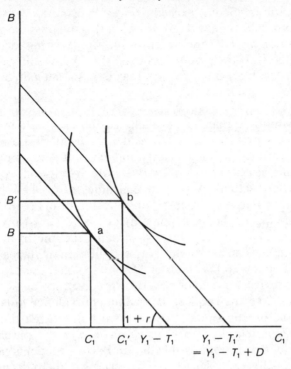

Figure 7.2 Ricardian equivalence fails when parents' bequest motive is absolute

intergenerational bequests. Poterba and Summers show that, for reasonable specifications of the probabilities of dying and the pattern of repayment of debt, very little of any addition to the debt will be treated as net wealth just because people show no concern for their off-spring. Their argument does not rule out any other objections to Ricardian equivalence.

In any case, the argument of Poterba and Summers depends critically on the assumption that government debt will be paid off over a short horizon. The financing of wars is the main evidence for this as-sumption: debt was run up to astronomical heights to support the war and was then paid off or inflated away as soon as peace was restored. It is not clear that large peacetime increases in debt will be treated in the same fashion. The question remains open.

There are a number of other objections to Barro's analysis of which at least six are worth noting.

1 Barro supposes that the debt must eventually be paid off. Just as in the case of monetarist arithmetic (chapter 4, section 4.2), if the rate of

growth of national income exceeds the real rate of interest, the ratio of debt to national income will fall. It would then be possible to issue additional bonds to pay the interest on the existing debt without increasing taxes. If the parents believed that this would be true, they could safely treat any bond-financed tax cut as a net gain and use it to increase their consumption.[8]

2 Barro supposes that, given a choice, parents will in fact leave bequests. This may not be so. Consider a parent whose indifference curve is tangent to the budget constraint at point e in figure 7.1 (interpret the figure as referring to individuals who live for only one period). Such a parent actually wants to consume more than his income $Y_1 - T_1$. Since that is infeasible, consumption of his entire income at point a, leaving no bequest, maximizes his utility. Now a shift in finance from taxes to debt alters disposable income from point a to point c, and he consumes the entire reduction in taxes while still leaving no bequest to his children. If some people, therefore, are in a position in which they favour their own consumption so much that they do not leave any bequest, Ricardian equivalence fails.

Ideally, the parent wants to consume at point e, but that would in fact require the children to transfer income to the parents. In our simple model that is not possible, but in Barro's model, since parents' and childrens' lives overlap, it is. If we assume that children care about their parents' utility, so that they make transfers to them (something like pensions or social security), then Ricardian equivalence will still go through. A tax cut that benefits the old will cause the young to reduce their transfers to the old to offset it exactly.

3 Barro supposes that capital markets are perfect in the sense that everyone may borrow or lend as much as he wants at a constant rate of interest, *and* the government and private individuals face the same rate of interest. Ricardian equivalence will not withstand relaxing either assumption. Consider the case shown in figure 7.3. Individuals are assumed to be able to lend at a rate r_L, which, for convenience, is the same as the government's borrowing rate. Individuals borrow, however, at the higher rate r_B. Their budget constraints are thus kinked at the point of disposable income for parents and children, say point a. Some parents will find their equilibria on the flatter upper portion of the budget constraint. For them, Ricardian equivalence would follow. Many would, however, find their equilibria at the kink or on the lower portion. Consider a parent whose equilibrium is at point a; he leaves no bequest. A switch of debt for taxes raises his disposable income. The kink of the budget constraint shifts to b, as he now no longer has to

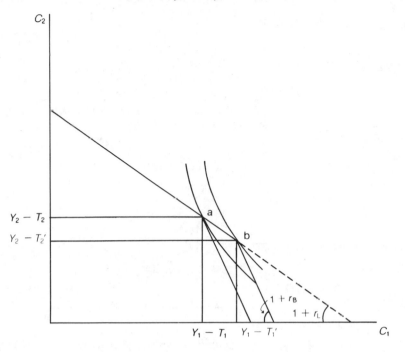

Figure 7.3 Ricardian equivalence fails when capital markets are imperfect: liquidity constraint

borrow to consume more than $Y_1 - T_1$ but less than $Y_1 - T_1'$. If, as is likely, his optimum remains at the kink (now point b), he still leaves no bequest: Ricardian equivalence fails.[9]

Consider another case. Suppose that the government can borrow at a better rate than private individuals ($r_g < r_p$). Figure 7.4 illustrates such a situation. If the government and private individuals had the same rate, a shift from taxes to debt would shift disposable income from point a to point c, as in figure 7.1. Since the government gets a better rate, however, the reduction in the children's income to pay off the debt is $(1 + r_g)D$ which is less than $(1 + r_p)D$, so that the point of disposable income is at b and the new budget constraint is to the right of the original one. Parents can afford to leave a bigger bequest *and* to consume more: Ricardian equivalence again fails. Barro denies that the government actually receives a better rate of interest than any other borrower with the same risk characteristics. The point is moot, however, as no other borrower ever does have the same risk characteristics. Government debt denominated in its own currency is free of default risk because the government can levy taxes and print money. A

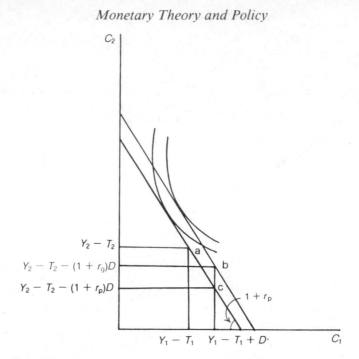

Figure 7.4 Ricardian equivalence fails when capital markets are imperfect: the government borrows at a better rate than the private sector

swap of government debt for private debt must lower the overall risk of the lenders' portfolio to his advantage and so lower the yield he demands. This advantageous yield is then passed on to the beneficiaries of tax cuts.

4   Barro supposes that taxes are lump sum, i.e. they are levied irrespective of income, expenditure or other characteristics of the taxpayer. If taxes are on income, then a debt-financed tax cut raises the marginal cost of leisure and encourages people to work more. Current consumption is then likely to rise. Sales taxes would have the opposite effect – encouraging saving. In either case, Ricardian equivalence fails.

Even if non-lump-sum taxes do not change the incentives to work or to save or otherwise distort economic choices, they may nonetheless have real effects. Suppose that the supply of labour is inelastic, that taxes are levied on income from labour and that income from future labour is uncertain. A tax cut then puts *certain* income into taxpayers' hands. Individual shares of future taxes used to repay the debt are *uncertain*, varying with uncertain future income. The overall riskiness of the taxpayer's lifetime income is thus reduced. Depending on his taste for risk and return he may reduce any savings he had planned as a precaution against a fall in future income. Reduced savings means additional consumption. Ricardian equivalence fails.[10]

5   Barro supposes that there are no distribution effects. Consider, however, a case in which the net transfers resulting from a debt-financed tax cut disproportionately aid the poor, while the taxes to pay off the debt fall mainly on the rich. The poor are, then, genuinely better off, and the rich are genuinely worse off. There will be real aggregate effects on the economy (i.e. Ricardian equivalence again fails) unless the rich and poor have the same tastes and these tastes are independent of their actual wealth. In such a case any distribution of wealth would generate exactly the same choices.

6   Finally, if tax and debt finance are truly equivalent, why do government budget deficits cause so much political heat? Barro cannot argue that it is because people are irrational, because too much of his argument hinges on their rationality. Governments do seem to care about the mode of finance. Barro needs to give some explanation of why.

Most of the objections to Ricardian equivalence (1–5) were mentioned in Barro's original article, only to be dismissed as being of the second order of importance. Whether or not this is so is an empirical question, detailed consideration of which is beyond the scope of this chapter. The evidence, however, is mixed: some studies support Barro's assessment, and others do not.[11]

Even if objections 1–5 could be dismissed as second-order effects, Barro is left to explain objection 6: why do governments seem to care about the mode of finance? Witness current American concerns about the federal deficit or Mrs Thatcher's passionate desire to cut the public sector borrowing requirement (PSBR). Barro tackles this question head on by expounding a positive theory of the determination of public debt.[12] The gist of his theory is that the mode of finance determines second-order costs that have small aggregate effects but still encourage governments to choose cost-minimizing patterns of taxation and deficit spending.

Suppose, for example, that taxes are costly to raise at an increasing rate. The rule is that the government should plan for the marginal cost of raising funds to be equal in every period. A cost-minimizing government would raise large transitory sums needed, say, to fight a war by issuing debt. It is not that it cares about the absolute level of the debt – it does not have any target value; it is rather that it will allow the debt to assume any level which reduces the cost of tax collection over all future time. Again, empirical evidence has run for and against Barro's theory, although Barro has himelf conceded that the theory is unable to explain the recent behaviour of United States debt.[13]

7.2   Open-market Operations

If Ricardian equivalence holds, it is often said that government bonds are not net wealth: the volume of bonds is not relevant to individuals' decisions about consumption or asset demands. Ricardian equivalence would then seem to be a prerequisite for money to be neutral in models of policy ineffectiveness (see chapter 4, section 4.1).[14] For as Metzler (1951) and Patinkin (1956, 1965) have shown, when bonds are net wealth, an increase in the supply of money, holding the stock of bonds constant, decreases the demand for money so that a greater than proportional increase in prices is needed to restore actual real balances to their desired levels. Even though neutrality may fail in this case, policy is unlikely to affect output as long as aggregate supply is described by a Lucas supply function, which insulates output from all anticipated movements in aggregate demand.

Ricardian equivalence seems critical to neutrality and therefore to monetarism in aggregate models, yet it is problematic in new classical microeconomic models since it presupposes the coexistence of non-interest-bearing money with interest-bearing bonds. Let us now consider three microeconomic models that permit money to coexist with bonds in order to consider to what degree Ricardian equivalence and neutrality are compatible with each model.

A Modigliani–Miller Theorem

Wallace (1981) explores a model in which Ricardian equivalence holds in principle and in which a far stronger proposition also holds: the price level is invariant to open-market operations. An open-market operation is an exchange of money for some other asset of equal value. In principle when a central bank conducts an open-market operation, the composition of private portfolios is altered while their value remains unchanged.

In order for open-market operations to be modelled, it must be possible for money and some other asset to coexist. Wallace uses an overlapping-generations model with a real investment good similar to those discussed in chapter 6, sections 6.1 and 6.2. An open-market operation is then a swap of money for the real asset. This is a peculiar characterization, since central banks generally deal only in financial assets. Wallace's result, however, can easily be extended to a financial asset.[15]

In Wallace's model, the young can choose between consumption and saving for their old age in the form either of money or of a real asset. They do not leave bequests. The real asset gives a different return in each possible state of the world (say 10 per cent if there is a fine season, -5 per cent if there is a drought and so forth). The young do not know what the state of the world will be in their old age, but they do know the probability of each state's occurring. A standard result in the theory of choice under uncertainty is that risk-averse agents will hold part of their portfolios in a risk-free asset if it is available. Wallace assumes that the young are risk averse; money is risk free since the price level is perfectly foreseen, and therefore money will be held even though the real asset dominates it in rate of return in *some* states of the world. It is a hedge.

The government (or central bank) also buys some of the risky real asset in each period in order to sell it in the next. Through open-market purchases (exchanging money for more of the real asset), the government can increase its total real capital. It may use the profits from its investments to finance its own real activities, but Wallace assumes that any profits above and beyond this use are distributed in some known way to individual agents. Wallace then demonstrates that if the government creates money in order to buy more of the asset, then utility-maximizing agents will choose to store less of it themselves *and* this open-market purchase will not affect the price level. This is a Modigliani–Miller theorem for open-market operations: the real consumption choices and the price level are independent of the composition of government and central-bank portfolios.

Wallace's main point is very simple and can be made in a model far less complex than his own. Begin with an overlapping-generations model such as that of Barro in section 7.1. Let there be a real asset K with a zero rate of return (i.e. $r - 0$) so that the budget constraint in fig. 7.5 is a 45° line. Assume that the level of prices is the same in each period, so that the rate of return on money is also zero. Money and real assets can now coexist in equilibrium. Let K^p be the amount of the real asset the young choose to hold for their old age, let K^g be the amount the government chooses to hold and let M/P be the amount of real money balances the young choose to hold.

Assume that there is no uncertainty and that there is perfect competition between private investors and the government, so that the government makes no profits from its real investment. There are, therefore, no profits to distribute to individual agents. Total resources available to the young are, then, their initial endowment (Y_1, Y_2) (point a in figure 7.5). The young choose to consume (C_1, C_2) (point b) and to save S. This saving can be held either as real money balances or as holdings of the real asset:

$$S = \frac{M(t)}{P_t} + K^p(t). \tag{7.2}$$

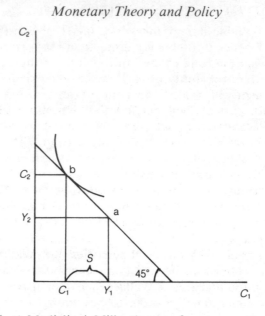

Figure 7.5 A Modigliani–Miller theorem for open-market operations

The important point is that the preferences and endowments of the young determine the total amount of real savings, and, since real money balances and the real asset are perfect substitutes, the division of the portfolio between them does not affect the total.

The total resources of the economy in each period are divided between consumption of the young and the old and savings of the young and the government:

$$Y_1 + Y_2 + K^p(t-1) + K^g(t-1) =$$
$$C_1(t) + C_2(t-1) + K^p(t) + K^g(t). \qquad (7.3)$$

The old consume all their savings and endowments as well as whatever their money will buy $(C_2(t-1) = Y_2 + K^p(t-1) + M(t-1)/P_t)$. By definition $S = Y_1 - C_1$. Equation (7.3) can then be rewritten as

$$S - [K^g(t) - K^g(t-1)] - K^p(t) - \frac{M(t-1)}{P_t} = 0. \qquad (7.3')$$

Substituting equation (7.2) into (7.3') yields

$$\frac{M(t) - M(t-1)}{P_t} = K^g(t) - K^g(t-1). \qquad (7.4)$$

Equation (7.4) says that the government can change its holdings of real assets through an open-market purchase that increases real money balances by the same amount.

Given these identities, the proof of the Modigliani–Miller theorem for open-market operations is simple. Define $\Delta K^g(t) \equiv K^g(t) - K^g(t-1)$. Suppose that government holdings of real assets are constant ($\Delta K^g(t) = 0$). Individual agents then choose their consumption levels and holdings of money and real assets, and the equilibrium condition determines the price level. Now suppose that the government adds $\Delta K^g(t)$ (> 0) to its real capital through an open-market purchase. The Modigliani–Miller theorem for open-market operations holds if it can be shown that there is a countervailing change in private portfolios which leaves both consumption decisions and the price level unchanged.

In order to purchase $\Delta K^g(t)$, the government creates $\Delta M(t) = P_t\Delta K^g$. For a given S, the increase in $M(t)$ would violate equation (7.2) unless $K^P(t)$ were decreased. Noting both the increase in government holdings and the decrease in private holdings of the real asset, the analogue of equation (7.2) is

$$S = \frac{M(t) + \Delta M(t)}{P_t} + K^P(t) + \Delta K^P(t). \tag{7.5}$$

Subtracting equation (7.2) from (7.5) yields

$$\Delta K^P(t) = -\frac{\Delta M(t)}{P_t} \tag{7.6}$$

or

$$\Delta K^P(t) = -\Delta K^g. \tag{7.6'}$$

Thus, in order to fulfil their own budget constraint, the young must reduce their holdings of the real asset by the exact amount that the government increases its holdings.

The composition of their savings portfolio does not affect the consumption patterns of the young. In order to show that the open-market purchase also leaves the consumption of the old and the price level unaffected, consider equation (7.3'). Before the open-market operation, it can be written

$$S - K^P(t) - \frac{M(t-1)}{P_t} = 0.$$

Afterwards and after the countervailing adjustment to private portfolios, it can be written

$$S - \Delta K^g(t) - [K^p(t) + \Delta K^p(t)] - \frac{M(t-1)}{P_t}$$

$$= S - \Delta K^g(t) - [K^p(t) - \Delta K^g(t)] - \frac{M(t-1)}{P_t} \qquad \text{by (7.6')}$$

$$= S - K^p(t) - \frac{M(t-1)}{P_t} = 0.$$

That is, the net effect of the open-market operation and the counter-vailing adjustment to private portfolios is to leave claims on the total resources of the economy unaffected. There is therefore no pressure for the level of prices to change; the real money balances of the old are unaffected and consequently their consumption remains unchanged.[16]

The intuitive explanation of the Modigliani–Miller theorem for open-market operations under perfect certainty when real assets do not dominate money in rate of return is simple. The young do not care whether they hold money or real assets because they are equally good ways of storing value. They therefore reduce their holdings of real assets one-for-one with any increase in the stock of money. The total supply of real goods to the private sector is unaffected because the government must sell any additional holdings of real assets back to the public after one period; otherwise, fiscal policy would not be constant as the real assets would lower the government's deficit. The open-market operation simply switches money and goods between pockets in one period and switches them back in the next. It is really quite trivial.

Wallace attempts to remove this triviality by allowing the real asset to have different rates of return in different states of the world, so that money is held as a hedging device even though it is dominated *ex post* in some states of the world. Unfortunately, the theorem remains essentially trivial and of highly restricted application. In the form stated, it still applies only when money is not dominated *ex ante* in rate of return in the following sense: there cannot exist *any* asset with returns greater than money in every state of the world, otherwise money would not be held as a hedging device. It is hard to believe, especially in times of inflation, that some assets do not dominate money in every state of the world.

Wallace's model is another example of the non-monetarist con-clusions of some new classicals. His model is very much in the spirit of Sargent and Wallace's 'Some Unpleasant Monetarist Arithmetic'. Prices can rise in Wallace's model if, for example, the central bank drops money out of Friedman's famous helicopter onto the populace below or, more to the point, if it monetizes the debt. They cannot rise, however, if money is simply exchanged for another asset. In complete contrast with typical monetarists, new classicals such as Wallace place the emphasis, not on the level of the stock of money, but on its mode of creation, particularly its relation to fiscal policy.

Wallace does not mean his model to be taken as a true description of economic reality, but as an ideal case from which to begin the correct analysis of open-market operations.[17] Unfortunately, since his theorem applies only when money is not dominated in rate of return, it seems unlikely to be a fruitful basis for analysing open-market operations in a world in which this condition never seems to hold.

Despite their anti-monetarist nature, models of Wallace's type have essentially the same structure as Barro's overlapping-generations model without money, so that Ricardian equivalence holds in them as well. The presence of money does present the monetary authority with the option – not available in Barro's model — of monetizing the debt. Since the net effect of such an action is to finance government expenditure with new money, rather than simply to exchange existing assets for money with government expenditure held constant, the price level will rise. But, given perfect foresight of government policy, individuals are able to adjust their savings to offset the 'inflation tax' just as they would any other tax.

Models with Finance Constraints

Another way in which the coexistence of money and other assets can be modelled is through the finance constraint (see chapter 6, section 6.3). In such models, money must be held as a means of exchange. It may happen that every asset has a return lower than money in some states of the world and higher than money in other states, so that some money would be held as a hedge in finance-constrained models as well. In such cases the finance constraint may not bind, i.e. all the money is willingly held as a store of value. At any given price level, however, the demand for money is inversely related to the probability of the occurrence of unfavourable states of the world. Hence, if the probability of the occurrence of an unfavourable state of the world is very low, the supply of money will exceed the demand for it as a store of value and the finance constraint will bind.

As we saw in chapter 4, when finance constraints bind, the price level is typically determined according to a quantity equation. The Modigliani–Miller theorem for open-market operations could not hold in such a model. An open-market purchase, for example, would raise the price level and lower the real balances and therefore the consumption of the old.

In an overlapping-generations model with a binding finance constraint, if taxes are levied in real goods – as they are in Barro's original model – then Ricardian equivalence can be demonstrated subject to the same reservations as Barro's model. The models have essentially the same structure. If, however, taxes are, more realistically, levied in money, then Ricardian equivalence fails. A debt-financed tax cut, for example, releases cash to the young. Since the young are cash constrained this actually changes their opportunity set, so that, in general, their consumption and investment choices will not remain unaltered.[18]

Models with Legal Restrictions

An open-market operation is usually thought of as a direct exchange of money for another asset between the central bank and some member of the private sector. A legal-restrictions model (see chapter 6, section 6.2) will allow open-market operations only in special circumstances: either when money is not dominated in rate of return, so that there is no kink in the budget constraint in figure 6.4 of chapter 6, or when the equilibrium is such that people happen to be indifferent between holding money and bonds (an indifference curve such as u_1 in figure 6.4 of chapter 6). Otherwise, since the rich hold only bonds and the poor hold only money, no exchange of bonds for money would be possible.

Barro, however, defines an open-market operation somewhat differently as a combination of two policies.[19] First, a tax or transfer is levied in money. Second, an offsetting transfer or tax is financed through an increase or decrease in government debt, which in turn is paid off with interest in a later period. All the while, fiscal policy is held constant, i.e. the real government deficit is unchanged. For example, suppose that the government issues £100 (or $100) of new currency and, at the same time, retires £100 of debt through an increase in current taxes of £100; this reduces the need for future taxes to repay this debt and results in a movement of debt and currency in equal but opposite directions. Such a policy could be carried out in a legal-restrictions model, but in general it would not fulfil the conditions either for the Modigliani–Miller theorem for open-market operations or for Ricardian equivalence.

Since the poor alone hold money and since the price level is proportional to their holdings, the increase in money would raise prices, reducing the real balances and consumption of the old poor and perhaps raising the consumption of the young poor, depending upon the distribution of future taxes. Therefore the Modigliani–Miller theorem fails. Since the rich alone hold bonds, the tax–debt exchange raises their current tax bill. If future taxes are reduced for them alone, Ricardian equivalence holds for them and their consumption plans are unaffected. If, however, taxes are reduced for both rich and poor, the rich are net losers and the poor are net gainers.

This is the general result: prices and consumption decisions are not invariant to open-market operations in a legal-restrictions model. Smith and Sargent show that with suitable adjustments to fiscal policy, prices and the real economy may yet be invariant.[20] A typical open-market operation for Smith and Sargent would consist of a transfer of money to the young poor with a tax of an equal amount to be levied in their old age and a tax in real goods on the young rich with a transfer to be made with interest in their old age. The ratio of money to real assets in government portfolios would be altered in the first period, as one expects of an open-market operation, but would not affect the deficit, as it must be reversed in the second period. The poor do not benefit from their transfer nor do the rich suffer from their tax because these two are reversed in the second period. Again, it is simply a case of shuffling assets between pockets and back again, so that invariance is no surprise.

Smith and Sargent take their result to show that the Modigliani–Miller theorem for open-market operations *may* still hold when other assets dominate money in rate of return. In a weak sense this is true: if open-market operations are as they describe them, if fiscal policy is adjusted so that earnings on real assets (or interest on bonds) is distributed to just the right people and if (crucially) the legal-restrictions model makes sense, the Modigliani–Miller theorem holds. But, as we have already argued (chapter 6, section 6.2), the legal-restrictions model is a poor basis for monetary analysis. Furthermore, open-market operations in the real world are never conducted with the distributional precision that Smith and Sargent require. The final conclusion must be that neither the Modigliani–Miller theorem for open-market operations nor Ricardian equivalence holds in legal-restriction models except with an attention to current and future taxes and distribution effects so precise that 'fine tuning' would have to be withdrawn from the Keynesian lexicon and restricted for the sake of accuracy to new classical economics.[21]

7.3 The Real Bills Doctrine

Real Bills and Monetarism

At a casual macroeconomic level monetarist claims for the neutrality of money, and therefore for the essential unimportance of monetary policy for every aspect of the economy except the rate of inflation, seem to require Ricardian equivalence. Examination of a series of overlapping-generations models – for many new classicals the preferred basis for the microeconomic analysis of monetary economies – shows, however, that the circumstances in which Ricardian equivalence generally holds are just the circumstances in which prices are invariant to open-market operations. The monetarist presumption that it is only the total quantity of money, and not its mode of creation, which matters for prices is false in such models. Models that show both Ricardian equivalence and invariance of prices to open-market operations stand at one anti-monetarist extreme. At the other extreme, models in which money is dominated in rate of return (finance-constrained and legal restrictions models) seem to be monetarist at least to the degree that they generate prices according to a quantity equation. One must nonetheless still attend in such models to fiscal policy and its effect on the stock of money and real consumption and investment decisions, as is shown by both the failure of Ricardian equivalence to hold in them generally and the analysis of monetarist arithmetic (chapter 4, section 4.2).

In reality other assets dominate money in rate of return. This fact combined with a disdain for the finance constraint leads a number of new classicals to advocate legal-restrictions models. In the context of legal-restrictions models yet another blow can be struck against monetarist policy prescriptions. Sargent and Wallace (1982) argue that control of the level of prices is not as self-evidently desirable as monetarists generally assume. True to the fundamental new classical tenets, they argue that the desirability of control over the price level can be judged only with respect to the welfare of individuals and hence only in the context of well-specified models of individual choice. Using the legal-restrictions model of money as a framework for their analysis, Sargent and Wallace conclude that it may be desirable to allow the price level to fluctuate as the demand for credit fluctuates and that the 'real bills doctrine' may be sound economic policy.

The real bills doctrine was the belief once common in both the United States and the United Kingdom that central banks should freely discount (i.e. lend) newly created currency against short-term commercial paper backed by firm orders for goods ('real bills'). The doctrine fell into disrepute because the newly ascendant quantity theory suggested that free discounting would be inflationary.[22]

Three Regimes

In order to investigate the real bills doctrine, Sargent and Wallace adopt a version of the overlapping-generations model with legal restrictions (see chapter 6, section 6.2). They assume that there are three classes of individuals with identical tastes and Engel curves that are straight lines through the origin.[23] 'Rich savers' are endowed with a quantity Y_R of a real perishable consumption good in the first period of their lives and nothing in the second. 'Poor savers' are endowed with a smaller amount Y_P of the consumption good only in the first period of their lives. 'Borrowers' are endowed with an amount Y_B of the consumption good only in the second, final, period of their lives. Clearly if savers are to consume at all in their old age, they must trade some of their endowment in their youth either to the old, who are assumed to hold money, or to the borrowers in exchange for repayment in the second period. Equally, if the borrowers are to consume in their youth, they must exchange a promise of repayment (at interest) with savers. Both sides evidently gain from trade. In order to generate a fluctuating demand for credit, Sargent and Wallace assume that the endowment of borrowers itself fluctuates between periods.

Sargent and Wallace investigate three monetary regimes.

Laissez-faire There are no legal restrictions on intermediation. In this regime, prices and consumption patterns are determined in an analogous manner to the simple overlapping-generations models of chapter 6. Since there is perfect competition and money to remove intergenerational inefficiency, everyone is able to set his marginal rate of substitution between consumption in the two periods equal to the marginal rate of transformation. Equilibrium is therefore Pareto-efficient. Since money and private borrowing and lending coexist, money must not be dominated in rate of return and the rate of interest must be zero. The real marginal rate of transformation is then the inverse of the rate of inflation.

Using the apparatus of chapter 6, it is easy to show that the price level is higher when credit demand is higher and lower when it is lower. The assumption that everyone has identical tastes and straight-line Engel curves that pass through the origin justifies treating them as one agent under *laissez-faire*.[24] Figure 7.6, which is closely related to figure 6.1 in chapter 6, shows the combined choice problem and the determination of prices under *laissez-faire*. Total endowments of the young in their youth are $Y_R + Y_P$. Expected endowments are Y_B in periods of low credit demand and Y_B' in times of high credit demand. The slope of the budget constraint is the inverse of the rate of inflation. The budget constraint must pass through the endowment point, so that the budget constraint shifts out as credit demand rises. Since the rate of interest is necessarily zero, savers are indifferent between holding money or IOUs (bonds) from young borrowers. All borrowing among the young nets out when they are treated as a single agent, so that $Y_P + Y_R - C_1$ and $Y_P + Y_R - C_1'$ represent *net* demand for real money balances in the two states of demand for credit.

When the endowment of borrowers in their old age is high, their demand for consumption in their youth and hence for credit is high. In this case, aggregate choice for the young is governed by the higher budget constraint. Given the assumptions about tastes, the young

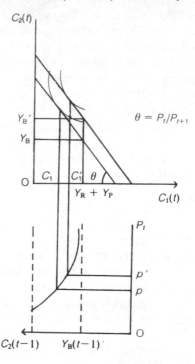

Figure 7.6 A *laissez-faire* regime

consume more in their youth and wish to hold fewer real balances (this is generally true as long as consumption in youth is not an inferior good). For fixed nominal balances this implies a higher price level and lower consumption for the old as shown in the lower panel.

The simple quantity theory does not appear to hold in this case: the price level changes even though the stock of money and total income in the current period are constant. Sargent and Wallace suggest that a monetarist might find this undesirable and might see the source of the problem in unfettered private intermediation.[25] They observe, however, that equilibrium under *laissez-faire* is Pareto-efficient.

Quantity Theory In contrast with *laissez-faire*, the quantity theory does hold under a legal restrictions regime. Suppose that the government sets a minimum size for private loans so that only the rich are able to lend. Even if all agents have identical tastes and straight-line Engel curves, they can no longer be treated as one aggregate individual because they face budget constraints that are very differently shaped.

The budget constraint for the young poor (figure 7.7) starts at their endowment, Y_P and again rises at the inverse of the rate of inflation.

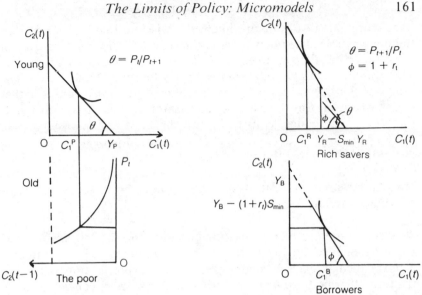

Figure 7.7 A quantity-theory regime

The old poor have no endowment in their old age and therefore consume only the real value of the money carried over from their youth. Together the old and the young poor determine the price level. A simple quantity theory now holds: an increase in the stock of money held by the old increases their real balances above the amount that the young poor wish to save; the price level must therefore rise proportionally to restore equilibrium.

Rich savers and borrowers, however, hold no money at all. The budget constraint is kinked as in figure 6.4 at a point determined by the minimum legal size for private loans. To the left of the kink its slope is given by the rate of interest on private loans. The borrowers budget constraint starts at Y_B on the vertical axis and also has a slope given by the rate of interest. Since borrowers cannot borrow less than the legal minimum, the constraint is inoperative above $Y_B - (1+r_t)S_{min}$. In equilibrium the amount $Y_R - C_1^R$ that rich savers wish to save must equal the amount C_1^B that borrowers wish to borrow. The interest rate and therefore the relevant portions of both budget constraints adjust until this equilibrium condition is fulfilled. The rich and the borrowers, then, determine the rate of interest independently of the poor, just as the poor determine the price level independently of the rich. The interest rate now fluctuates with credit demand, but the price level remains stable.

Equilibrium in the model with legal restrictions is clearly not Pareto-efficient. Pareto-efficiency requires each individual to have the same marginal rate of substitution. Otherwise, mutually advantageous trade is possible. The poor, however, face a different marginal rate of substitution (P_t/P_{t+1}) from the rich savers and the borrowers $(1+r_t)$. This equilibrium is not, however, Pareto-inferior to *laissez-faire*. The utility of the rich savers is lower and that of the borrowers is higher under *laissez-faire* as their budget constraints become flatter as r_t falls to P_t/P_{t+1}. The budget constraint and the utility of the young poor remains the same in both cases; utility of the old poor may rise or fall depending on whether the net savings of the young exceed or fall short of $Y_P - C_1{}^P$. Since there are losers and gainers, a shift to *laissez-faire* is not a Pareto-improvement. Its desirability must be judged on its distributional consequences.

Real Bills   A third regime arises when the central bank lends newly created money to borrowers in any amount at market rates of interest. This is called a 'real bills' regime because the loans are fully backed in the sense that no borrower will borrow more than he can repay given his second-period endowment. Furthermore, since the endowments fluctuate, borrowing from the central bank ('discount window' borrowing) and therefore the supply of money fluctuate just as the original real bills doctrine envisaged. The unlimited availability of discount window credit drives the market rate of interest down to zero, the rate on money. Facing identical rates of interest, borrowers are indifferent between borrowing from rich savers or the central bank. This indifference to the composition of their liabilities is another example of the Modigliani–Miller theorem. This closes the gap between the two portions of the rich savers' budget constraint, and effectively re-establishes the conditions of *laissez-faire*. Now that all agents face a common marginal rate of transformation (parallel budget constraints), it is again legitimate to treat them as an aggregate individual. If we aggregate over the central bank as well, discount window borrowing and lending net out, so that figure 7.6 once again represents the equilibrium. The equilibrium under a real bills regime is thus identical with that under *laissez-faire*.

Sargent and Wallace conclude that if *laissez-faire* is desirable but unobtainable because of legal restrictions on intermediation, then a real bills regime is also desirable – contrary to monetarist prejudices. The fact that a move from their so-called quantity theory regime to *laissez-faire* is not a Pareto-improvement, even though the quantity-theory regime is not Pareto-efficient, casts considerable doubt on the desirability of *laissez-faire*.

Sargent and Wallace's conclusion depends critically once more on the assumption that no real asset dominates money in rate of return under *laissez-faire* or the real bills regime. If it were dominated under *laissez-faire*, either no one would hold it or they would have to invoke some other device to guarantee its coexistence with other assets. Under the real bills regime, there are two possibilities. First, if the assets which dominate money are available to rich and poor, then, just as under *laissez-faire*, money is driven out of use. Second, if the poor face a legal restriction so that they cannot hold the asset, discount window lending cannot force the market rate of interest below the real rate. The rich and the poor therefore face different rates of transformation, and the real bills regime is not even Pareto-efficient, much less identical with *laissez-faire*.

The rehabilitation of the real bills doctrine – like other new classical conclusions about monetary policy reached in overlapping-generations models – rests on special and not very plausible assumptions. The underlying point of Sargent and Wallace's analysis, however, was to question the automatic presumption that inflation or variability of the price level is undesirable. While they have raised a legitimate question, they have given no compelling reason to believe that traditional answers are incorrect.

Part IV   Econometric Issues

8 Econometrics and the Analysis of Policy

In earlier chapters we have examined aspects of the new classical macroeconomics from a theoretical perspective. And there is a strong case for regarding it as largely a theoretical doctrine. It is important, nonetheless, to recall that the new classical economics grew out of empirical problems – the breakdown of the Phillips curve in the early 1970s and the perceived failure of macroeconomic forecasting models to chart the course of the economy accurately. The principal plank of the new classical's positive programme has been to provide a certain class of market-clearing microfoundations for macroeconomics and monetary theory, while one important plank of the critical programme has been to use these microfoundations as a basis for criticizing 'Keynesian' and monetarist econometric practice.[1] The title of Lucas and Sargent's (1981) anthology of important new classical articles, *Rational Expectations and Econometric Practice*, underscores the importance of this critical programme in new classical thinking.

Just as with the analysis of monetary and fiscal policy examined in earlier chapters, new classical economists do not speak with one voice. Disagreement over econometric issues indeed parallels disagreement over the correct analysis of policy. Lucas and Sargent, for example, argue that typical macroeconometric models shed no light on the consequences of alternative policies because they are not constructed in accord with the tenets of the new classical economics. Rational expectations, together with the general principle of Walrasian models that everything depends upon everything else, implies, they believe, that estimated macroeconomic relations are not invariant to alterations in policy rules. The Phillips curve, in an instance already examined, would have a steeper slope under a policy of high variability in money growth than under a policy of low variability (see chapter 2, section 2.2). Lucas concludes from his analysis that empirical evidence is obtainable and relevant only for steady states – not for periods of transition between policy regimes. Sargent, however, tries to estimate macroeconomic relations, using economic theory to identify the precise manner in which they are connected to the choice of policy regime.

In contrast, Sims and some of his students and colleagues argue in a manner remarkably similar to that of Barro and Gordon (see chapter 4, section 4.3) that new classical principles consistently applied to the authorities as well as the public imply that the choice of alternative policy regimes is not usually open. Unlike Barro and Gordon, Sims does not conclude that this leaves no role for the policy adviser – merely that his role is to help implement the best rule, rather than to discover what the rule is.

The purpose of this chapter is to examine and assess these contrasting attempts to apply new classical principles to the econometric analysis of policy. The emphasis is not on the application of econometrics to the evaluation of particular new classical propositions. Systematic consideration is given neither to the many empirical studies of new classical propositions nor to detailed econometric techniques. The emphasis is rather on the more conceptual question: do new classical principles correctly limit the scope and method of econometrics applied to the evaluation of macroeconomic policy? Empirical studies and particular techniques are cited only when they shed light on this issue.

New classical econometricians frequently advocate the use of tests of 'Granger-causality' in order to assess whether or not a variable is statistically exogenous. The notion of Granger-causality is not unique to new classical econometrics. Nevertheless, because it is important to the new classical approach, and because there has been a great deal of confusion about its relation to other senses of causality and to various notions of exogeneity, we must consider it before moving on to peculiarly new classical approaches.

8.1   Granger-causality

A Definition

In his seminal paper of 1969, C.W.J. Granger suggests that an operational definition should treat causality as a matter of the ordering of events in natural time: the future cannot cause the past. Granger traces his definition of causality back to Norbert Wiener: A causes B if A precedes B, and knowledge of A helps to predict B, while knowledge of B does not help to predict A (i.e. there is no feedback).

Granger reformulates Wiener's notion into a general definition of cause in dynamic stochastic systems: Y in one period causes X in the next period if the probability distribution of the one-period-ahead prediction of X conditional on all past and present information is different from the probability distribution when information on past Y is omitted from the information set.[2]

Granger seeks an operational definition of causation. It is therefore necessary to restrict his general definition in various ways. The information set must be restricted to some practically manageable subset of data: only a limited number of variables and only a limited number of their past values can be considered. The complete population probability must be replaced by estimated sample distributions, characterized by only a few moments, e.g. the mean and standard deviation. Granger's original statistical criterion is the error variance of the optimal linear predictor of a variable.[3] A variable Y *causes* a variable X by Granger's criterion, if the error variance of X conditional on all past values of all variables is less than the error variance of X conditional on all past variables except Y. If X causes Y and Y causes X, then there is *feedback* between X and Y. If the present current value of Y reduces the error variance, then Y *instantaneously* causes X. Granger argues that instantaneous causation is simply an artefact of data which is not collected frequently enough to reveal the true temporal ordering.

Granger's definition immediately suggests a simple test of causality. An investigator would run a regression of X on a number of lags of itself and on a number of lags of Y.[4] If a standard test showed that the lagged values of Y were not statistically significant in explaining X, then the null hypothesis that Y does not cause X could not be rejected.

The upshot of these definitions is that Granger-causality is a purely stochastic notion. The residual variance of any deterministic relationship is definitionally zero; nothing can reduce it and so no causal links exist. Similarly, since non-stationary time series do not have well-defined variances, Granger's definition applies to stationary time series only.[5] Thus there are no causal links between the trend (non-stationary) components of different time series. Granger concedes that these limitations are contrary to commonsense notions of causality, but he argues that testable definitions are difficult to obtain without them.

A problem arises with the definition of Granger-causality from the practical necessity of restricting the information set to a manageable number of lags of a manageable number of variables. Ideally, only irrelevant variables would be excluded. Unfortunately, there is no way of knowing in advance which variables are relevant. Thus causality is defined relative to a particular data set. A relation judged not to be causal on Granger's original definitions might be accepted as causal if the data set includes A and B only, and they are not related except that C, not included in the data set, Granger-causes them both.

An Example

Exactly what Granger-causality amounts to can be made clear in a simple example.[6] Let the following model be the actual structural relationship between Y and X:

$$Y_t = \theta X_t + \beta_{11} Y_{t-1} + \beta_{12} X_{t-1} + e_{1t} \tag{8.1}$$

$$X_t = \gamma Y_t + \beta_{21} Y_{t-1} + \beta_{22} X_{t-1} + e_{2t} \tag{8.2}$$

where e_{1t} and e_{2t} are random errors with means of zero and variances of σ_1^2 and σ_2^2. Both errors are serially uncorrelated and uncorrelated with each other.

The simultaneous system (8.1) and (8.2) can be rewritten as a reduced form in which each variable depends only on past values of itself and other variables. Equation (8.2) is substituted for X_t in (8.1) and equation (8.1) is substituted for Y_t in (8.2); both are then rearranged to yield

$$Y_t = \Pi_{11} Y_{t-1} + \Pi_{12} X_{t-1} + u_{1t} \tag{8.3}$$

$$X_t = \Pi_{21} Y_{t-1} + \Pi_{22} X_{t-1} + u_{2t} \tag{8.4}$$

where

$$\Pi_{11} = \frac{\beta_{11} + \theta\beta_{21}}{1 - \theta\gamma}$$

$$\Pi_{12} = \frac{\beta_{12} + \theta\beta_{22}}{1 - \theta\gamma}$$

$$\Pi_{21} = \frac{\gamma\beta_{11} + \beta_{21}}{1 - \theta\gamma}$$

$$\Pi_{22} = \frac{\gamma\beta_{12} + \beta_{22}}{1 - \theta\gamma}$$

$$u_{1t} = \frac{e_{1t} + \theta e_{2t}}{1 - \theta\gamma}$$

$$u_{2t} = \frac{\gamma e_{1t} + e_{2t}}{1 - \theta\gamma}.$$

Equations (8.3) and (8.4) are the best linear predictors of Y and X, given the past values of each variable. To say that X Granger-causes Y is to say that $\Pi_{12} \neq 0$, while to say that Y Granger-causes X is to say that $\Pi_{21} \neq 0$. As long as X Granger-causes Y, a regression of Y on several lags of itself and on several lags of X would turn up statistically significant coefficients on Y_{t-1} and on X_{t-1}, although, in this particular example, not on any longer lags. Of course, if the true structural model, (8.1) and (8.2), had involved longer lags, so would the reduced forms, (8.3) and (8.4).

Exogeneity

Granger's 1969 paper is the foundation of a large literature.[7] But if Granger's work is the essential chemical ingredient of the recent applied literature on causality, Christopher A. Sims's paper 'Money, income and causality' (1972) is the equally essential catalyst. Sims developed a statistical test for Granger-causality and demonstrated that a variable X is *strictly exogenous* with respect to a variable Y if and only if Y does not Granger-cause X. Sims further claimed that, in order for a distributed lag regression to be valid, the independent (right-hand-side) variables must be strictly exogenous from the dependent (left-hand-side) variables, i.e. Granger-causality must run one way from the independent to the dependent variables.[8] He also claims that for a regression of Y on lagged X to be reasonably interpreted as a causal relation Y must not Granger-cause X.[9]

Discussions of exogeneity and causality must proceed gingerly through a terminological minefield: there are no standard and universally accepted definitions of these terms, and there are many variants.[10] In order to remain consistent, we shall follow the usage of Engle et al. (1983). In order to see exactly what the concept of Granger-causality can and cannot be used for, we shall refer to the example of equations (8.1)–(8.4).

Sims claims that an estimate of the single equation (8.1) will yield a consistent estimate of θ if and only if Y does not Granger-cause X, i.e. if and only if $\Pi_{21} = 0$. The problem of consistent estimation, which is explained in any elementary econometrics text, can easily be understood through a simple example. Suppose that one wants to estimate the parameter a in the relation

$$q_t = ap_t + v_t \tag{8.5}$$

from N observations of each variable q and p, where v_t is a random error. The ordinary least squares estimator of a is

$$\hat{a} = \sum_{t=0}^{N} q_t p_t \bigg/ \sum_{t=0}^{N} p_t^2.$$

The question of whether or not this is a consistent estimate is a question of whether it approaches the true value of a as the number of observations becomes larger. To check this, multiply both sides of equation (8.5) by p_t and sum over the N observations to yield

$$\sum_{t=0}^{N} q_t p_t = a \sum_{t=0}^{N} p_t^2 + \sum_{t=0}^{N} p_t v_t.$$

Now divide both sides by $\sum_{t=0}^{N} p_t^2$ to yield

$$\sum_{t=0}^{N} q_t p_t \bigg/ \sum_{t=0}^{N} p_t^2 = a + \sum_{t=0}^{N} p_t v_t \bigg/ \sum_{t=0}^{N} p_t^2 \tag{8.6}$$

The left-hand side of (8.6) is simply $\hat{a}$. If the second term on the right-hand side of (8.6) were equal to zero, then $\hat{a}$ would equal a and the ordinary least squares estimator would be consistent. Therefore consider this term. Divide the numerator and the denominator by N:

$$\frac{\sum_{t=0}^{N} p_t v_t}{N} \bigg/ \frac{\sum_{t=0}^{N} p_t^2}{N}.$$

The denominator of this new expression is the sample variance of p, and the numerator is the sample covariance of p_t and v_t. Therefore what consistency seems to require is that, as N becomes large, the sample covariance of p_t and v_t approaches zero. If p_t and v_t are not correlated, this is bound to be true.

This lesson from a simple two-variable model can be generalized to models with more variables, such as equations (8.1) and (8.2). In order to obtain consistent estimates of θ, β_{11} and β_{12} the independent variables X_t, Y_{t-1} and X_{t-1} in equation (8.1) must not be correlated with the error e_{1t}. Since e_{1t} is a serially uncorrelated random variable that is not realized until time t, it is clear that neither of the earlier-dated variables Y_{t-1} or X_{t-1} could possibly be correlated with it. Therefore the question is only: is it correlated with X_t? Equation (8.2) determines the value of X_t. Since e_{1t} helps to determine the value of Y_t, and Y_t appears in equation (8.2), e_{1t} indirectly helps to determine the value of X_t. X_t and e_{1t} must therefore be correlated unless $\gamma = 0$, which would remove Y_t from (8.2) and eliminate the indirect link with e_{1t}.

Consistent estimation of θ requires that $\gamma = 0$. Is this related to the absence of Granger-causality from Y to X, i.e. is this related to the condition that

$$\Pi_{21} = \frac{\gamma \beta_{11} + \beta_{21}}{1 - \theta \gamma} = 0$$

in the reduced form (equation (8.3))? The answer is: no. The absence of Granger-causality from Y to X is neither necessary nor sufficient for the consistent estimation of θ. It is not necessary because, even if $\gamma = 0$, Π_{21} will not equal zero unless $\beta_{21} = 0$. It is not sufficient because if $\beta_{11} = -\beta_{21}/\gamma$, Π_{21} will equal zero even when $\gamma \neq 0$.

In general, the true necessary and sufficient condition for consistently estimating θ in equation (8.1) is that X_t be *weakly exogenous* for the parameters one wishes to estimate.[11] Roughly speaking, X is weakly exogenous for a parameter such as θ in (8.1) if the simultaneous system that determines X and Y can be partitioned in such a way that an efficient estimate of the parameter can be obtained from the part of the partition in which X is an independent variable without regard to the part in which X is a dependent variable. This definition is not circular because, in particular contexts, it makes substantive claims about the relationships between the variables. For example, in the linear model (8.1) and (8.2) X_t is weakly exogenous for θ if and only if X_t is *predetermined* in (8.1), i.e. if it is not correlated with the current or future error terms or, equivalently, if $\gamma = 0$.[12]

Cause and Control

If tests of Granger-causality do not help us know when it is possible to estimate a parameter of interest to us consistently, what do they help us do? There has been much equivocation about the answer to this question.

Sims (1972) clearly implies that if X Granger-causes Y, we are entitled to believe that X causes Y in the ordinary sense of the word. He even goes as far as to say that tests for Granger-causality ' . . . rest on a sophisticated version of the post hoc ergo propter hoc principle', seemingly unaware that sophistication does not transform a notorious fallacy into a valid principle of inference.[13] In particular, Sims (1972) shows that money Granger-causes income in United States data. Sims takes this finding to support monetarist claims that money causes income.

In later work, Sims clarifies his views somewhat. He endorses the view that correlation does not prove causation and observes that *post hoc ergo propter hoc* is indeed a fallacy.[14] He also finds that money does not Granger-cause income when additional variables, such as interest rates, are included.[15] He maintains, nonetheless, that the concept of Granger-causality captures what economists normally mean by 'cause'.[16] Short of a comprehensive poll of economists, such a claim is not easily adjudicated. Sims is not unaware, however, that an alternative definition of 'cause' is widely acknowledged: A causes B if control of A renders B controllable. A causal relation, then, is one that is invariant to interventions in A in the sense that if someone or something can alter the value of A the change in B follows in a predictable fashion.[17] If, for example, the relation between A and B could be stated as an equation, the relation would be causal if, when A changed value, the coefficients of the equation remained constant so that it determined the value of B.

On this definition, equation (8.2) is a causal relation if its structure (i.e. its parameters) remain unaltered as Y takes different values. It can therefore be used to predict the value of X conditional on knowing the value of Y.

A test of Granger-causality cannot tell us whether or not a relation is causal in this sense. For example, suppose that equation (8.1) is a policy rule.[18] Let Y_t be, say, the level of the money stock and let X_t be the level of GNP. Equation (8.1) would then say that the authorities set money according to a feedback rule from its own past and the current and past values of GNP. Equation (8.2) would then say that GNP is determined from its own past and from the current and past levels of the money stock set by the authorities. Now suppose that the authorities wish to minimize the variability of GNP. They do not control it directly; the best they can do is to influence it through their choice of the money stock, Y_t. The error term e_{2t} is random and beyond the control of the authorities; they cannot eliminate its contribution to the variability of GNP. If, however, they are able to reduce the non-random elements of (8.2) to zero, they will eliminate all the variability from that source: i.e.

$$0 = \gamma Y_t + \beta_{21} Y_{t-1} + \beta_{22} X_{t-1} \tag{8.7}$$

or

$$Y_t = -\frac{\beta_{21}}{\gamma} Y_{t-1} - \frac{\beta_{22}}{\gamma} X_{t-1}. \tag{8.7'}$$

Recall equation (8.1):

$$Y_t = \theta X_t + \beta_{11} Y_{t-1} + \beta_{12} X_{t-1} + e_{1t}.$$

Compare (8.7') with (8.1) term by term. Clearly, the authorities should choose the parameters of their policy rule as $\theta = 0$, $\beta_{11} = -\beta_{21}/\gamma$ and $\beta_{12} = \beta_{22}/\gamma$. This choice reduces the variability of X_t as much as possible. Since

$$\Pi_{21} = \frac{\gamma\beta_{11} + \beta_{21}}{1 - \theta\gamma}$$

if $\beta_{11} = -\beta_{21}/\gamma$, as the second of the three conditions suggests, $\Pi_{21} = 0$, i.e. Y does not Granger-cause X. Thus, just when the causal relation between money (Y) and GNP (X) is being used to control GNP most effectively, a test of Granger-causality would indicate that money does not Granger-cause GNP. Clearly, Granger-causality and causality as it is normally analysed are not closely related concepts.

Prediction

Do tests of Granger-causality tell us anything at all? The answer is: yes, they tell us whether or not the current value of a variable carries any information about future values of another variable once the second variable's past is taken into account. As such, they are tests of incremental predictability, and a great deal of confusion could be spared if the word 'causality' were omitted from their name.[19]

To illustrate how knowledge of Granger-causality can sometimes be useful, consider using equation (8.1) to predict the value of Y one period in the future. Suppose that it is now time $t-1$. The value of the random error in the next period (i.e. e_{1t}) is not predictable this period, and so the prediction equation can be written as (8.1) without the error term. However, the value of X_t is also not known at time $t-1$ and therefore must itself be predicted. Prediction of Y_t is then generally simultaneous with prediction of X_t. The reduced-form equations (8.3) and (8.4) are in fact expressions of this complex interrelationship.

In general, equation (8.1) cannot be used to make a valid prediction of X because of the problem of simultaneously predicting Y. But if X is strongly exogenous with respect to Y, equation (8.1) can be used for valid predictions. A variable X is *strongly exogenous* in an equation with Y as the dependent variable if and only if it is weakly exogenous for its parameter *and* Y does not Granger-cause X.[20] In the system (equations (8.1) and (8.2)) X is strongly exogenous if it is weakly exogenous with respect to θ (i.e. $\gamma = 0$) and if Y does not Granger-cause X (i.e. $\Pi_{21} = 0$). Together these imply that $\beta_{21} = 0$ and that $\theta\gamma = 0$. Substituting these facts into the Π_{ij}s in equations (8.3) and (8.4) and omitting the unpredictable error terms yields

$$Y_t = \beta_{11}Y_{t-1} + \beta_{12}X_{t-1} + \theta\beta_{22}X_{t-1} \tag{8.3'}$$

and

$$X_t = \beta_{22}X_{t-1} \tag{8.4'}$$

or

$$X_{t-1} = \frac{X_t}{\beta_{22}}. \tag{8.4''}$$

Substituting (8.4'') into the final term of (8.3') yields

$$Y_t = \theta X_t + \beta_{11}Y_{t-1} + \beta_{12}X_{t-1}, \tag{8.3''}$$

which is simply equation (8.1) without the error term.

Equations (8.3) and (8.4) together are the optimal linear predictors of X and Y. The assumption of the strong exogeneity of X implies that they collapse back into the form of equation (8.1). The example shows, therefore, that, when the independent variables are strongly exogenous, not only can the parameters be estimated efficiently but the equation can also be used for prediction without attention to the process that determines the values of the independent variables.

This result sheds light on a controversy over the interpretation of Sims's theorems in his 1972 paper. Some commentators interpret Sims as showing that if Y does not Granger-cause X, then there is *some* regression model in which Y is a function of lagged Xs only *and* for which the Xs are not correlated with the error terms so that estimates are consistent.[21] To rephrase this, if Y does not Granger-cause X, it is possible to formulate a valid *predictive* equation in which the Xs are the dependent variables. In such an equation X is strongly exogenous with respect to Y and its parameters. This is true, although it is an extremely uninteresting claim; for the parameters of such an equation do not generally correspond to the parameters that happen to interest us such as θ or β_{12} in equation (8.1).[22]

8.2 Early New Classical Econometrics and the Natural Rate Hypothesis

Sims's early application of tests of Granger-causality to macroeconometric problems appeared at about the same time as Lucas's important theoretical work in which the hypothesis of rational expectations was applied to the analysis of the natural rate of unemployment and the neutrality of money (see chapter 2). In this section we examine some of the early work on econometric testing of the natural rate hypothesis. The point is not to provide a definitive empirical analysis or even to give a detailed history. Rather, it is to expose the roots of some of the econometric issues that converge in new classical reactions to Lucas's famous criticisms of econometric policy evaluation. It is a sort of prehistory or stage-setting to the discussion of the central issue in new classical econometrics.

Lucas

Let us first step back from the analysis of Granger-causality. Eventually, Sims's techniques for assessing Granger-causality would become widely used tools of new classical econometricians, but in the meantime Lucas's theoretical work suggested two separate lines of empirical enquiry.

Lucas's theoretical work explained a paradox: rational expectations and the natural rate hypothesis imply that there is no exploitable trade-off between unemployment (or output) and inflation as long as markets clear, yet empirical evidence consistently finds a negatively sloped Phillips curve. Lucas's resolution of this paradox (as described in chapter 2, section 2.2) is that the Phillips curve is not a structural relationship, but merely an artefact: a random fluctuation of the price level above its expected value is correlated with a rise in output and a fall in unemployment, while a random fluctuation below is correlated with a fall in output and a rise in unemployment. This explanation relies on people temporarily mistaking absolute and relative changes in prices. It is not, however, the only explanation for the shape of the Phillips curve, and so needs to be tested empirically.

Lucas's first test is very simple. In chapter 2, section 2.2, we showed that in a simple natural rate model with rational expectations the slope of the estimated aggregate supply function is

$$\hat{\alpha} = \frac{\gamma \tau^2}{\sigma^2 + \tau^2},$$

where σ^2 is the variance of the price level and τ^2 is the variance of relative prices. The expression indicates that the more variable is the general price level, the steeper is the Phillips curve. The more likely that a change in the prices observed by individuals is general inflation and not a change in relative prices, the less likely people are to adjust output and employment in response to it. In order to test this relationship, Lucas (1973) estimated aggregate supply functions for 18 countries and correlated the estimated slopes with collected data on the variability of inflation in each country. The countries divided into two groups – those with moderate rates and variability of inflation and just two countries (Argentina and Paraguay) with very high rates and variability. As predicted the high variability countries had very steep Phillips curves in comparison with the low variability countries. The strong correlation reported by Lucas depends greatly on the inclusion of Argentina and Paraguay. If these countries are omitted, the results are not clear cut. Although there is some evidence of the same general pattern even when these countries are omitted from the data, this dependence on just two observations for most of the statistical strength of the test must somewhat diminish its persuasive power.[23]

Lucas's (1972b) second test is somewhat more complex. Consider the aggregate supply and demand model of chapter 4, section 4.1 (equations (4.1)–(4.4)), which is reproduced here:

$$\tilde{y}_t = y_t - \bar{y} + \alpha(p_t - {}_{t-1}p_t^e) + \varepsilon_t \qquad \text{aggregate supply} \qquad (8.8)$$
$$p_t = m_t - y_t + u_t \qquad \text{aggregate demand} \qquad (8.9)$$
$$m_t = \lambda + m_{t-1} + e_t \qquad \text{money supply rule} \qquad (8.10)$$
$${}_{t-1}p_t^e = E(p_t | I_{t-1}) \qquad \text{rational expectations} \qquad (8.11)$$

Equations (8.8)–(8.11) can be solved to yield

$$_{t-1}p_t^e = \lambda + m_{t-1} - \bar{y}. \tag{8.12}$$

Equations (8.9) and (8.12) can be substituted into equation (8.8) and the results rearranged to yield

$$\tilde{y}_t = -\frac{\lambda\alpha}{1+\alpha} + \frac{\alpha}{1+\alpha}(m_t - m_{t-1}) + \varepsilon_t + \frac{u_t}{1+\alpha}. \tag{8.13}$$

In the context of this model, Lucas's second test is to estimate two regressions:

$$m_t = a_0 + a_1 m_{t-1} \tag{8.14}$$

and

$$\tilde{y}_t = b_0 + b_1 m_t + b_2 m_{t-1}. \tag{8.15}$$

Compare (8.14) with (8.10) and (8.15) with (8.13). If the model is correct,

$$a_0 = \lambda$$
$$a_1 = 1$$
$$b_0 = -\frac{\lambda\alpha}{1+\alpha}$$
$$b_1 = \frac{\alpha}{1+\alpha}$$
$$b_2 = -\frac{\alpha}{1+\alpha}.$$

Together these imply that the following restrictions should hold:

$$b_0/a_0 = -b_1$$

and

$$b_1 = -b_2.$$

A standard statistical test of the validity of these restrictions then constitutes a joint test of (8.8)–(8.11), i.e. of the specification of aggregate supply and demand and of rational expectations.

Although Lucas (1973) does analyse a formal model, his first test relies principally on readily computable descriptive statistics and does not impose much structure on the data. Lucas's second test is, however, model specific. Failure of this test could result from any one of a failure of rational expectations, a failure of the natural rate hypothesis or a failure to specify aggregate demand properly. Unlike the first test, Lucas does not actually carry out the second test. The reason no doubt is that he does not take the detailed specification of the underlying model as correct in any but its broadest outlines. Nevertheless, Lucas's point is clear: the proper structural test of a new classical model with rational expectations is not a test simply of the significance of various parameters; rather it is a test of the relationship between parameters – of the model's implication that certain restrictions hold on the parameters within and across equations. Tests of cross-equation restrictions in particular have become the hallmark of one brand of new classical econometrics.[24]

Sargent and Wallace

An early example of the use of tests of Granger-causality in new classical econometrics is Sargent and Wallace's (1973) reconsideration of Cagan's (1956) famous study of the monetary dynamics of hyperinflation. The heart of Cagan's analysis is a function in which the demand for real money balances depends, among other things, inversely on the expected rate of inflation. Thus, if an expanding supply of money generates inflation, that inflation lowers the demand for real balances. In the face of given nominal balances, the price level must rise in order to reduce the supply of real balances to its demand. Consequently, in hyperinflation, prices rise faster than the nominal supply of money.

Cagan assumed that the supply of money in a hyperinflating economy was expanded exogenously in the sense that the monetary authority did not consider the price level or the state of the economy in deciding how much money to supply. Cagan also assumed that expectations of the rate of inflation were formed autoregressively as a function of past actual inflation rates.

Autoregressive expectations have been frequently seen as incompatible with rational expectations.[25] Sargent and Wallace confirm that, as long as the supply of money is exogenous as Cagan assumes, autoregressive expectations are not rational. Nevertheless, they show that, if the money supply is not exogenous, Cagan's autoregressive scheme may coincide with rational expectations.

If the supply of money is exogenous in Cagan's sense, it is hard to see why the monetary authority would continue pumping it up, generating more inflation. Sargent and Wallace suggest that it is more plausible to believe that the government has some target level of revenues that cannot be met through taxation, so that money creation is a substitute for explicit taxation. As a result, when the price level rises, the real value of government revenues falls, and the monetary authority must supply more money in order to make up the shortfall. There is, then, a feedback from the price level and the economy to the supply of money.[26]

The two hypotheses, Sargent and Wallace believe, can be stated in terms of Granger-causality: first, if the supply of money is exogenous, money Granger-causes inflation; second, if the supply of money is not exogenous, inflation Granger-causes money and money does not Granger-cause inflation. Sargent and Wallace perform tests of Granger-causality and are able to reject the first but not the second hypothesis. Cagan's scheme for forming expectations is, they believe, therefore vindicated at the expense of his exogeneity assumption.[27]

Sargent and Wallace (1973) use tests of Granger-causality in an attempt to decide how best to apply rational expectations in a particular econometric model. Sargent (1976a) uses these tests more directly to address Lucas's main concern, the hypothesis of the natural rate of unemployment. Sargent sets up a simple IS–LM model with a Lucas aggregate supply function (similar to equation (8.8)). He then proposes that a 'strong' form of the natural rate hypothesis is that macroeconomic policy variables cannot be used to manipulate the rate of unemployment.

In order to check both direct and indirect channels of influence, Sargent runs tests of Granger-causality between the unemployment rate and the interest rate on the one hand, and between measures of policy (the money supply, the govenment budget surplus and government expenditures) and price variables (the GNP deflator and the wage rate) on the other. With three exceptions the policy and price variables do not Granger-cause unemployment or interest rates, which Sargent takes as support for the natural rate hypothesis. The exceptions are that wages Granger-cause unemployment and interest rates, and, in one of two versions of the test, that money Granger-causes unemployment. Sargent concludes, nonetheless: 'All in all, the empirical results provide some evidence that the causal structure imposed on the data by [his] classical model . . . is not obscenely at variance with the data.'[28]

Barro

Applying Granger-causality tests to new classical models is an indirect method. In contrast, Barro (1977) takes a more direct approach related to Lucas's test of the cross-equation restrictions in a natural rate model. To understand his method, consider a model similar to equations (8.8)–(8.11). Substitute (8.9) into (8.8) to eliminate p_t, apply (8.11) to (8.9) and then substitute the result into (8.8) to eliminate $_{t-1}p_t^e$, leaving

$$\tilde{y} = \frac{\alpha}{1+\alpha} (m_t - {}_{t-1}m_t^e) + \varepsilon_t + \frac{u_t}{1+\alpha}, \qquad (8.16)$$

where $_{t-1}m_t^e$ is the expectation at time $t-1$ of the level of the money stock at time t. Equation (8.16) says that only unexpected changes in the stock of money affect output. Since output and employment are related, a similar equation would obviously link unemployment and money.

Barro actually estimates an equation of the form

$$U_t = a_0 + a_1\Delta MS_t + a_2\Delta MS_{t-1} + a_3\Delta MS_{t-2} + \text{other variables,}$$
$$(8.17)$$

where U is the rate of unemployment, ΔMS (money surprise) is the difference between the actual and the expected rate of growth of the money stock and the other variables are factors which affect aggregate supply (in particular, for the United States, Barro singles out the legal minimum wage rate and the proportion of the population in military service).[29]

In order to generate ΔMS, it is necessary to know how expectations of the rate of growth of the money stock are formed. Barro considers it more likely that the United States monetary authorities followed a feedback rule rather than a simple fixed rule such as equation (8.10). He actually estimates a rule of the form

$$\Delta M_t = b_0 + b_1\Delta M_{t-1} + b_2\Delta M_{t-2} + b_3\text{GOV} + b_4U_{t-1}, \qquad (8.18)$$

where ΔM is the rate of growth of the money stock and GOV is the level of difference between the level of government expenditure and its trend. If ΔM_t is the actual value of the rate of growth of the money stock and $\Delta \hat{M}_t$ is the value calculated from equation (8.18) once its parameters have been estimated, then $\Delta MS_t \equiv \Delta M_t - \Delta \hat{M}_t$, i.e. ΔMS_t is the residual from the regression equation (8.18). The identification of the residual from equation (8.18) with the surprise in the rate of growth of the money stock amounts to the bold untested assertion that the equation actually captures the way that agents form their rational expectations.

Having made this assumption, Barro estimates equation (8.18) and uses its residuals as variables in order to estimate equation (8.17). Not only does he find that these variables are statistically significant, but also that, if added to the regression, the actual values of the rate of growth ΔM_t of the money stock are not significant. This he sees as confirming the hypothesis that only unexpected changes in the stock of money affect employment and output.

In a later paper, Barro (1978) used the same approach to money surprises to investigate the influence of money on the price level. The quantity theory embedded in equation (8.9) implies that perfectly anticipated increases in the stock of money are matched one-for-one with increases in the level of prices. In contrast, equation (8.16) implies that unexpected increases in the stock of money raise aggregate supply above trend. A higher value of y_t in (8.9) implies a lower price level. Barro estimated an equation in order to test whether the level of prices was positively related (with an elasticity of unity) to the level of the money stock and negatively related to surprises in the stock of money. On the basis of the predicted signs and values of the coefficients, he was not able to reject the hypothesis that prices are related to money as the quantity theory in conjunction with a Lucas aggregate supply function suggests.

He also estimated an output equation similar to equation (8.16) (or, more nearly, to (8.17) with y_t in place of U_t). The underlying theoretical analysis implied that the pattern of coefficient values on the money surprise terms in the price equation should be related to those in the output equation. Barro's statistical test rejects the implied cross-equation restrictions, casting doubt on the validity of the model as a whole.[30]

Observational Equivalence

Sargent wrote that his tests of Granger-causality between policy and price variables and the unemployment and interest rate constitute ' . . . tests of a naive but powerful formulation of the hypothesis that there is a natural rate of unemployment'.[31] He soon discovered, however, that these tests were in fact more naive than powerful. Sargent (1976b) shows that models compatible with the natural rate hypothesis and models that are incompatible with it can both generate the very same Granger-causal relations.

In order to understand how this is possible, consider an example:

$$y_t = \alpha m_t + \beta m_{t-1} + \gamma y_{t-1} + \eta_t \tag{8.19}$$

and

$$m_t = \delta m_{t-1} + e_t, \tag{8.20}$$

where y is output and m is the stock of money. This model is similar in structure to equations (8.1) and (8.2) with $\Pi_{21} = 0$. In any case, it is obvious that money Granger-causes income in it, but that income does not Granger-cause money.

Having estimated such a model, one might well believe that the money stock could be used to control income or, equivalently, that the natural rate hypothesis did not hold. But this would be jumping to an unwarranted conclusion. Observe first that equation (8.20) implies that the expectation at time $t-1$ of the value of the money stock at time t is $_{t-1}m_t^e = \delta m_{t-1}$. Next move all the subscripts in equation

(8.19) back one period to obtain an expression for y_{t-1} and substitute this expression back into equation (8.19) to yield

$$y_t = \alpha m_t + (\beta + \alpha\gamma)m_{t-1} + \beta\gamma m_{t-2} + \gamma^2 y_{t-2} + \eta_t + \gamma\eta_{t-1}. \quad (8.21)$$

Repeated substitutions to eliminate lagged y terms yields

$$y_t = \alpha m_t + \sum_{j=0}^{\infty}[(\alpha\gamma^{j+1} + \beta\gamma^j)m_{t-j-1} + \gamma^j\eta_{t-j}]$$

$$= \alpha m_t + A_1 m_{t-1} + A_2 m_{t-2} + \ldots + \sum_{j=0}^{\infty}\gamma^j\eta_{t-j}. \quad (8.22)$$

y_t is now a function of the infinite past history of the money stock and of an infinite number of error terms. Now add and subtract $\alpha\delta m_{t-1}$ on the right-hand side of equation (8.22):

$$y_t = \alpha m_t - \alpha\delta m_{t-1} + (A_1 + \alpha\delta)m_{t-1} + A_2 m_{t-2} + \ldots + \sum_{j=0}^{\infty}\gamma^j\eta_{t-j}$$

$$= \alpha(m_t - {}_{t-1}m_t^e) + (A_1 + \alpha\delta)m_{t-1} + A_2 m_{t-2} + \ldots + \sum_{j=0}^{\infty}\gamma^j\eta_{t-j} \quad (8.23)$$

If this process of adding and subtracting the appropriate term and replacing δm_{t-j} by ${}_{t-j}m^e_{t-j+1}$ is continued, equation (8.23) can eventually be written as

$$y_t = B_0(m_t - {}_{t-1}m_t^e) + B_1(m_{t-1} - {}_{t-2}m^e_{t-1}) + \ldots$$
$$+ \eta_t + \gamma\eta_{t-1} + \gamma^2\eta_{t-2} + \ldots, \quad (8.24)$$

where the terms B_i, $i = 0, 1, 2, \ldots$, are complicated functions of α, β, δ, and γ. To eliminate the series of infinite errors, move the subscripts in equation (8.24) back one period to obtain an expression for y_{t-1}. Multiply this by γ and subtract it from (8.24) to yield

$$y_t - \gamma y_{t-1} = B_0(m_t - {}_{t-1}m_t^e) +$$
$$(B_1 - \gamma B_0)(m_{t-1} - {}_{t-2}m^e_{t-1}) + \ldots + \eta_t \quad (8.25)$$

or

$$y_t = \Gamma_0(m_t - {}_{t-1}m_t^e) + \Gamma_1(m_{t-1} - {}_{t-2}m^e_{t-1})$$
$$+ \Gamma_2(m_{t-2} - {}_{t-3}m^e_{t-2}) + \ldots + \gamma y_{t-1} + \eta_t \quad (8.25')$$

where $\Gamma_0 = B_0/(1-\gamma)$ and $\Gamma_i = (B_i - \gamma B_{i-1})/(1-\gamma)$ for $i = 1, 2$, ... ∞.[32]

   Equations (8.19) and (8.25′) both fit the data equally well. This is evident from the fact that they have exactly the same error term η_t. Yet (8.25′) is closely related to a surprise-only aggregate supply equation, such as that of Lucas or Barro.

Equations (8.19) and (8.20) imply that the monetary authorities can control the level of output through their control over the stock of money; equation (8.25') implies that at best they can subject it to random shocks. The data give us no direct way of distinguishing which is right. These apparently contradictory but equally accurate representations of the data are another indication that Granger-causality has little to do with control or causality as it is usually analysed. The real question is which set of parameters – α, β and γ or the Γ_i – are primary in the sense that they remain constant when policy-makers alter the parameter δ. If the parameters of (8.19) are invariant to changes in δ, then the Γ_i, which are functions of those parameters and δ, will change every time policy changes. If, however, the Γ_i are invariant to change in δ, then α, β and γ cannot remain constant when δ changes. The problem of *observational equivalence* is that a set of data drawn from a regime in which δ is constant cannot discriminate between these two possibilities.

Neftci and Sargent (1978) attempt to use different regimes to discriminate between the two hypotheses. They examine United States output and money stock data for periods before and after the Second World War. In each case, they break the sample into two parts, estimate equations similar to (8.19), (8.20) and (8.25'), and test for the constancy of the parameters between the parts. For both the pre-war and the post-war period, the policy equation (similar to (8.19)) rejects the null hypothesis of stable parameters, indicating a shift of policy regimes. In the face of this shift, the natural rate model (similar to (8.25')) appears to be more stable than the non-natural rate model (similar to (8.20)), although the statistical evidence is not over-whelming. Neftci and Sargent interpret this as 'a little bit of evidence' in favour of the natural rate hypothesis.

Sargent's (1976a) use of Granger-causality is an early example of an 'atheoretical' approach to macroeconomics – an attempt to let the data speak for themselves without imposing theoretical structures on them. Sargent's (1976b) discovery of observational equivalence, however, alerts us to a major pitfall of such an approach. In contrast with Sargent (1976a), Barro's uses of models which distinguish between expected and unexpected growth of the money stock are not open to the same objection. To see this, observe that equations (8.19) and (8.25') are observationally equivalent because both can be represented as the same unrestricted distributed lag equation (8.22). Two features of the process of converting one equation into the other are important. First, expected future values of the money supply depend only on past values of the money supply (equation (8.20)). Second, the surprise-only aggregate supply equation involves an infinite number of past surprises ($m_t - {}_{t-1}m_t^e$ etc). If there are variables other than past values of the stock of money in the money supply equation which do not occur in the aggregate supply equation (8.25′), these will be introduced into the unrestricted distributed lag (reduced-form) when the levels of the money stock are reformulated as surprises (as in (8.23) and (8.24)). Since this reformulated equation contains different variables from (8.25′), the two are not observationally equivalent. Similarly, if the aggregate supply equation involved only a finite number of past surprises (i.e. $\Gamma_i = 0$ for all i greater than some finite number), the reformulated equation with its infinite past surprises would not be observationally equivalent.[33]

Barro's money supply equation (8.18) could, of course, be used to eliminate the $\triangle MS$ terms from his surprise-only aggregate demand equation (8.17). Unemployment would then be a function of the actual and lagged rates of growth of the money stock, actual and lagged government expenditure, lagged rates of unemployment and other variables. Equation (8.17) is therefore observationally equivalent to a distributed lag equation. Unlike equation (8.25′), however, it is not equivalent to an *unrestricted* distributed lag. Because Barro's 'other variables' in (8.17) do not include GOV or U_{t-1}, these variables and their lagged values would show up in a reduced-form regression only with the particular structure imposed by equations (8.17) and (8.18). The natural and non-natural rate models could therefore be distinguished. Later empirical studies suggest, however, that Barro's model is still subject to the more mundane, but powerful, objection that it is simply not true.[34]

8.3 The Lucas Critique

Observational equivalence implies that, within any policy regime, there are an infinite number of equally accurate representations of the data. Sargent's (1976b) analysis also shows that, if one of these forms is invariant to changes in the policy regime, then the other forms will in general not also be invariant. Models such as that of Barro (1977, 1978) implicitly assert (usually without any test) selection of the invariant form. In his celebrated paper of 1976, Lucas argues that typical macroeconometric models have not selected invariant forms, principally because they have ignored rational expectations.

Lucas's point is very simple. Most macroeconometric models estimate equations labelled 'consumption function', 'money demand function' and so forth. In principle, these functions include expectations. For example, a permanent-income or life-cycle consumption function assumes that individuals decide how much to consume now partly on the basis of their expected future income. Typical 'Keynesian' econometric models, however, either ignore expectations or form them from some autoregressive or adaptive scheme which is in general not compatible with rational expectations or, in some rare cases, uses direct survey data about expectations. Rational expectations, however, implies that individuals actually use not just the past values of a variable in order to form their prediction of its future value as autoregressive or adaptive expectations assumes, but rather all the available information including the structure of the actual underlying economic model. Policy rules are part of this structure. When policy regimes change, therefore, one should expect people's expectations to change as well. Yet autoregressive or adaptive expectations schemes form predictions mechanically without regard to the policy regime. Consequently, any estimate that either fails to account for expectations or accounts for them in some mechanical or non-rational manner is likely to break down when the policy regime changes.

As an illustration, consider one of Lucas's examples.[35] In Friedman's permanent-income model of the consumption function, agents are assumed to form expectations of future income streams in order to calculate their permanent incomes. Friedman assumes that in practice agents use past actual income as the data from which future expected income is predicted according to an autoregressive scheme with geometrically declining weights. Under some circumstances, this scheme coincides with rational expectations.[36] One of the circumstances is that the policy regime is constant.

Imagine what would happen if the government were to make a credible announcement that taxes would be cut for all future time. Under rational expectations, estimates of permanent income would rise and consumption would rise; but the adaptive expectations scheme would underpredict future income because it is based only on past income, and the consumption function would therefore underpredict consumption. Over time the adaptive expectations scheme would tend to correct its mistake. The optimal weights that make adaptive expectations coincide with rational expectations would nonetheless be different in general under the new policy regime than under the old.

Alternatively, suppose that the government announced a credible one-year-only tax cut. Under rational expectations, expected future income would rise only by the amount of interest earned from saving the entire tax cut, so that permanent income and consumption would rise very little. In the period in which the announcement was made, the adaptive expectations scheme would miss even this small rise as current and past incomes remained unchanged. But in the period after the tax cut actually took place, the adaptive scheme would overpredict permanent income and consumption because it could not anticipate that taxes would return to their old levels.

Estimates of the consumption function with adaptive expectations would not predict well from one regime to another and would yield different parameters under different regimes. Lucas's point is not that all estimated macroeconomic relations are necessarily not invariant. It is rather that, in order to obtain an invariant relation, one must derive the functional form to be estimated from the underlying choices of individual agents. Lucas supposes that this means that one must derive aggregate relations from individual optimization problems taking only tastes and technology as given.[37]

A Formal Example

Exactly how the Lucas critique works in a concrete case can be made clear with a simple formal example.[38]

Consider Cagan's (1956) equation showing the demand for real balances in hyperinflation:

$$m_t - p_t = \alpha(_t p_{t+1}^e - p_t) + v_t, \qquad (8.26)$$

where $_t p_{t+1}^e$ is the expectation at time t of the price level at time $t+1$ and v_t is a random error. (All variables are in natural logarithms.) Equation (8.26) asserts that, in hyperinflation, the opportunity cost of holding money in the face of high inflation outweighs the effects of all the usual arguments in the demand-for-money function, e.g. income and interest rates. In order to keep the example simple, we assume that $\alpha = -1$, so that (8.26) can be written

$$m_t - p_t = p_t - _t p_{t+1}^e + v_t. \qquad (8.26')$$

Assume that the central bank supplies money according to the rule

$$m_t = \lambda m_{t-1} + e_t, \qquad (8.27)$$

where e_t is a random error. The error terms v_t and e_t are assumed to be serially uncorrelated and uncorrelated with each other and to have means of zero. Each possible value of λ characterizes a different policy regime.

Assume also that expectations are rational:

$$_t p_{t+1}^e = E[p_{t+1} | \Omega_t], \qquad (8.28)$$

where Ω_t is the information available at time t. For our purposes Ω_t will be taken to include only the current and lagged values of the variables of the model *and* the structure of the model itself.

In order to solve the model, equation (8.26') can be rewritten as

$$p_t = \tfrac{1}{2}m_t + \tfrac{1}{2}{}_t p_{t+1}^e - \tfrac{1}{2}v_t. \qquad (8.29)$$

This expression contains the unobservable term $_t p_{t+1}^e$. In order to eliminate this term, advance the subscripts in equation (8.29) in order to obtain an expression for p_{t+1}. Take expectations of both sides conditional on Ω_t:

$$E[p_{t+1}|\Omega_t] = \tfrac{1}{2}E[m_{t+1}|\Omega_t] + \tfrac{1}{2}E[_{t+1}p^e_{t+2}|\Omega_t]$$
$$- \tfrac{1}{2}E[v_{t+1}|\Omega_t]. \qquad (8.30)$$

Equation (8.27) shows that $E[m_{t+1}|\Omega_t] = \lambda m_t$. Since v_t has a mean of zero by assumption, its expectation is zero. The best expectation at time t of what the expectation will be at time $t+1$ of the price level at time $t+2$, i.e. $E[_{t+1}p^e_{t+2}|\Omega_t]$, is obviously simply the expectation at time t of the price level at time $t+2$, i.e. $_tp^e_{t+2}$. Using these facts and applying equation (8.28) to (8.30) yields

$$_tp^e_{t+1} = \tfrac{1}{2}\lambda m_t + \tfrac{1}{2}{}_tp^e_{t+2}. \qquad (8.30')$$

This expression still contains an unobservable term on its right-hand side. The process of advancing the subscripts in equation (8.29), taking expectations and substituting can, however, be repeated. After n substitutions, equation (8.30) can be written

$$_tp^e_{t+1} = \frac{\lambda}{2}m_t \sum_{j=0}^{n}\left(\frac{\lambda}{2}\right)^j + \left(\frac{1}{2}\right)^{n+1}{}_tp^e_{t+n+1}. \qquad (8.30'')$$

As long as $|\lambda| < 2$, the second term will vanish as n becomes infinitely large and the first term will converge to the finite value $\lambda/(2-\lambda)$, so that (8.29) can be written

$$p_t = \frac{1}{2-\lambda}m_{t-1} - \frac{1}{2}v_t \qquad (8.29')$$

or, substituting from equation (8.27),

$$p_t = \frac{\lambda}{2-\lambda}m_{t-1} + \frac{1}{2-\lambda}e_t - \frac{1}{2}v_t. \qquad (8.29'')$$

Suppose that a policy maker wished to assess the effect of the money supply rule on the economy. He might estimate a regression equation of the form

$$p_t = a_0 + a_1 m_{t-1}. \qquad (8.31)$$

If the model of hyperinflation is true, then equation (8.29') says that, up to a random error, our estimate should find $a_0 = 0$ and $a_1 = \lambda/(2-\lambda)$. The Lucas critique, then, is simply the observation that if the regime is constant (i.e. λ is a constant) the estimated parameters of (8.31) will be constant, but if the regime changes (i.e. λ becomes some other constant) the estimate of the parameter a_1 will change. Lucas argues that estimates of an equation such as (8.31) are useless for evaluating alternative policies (i.e. alternative values for λ) because, having been estimated under one regime, they will necessarily mispredict under a different regime. Only if the effect of the regime change on the underlying model can be adequately specified would an empirically estimated equation be helpful. In this example a direct estimate of the system of equations (8.27) and (8.29″) would be useful for policy analysis. This, of course, assumes that the underlying model (equations (8.26)–(8.28)) is in fact the true model – a very bold assumption to make in advance of all empirical investigation.

The Role of Rational Expectations

The simple formal example illustrates a number of characteristic features of rational expectations models and of the Lucas critique. The first is that, in order for objective expectations to be put in place of subjective expectations – the rational expectations hypothesis (equation (8.28)) – the information set Ω_t must be specified explicitly. In this model it comprises the non-expectational variables and the structure of the model itself. Outside information (e.g. the stochastic structure of the non-expectational exogenous variables) could be introduced into more complicated models. Second, if the value of any variable depends on expectations of its value in a future period, it generally depends on expectations of its value in all future periods (e.g. equation (8.30)). Rational expectations, as a rule, involve infinite horizons. Third, the solutions to rational expectations models generally involve cross-equation restrictions. The coefficient $\lambda/(2-\lambda)$ on m_{t-1} in equation (8.29″) is a function of the coefficient λ on m_{t-1} in (8.27). Futhermore, the error term $[1/(2-\lambda)]e_t - \frac{1}{2}v_t$ in (8.29″) is a function of λ and of the error term in (8.27). These cross-equation restrictions are the reason that regression equations such as (8.31) are supposed not to be invariant. They also form the basis for joint tests, such as Lucas's test of the natural rate hypothesis (see section 8.2), the structure of a model and rational expectations.

In this model, as with other typical examples, the characteristic features of the Lucas critique seem to arise because of rational expectations. It is important to observe, however, that it is general interdependence rather than rational expectations *per se* that generates cross-equation restrictions and the failure of invariance.[39] If expectations of prices were to be formed only on the basis of past prices, this model would be invariant. Suppose, however, that expectations of prices are formed from expectations of the level of the money stock which, to keep things simple, are formed according to the true money supply rule (equation (8.27)). Let equation (8.28) be replaced by

$$_t p^c_{i+1} = \theta_t m^c_{i+1} = \theta \lambda^2 m_{t-1}. \tag{8.32}$$

Unless $\theta = 1/(2-\lambda)$ this expression does not coincide with rational expectations. Even though expectations are not rational, the model (equations (8.26), (8.27) and (8.32)) implies that coefficient a_1 of the regression equation (8.31) (now equal to $\lambda^2/(2-\lambda)$) changes with every change of regime. The important point is not that agents have rational expectations, but that they take *some* account of the policy rule.

The Lucas critique, whether it derives from rational expectations or not, points to a possible incompatibility in the early new classical econometric literature. Barro (1977, 1978) assumes that the regression equation (8.18) is the policy rule and, invoking rational expectations, coincides with agents' own expectations of the rate of growth of the stock of money. The Lucas critique implies that the parameters of his unemployment (aggregate supply) equation (8.17) are not invariant to changes in the policy regime (i.e. to changes in the parameters of the rule). Barro estimates (8.18) as if its parameters were invariant. Yet Neftci and Sargent (1978) find that the money supply rule, over a period which overlaps with Barro's estimation period, is not invariant. Both cannot be right. Barro does not present tests of the invariance of his estimated equation, while Neftci and Sargent do not include government expenditure as an independent variable, which could be why their estimates are not invariant.

Interpretations of the Lucas Critique

The Lucas critique is related to the identification problem in econometrics. The root of the problem is this: economic theory uses variables to describe economic processes which are not observable; observable variables are, in part, the outcome of interactions among these unobservables, and without further information it is, in general, not possible to infer the behaviour of the unobservables from the observables. The paradigmatic identification problem is the simple system in which desired or planned supply is an increasing function of price alone and desired or planned demand is a decreasing function of price alone. Together these functions determine an equilibrium observable outcome: the amount sold. The identification problem is that one cannot infer what the underlying functions are from the observation of this single price–quantity combination. The problem is no easier if the functions are subject to random shocks. A scatter of points randomly distributed about the equilibrium then replaces the single observed point. If we have enough additional information, however (say that the variance of the random shocks to the supply curve is much greater than that of shocks to the demand curve or that supply is also a function of rainfall), then it may be possible to infer the shape of the underlying functions (subject to some random error) – in this case because movements of the supply curve from random shocks or variability in rainfall force the observed price–quantity combinations to trace out the demand curve.

The Lucas critique is a variation on the theme of the identification problem. Just as we find observed price–quantity patterns (a point, a scatter or a line, depending on the nature of the actual underlying relation) jumping about when underlying but unaccounted for factors such as the level of rainfall change, we notice that estimated (presumed) behavioural functions appear not to be stable in the face of policy changes not accounted for in the estimate. When seen in this light, the Lucas critique clearly did not originate with Lucas and deserves to bear his name only because he brought the invariance problem home to most economists more forcibly than any earlier author and because it serves as a convenient shorthand.

Lucas (1976) himself claims no originality for the non-invariance argument, suggesting that it is implicit in the work of Frank Knight, Milton Friedman and John Muth. However, Lucas does not notice the explicit statement in Trygve Haavelmo's famous paper 'The Probability Approach in Econometrics' (1944). Haavelmo compares the estimation of simple econometric relations to working out the relation between the amount of throttle and the speed of a car on a flat track under uniform conditions. The relations may be precise, but if the surrounding conditions are changed (e.g. take the car off the track or allow the engine to go out of tune) the relation will almost certainly break down. Haavelmo contrasts the lack of autonomy of such empirical regularities with such things as the laws of thermodynamics, friction and so forth, which are autonomous because they '... describe the functioning of some parts of the mechanism *irrespective* of what happens in some *other* parts'.[40] If, as was suggested earlier, we define 'causality' in terms of controllability and therefore as invariance under interventions of control, then Haavelmo's point can be restated as follows: non-autonomous relations do not represent the underlying causal ordering. It will not do to overstate the case, so Haavelmo goes on to argue that autonomy is a matter of degree. Haavelmo does not himself state the invariance problem in terms of representing causal relations, but Simon puts it in exactly such terms and is, therefore, another precursor of Lucas.[41]

Although Lucas was not the first to recognize the invariance problem explicitly, his own important contribution to it is to observe that one of the relations frequently omitted from putative causal representations is that of the formation of expectations. He notes, further, that the formation of expectations may depend upon people's understanding of the causal structure of the economy in general and of the process of policy formation in particular. This is why the rational expectations hypothesis is so often linked with the Lucas critique. The important point about Haavelmo's and Simon's analysis of non-invariance is that it reminds us that rational expectations is simply one means by which causal relations may be linked, and, in general, it is the omission of *any* relevant causal relation that produces non-invariance.

8.4   Reactions to the Lucas Critique

Lucas's (1976) paper on econometric policy evaluation is widely seen as the most formidable challenge ever made to the legitimacy of econometrics applied to macroeconomics. Lucas himself clearly intended it to show that the use of traditional econometric models for any serious analysis of microeconomic policy was invalid. New classical economists have made two prominent responses to Lucas's argument. The first, most popular, response is to attempt to develop new classical microfoundations in order to generate theoretically sound identifying restrictions. If successful, such a project would uncover invariant parameters and enable accurate predictions of the effects of changes in policy regime. The work of Sargent and some of his colleagues exemplifies this response.[42]

The second response argues that, while the Lucas critique is correct in principle, it is, in Sims's words, '. . . a cautionary footnote to such analysis rather than a deep objection to its foundations'.[43] On this view true changes of policy regime are rare, so that even models which would not be invariant across such regime changes will still be useful for forecasting and policy analysis within a given regime. This approach argues that theory is unlikely to provide enough sufficiently convincing identifying restrictions actually to permit estimation of the true underlying invariant parameters. Consequently, it turns the problem around and asks: what can be learned from the data with little reference to theory?

The second response is paradoxical. It argues that when there is no change of regime, it is possible to evaluate policy without worrying about the Lucas critique. But if policy makers acted on the advice generated in such an evaluation, would the regime not then have changed, invalidating the exercise?[44] This paradox turns on the problem of how policies should be characterized – the problem which we now examine.

The Characterization of Policy

In section 8.3 as well as in chapter 4, a policy (or policy regime) was identified with a rule governing the evolution of a policy variable. For example, equation (8.27) (and, similarly, equation (8.10)) is a rule specifying for each time what the level of the money stock will be. The parameter λ is an index of the policy regime: there are as many possible regimes of the same general form as there are values of λ. To evaluate a change of policy regime within a model, the model is usually solved with different values for the policy parameter. Since rational expectations usually involves infinite time horizons, this procedure implicitly assumes that once the policy is changed it will be maintained without further change forever.

Several authors have argued that this characterization of a change of policy regime is faulty for at least two reasons. First, it assumes a strict form of rational expectations: people understand the new policy and incorporate its effects into their decisions immediately. A weaker form of rational expectations is, however, more plausible: people learn from their mistakes. If such a weaker form in fact holds, it is important to model the learning process. The characteristics of an economy in transition between regimes is likely to be quite different from its characteristics after the policy has been in force for some time and is widely understood.[45]

Lucas seems to accept the critical, but not the substantive, thesis of this argument. He argues that the domain of economic theory is recurrent phenomena. There are many possible paths between one steady state and another. Economics is about the common steady states and has nothing to say about these transitional paths.[46] Empirical investigation, on this view, must wait for people to adjust to a change of regime and for the economy to settle down close to its steady state path.

The method adopted by Lucas (1973) (see section 8.2) is meant to be appropriate to this emphasis on steady states. An investigation of the slope of the Phillips curve in one country, as its rate of inflation became more or less variable, would have involved identifying different regimes and worrying about transitional behaviour between them. Instead, Lucas treats each country as if a single regime had prevailed over his 24 year estimation period and uses *average* data from the whole period in making a cross-country comparison. Long averages are supposed to smooth out any transitional aberrations in the data and allow approximately steady state behaviour to shine through. Each country is then seen as a single observation of a particular regime, and the relationship between the slope of the

Phillips curve and the variability of inflation is read as a relationship between steady states under different regimes.

Lucas (1986) justifies this method more explicitly and applies it to a test of the quantity-theoretic relationship of the rate of growth of the money stock to the rate of inflation for 16 Latin American countries over the period 1950–69.[47] He confirms the quantity theory's prediction of a one-for-one relationship. In order to construct a related test of the quantity theory in a single country, Lucas replaces quarterly observations by long moving averages of the rate of growth of the stock of money and the rate of inflation for the United States for the period 1955–75. Once again, he finds a one-for-one relationship.

Lucas's method, especially in the single-country case, strikingly resembles Phillips's original method of uncovering the wage–unemployment relationship.[48] Like many 'Keynesians' of the 1960s with their Phillips curves, but unlike Phillips himself, Lucas treats the empirical inflation–money growth relationship as if it were a menu of choices for the policy maker.[49] Even though he asserts the stability of the quantity theory only in the long run, there is a certain irony in the man who more than any other taught the profession to question the stability of empirically estimated relationships as guides to policy offering such a crude correlation as persuasive evidence of a controllable relationship. Correlation does not prove causation – even in the long run.

The second objection to characterizing policy as a parameter (or set of parameters) held at a constant value forever is simply that policies do in fact change and are known to change. Consequently, rational agents would assign probabilities to the current policy remaining in force and to each possible policy succeeding it at some definite time.

While two of his examples of non-invariance to regime changes are of the constant-parameter type, Lucas (1976) does provide one example in which agents account for possible future changes of regime. He considers the case of a newly enacted investment tax credit. If it is only temporary, its immediate effects are much more powerful, as firms reschedule their investments in order to take advantage of a temporary windfall. If it is permanent, firms now find some previously unprofitable investments to be worth undertaking but they have no special incentive to undertake them quickly. How powerful the net effect is depends on the degree to which firms believe that the tax credit is temporary, i.e. on the probability, once it is in effect, that it will be reversed. The expected value of the tax credit is, then, the sum of its values when expected to be permanent and when expected to be temporary, weighted by the probabilities of the policy's being maintained and being reversed. The calculation of the net effect on investment uses this expected value.

Cooley et al. (1984a, b) argue strongly that policy should always be described, as in Lucas's investment example, as variables and not as fixed parameters.[50] People observe that policies change, and, even if a particular policy has never changed so far, as soon as one actually establishes a new policy only a myopic agent could regard it too as unchangeable. Once a parameter is viewed as changeable, it is more accurately described as a variable:

> ... any variable which changes over time in a way that is not completely predictable should be assumed to be perceived by agents as a sequence of random variables, the distribution of which coincides with the corresponding objective distribution.[51]

Cooley et al. draw

> ... the essential distinction between parameters as representing things which are assumed not to change, such as measures of preferences and technology, and variables as representing things which do, like policy regimes. Different policy regimes are then represented by different realizations of a random process ...[52]

On this view, the money supply rule in the illustration of the Lucas critique in section 8.3 (equation 8.27)

$$m_t = \lambda m_{t-1} + e_t$$

might still be taken to describe policy, but λ would now be regarded as permanently fixed and a change in policy regime would be represented as different sequences of e_t. An expansionary regime, for example, would consist of a sequence of positive values for e_t, while a contractionary regime would consist of a sequence of negative values.

This view appears to be an attractive alternative to the difficulties implicit in Lucas's parametric characterization of policy. It suffers, nonetheless, from its own problems. The public views e_t as a serially uncorrelated random variable. So in what sense can the authorities be said to choose it? One way to think about this would be to say that e_t is random from the point of view of the public although it is chosen by the authorities, i.e. the public views the authorities as a black box which generates values for m_t by an unknown process.[53]

Such a view does not seem to be compatible with rational expectations and is not, therefore, appropriate to new classical analysis. For if the public has rational expectations then its subjective beliefs about e_t correspond to what is objectively true. It they believe that e_t follows a particular random process, then the authorities can choose e_t only in a way that appears to follow that process. Such a constrained choice is no choice at all. One may as well throw dice.[54]

A better representation of the problem might be to leave e_t as an un-controlled random error and permit the authorities to choose λ to be, say, λ_1 or λ_2. Cooley et al. would then argue that λ is a variable and that a public with rational expectations would know the probabilities of a switch between λ_1 and λ_2 so that both would belong to the same (more complicated) regime. But, then, all the same questions arise: if subjective beliefs about the probabilities of switching between λ_1 and λ_2 are objectively true, then the authorities have no real choice about λ. We might think that the authorities choose not λ_1 and λ_2 but rather the probabilities of switching. Of course these probabilities need not be fixed so that a regime change would then be a change in the probabilities of switching. But then a rational public would know the probabilities of switching between λ_1 and λ_2. The problem can ramify to ever higher levels. At each stage, the policy maker has no real choice if the public's estimates of transition probabilities are objectively true.

The process cannot be ramified forever. Cooley et al.'s view is that the public situates 'new' events as repetitions of previous patterns, but the public's expectation can be rational only if the authorities in fact stick to the previous pattern, complicated as it might be. At some level the authorities can surely choose probabilities or parameters for which there is no precedent. The public would not then be able to form objectively correct assessments of the probabilities. This is a change of regime.

It has been objected that the problem of the authorities *choosing* a variable such as m_t, which is at the same time accurately described by a stochastic process such as (8.27), is closely analogous to a person choosing consumption goods, which is at the same time accurately described by maximization of a utility function subject to a budget constraint; both really are choosing.[55] The analogy is close. Just as there are situations that we best describe as changes of taste, there are situations that we best describe as changes of policy regime.

To summarize the issue: either the policy is random, in which case it is not policy, or it is described by a changeable parameter and is subject to Cooley et al.'s objection. To put it another way, Cooley et al. believe that any changeable variable should be described by a probability distribution; however, if the variable is a policy variable, a policy maker must be able to affect the probabilities assigned to different realizations of that distribution. All Cooley et al. have done is to move the problem up one level from Lucas's original fixed- and random-parameter illustrations of the Lucas critique.

Sims (1980a, 1982) anticipates Cooley et al.'s argument that policy should be described by a variable with a well-defined probability distribution. He later notes, however, that the distinction between choosing a fixed parameter in a policy rule and choosing a sequence of policy variables is, in fact, superficial.[56] Sims seems to agree with Lucas that a true regime change is *sui generis*; it may as well be represented by a permanently fixed parameter and may pose difficulties for the application of rational expectations in the transition between regimes.[57] Where Sims seems to differ from Lucas is that he believes that private individuals have seen a sufficient range of government actions and are able to attach probabilities to these actions recurring, so that true regime changes are really very rare.[58] An episode of tight monetary policy, on this view, is unlikely to represent a true change of regime, having occurred any number of times in the past, while the end of the gold standard or the breakdown of the Bretton Woods system might well be examples of regime changes. Sims does not object to the Lucas critique in principle, only to its practical applicability in most cases.

Nonetheless Sims's view is close to that of Cooley et al.: policy should usually be thought of not as a choice between fixed rules, but as the implementation of a single rule. Sims sees both the public and the policy maker as optimizing agents. Thus, game theory, in which players interact, rather than control theory, in which the public is passively manipulated, should be the basis for policy analysis.[59]

Sims's view of policy making from an econometric perspective is remarkably similar to Barro and Gordon's view of it from a theoretical perspective (see chapter 4, section 4.3), and it raises the same issues. If policy makers and the public are already behaving optimally and if it is wrong to see them as choosing among alternative rules, what possible role is left for giving advice on policy? Sargent (1984) worries that Sims pushes the hypothesis that agents optimize one step too far. Sargent's concern is that Sims has adopted a fundamentalist interpretation of what Craine and Hardouvelis (1983) so aptly call 'stochastic Calvinism' – the doctrine of predestination implicit in rational expectations models.[60] Barro (1986) is a willing fundamentalist, claiming that all economics is positive economics. Sims, however, while not apostate, claims to profess a more moderate line. Unlike Barro and Gordon, he is unwilling to accept that his analysis eliminates the usefulness of policy advisers. Instead, he proposes his own controversial analysis of what policy advisers do and how policy advice should be formulated.

The Vector Autoregression Programme

The roots of Sim's alternative analysis are found in his early work. His application of tests of Granger-causality (Sims 1972) can be seen as an attempt to gain substantive economic knowledge without resort to economic theory. His intent is clear in the title of Sargent and Sims

(1977), 'Business Cycle Modeling Without Pretending to Have Too Much *A Priori* Economic Theory'. In section 8.3 we observed that the Lucas critique can be interpreted as an identification problem. It is hardly surprising, then, that Sims's earliest version of his proposal on how to conduct policy analysis without falling foul of the Lucas critique should concentrate on the 'incredible identifying restrictions' adopted in most large-scale econometric models.[61] The problem as he sees it is this. In order to identify the parameters of large macroeconomic models, econometricians have typically placed a vast number of arbitrary restrictions – neither suggested by economic theory nor by institutional knowledge – on the structure of the estimated equations. For example, variables that might be theoretically important are simply omitted from some equations or lag lengths are truncated without any theoretical justification. To the degree that these restrictions are invalid, one would expect the models to forecast badly. Yet, according to Sims, they forecast surprisingly well.

This relatively good performance is possible, Sims believes, simply because true changes of regime, which would open these models to attack along the lines of the Lucas critique, are few and far between. Consider Sargent's (1976b) analysis of observational equivalence (see section 8.2). The natural and non-natural rate hypotheses both generate identical observable consequences and both form the basis for equally good forecasts, as long as the policy regime in Lucas's and Sargent's parametric sense remains constant. Whichever theory is right, the common reduced-form equation is the same, and if there is no change of regime it will have stable parameters.

While admitting that it has resulted in some improvements in short-term forecasting, Lucas derides Lawrence Klein's work on large-scale macromodels for its lack of theoretical basis:

> I recall . . . an illustration of his in which the *same* price equation is derived from a competitive model, a pure-monopoly model, and a behavioral markup pricing model! The point was clear: Pick the 'story' that suits your prejudices, but do not be deluded that this choice matters operationally.[62]

Rather than recoil in horror, as Lucas does, from this lack of connection between theory and empirical models, Sims argues for the legitimacy of concentrating on uninterpreted reduced forms.

In earlier work, Sims (1977) argued that structure is a matter of degree. An econometric relation is *structural* if it is invariant to a specified class of intervention. A structural relation is therefore a *causal* relation in the sense of Hurwicz (1962) or Simon (1953) (see section 8.1). Sims points out that, on this definition, reduced forms may be structural. Take the example of equations (8.3) and (8.4), which are the reduced forms of equations (8.1) and (8.2). These are not invariant to the class of interventions represented by changes of the parameters θ, γ or the β_{ij}s. They are invariant, nonetheless, to the interventions of the class represented by different shocks to e_{1t} and e_{2t}. The interventions of the first class are regime changes in Lucas's sense, while those of the second class are what Sims calls 'normal policy making'.[63] This distinction is the same as Cooley et al.'s distinction between changes of a parameter and alternative realizations of a random variable. As long as the regime is constant, i.e. as long as we are restricted to normal policy making, Sims believes that reduced forms are adequate to provide policy advice.

Large-scale macromodels perform reasonably well in Sims's view because they are approximations to reduced-form optimal forecasting equations. The 'incredible' identifying restrictions have little to do with uncovering underlying parameters which are theoretically invariant to regime changes, but are simply artfully employed simplifications which help to make estimation tractable.[64] Sims's own proposal for vector autoregressions (commonly known by the acronym VAR) as a source of policy advice is to systematize the haphazard manner in which such reduced forms are specified and estimated.

Sims (1980a, 1982, 1986b) proposes that we treat all variables – policy and behavioural – on a par, and estimate vector autoregressions (i.e. reduced forms such as equations (8.3) and (8.4) estimated as a joint system, so that the covariance between u_{1t} and u_{2t} can be taken into account). Sims (1980a) illustrates this method with six variables (money, real income, unemployment, wages, prices and import prices) and six vector autoregression equations. Sims believes that, once estimated, such a system is of great use of the policy maker.

Why does Sims believe that this programme of vector autoregressions is not subject, on the one hand, to the Lucas critique and, on the other hand, to Sargent's concern that the policy adviser has no function when both the public and the policy maker are optimizing agents in the same game? The Lucas critique could apply, Sims believes, but does not apply in practice because changes of regime are rare. Sims also believes that nothing as simple as, say, a rule setting a constant rate of growth for the stock of money has ever characterized policy in practice. Instead, policy makers have followed complex feedback rules or, to put it into their own parlance, have practised 'leaning against the wind.'[65] Such policy is not well described by a simple rule, and so regime changes would not be as obvious as changing one parameter to another.

While the absence of changes of regimes justifies Sims's ignoring the Lucas critique, the presence of feedback rules seems to bolster Sargent's concern. To see this, consider the following equation in which current output y is a function of past output and a policy variable x:

$$y_t = \alpha y_{t-1} + \beta x_t + e_t, \tag{8.33}$$

where e_t is a random error. Suppose that the authorities have followed a deterministic feedback rule of the form

$$x_t = \gamma y_{t-1}. \tag{8.34}$$

One might think that an econometrician could estimate the effect of the policy variable on output in order to help the authorities choose a sensible rule, i.e. a desirable value for γ. Unfortunately, if the authorities have been following *any* feedback rule in the past, this is not the case. To see this, substitute (8.34) into (8.33) to yield

$$y_t = (\alpha + \beta \gamma)y_{t-1} + e_t = \pi y_{t-1} + e_t. \tag{8.35}$$

Equation (8.35) says that, because of the deterministic nature of the feedback rule, the control variable x_t disappears from the estimated relation. Even if one knows the exact value of γ, the parameters α and β cannot be recovered from the estimate of π: they are not identified. Although x_t is used to control y_t, x_t does not Granger-cause y_t. This is a slightly simpler illustration than the one in section 8.1 of the general point that Granger-causality and controllability may run in opposite directions.

Optimal policy rules are generally deterministic; and calculating the optimal coefficients requires knowledge of the parameters of behavioural relations such as equation (8.33). The fact, therefore, that the authorities have followed some deterministic policy rule (not necessarily optimal) undermines the ability of the econometrician to obtain the requisite information to give useful policy advice.

While recognizing that this argument is correct, given its premises, Sims believes that it is wrongly formulated because policy rules in the real world are not deterministic but subject to capricious variation.[66] Interestingly, he does not believe that this capricious variation undermines the general new classical view that agents – including policy makers – are successful optimizers. A single unified authority does not make policy. Rather, policy is the outcome of a political process in which competing groups pursue incompatible goals. Any group may select an optimal deterministic policy, given its goals, but this will in general differ from the optimal deterministic policy of other groups with different goals. The final policy is unlikely to be precisely what any group sought, or even if it is today, the policies of the other groups may dominate tomorrow.[67]

In our simple example, Sims's view suggests replacing equation (8.34) with, say,

$$x_t = \gamma y_{t-1} + v_t \tag{8.34'}$$

where v_t is a random error representing the capricious element of policy. Substituting (8.34') into (8.33) yields

$$y_t = (\alpha + \beta\gamma)y_{t-1} + \beta v_t + e_t. \tag{8.36}$$

Substituting once more from (8.34') in order to eliminate v_t yields

$$\begin{aligned} y_t &= (\alpha + \beta\gamma)y_{t-1} + \beta x_t + \beta\gamma y_{t-1} + e_t \\ &= \alpha y_{t-1} + \beta x_t + e_t \end{aligned} \tag{8.36'}$$

Equation (8.36') is, of course, identical with equation (8.33). It demonstrates that, in the presence of capricious variation in the realization of policy rules, the econometrician may once more be able to estimate controlled behavioural relations.[68]

In a world of capricious variation in the political process, deterministic feedback rules may no longer blind the econometrician, yet, if the capricious element results not from a failure of individual groups to pursue their own goals optimally but from the interaction between different groups with competing goals, it remains difficult to see what use any group would find for information obtained econometrically.

If a group already follows an optimal policy, it has no need to evaluate alternative policies – changes of regime are not in question. To resolve this puzzle, Sims distinguishes between the *evaluation* of policy (to use Lucas's term) and the *implementation* of policy (to use Sims's own term).[69] If the authorities' goals and instruments are constant, the Lucas critique is not an issue. Sims believes, therefore, that the evaluation of policy is moot. The authorities know what they want to do, but exactly how to implement such a policy is an open question. What precise levels of the money stock or the government deficit should they choose to achieve their invariable goal? Sims denies the econometrician a role in the evaluation of policy, but reserves for him a more modest role in the implementation of policy.

To make this clear, continue with the previous example. Suppose that the desired policy is to minimize the variability of output. The best that the authorities can do is to set x_t such that the deterministic part of the right-hand side of (8.34) is zero, i.e. $\alpha y_{t-1} + \beta x_t = 0$ or $x_t = -(\alpha/\beta)y_{t-1}$ or, equivalently, set $\gamma = -\alpha/\beta$. One way to implement this is, of course, to estimate α and β, and then to calculate γ. Because the present example is so simple, this seems to be straightforward. A more realistic model, however, would have to reflect the complexities of the real world. It would be difficult to determine the structure of such a model theoretically or econometrically. The problem of observational equivalence would loom large. It would be impossible to know the analogues to α and β in order to choose γ,

Sims suggests an alternative method of implementation. If one regime comprises the possible range of policy actions i.e. if, as Cooley et al. also suggest, the public assesses the probabilities of alternative policy actions and does not treat particular policy actions as new policy strategies, then the Lucas critique can be ignored. The reduced-form equations which forecast goal variables (output in the example above) would then have invariant coefficients. Different paths for the control variable (x_t in the example above) could be tried out in the reduced form. The path which produced the most favourable outcome for the goal variable (say, gave the lowest variability), assuming that *all* possible paths are tested, would be chosen. This path in fact will be the same path that would be chosen by direct optimization if structural information were available. The advantage of this procedure is that neither structural information nor complicated calculations are required. In our simple example this procedure seems to be more complex than direct calculation, but the more complicated are the behavioural relations in the world and the more control variables are available to the authorities, the less likely the authorities are to have the required structural information and the more complex direct calculation will be, and so the greater are the advantages of this method of approximation.

Sims's conception of the policy adviser as helping to implement existing policies is far less grand than Lucas's conception of him as helping to evaluate alternative policy regimes. In principle, one could imagine the econometrician's being replaced completely by a computer. His only role would have been to set up the original program. Sims's method works, however, only if the reduced forms are themselves correct and all alternative combinations of policy paths are checked. It is hard to believe that this is practicable even with a computer. It is consistent with Sims's argument, then, that *feasible* implementation of his procedure would still require the econometrician's art.

Although Sims has reduced the econometrician to a minor role in order to preserve any role for him at all, this is, Sims believes, what day-to-day normal policy making is really about. Barro and Gordon infer from their belief that policy makers are already optimizers that policy advisers have no day-to-day role to play.[70] In contrast, Sims concludes that it is *because* policy makers are optimizers that they need policy advisers to help them find the optimal policy, which, although it may be transparently obvious in simple models such as that of Barro and Gordon, may still require great ingenuity to find in a complex world.

The Interpretation of Vector Autoregressions: Problems and Equivocations

Sims admits that the Lucas critique is correct in principle, and Sims's own argument for the usefulness of reduced-form estimation in implementing existing policy also seems to be correct in principle. Sims suggests that the Lucas critique is really a minor qualification in the analysis of policy advice, and yet he also acknowledges that many may see his own view as simply a minor qualification of the Lucas critique.[71] It finally comes down to whether one believes that changes of policy regime (i.e. the adoption of new rules governing the authorities' behaviour, which are both surprises and expected to continue in force indefinitely) are the rule or the exception. The relative fruitfulness of these assumptions in practical policy analysis is the ultimate test.

Even if Sims's own assumption is adopted, the application of his programme of vector autoregressions to the analysis of policy is not completely straightforward. In practice, each equation of the vector autoregression is a long distributed lag on several variables. Interpreting the pattern of estimated coefficient values is difficult. The usual method for handling this problem involves two steps: imposing a 'causal' order on the variables, and using statistical or graphical techniques to indicate the implied quantitative interrelationship between the variables.

Causal Order

1   Wold-causal chains. Simultaneity suggests mutual causality. Causality is sometimes interpreted as always running in just one direction and never being reciprocal. Thus, if money causes output, output does not cause money. A Wold-causal chain orders variables so that the current values of 'causally' prior variables appear as independent variables in the equations for 'causally' posterior variables, but not vice versa.[72] Any vector autogression can be rewritten so that its variables are causally ordered and there is no contemporaneous correlation between the errors of the rewritten equations. A completely causally ordered vector autoregression is said to be *recursive*.

To illustrate, consider the reduced forms (equations (8.3) and (8.4))

$$Y_t = \Pi_{11} Y_{t-1} + \Pi_{12} X_{t-1} + u_{1t} \tag{8.3}$$
$$X_t = \Pi_{21} Y_{t-1} + \Pi_{22} X_{t-1} + u_{2t}, \tag{8.4}$$

where

$$u_{1t} = \frac{e_{1t} + \theta e_{2t}}{1 - \theta\gamma}$$

and

$$u_{2t} = \frac{\gamma e_{1t} + e_{2t}}{1 - \theta\gamma}$$

Since both u_{1t} and u_{2t} involve e_{1t} and e_{2t}, the error terms from the original equations (8.1) and (8.2), they are obviously contemporaneously correlated. To eliminate this simultaneity, assume that Y is causally prior to X. Multiply equation (8.3) through by $\delta = \text{cov}(u_{1t}u_{2t})/\text{var}(u_{1t})$ and subtract the result from equation (8.4) to yield

$$X_t = \delta Y_t + \rho_1 Y_{t-1} + \rho_2 X_{t-1} + \eta_t \tag{8.37}$$

where $\rho_1 = \Pi_{21} - \delta\Pi_{11}, \rho_2 = \Pi_{22} - \delta\Pi_{12}$ and $\eta_t = u_{2t} - \delta u_{1t}$. Equations (8.3) and (8.37) are a 'causally' ordered system: the current value of X does not appear in equation (8.3), while the current value of Y does appear in (8.37) and the error terms are no longer correlated – $\text{cov}(u_{1t}\eta_t) = 0$.[73]

The new system (equations (8.3) and (8.37)) is simply an alternative way of representing the data of the old system (equations (8.3) and (8.4)). Since each is a transformation of the other, they fit the data equally well, i.e. they are observationally equivalent. Of course the 'causal' ordering is arbitrary: X could have been ordered 'causally' prior to Y, and then a system with equation (8.4) and a new equation for Y with current X as a dependent variable would replace the original reduced forms.

2 **Block recursive orderings.** In recent work, Sims suggests that Wold-causal chains may be too restrictive a way to display the relationships between variables in a vector autoregression.[74] When there are more than two variables and equations, the alternative is to order groups or blocks of equations 'causally', while allowing simultaneity among the equations within each group. Such simultaneity shows up either as the inclusion of the current value of each variable or as the correlation between the contemporaneous error terms of each equation in the group.[75]

Display of Quantitative Relationships

1 **Impulse response analysis.** The interrelationships between the data of 'causally' ordered vector autoregressions have usually been displayed in one of two ways. One method is to suppose that there is a shock of some standard size (say, one standard deviation) to the error term in one of the equations, holding everything else constant, and then to calculate the response of each variable over several periods into the future. The paths of these variables in response to this impulse can be displayed on a graph or numerically.

'Causal' ordering is of course important to the actual response. For example, suppose that Y is 'causally' ordered ahead of X as in our previous example and that the effects of a one-standard-deviation shock to u_{1t} in equation (8.3) were traced out. Y_t would rise by the amount of the shock; X_t (see equation (8.37)) would rise by δ times the shock, while the effects on Y_{t+1} and X_{t+1} and later values of these variables are easily calculated from (8.3) and (8.37) once the current effects are known. Suppose instead that the shock was not to u_{1t} but to η_t in (8.37). X_t would rise by the amount of the shock, but, since u_{1t} and η_t are not correlated and since X_t does not appear in (8.3), Y_t would not be affected. X_{t-1} does appear in (8.3), and so Y_{t+1} and later values of Y would be affected, and (8.3) and (8.37) can be used to calculate those effects. However, suppose that X had been 'causally' ordered ahead of Y. Then the appropriate system would be equation (8.4) and an analogue to (8.37) that had Y as the dependent variable and included current X among the independent variables. A shock to u_{2t}, the error of (8.4), would be immediately transmitted to both X and Y, while a shock to the error on the analogue to (8.37) would immediately affect only Y and would be transmitted to X only in subsequent periods.

2   Innovation accounting. A second method of displaying the interrelationships among the variables in a vector autoregression is closely related to impulse response analysis. It is possible to calculate what proportion of the variance of the forecast error of each variable is accounted for by each of the error (innovation) terms. In the system described by equations (8.3) and (8.37) the innovation u_{1t}, in the equation for Y, necessarily accounts for 100 per cent of the forecast error one step ahead because no currently dated variables appear on the left-hand side of (8.3). u_{1t} simply *is* the forecast error of (8.3). How much of the forecast error in (8.37) u_{1t} accounts for depends on the variance of η_t and on the coefficient δ. It is possible to compute for any number of periods ahead the proportions of the forecast error accounted for by innovations to each variable.

Once again, the particular 'causal' ordering is crucial. Had X been 'causally' ordered ahead of Y, so that equation (8.4) was part of the system, u_{2t} would necessarily account for 100 per cent of the forecast error in X one step ahead. There is no unique method of displaying the quantitative interrelationships of a vector autoregression.

All the many possible 'causal' orderings of the variables of a vector autoregression fit the data within any sample period equally well. This is exactly the observational equivalence which Sargent (1976b) discovered in the particular context of natural and non-natural rate models. The general point, however, was known long before.[76] Once one looks beyond the sample period, each 'causal' ordering displays a different pattern of responses of the variables to shocks. They cannot, therefore, all be correct. As in Sargent's analysis, the crucial question is: which set of parameters remains invariant? Suppose, for example, that equations (8.1) and (8.2) are the true model, so that the parameters θ, γ and the β_{ij} are invariant. The error terms u_{1t}, u_{2t} and η_t, are then complicated functions of these parameters and of the error terms e_{1t} and e_{2t} of equations (8.1) and (8.2). To perform the experiment of a one-standard-deviation shock to u_{1t} in the system represented by equations (8.3) and (8.37) thus requires that either e_{1t} or e_{2t} or some combination of the two be shocked. The ultimate effects on X and Y depend on which combination is chosen. It is not possible, in general, to shock u_{1t} while holding η_t constant as impulse analysis and innovation accounting assume, for both are functions of e_{1t} and e_{2t}. If equations (8.3) and (8.37) were invariant, then this experiment would be possible but it would imply that equations (8.1) and (8.2) were not invariant.

Vector autoregressions provide compact summaries of the properties of data within a given sample. Impulse analysis and innovation accounting may be methods of displaying this information effectively. In the absence of further justification, however, no particular 'causal' ordering can be singled out for policy analysis. Careful users of vector autoregressions have not claimed otherwise, but equivocations about their usefulness in policy analysis are fairly common.[77] The situation is similar and related to the equivocations that often surround the use of tests of Granger-causality. Just as it is tempting to conflate Granger-causality with controllability, it is tempting to impose an ordering on the data and then treat it as if it were the invariant ordering that actually generated the data.

Apriorism

Cooley and LeRoy (1985) stigmatize the programme of vector autoregressions as 'atheoretical macroeconometrics'. Its response to the Lucas critique is to argue that regime changes are rare, and that in their absence reduced-form estimation is sufficient for policy analysis. It asks: what can be learned from the data alone prior to any theorizing? The alternative approach – more common among new classical economists – starts from theory and asks: how must the data be arranged in order to confirm our *a priori* theoretical conjectures?

Apriorism, as we might call this alternative approach, treats the Lucas critique as a problem of econometric identification. Apriorism comes in two forms: strong and weak. Strong apriorism can be traced back to Koopmans's attack, in his paper, 'Measurement without Theory' (1947), on the atheoretical methods of Wesley Mitchell and his colleagues at the National Bureau of Economic Research. The strong apriorist view is that, in order to obtain estimates of structural parameters, identifying restrictions must be placed on the data.[78] Such restrictions are seen as untestable.

To take the most hackneyed example, if both the demand and supply for a crop depend only on price, it is not possible to distinguish the demand and supply curves in econometric estimates of the data. If one believes, however, that supply also depends on rainfall, the supply curve will shift with every change in rainfall and so trace out the demand curve. The demand curve is then identified *conditional* on rainfall affecting supply and not demand. We cannot use the demand curve estimated in this way to *test* that rainfall does not influence demand, for that would be to prove what we had already assumed, to beg the question. Of course, if supply but not demand also depended on temperature, we could test that demand conditional on being identified by the exclusion of rainfall did not depend on temperature. Tests of such redundant or *over-identifying* restrictions are often central to new classical econometric strategies.

The only possible basis for imposing untestable restrictions in the view of strong apriorists is that they are derived from a well-articulated economic theory. New classicals typically argue that econometric estimates will be secure from the Lucas critique only if the theories used to identify them are grounded in well-specified optimization problems, taking tastes and technology alone as given.[79] Rational expectations, which often generates a high degree of inter-dependence between variables in theoretical models, suggests that even economic theory may not be able to provide the restrictions needed to identify large-scale macroeconometric models.

An example of the application of this strategy is Sargent's (1978) paper, 'Estimation of Dynamic Labor Demand Schedules under Rational Expectations'. In this paper Sargent attempts to derive enough restrictions from economic theory to identify the parameters of dynamic labour demand schedules and enough additional ('over-identifying') restrictions to test the rational expectations hypothesis along the lines first suggested by Lucas (see section 8.2). His conclusions are interesting in the light of the attack on atheoretical macroeconometrics:

> ... optimizing, rational expectations models do not entirely eliminate the need for side assumptions not grounded in economic theory. Some arbitrary assumptions about the nature of the serial-correlation struc-ture of the disturbances and/or about strict econometric exogeneity are necessary in order to proceed with estimation.[80]

Sargent's conclusions suggest a softening of the strong apriorist hardline of many classical economists. It is a step towards what might be called 'weak apriorism'. The weak apriorist recognizes that belief and inference stand in a reciprocal relationship: inferences are founded partly on unexamined beliefs, but these inferences, in turn, may suggest the modification of those beliefs. Thus theory presents us with some *a priori* (in the sense of not *currently* questioned) restrictions on empirical investigations, while the empirical results help generate beliefs (or new theories) which are prior to further investigations. Haavelmo expresses the essentials of weak apriorism clearly:

> How can we actually distinguish between the 'original' system [i.e. the structural model] and a derived system [i.e. an observationally equivalent model] . . . ? That is not a problem of mathematical independence or the like; more generally, it is not a problem of pure logic, but a problem of actually *knowing something* about the real phenomena, and of making realistic assumptions about them. In trying to establish relations with a high degree of autonomy we take into consideration various *changes* in the economic structure which might upset our relations, we try to dig down to such relationships as actually might be expected to have a great degree of invariance with respect to certain changes in structure that are 'reasonable'.[81]

The objection to strong apriorism is not that it involves non-empirical principles (beliefs) – all empirical research does that. Rather, it is that it is committed so strongly to these beliefs that it does not permit them to adjust in the interplay of theorizing with the testing of theories. The strength of weak apriorism is precisely that it recognizes the need for such interplay.

The strong apriorist approach is probably wrong to stigmatize Sims and his followers as 'atheoretical'. Equivocations aside, they admit that models must be identified to be used in policy analysis. Where the two sides differ is over the nature of the identifying restrictions. Sims prefers to make broadly based restrictions (e.g. simply to divide variables into policy variables and behavioural variables) and to impose 'reasonable' 'causal' orderings. Strong apriorists prefer to derive detailed restrictions from optimization problems. As Sargent already noted, theory alone is usually inadequate to this task. Sims agrees:

> . . . a rational expectations equilibrium model . . . will almost invariably have a weaker, more heuristic connection to the data than a VAR model, so that all its implications are suspect from the start. It will rely on approximate assumptions about functional forms for tastes and technology in the economy . . . It will make assumptions about market structure and individual rationality which are sure to be incorrect to some degree. Since the limitations of such a model are different from the limitations of a VAR model, even though conceptually similar, it will often be useful to think about the consequences of policy changes in the

context of such rational expectations models as well as in the context of VAR models. There is a tradeoff between types of models for policy analysis, not a hierarchy of them.[82]

Like Sargent (1978), Sims's views seem to approach weak apriorism.

A Suggestion

The dispute between the advocates of the programme of vector autoregressions and the strong apriorists arises partly because both concentrate on data drawn from a single sample period or regime. But as Sims writes:

> ... data will obviously not determine directly the outcome of debate between various schools of thought; it does, however, influence the conflict by defining what battlefield positions must be.[83]

Whatever one's theoretical position, it must somehow rationalize the facts.

In seeking such a rationalization, the strong apriorist would like to estimate the fundamental ('deep') parameters of individuals' optimization problems from a single set of data and so needs theoretical identifying restrictions in order to guard against the Lucas critique. The advocates of vector autoregressions dismiss the practical relevance of regime changes and impose a 'causal' order on the data in order to make conditional forecasts. Both seem to ignore the insight implicit in Sargent (1976b) and applied in Neftci and Sargent (1978) that the test of having selected the correct identifying restrictions or hypothesized causal orderings is the stability of models based on such restrictions across regime changes.

A fruitful common approach would be to choose events that may represent regime changes (e.g. the imposition of wage and price controls, the adoption of monetary targeting, changes in central-bank operating procedures, adoption of new exchange rate regimes or oil price shocks) and to test models constructed according to theoretically derived identifying restrictions or models incorporating some particular 'causal' ordering for their stability across such possible regime changes.[84] If Sims is correct and true regime changes are rare, reduced-form models will have stable parameters, although some causal orderings may generate better conditional forecasts than others. But if Lucas, Sargent and others are correct that regime changes are of practical importance, then the fact that some models remain stable and others do not should yield useful information on the true causal ordering of variables and, equivalently, on the theoretical identifying restrictions which the data in fact support.[85]

Part V   The New Classical Methodology

9 Two Types of Monetarism?

Novelty is a mixed blessing: although theoretical originality wins wide approval, especially among the young, deep roots in established doctrine lend greater authority to any innovation. How novel is the new classical economics?

In chapter 1 we asked: what is *new* and what is *classical* about the new classical economics? The answer to what is classical was fairly straightforward: all markets clearing over some time horizon, so that aggregate supply is insensitive to aggregate demand, is the essence of classicism. What is new is much harder to judge. On the one hand, the new classical economics has been hailed as a revolution; on the other, it has been closely associated, sometimes by its advocates as well as its opponents, with the older doctrines of monetarism and the Austrian school. In this chapter and the next, we shall explore these associations. In each case, the central theme is that, while there are many superficial similarities and even some deeper harmonics, the new classical economics is clearly methodologically distinct from these older schools of thought.

The question of whether or not the new classicals are monetarists loomed large in early discussions of the new classical economics. James Tobin (1980, 1981) calls the new classicals 'monetarists mark II'. He bases the title on the similarity of the two schools' policy prescriptions. Frank Hahn (1980) agrees that they are monetarists, but bases the judgement on the similarity of their theoretical presuppositions. David Laidler (1981, 1982), however, finds that they are not monetarists, but rather more closely related to the Austrian school.[1] He rejects Hahn's classification as misleading, because it is precisely theoretical differences which, he believes, separate the new classicals from the monetarists.

In this chapter we shall not enter the debate over titles – 'monetarist' or 'not monetarist'. We shall try to *clarify* the relationship between some sorts of monetarism and the new classical school. To do this we shall compare Milton Friedman, indisputably a monetarist, with Robert Lucas, Thomas Sargent, Neil Wallace and others as representatives of the new classical school. The principal theme of this chapter is that, although we may wish to classify the new classicals as monetarists (for Tobin's or Hahn's reasons) or we may not (for Laidler's reasons), Friedman, as one important monetarist, differs from the new classicals on a fundamental point of methodology: he is a Marshallian, whereas they are Walrasians.

9.1 Friedmanian Roots, New Classical Conclusions

The new classical economics grew up as a response to the perceived failure of modern-day Keynesian macroeconomics, particularly as a result of the apparent breakdown of the Phillips curve – ever-higher inflation in times of historically high unemployment (see chapter 2). Friedman's work suggested that inflation was associated most closely with changes in the supply of money, that unemployment was a response to the real wage and that as soon as agents grasped that inflation erodes their real wage they would press for compensating rises in the money wage.[2] The Phillips curve trade-off between unemployment and the rate of increase of wages would thus prove to be a will-o'-the-wisp. These insights were the starting place for the new classical analysis, and the new classicals openly acknowledged their debt to Friedman.[3]

In contrast, until Friedman's publication (with Anna J. Schwartz) of *Monetary Trends in the United States and the United Kingdom* (1982), it was difficult to know how he regarded the new classicals.[4] It is clear from this work that he sees rational expectations as a potentially useful modelling technique, but stops short of embracing the new classical research programme. In the rest of this section we examine how the new classicals begin with Friedman's insights and reach similar conclusions, but offer a different analysis along the way.

Neutrality, the Natural Rate of Unemployment and the Phillips Curve

The old distinction between real and nominal quantities is the most fundamental element in Friedman's rehabilitation of the quantity theory of money.[5] We observed in chapter 1, section 1.3, that it was one of the defining characteristics of the new classical school as well.

This distinction enables Friedman to formulate a theory of inflation. The government in conjunction with the commercial banks determines the *nominal stock of money* The public in response to real factors such as (real) income or (real) interest rates determines the *real demand for money*. The price level adjusts to equate the nominal stock to the real demand. Given a stable real demand for money, a continuing rise in prices thus requires a continuing increase in the nominal stock of money. This view of the inflation process is captured in most new classical macromodels (see chapter 4, section 4.1).

Friedman's theory of the inflation process implies that money is neutral, but only in the longer run. Initially an increase in the stock of money swells real balances at existing prices. It is only when these are spent, stocks of goods run down and production temporarily increased that prices rise. Some new classicals go further: money is neutral in the shorter run as well. Rational expectations implies that agents understand the connection between money and the price level and that they correctly anticipate the systematic components of government monetary policy. Continuous optimization implies that they use this information to discriminate between nominal and real changes. Only real changes affect their real decisions. Actual shorter-run non-neutralities are the result of random shocks, say in government monetary policy, which could not be anticipated. Their effect disappears as soon as it is realized that they have occurred.

Both versions of the neutrality thesis are closely related to the notion of a natural rate of unemployment. Full employment in the sense used above is not an absolute technical limit. Rather, it is the equilibrium optimizing choice of economic agents. Recall Friedman's definition of the 'natural rate of unemployment' (chapter 2, section 2.1): '. . .the level that would be ground out by the Walrasian system of general equilibrium equations, provided there is embedded in them the actual structural characteristics of the labor and commodity markets . . .'. He also recognizes a natural real rate of interest and, presumably, a natural rate of output as well. This notion of a natural rate of unemployment accords well with the tenets of new classicism (chapter 1, section 1.3).[6]

The importance of the natural rate of unemployment and the neutrality of money is clearly seen in the expectations-augmented Phillips curve. Friedman argues that a sudden monetary expansion temporarily expands output and depresses the rate of unemployment below the natural rate. It also produces an acceleration in the rate of inflation. Prices rise faster than wages, so that the real wage is cut. Observing that the volume of employment is greater than they would wish at this real wage, workers endeavour to restore real wages to their old level, and the actual rate of unemployment rises towards the natural rate. Prices (i.e. wages) here respond to quantity (i.e. employment) signals.

The Phillips curve in this version cannot be exploited in the long run, for once workers anticipate any constant rate of inflation, they adjust their wage claims in line with it. Nevertheless, there is a real shorter-run trade-off between unemployment and inflation.

As with the neutrality of money, the new classicals deny even this shorter-run trade-off. They recast the Phillips curve as the 'Lucas short-run aggregate supply function'. Aggregate supply in this presentation is positively related to the deviation of actual from expected prices (or wages) as each producer (or worker) at first perceives (falsely) a general price (wage) rise as a favourable shift of relative prices.

The aggregate supply version of the Phillips curve reverses Friedman's adjustment mechanism: quantities (labour or output) respond to price signals. The shift in relative prices is only *apparent* and not *actual*. No appeal is made to wage stickiness. As with the new classicals' analysis of neutrality, agents are continuously in equilibrium given their information. Rational expectations guarantee that, except for random shocks, this information is correct. Hence an inverse relation of unemployment to inflation is observed, but it cannot be exploited deliberately and consistently, even in the shorter run, because it reflects the unsystematic or random component of the relation between changes in individual workers' wage levels (or producers' prices) and the general rate of inflation.

In later work, Friedman sometimes offers an aggregate supply explanation of the Phillips curve.[7] Nevertheless, he does not take over the full new classical position. He does not, as the new classicals do, rule out prices adjusting to quantities. Indeed, his adjustment functions for both prices and real income have actual and anticipated income as arguments.[8] Furthermore, in *Monetary Trends*, as in his presidential address to the American Economic Association (1968a), he still maintains that expectations of inflation are slow to develop.[9] The process has speed up over the past two decades, but it still takes years, not weeks or months, for expectations of inflation to adjust fully to actual changes.

Government Policies: Rules versus Discretion

Following Henry Simon, Friedman has long preferred rules over discretion or authorities in the conduct of monetary policy (and other policies as well, e.g. tax and expenditure policies).[10] His advocacy of fixed rules is based on the authorities' ignorance of the sources and timing of economic disturbances. Discretionary policies may or may not be perverse or adverse on average, but they do increase noise in the economic system, which interferes with prices acting as efficient signals.[11]

Lucas comes down squarely in Friedman's camp, acknowledging the same intellectual debt.[12] Furthermore, the signal extraction problem in the context of rational expectations has been developed with great theoretical nicety by the new classical school (see chapter 2, section 2.2). Sargent and Wallace declare somewhat tendentiously: 'there is no longer any serious debate about whether monetary policy should be conducted according to rules or discretion.'[13]

Friedman has advocated a particular rule for monetary policy: namely, that money should be allowed to grow at a constant X per cent per year, where X is determined to equal the secular rate of GNP growth after allowing for secular changes in the velocity of circulation of the money stock. Authorities should not use money in an attempt to offset cyclical movements in economic activity. This rule is related to Friedman's belief that expectations of inflation are slow to develop. He believes that holding the growth of the money stock to a constant X per cent rate will result in a steady rate of inflation (zero if X is low enough) over the longer run. Once agents have adjusted to this steady rate, no important and unpleasant surprises await them as long as the rule continues to be followed.

Friedman's X per cent rule receives weak support from the new classical school. Their argument is derived from their belief that monetary policy cannot *systematically* trade off inflation for output or employment (see chapter 2, section 2.2, and chapter 4, section 4.1). At a formal level any determinate (i.e. non random) rule will have no real effects, because agents with rational expectations will understand the rule and not be fooled by changes in the money stock into moving away from the natural rate of unemployment or output. Random policies may have real effects since agents cannot anticipate them, but of course they cannot be systematically pursued and hence are hardly policies at all.

It is, then, the determinateness or non-randomness of Friedman's rule that the new classicals support, and not its particular simple form. Yet the new classical argument is that agents act *as if* they know the structure of the economy. Of course, they must infer most features, including money supply rules, from past experience. Simple rules may be easier to infer and therefore may be preferred.[14]

A Paradox: Empirical Agreement, Theoretical Difference

Friedman argues that what separates monetarists from Keynesians are differences of empirical judgment and not of theoretical principle.[15]

His relation to the new classicals appears to be just the reverse: their empirical judgements are broadly similar, while their theoretical paths to those judgements are, at times, strikingly different.

There are, of course, important theoretical similarities, e.g. the supposition of a natural rate of unemployment. But it is the similarity of their policy prescriptions which leads many to classify the new classicals as 'monetarist', and it is the radical nature of those prescriptions which leads observers such as Tobin to distinguish them from older monetarists by labels like 'mark II'.

It is commonly believed that the rational expectations hypothesis is the source of new classical radicalism. But this is only partly true. The examples in the two preceding sections show that the characteristic new classical conclusions require both the other tenets of their doctrine – only real quantities matter for real decisions and continuous optimization.

Indeed, Friedman and Schwartz take the rational expectations hypothesis to be equivalent to the proposition that agents make no consistent mistakes about real variables *in the long run*.[16] Later they write:

> The formalization in the theory of rational expectations of the ancient idea that economic actors use available information intelligently in judging future possibilities is an important and valuable development. But it is not the open sesame to unraveling the riddle of dynamic change that some of its more enthusiastic proponents make it out to be.[17]

This quotation gets to the nub of the matter. The new classicals wish to analyse economic dynamics using the rational expectations hypothesis. To do this they must collapse the long run into the short run, appealing to the other tenets of the new classical doctrine. Friedman wishes to analyse economic dynamics by retaining the Marshallian distinction between the market, short periods and long periods. We shall examine this difference in approach more closely in section 9.3. Before that, however, we must examine the even more fundamental distinction between Friedman's Marshallian incrementalism and the new classicals' Walrasian globalism.

9.2 Walrasian and Marshallian Economics

The Cournot Problem

Friedman's most famous and controversial contribution to economic methodology is his essay, 'The Methodology of Positive Economics' (1953). Also well known, if less frequently discussed, is the earlier essay 'The Marshallian Demand Curve' (1949). Here Friedman introduces the key distinction that separates him, as it turns out, from the new classicals. Friedman argues that the common view that Marshall deals with partial equilibrium while Walras deals with general equilibrium is false. Rather, both deal with general equilibrium. Partial equilibrium must be conceived of as just a special case of general equilibrium. Marshall, too, is an advocate of the view that in economics everything depends on everything else.

In place of this common and, he says, erroneous distinction between Marshall and Walras, Friedman proposes another. He argues that Marshall and Walras conceive of economic theory differently. To Marshall it is but 'an engine for the discovery of concrete truth' as well as 'substantive hypotheses, based on factual evidence about the "manner of the action of causes" '.[18] Counting equations and unknowns and so forth is useful only as a check on the consistency of reasoning.

In contrast with Marshall's view of economic theory, Friedman argues that Walras and the Walrasians see theory as a comprehensive formal structure to be judged on the one hand by its abstractness, generality and mathematical elegance, and on the other hand by the accuracy of its assumptions as a photographic description and not by the correctness of its predictions.[19]

A Walrasian theory cannot be used as a tool because its comprehensiveness prevents one from focusing on a manageable bit of reality, ignoring or summarizing those parts whose influence on the problem at hand is small. For example, the Walrasian observes that the demand for a good depends upon the price of every good. The Marshallian replies that for practical purposes the prices of all but a few related goods can be summarized in the general price level. Similarly, the Walrasian abolishes the useful notion of an industry, because the products of each firm, no matter how alike, are not identical.

Friedman (1955) makes his distinction clearer in a review of the English translation of Walras's *Elements of Pure Economics*. He observes that the problem of economic interdependence has been neatly summarized by Augustin Cournot:

> So far we have studied how, for each commodity by itself the law of demand in connection with the conditions of production of that commodity, determines the price of it and regulates the income of its producers. We considered as given and invariable the prices of other commodities and the incomes of other producers; but in reality the economic system is a whole of which all the parts are connected and react on each other. An increase in the income of the producers of commodity A will affect the demand for commodities B, C, etc., and the incomes of their producers, and, by its reaction, will involve a change in the demand for commodity A. It seems, therefore, as if, for a complete

and rigorous solution of the problems relative to some parts of the economic system, it were indispensable to take the entire system into consideration. But this would surpass the powers of mathematical analysis and of our practical methods of calculation, even if the values of all the constants could be assigned to them numerically.[20]

For Friedman, Cournot's problem is, given economic interdependence, how to cope with economic analysis using *practical* methods. Walras's achievement, however, is to solve the different problem of showing, as Cournot does not, what the rigorous solution to the problem of economic interdependence would look like *in principle*. 'His problem is the problem of form, not of [empirical] content: of displaying an idealized picture of the economic system, not of constructing an engine for analyzing concrete problems'.[21]

Marshall's method is a response to Cournot's problem. It attempts to keep an investigation manageable by examining one problem at a time. It can be illustrated by specific examples of Friedman's work. Friedman generally employs single-equation methods in his empirical work. Hence, although he claims as his theoretical framework a multi-equation macromodel that includes a money supply equation as well as a money demand equation, in his empirical work he estimates only money demand, making the practical judgement that the money supply is too unstable to model and can be treated as exogenous.[22] Similarly, he holds that the whole range of implicit returns on assets might affect money demand or consumption, but in his applied work these are reduced to portmanteau variables or ignored altogether.[23] Likewise, he estimates expectations or permanent values of variables by distributed lags on their own actual past values, even though they may in principle depend in part on the present and expected future values of the dependent variables of the equations in which they appear as independent variables.[24] It is not that Friedman *must* use this method in every particular case. It is just that only a practical advantage of another method, say rational expectations, in generating successful predictions would obligate him to abandon it.

Positive Economics

In drawing the distinction between the Marshallian and Walrasian approaches, Friedman makes much of his belief, developed at length in 'The Methodology of Positive Economics', that success at predictions is the sole criterion for judging theories. Predictive success is the standard of efficacy by which the engines of economic analysis are to be evaluated.

The question of the appropriate standard of efficacy is, nevertheless, separable from the Marshallian response to the Cournot problem.

Even if there were – contrary to Friedman's view – another standard of efficacy for the empirical policy problems that interest him, it would not affect his analysis of the Cournot problem. For the point of the Cournot problem and Marshall's (and Friedman's) solution to it is that, whatever the economic problem, any practically significant analysis of it requires that reality be partitioned. The most important bits with respect to the problem at hand are analysed in detail; the rest are summarized in less detail (but not forgotten of course).

A Marshallian approach does, however, rule out one sort of criticism of theories. It is pointless to attack a theory as 'unrealistic' or 'incomplete' solely on the grounds that it partitions reality: all useful theories must do so.

The question naturally arises about how this defence of 'unrealism' relates to Friedman's (1953) famous claim – the so-called F-twist – that the less realistic a theory is, the more useful it is. There is considerable debate about what Friedman means by 'unrealism', and it is not to our purpose to try to decide the matter here. It is enough to note that if 'unrealism' means nothing more than partitioned, then Friedman's advocacy of unrealistic theories follows naturally from his Marshallian method. Of course, the Marshallian method requires an *appropriate* degree of partition, not necessarily the greatest possible degree. So if this is what Friedman means by 'unrealism', the F-twist may be an exaggerated claim. If 'unrealism' means something more than partitioned, then Friedman's claim must be supported on other grounds. A supporter of the Marshallian method might then reject the F-twist.[25]

The New Classical Economics' Walrasian Solution

The desirability of predictive success is not at issue between Friedman and the new classicals. Again and again they praise predictive success as a standard of efficacy.[26] Oddly enough, the importance of practical tractability implicit in the Marshallian approach is in some respects also not at issue. Lucas's preference for quantities adjusting to prices over prices adjusting to quantities is based on the fact that the theory of the former is better developed and easier to handle than the theory of the latter.[27] Lucas accepts that theoretical techniques develop over time and, consequently, that it is misguided to criticize our forerunners for not developing theories which would have been intractable, given the techniques then available.[28]

On the surface, then, Friedman and the new classicals agree about the desirability of predictive success and analytical tractability. Friedman, however, anticipated his essentially false concord. 'Most modern theorists would accept [the Marshallian view] of the objectives of economic theory. But our work belies our professions.'[29]

Friedman is, in his own view, primarily an empirical economist who uses a few deeply held principles to sift through facts in search of predictions. The 'new classicals' recognize the challenge of the facts, but see the problem more as one of consistently reconciling the facts with their world view.

The new classicals are Walrasians in two senses. First, they advocate general equilibrium analysis.[30] Friedman admires the Walrasian system for '. . . its beauty, its grandeur, its architectonic structure . . . ', but he does not expect to obtain useful predictions from it.[31] The new classicals do. Lucas (1977) argues that, given business cycles in the data, the theorist's challenge is to reconcile them with general equilibrium theories.

The second sense in which the new classicals are Walrasian is obviously related to the first: partition is a legitimate ground on which to criticize an applied theory. Sargent and Wallace (1975) strongly criticize their own and Keynesian macromodels for the lack of consistent assumptions about firms and individuals' objective functions. Friedman, while believing in rational optimizing man to a first approximation, could not sustain that sort of objection if the model yielded accurate predictions, whatever its theoretical assumptions.[32]

An explicit insistence on a general equilibrium foundation is the basis for the famous 'Lucas critique' of macroeconometric models (see chapter 8, section 8.3). Expectations terms cannot be observed, and so in most econometric models they are replaced by some function of the observable terms upon which expectations are formed. The rational expectations hypothesis implies that the structure of the model itself is part of the information upon which expectations are formed. If some part of the structure changes, say the money supply rule, then the proxy function for, say, the price expectations terms will itself change, even if the underlying behavioural relations remain fixed. A model based on the old function will no longer forecast well.

The new classical alternative to conventional (i.e. structurally non-invariant) econometric models is to posit the model with its expectational terms in place. These are then solved using the rational expectations hypothesis in such a way that the interrelationships between the coefficients of different equations become explicit. Now when a policy rule changes, the appropriate changes to the expectations function and therefore to the solutions of the full model are automatic. So far, this has been done only for relatively simple models.

To see that the Lucas critique result follows from the insistence on general interdependence and not from the rational expectations hypothesis itself, consider Friedman's (1957) permanent-income hypothesis. Permanent income is the flow of income from wealth defined as the subjective expectation of the discounted stream of the agent's future income. In order to apply the permanent-income hypothesis, Friedman supposes that the subjective expectation equals what in fact *actually* happens on average. This is a simple form of rational expectations. Permanent income can thus be represented as an optimal forecast. Friedman represents it by a geometrically declining lag on past income, which has since been shown by Muth (1961) to be statistically optimal under some circumstances. One of the circumstances is that there are no policy changes. If there are policy changes – say, a change in taxation affecting income – then the predictions are no longer optimal. Thus Friedman implicitly uses the rational expectations hypothesis, but still falls victim to the Lucas critique in failing to account for interdependence with the policy rule.[33]

Friedman concedes the principle of the Lucas critique, that a function of past values of a variable *may* not be a stable proxy for its expected value.[34] Nevertheless, his Marshallian method does not force him to take account of it unless it proves to be a *practical* barrier to accurate prediction in a specific case. Even then his preferred method is to work backwards incrementally to the minimum necessary level of complication, rather than to impose a fully interdependent structure on the problem, as Lucas suggests.[35]

In addition to such explicit applications of the Walrasian method, it is applied implicitly in other cases: partition is taken as a sufficient ground for criticism. For example, the rational expectations models of Fischer (1977) and Phelps and Taylor (1977) are criticized because they impose unexplained wage or price rigidities.[36] It is only if these rigidities (e.g. long-term labour contracts) can be deduced from first principles – say, from a general equilibrium system with contingent contracts – that the models can be accepted, even if they fit the data. Only then can their predictive success rest on more than the accidental constancy of a theoretically variable bit of reality.

The Tenets of New Classicism Re-examined

In chapter 1, section 1.3, we suggested that three tenets characterize the new classical doctrine: namely, that agents attend to real factors only in making real economic decisions, that they are consistent and successful optimizers and that they hold rational expectations. So far, we have argued in this chapter that the most important distinction between Friedman's doctrine and that of the new classicals is that, in Friedman's own usage, they are Walrasians while he is a Marshallian. Now let us consider how this fundamental distinction relates to the tenets of new classicism.

The first tenet, that only real factors matter for real economic decisions, is not fundamentally at issue, at least for longer time horizons. It is the basis for the general agreement between Friedman and many new classicals about the neutrality of money, the natural rate of unemployment and the Phillips curve. The differences that remain between them on these matters should be ascribed to the second tenet.

The proposition that economic agents are consistent and successful optimizers is in some sense agreed by all those – including Friedman and many new classicals – imbued with the so-called Chicago tradition in economics.[37] Precisely in what sense to take the proposition is the fundamental point at issue between them. Friedman takes consistent optimization as an article of faith. Because of the Cournot problem, he cannot detail every aspect of agents' economic behaviour. Thus he applies the optimization proposition to a part of the problem, while retaining a faith that agents do optimize with respect to those parts not worked out in detail. For example, in his analysis of the Phillips curve, he sets out agents' longer-run behaviour in order to show that, if they are optimizers, any trade-off between inflation and unemployment will not endure. He does not analyse their shorter-run behaviour in detail: he uses the Marshallian method to partition the problem. Nevertheless, he does not assert at any point that agents are not optimizing in the shorter run. If agents' shorter-run behaviour differs from their longer-run optimal behaviour, he supposes that they are still optimizing under unspecified constraints. The Marshallian method is in large measure the view that it is legitimate not to analyse those constraints explicitly when the longer-run behaviour is itself largely independent of the shorter run and when one is primarily interested in the longer run.

It might be argued that the contrast between Friedman's view that agents are optimizing under unspecified constraints and the new classical view that agents optimize to the limits of their information draws a distinction without a difference. This would, however, confuse the agent's point of view with the observer's (or economist's) point of view. Friedman argues that we can have faith that agents do their best, but that, as observers, we need not specify how they do it. The new classicals, however, require that the informational limits which constrain agents be specified precisely if the observer is to understand their behaviour at all.

Friedman is a pessimist about solving the Cournot problem. His Marshallian method is a way of pursuing economic analysis in the face of the problem, but it does not dissolve it. The new classicals, however, are optimists with respect to the Cournot problem. They believe that a Walrasian programme of fully specifying the optimization problem which agents face is a real possibility.[38] To return once more to the example of the Phillips curve, they argue that when it is cast as an optimization problem with the constraints on agents fully set out the possibility of an *exploitable* shorter-run trade-off vanishes.

The new classicals' conclusion about the Phillips curve hinges, as we observed in section 9.1, on the assumption of rational expectations. We can now see why this third tenet is a necessary, but subsidiary, element of the new classical doctrine. Expectations become important as soon as one turns to a dynamic problem. The Walrasian interpretation of the second tenet, i.e. consistent optimization, does not allow one to partition off the formation of expectations from the general optimization problem. If one is making systematic errors, one could do better. Walrasian optimization thus implies the absence of systematic error, i.e. it implies rational expectations.

Rational expectations has frequently been taken to be the most characteristic feature of the new classical doctrine. We can now see that this is a mistake. It is rather the Walrasian interpretation of the assumption that, to the limits of their information, agents are consistent and successful optimizers that is the distinctive feature of the new classicism. Rational expectations is but an implication of this assumption.

9.3 Equilibrium and Dynamics

We have already observed that the new classicals use the rational expectations hypothesis as a means of bringing optimization into the analysis of economic dynamics and that, in their hands, this has the effect of collapsing the distinction between the long run and the short run, which Friedman wishes to preserve. Now that we have examined the principal methodological difference between Friedman and the new classicals and have seen how it relates to the tenets of the new classicism, we are in a position to examine further the difference between Friedman's and the new classicals' analysis of economic dynamics. It will come as no surprise that the contrast of their treatments of dynamics illustrates in a concrete case the fundamental difference between the Marshallian and Walrasian methods.

Equilibrium Defined

Friedman writes: 'An equilibrium position is one that, if attained, will be maintained'.[39] This definition – drawn by analogy with the physical sciences – is consistent with the new classical view that an agent is in equilibrium when he is where he chooses to be, given what he knows.[40] Both Friedman and the new classicals agree on the formal correctness of these definitions. Friedman, however, finds them 'unilluminating and uninteresting' as they stand.[41] Similarly, Lucas and Sargent (1979) believe that data cannot reveal whether they come from an equilibrium process or not.

Friedman responds to the vacuousness of the formal definition by drawing the distinction between market, short-run and long-run equilibria.[42] This distinction is Marshallian both in that it derives directly from Alfred Marshall and in that it illustrates Friedman's method of coping with the Cournot problem discussed above.[43] Friedman grants in principle that agents are optimizing at all times and are therefore on some demand and supply curves which fully incorporate the constraints they face. This is practically useless, however, when the investigator cannot accurately specify all the constraints (i.e. he faces the Cournot problem). In this situation a practical approach is to partition the problem. One may, for instance, specify a *long-run* demand-for-money function. Then, with respect to that *particular* function, an agent may be in *short-run* disequilibrium. The essence of much of Friedman's work is that much may be known about the long run, yet little about the short run. For example, there is, he argues, a stable long-run relation between money and prices, and yet the lags are long and variable.[44]

Dynamic Equilibrium versus Long-run Equilibrium

We have seen that the rational expectations hypothesis is an implication of applying the Walrasian interpretation of the consistent optimization proposition, i.e. the second tenet of the new classical doctrine, to a dynamic problem. Agents are subject to error arising from their own ignorance of the future. But their ignorance can be characterized as risk in Frank Knight's (1937) sense. Over any length of time or over many independent agents the errors that result from risk take on a pattern that can be summed up in an objective probability distribution. One can insure against such errors.

The rational expectations hypothesis amounts to identifying the objective probability distribution of forecast errors with the agent's own subjective assessments. This rules out Knight's other category of ignorance – uncertainty or uninsurable error. Lucas accepts the risk–uncertainty dichotomy in order to restrict the scope of economic analysis to risk alone: 'In cases of uncertainty, economic reasoning will be of no value.'[45]

Friedman, however, rejects the risk–uncertainty dichotomy, adopting instead the 'personalist' (or Bayesian) interpretation of subjective probability associated with L. J. Savage and Bruno de Finetti.[46] This amounts to a rejection of the notion of risk, since probabilities are not taken to be objective but rather statements of a personal evaluation based on current knowledge. Such valuations change as knowledge accrues. In rejecting risk, Friedman implicitly defends the importance of uncertainty. He points out the difficulty of giving precise meaning to the identification of the subjective with the objective probability distribution and to the ambiguity of the time limit over which forecast errors are supposed to be uncorrelated.[47] In a counter-example, he distinguishes between *anticipations* of inflation during the 1890s owing to the rise of the free silver movement, reflected in high rates of interest, and the *realized* fall in the rate of inflation. Agents made persistent serially correlated errors in forecasting inflation, but whether their expectations coincided with the objective probability distribution is a moot point because a historical situation cannot be repeated in a controlled experiment in order to ascertain the objective frequency of its falling out one way or the other. Whether or not the United States would go on to free silver was a classic example of uncertainty. Observing their past forecast errors, agents might (rationally) not revise their current forecasts as long as they believed a move to free silver was a real possibility.

While Friedman does not accept the distinction between risk and uncertainty, it nonetheless suits his pessimism about solving Cournot's problem along Walrasian lines. It is a Marshallian distinction. It partitions the agent's ignorance into that which is quantifiable (risk) and that which is not (uncertainty). In the free silver illustration, Friedman also partitions time into the Marshallian short and long runs. Thus, he argues that if the time unit is long enough – say 20 years – forecast errors are uncorrelated, which we could characterize as risk. In the short run, however, uncertainty is relevant, at least in retrospect when we explain an episode like that of the 1890s historically.

The new classicals' view of uncertainty reflects their Walrasian optimism. If a model is sufficiently fully specified, uncertainty reflects a residual about which we can truly know nothing. Hence it is correct to hold that it cannot be usefully analysed. The new classicals' banishment of uncertainty from economic analysis is of a piece with their collapsing the long run into the short run. The actual dynamic path of the economy is a fully optimizing (i.e. equilibrium) path. Agents do not deviate from that path by more than a serially uncorrelated error.

The Problem of Business Cycles

The most pressing problem for the new classical economics is to give an explanation of business cycles, i.e. for the observed serial correlation and the co-movements of important economic aggregates, that does not invoke money illusion (violating the first tenet of new classical doctrine), disequilibrium (violating the second tenet) or serially correlated forecast errors on the part of agents (violating the third tenet). Lucas terms such an explanation as a *competitive equilibrium account*. He believes that it is '... the central problem of macroeconomics ... to find an analytical context in which [business cycles triggered by unanticipated monetary-fiscal shocks] can occur and which does not at the same time imply the existence of persistent, recurrent, unexploited profit opportunities.'[48]

We have already examined new classical models of business cycles in detail in chapter 3. Our purpose here is to show that business cycles pose an important and difficult problem for the new classicals because of their Walrasian method. As we have already observed, Friedman admires the Walrasian system on aesthetic grounds. Lucas, in contrast, denies that 'the attempt to discover a competitive equilibrium account of the business cycle ... [is] merely eccentric or, at best, an aesthetically motivated theoretical exercise.'[49] He believes that, because of the 'Lucas critique', it will not be possible to analyse the effects of counter-cyclical policies on the economy unless such an account can be given.

Lucas is clear that a competitive equilibrium account is Walrasian in the sense used in this paper. He quotes Friedrich von Hayek: 'By "equilibrium theory" we here primarily understand the modern theory of the general interdependence of all economic quantities, which has been most perfectly expressed by the Lausanne [i.e. Walrasian] School of theoretical economics.'[50] Furthermore, Lucas's insistence that there be no unexploited profit opportunities makes it clear that a competitive equilibrium account is one consistent with the Walrasian interpretation of the consistent optimization proposition, the second tenet of the new classical doctrine.

The chief difficulty in explaining business cycles is to show how it can be consistent with continuous competitive equilibrium for real quantities such as output to cycle fairly rapidly when real resources such as the labour force and the capital stock change rather slowly. In other words, why do rational agents not find it both desirable and feasible to eliminate such fluctuations from the system? The discussion of the Phillips curve and of policy ineffectiveness (section 9.1) suggest that only unexpected nominal shocks should matter at all. Even so, if real quantities can be altered at will, even unexpected nominal shocks should not have *persistent*, cyclical effects. This provides the key to Lucas's most explicit attempt to model the business cycle (Lucas, 1975).

Let us review Lucas's model, which is discussed in detail in chapter 3. He imagines, first, that agents have imperfect information, so that they make *unsystematic* mistakes in the face of monetary shocks, and, second, that they take decisions on the basis of those mistakes. Lucas's model is an elaboration of a neoclassical growth model in which, in a steady state with certainty, real quantities, the money stock and prices would grow at constant rates. In order to illustrate his explanation of business cycles, suppose that there is uncertainty and, in particular, that there is an unanticipated increase in the money supply which agents first perceive as increased demand. They expand output and, if they are ignorant of the shock's transient nature, increase their rate of investment in order to adjust the capital stock to the higher level of demand. By rational expectations, they soon learn of their mistake, but, since capital endures, they are stuck with a real change in their economic environment.

Even if there are no further shocks, a cycle has been generated. For now agents see that their capital stock is too high, and so they choose a lower rate of investment in order to reduce the capital stock optimally to its optimal level. Prices cycle as well: the initial effect of the increased supply of money is that prices rise faster than they otherwise would have. Once installed, however, the increased capacity resulting from the new investment retards the rate of increase of prices below the steady state rate until the optimal capital stock is restored. Other real quantities – employment, output and so forth – are connected by agents' plans to their decisions about the capital stock and investment cycles as well. Agents do not make persistent mistakes; their mistakes may nonetheless have persistent consequences, even when they act optimally.

Lucas is not happy with the details of the particular model just sketched.[51] He recognizes that a competitive equilibrium theory of the business cycle must solve the Cournot problem by adequately characterizing the constraints that agents face, and he is careful not to claim success too early. Nevertheless, as we have already observed, the new classicals are optimists about solving the Cournot problem: Lucas predicted in 1977 that an adequate equilibrium model may be '. . . five but not twenty-five years off.'[52]

Friedman does not believe that Cournot's problem will be so easily solved. In the meantime, the Marshallian method and its accompanying distinction between the long run and the short run are needed for practical purposes. Lucas writes: 'The idea that an economic system in equilibrium is in any sense "at rest" is simply an anachronism.'[53] Friedman's approach to economic dynamics requires no such assumption. He needs merely to maintain that our ignorance of the fine details of economic processes is such that we know more about the secular than the cyclical behaviour of the economy. It is, then, more useful to detail the secular in our description of the Marshallian long-run equilibrium, which may well be moving, and to summarize cyclical behaviour as a short-run adjustment towards this equilibrium.[54]

Indeed, Friedman's method of treating the business cycle has not altered much in the last 20 years. In the earlier empirical examination of the role of money in business cycles (Friedman and Schwartz 1963b), as well as in the theoretical sections of *Monetary Trends* (1982), Friedman imagines the economy in long-run equilibrium (an 'Elysian state of moving equilibrium') before and after a monetary shock. He then deduces general properties of the economic dynamics that must obtain if the economy is to move from one long-run equilibrium to the other. The picture he paints of the mechanism by which monetary shocks are transmitted to cycles in real quantities remains impressionistic and does not extend to the full specification of the agents' economic environment that is required by the new classical standards of adequacy.

The difference between Friedman and the new classicals here as elsewhere is not over the nature of the economy: both agree that at root it is a complex interdependent system. Rather, it is that, in the face of the Cournot problem, Friedman believes that only the Marshallian method of partitioning problems produces *fruitful* results, while the new classicals believe that only the Walrasian method of fully specifying the optimization problem that agents face produces *secure* results.

10 An Austrian Revival?

Sir John Hicks recounts how in the early 1930s *Prices and Production* ([1931] 1935) by the Austrian economist Friedrich von Hayek was the main rival to Keynes's *Treatise on Money* ([1930] 1971) as an analysis of the business cycle.[1] For Hicks, as for many others, Hayek's theories seemed at the time to hold the edge. But for Hicks and most other observers Keynes's *General Theory* (1936) shone a blaze of light on the economic problem of the Great Depression and, at the same time, placed the Austrian theories of the cycle into total eclipse.

Keynes's *Treatise* was still a part of the classical discourse. His *General Theory*, however, proclaimed the need to replace classical price theory with a new aggregative analysis if the problems of business cycles and depressions were ever to be understood. Lucas sees the *General Theory* as a false trail:

> Keynesian 'macroeconomics' was . . . a surrender (under great duress) to [the] temptation . . . to relieve the discomfort induced by discrepancies between theory and facts by saying that the ill-understood facts are the province of some other, different kind of economic theory.[2]

The new classical economics is an attempt to regain the high road by applying microeconomic analysis to all economic problems. Lucas casually, but self-consciously, presents new classical doctrine as the natural development of pre-Keynesian economic thinking – particularly of Hayek's theory of business cycles.[3]

Other observers have agreed with Lucas's general claim of pre-Keynesian antecedents for new classicism and have argued particularly for the link with the Austrian business cycle theorists of the 1920s and 1930s – most prominently, Hayek, Ludwig von Mises and Ludwig M. Lachmann.[4] In this chapter we shall explore the relationship between these two schools – both to appreciate the surface plausibility of regarding the new classicals as heirs to the Austrians and to expose the fundamental differences in their views of the nature and methods of economics.

10.1 A Common Research Programme?

Who are the Austrians?

The principle of marginal utility entered the mainstream of economic analysis from three independent sources: the English economist, William Stanley Jevons, the French economist Leon Walras and the Austrian economist Carl Menger. Each can be associated with a school of economic thought. A direct line runs from Jevons to Alfred Marshall and the Cambridge economists such as Pigou, Robertson and Keynes. Walras was the central figure in the so-called 'Lausanne school'; Vilfredo Pareto was his distinguished successor. The first of these schools lives on in our textbook analyses of partial equilibrium, while the second is the foundation for general equilibrium analysis.

Although it has modern descendants, the Austrian school has been pushed out of the mainstream of modern economics. Menger's work was extended in the late nineteenth and early twentieth centuries by Friedrich von Wieser and Eugen von Böhm-Bawerk among others. It is the students of this second generation – Mises, Hayek and Lachmann – to whom we shall most closely attend in this chapter. The principal concern of the earlier Austrians had been what we would now call the foundations of microeconomics. This later generation, however, focused on the theory of money, business cycles and the methodological foundations of economics. Austrian monetary theory 'virtually begins and ends with' Mises' *Theory of Money and Credit* ([1912] 1981), while his *Human Action* ([1949] 1966) remains the classic statement of the Austrian methodology.[5] Hayek's theory of the business cycle was once pre-eminent even outside Austrian circles.

Although Austrian economics has never re-entered the mainstream of economic thought since its high tide in the 1930s, it has neither died nor completely faded from the consciousness of the profession. Hayek was awarded the Nobel Prize in Economics in 1974. The winner of the 1986 Nobel Prize, James Buchanan, while not an Austrian fundamentalist, can be classified at least as an Austrian 'fellow traveller'. A small coterie of economists preserve the fundamentals of Austrian methods and analysis.[6]

Against Macroeconomics

The first step in the development of Austrian economic theory was Menger's discovery of the principle of marginal utility. Following

Jevons's parallel discovery, English economists, who were already steeped in the tradition of utilitarianism, immediately thought of utility as something palpable and measurable, and so elaborated a theory of objective cardinal utility. In contrast, the Austrians from the start saw marginal utility as simply an expression of an individual's rankings of his available choices, and so developed a theory of subjective ordinal utility.

The objective interpretation suggested that interpersonal comparisons of utility were possible and that social gains and losses could be measured in some objective fashion. The Austrians reject such notions. On their subjective interpretation, the individual is the locus of all utility and the source of all value. Interpersonal comparisons of utility are ruled out from the start because utility is not seen as an entity but as an expression of individual choice. The Austrians believe that an advantage of their theory of value over earlier theories of value is that it does not require any reference to abstract or super-individual social entities, such as Marx's 'socially necessary labour time', in order to obtain a consistent explanation of prices.

The Austrian theory of value thus illustrates the two essential and closely related aspects of Austrian methodology: radical subjectivism and methodological individualism. The fundamental distinction for Austrian economics is between means and ends. Radical subjectivism implies that the ends or goals of individuals are beyond economic analysis. Economics is the science of the rational attainment of given ends.[7] Methodological individualism implies that no explanation of economic phenomena is satisfactory unless it is derived from an analysis of individual choices.[8]

The new classicals (and many other modern economists) could easily embrace both the Austrians' radical subjectivism and their methodological individualism stated in such a broad, unelaborated form. After all, the standard new classical response to the Lucas critique is to return to microfoundations, to derive aggregate economic relations from the constrained choices of individual economic agents taking only tastes and technology as given. Individuals are characterized by ordinal utility functions, and Pareto-efficiency, which involves no comparisons of utility between individuals, is the standard of welfare gain or loss.[9]

Neither the Austrian nor the new classical analysis should be taken to deny the existence of social entities or aggregates. Mises, for instance, is explicit that the central problem of social science is to explain the apparent spontaneous regularity in society, e.g. the unplanned coordination of trading visible in the market-place every day and celebrated in Adam Smith's immortal coinage, 'the invisible hand'.[10] Individuals must take the organization and behaviour of such social ordering as given and, for the most part, beyond their direct manipulation. Social entities are real and subject to laws whose importance and logical status Mises compares to those of the laws of physics.[11]

Methodological individualism and subjectivism do not challenge the reality of social or aggregate entities; rather they insist that, since these entities are composed of individuals, the challenge is to provide an explanation of their characteristics which refers only to individuals and their subjective valuation.[12] While physical sciences are objective and analytical, working down from macrophenomena to their root causes, social sciences (not just economics) are subjective and compositive, building up an understanding of macrophenomena from prior knowledge of individual choice.[13] Social phenomena are complex and are not subject to controlled experimentation. Macrolaws in social sciences are not generalizations of empirically observed regularities but deductions from characteristics and general principles of rationality assignable *a priori* to individuals.[14]

Because of their subjectivism, the Austrians believe that social science has no choice but to attempt to *understand (verstehen)* the actions of individuals through a sort of imaginative leap – to see the world as they themselves see it.[15] Once again, Lucas seems to agree completely: 'real social science', he writes, is '[a]n attempt to model, to *understand* human behavior by visualizing the situation people find themselves in, the options they face and the pros and cons as they see them.'[16] Macroeconomics is illegitimate in Austrian eyes because it concentrates on the relationship of aggregates to each other, dispensing with reference to the individual actors and the meaning they assign to their actions which underlie the behaviour of the aggregates.[17] Similarly, Lucas states that the goal of the new classical school is to reincorporate aggregative problems into microeconomics. He concludes:

> If these developments succeed, the term 'macroeconomic' will simply disappear from use and the modifier 'micro' will become superfluous. We will simply speak, as did Smith, Ricardo, Marshall and Walras, of *economic* theory.[18]

Rationality, Expectations and Knowledge

Behind the new classical drive to reduce macroeconomics to microeconomics is the core notion that economics is the study of rational behaviour. Rationality is taken to be an axiom, and not a testable hypothesis or even a debatable methodological assumption. It is implicitly defined to be simply optimization of complete transitive preferences subject to the constraints on technology and non-produced resources.[19] This notion does not in itself distinguish new classical economists from many others. They are, nevertheless, more thoroughgoing in their application of the assumption of rationality. Rational expectations, for example, is often portrayed simply as the application of the rationality axiom to forward-looking behaviour.

Although their understanding of the relationship between rationality and expectations is different, the Austrians share a commitment to the axiom of rationality in economic analysis. 'Human action', according to Mises, 'is purposeful behaviour.'[20] Human action is also necessarily rational.[21] This is because Mises contrasts 'rational' behaviour not with 'irrational' behaviour but with 'reactive' behaviour.[22] Since action is purposeful, it must not be reactive. The term 'rational action' is therefore pleonastic and should be avoided.

Expectations must enter into Austrian analysis because human action is purposeful. It is impossible to analyse how people respond to conditions today (e.g. how their demand for a good responds to the current price) without some notion of their goals and of their beliefs about what conditions (e.g. future prices) will be like tomorrow. Agreement between the new classicals and the Austrians over expectations is more or less confined to recognition that they are a critical consideration in the economic analysis of forward-looking behaviour. It is possible to find scattered passages in which Austrians seem to anticipate rational expectations, but we shall see in section 10.2 that Austrian methodology is fundamentally at odds with this hypothesis.[23]

The new classicals faced a central problem with the introduction of rational expectations into macroeconomic models: rational expectations seemed to force the models too close to their equilibria to explain observed economic phenomena. The observed Phillips curve and business cycles appeared to be just the sort of *systematic* deviations from equilibrium that knowledgeable economic agents with rational expectations would eliminate. The solution offered to this conundrum (see chapter 2) was to make the realistic assumption that agents were not all equally knowledgeable; information was dispersed, and agents had to infer what they could not observe from what they could observe. Prices were seen as the carriers of information. But since current prices carried information on both relative prices and the general level of prices, neither of which were directly observable, agents faced the problem of separating these two components, i.e. they faced the signal-extraction problem.

These ideas have a remarkably Austrian flavour. The Austrians constantly stress the importance of prices as carriers of information. Mises and Hayek argue that, without market-determined prices, the whole problem of how to direct resources to secure given ends efficiently is insoluble. Complete central planning or socialism makes rational calculation infeasible.[24] The price system, on this view, acts as a computer which solves a planning problem that is impossible to centralize.

Prices obviate the need for any individual to have complete knowledge of every other individual's preferences and resources. Prices convey the most important information on the relative scarcities of goods and resources, but they do not convey complete information. For this reason, Hayek (1937) argues that economic analysis requires explicit assumptions about the dispersion of knowledge in society. 'Division of knowledge' surpasses 'division of labour' as the foundation of the economic organization of society. Persistent deviations from static equilibrium, according to Hayek, can be attributed to constantly changing information imperfectly conveyed between agents whose knowledge is different.

In some of its particulars the Austrian analysis of prices as carriers of knowledge is remarkably similar to new classical views. Mises maintains that with inflation of the stock of money, money prices cease to convey necessary information on relative prices.[25] This seems to anticipate Lucas's analysis of the Phillips curve: as inflation becomes large, economic agents attribute more of any observed price rise to inflation and less to relative prices; the elasticity of the Phillips curve is seen as purely a relative-price effect; therefore the Phillips curve becomes totally inelastic and prices no longer convey useful information (see chapter 2, section 2.2).

Lachmann anticipates the new classical analysis of signal extraction even more exactly:

> First, ... in a world of continuous changes prices are no longer in all circumstances a safe guide to action;
> Second, ... nevertheless even here price changes do transmit information, though now incomplete information;
> Third, ... such information therefore requires interpretation (the messages have to be 'decoded') in order to be transformed into knowledge, all such knowledge is bound to be imperfect knowledge.
> In a market economy success depends largely on the degree of refinement of one's instruments of interpretation. On the other hand, every act is a source of knowledge to others.[26]

Lachmann goes on to argue that in the formation of expectations we must in practice divide economic forces into major forces and minor or random forces and neglect the latter – essentially noise.[27] The problem is then, as it is in new classical business cycle models, to determine which price movements are meaningful, i.e. permanent, and which are merely noise, i.e. transitory.[28]

10.2   Open versus Closed Economics

The similarities between the Austrian and new classical research programmes are striking. This immediately raises the question of why the new classicals do not more frequently and explicitly appeal to the work of the Austrians of the 1930s and why there is so little communication between the new classicals and the Austrians of today.

A possible explanation of this puzzle consistent with Lucas's views of the development of economics is found in one obvious difference between Austrian and new classical work: Austrians write words; new classicals write mathematics and formal symbols.[29] Lucas views many of his predecessors – including Hayek in his theory of business cycles – as lacking the necessary technical facility to do modern economics. They are not to be faulted for this, as the techniques required were not available when they were writing. Still, it limits, in his view, the relevance of what they wrote for modern work. Modern Austrians have no such excuse. In continuing to eschew modern techniques, they allow misplaced piety to drain their work of any scientific relevance.[30]

The thesis of this section is that this view is wrong. While obviously not acquainted with the new classical school *per se*, the Austrians consciously rejected the essential elements of the new classical view not from technical or conceptual incapacity, but from a fundamentally different belief about the purpose and methods of economics. In many respects the Austrians carry the epistemological presuppositions of the new classical school out to their logical conclusion and so expose their hidden, and sometimes unpalatable, consequences.

The Scope of Economics: Prediction versus Understanding

In the last chapter we saw that the new classicals are Walrasian in the sense defined there. They are, of course, not committed to Walras's particular account but rather to the view that any acceptable explanation of economic phenomena must be based upon the completely specified interdependence of economic agents. While eschewing Friedman's Marshallian methods, they nevertheless agree with him that the goal of economic theory is to generate successful predictions.[31] As does Friedman, Lucas agrees with Marshall's characterization of economic theory as 'an engine for the discovery of truth'.[32] Where Friedman and the new classicals disagree is not over the role of theory in economic inquiry, but over the principles upon which the 'engine' is to be constructed.

Again, like Friedman, Lucas argues that lack of realistic assumptions is not in itself a telling criticism of an economic theory:

> Any model that is well enough articulated to give clear answers to the
> questions we put to it will necessarily be artificial, abstract, patently
> 'unreal'... At the same time not all well-articulated models will be
> equally useful.... The more dimensions on which the model mimics the
> answers actual economies give to simple questions, the more we trust its
> answers to harder questions. This is the sense in which more 'realism' in
> a model is clearly preferred to less.[33]

In this same vein, Lucas asserts that whether or not a model is true
in the sense that it is a valid nested case of a larger class of models is
simply not interesting: '... *any* effort in positive economics ... *at best*
– is a workable approximation that is useful in answering a limited set
of questions.'[34]

Unrealistic theoretical assumptions are unavoidable and often
useful in that they make models more tractable. Still, lack of realism is
not a virtue in every case. The new classicals are apriorists in the sense
that only equilibrium models which conform to the canons of
methodological individualism, as they understand it, are acceptable at
all. These principles are immune from empirical revision. The new
classicals are, nevertheless, willing to explore alternatives within this
acceptable class in order to obtain models which correspond better to
empirical observations. The ultimate standard of success for a theory
is, then, that it generates models which belong to the correct class and
accurately mimic reality. This is the standard that Lucas applies to
theories of the business cycle.[35]

The new classicals view economic science as essentially a predictive
enterprise. This conception helps to demarcate those phenomena
which economics is competent to explain from those which it is not.
Prediction must be grounded in empirically sound laws or rules.
Economics must therefore restrict itself to repetitive phenomena for
which general rules can be discovered. Empirical evidence, Lucas
maintains, shows that all business cycles are essentially alike. He
writes:

> To the theoretically inclined economists this conclusion should be
> attractive and challenging, for it suggests the possibility of a unified
> explanation of business cycles, grounded in the *general* laws governing
> market economies, rather than in political or institutional characteris-
> tics specific to particular countries or periods.[36]

Prediction also requires *determinate* rules which transform currently available information into predicted values. New classical
theoretical models with well-defined unique equilibria are one set of
determinate rules. Sargent and many other new classical economists
attempt to estimate such models empirically (see chapter 8). New
classical models often do not have unique equilibria – either because

of the many alternative assumptions one might make and still be consistent with essential new classical principles or because of intrinsic non-uniqueness, usually generated by rational expectations (see chapter 6, section 6.1). Long-run properties of models are often common to distinct models, independently of their differing theoretical assumptions, and unique, even when there exist multiple short-run dynamic paths. For this reason, Lucas tends to concentrate in his empirical work on evidence which can be reasonably interpreted as long run.[37] In either Sargent or Lucas's approach, the scope of economics is restricted to problems for which definite empirical predictions can be generated. New classical economics is *closed* or determinate.

The Austrians reject the view that economics is essentially a predictive enterprise. They do not dispute that there are economic laws, but they believe that the parallel which the new classicals implicitly (and Friedman explicitly) draw between economic laws and laws in the natural sciences, particularly physics, is false.[38] Economic laws are derived from the general laws of human action. As such they are based on the purposive conscious behaviour of individuals. They cannot be stated in the closed form necessary for prediction because any individual subject to a predictive law could not be regarded as making conscious choices; he would be reacting not acting.[39]

The new classicals use the rational expectations hypothesis as a means of closing the future and so of generating determinate solutions to models with expectations. This raises what Mises calls the paradoxes of omniscience. Rational expectations is a sort of practical omniscience: not everything is known, but the structure of what is unknown (its randomness) makes it effectively irrelevant to current decisions. Mises insists that such complete knowledge is incompatible with human action:

> If a man knew the future, he would not have to choose and would not act. He would be like an automaton, reacting to stimuli without any will of his own.[40]

Uncertainty about the future and human action are, for Mises, simply two aspects of the same thing. In order to work with rational expectations, Lucas places uncertainty outside the scope of economic inquiry. But for Mises, risk is a relatively simple calculation, a routine business decision; economics is about human action and therefore about uncertainty, which rules out rational expectations.[41]

The paradoxes of omniscience are well known to the new classicals.[42] Rational expectations strictly applied to the policy maker acting optimally as well as to the public means that there is effectively no policy to be made. In his recent lectures on business cycles, Lucas acknowledges these paradoxes. He notes that George Stigler observed that taking the view that the behaviour of the private sector is to be predicted, while the behaviour of the public sector is to be reformed, is 'deeply schizophrenic'. Despite this recognition, Lucas chooses to 'consistently tak[e] the schizophrenic, utopian point of view'.[43] As we saw in chapter 4, section 4.3, other new classicals (e.g. Barro and Sims) reach mental equilibrium through the consistent application of rational expectations to both the public and private sectors. Both are to be predicted: omniscience rules. The Austrians would equally wish to avoid Lucas's schizophrenia, but they take the position that neither the public nor the private sector can be predicted: human action rules.

To Mises, action and reason are simply two aspects of the same thing. The fundamental categories of reason, he believes, are given *a priori* and not discovered through experience. Some of these categories are the obvious principles of logic: A is not not-A, if A implies B and B implies C, then A implies C, and so forth. Significantly, Mises also believes that the distinction between means and ends is an *a priori* category. The essential principles of economics follow from this.[44] The concept of exchange precedes actual exchanges; the concept of money precedes the use of money. Without the category 'money', small round pieces of metal would have no significance for human action. It would be impossible even to experience an event as a monetary exchange.[45]

For many, Mises's apriorism is an extreme obscurely supported doctrine.[46] Mises believes that he states facts about the nature of the human mind: we cannot think unless we think in the categories of human action. As difficult as this doctrine is, it has important consequences for Austrian economics. The phenomena which a closed or predictive interpretation of economics rules as non-economic now fall within the scope of economic inquiry. Anything which can be viewed as human action is subject to economic analysis. Unlike the new classicals, the Austrians believe that economics applies with equal force to non-repetitive or unique events (i.e. to Knightian uncertainty), to disequilibria and to the mentally incompetent.[47]

The Austrians' general point is that, because the subject of economics is human action, the analogy from physics, in which the scientist stands to one side observing a process and learning to predict its outcome, is false. The only way to conduct economic analysis is to understand (*verstehen*) action as the actor sees it. New classical economists themselves sometimes seem to support such a view. The crucial difference is obvious, however, in the new classical practice of treating rationality as equivalent to the maximization of a utility function – more particularly, of a utility function with a particular content. New classical economists would not believe, for example, that a utility function with the level of prices as an argument was rational. Such a function would generate 'money illusion' and would be ruled out of their models.[48] Determinate predictions require such restrictions.

Nevertheless, Austrians would dispense with the maximization of utility as necessary for economic analysis, for this would imply that rationality depends upon actors possessing particular capacities (such as the ability to maximize) or particular tastes (such as a lack of preference over the *nominal* level of variables), which may or may not be true. Instead, rationality for the Austrians is the adaptation of means to ends and is always a characteristic of human action whatever the tastes or abilities of the actor.[49]

Economics in the Austrian view is, then, non-predictive or *open*. Economic principles are true *a priori* and cannot be contradicted by empirical evidence. Mises, for example, explicitly denies that empirical evidence purporting to show that people's preferences are intransitive shows anything of the sort. An experiment in which people are presented with a choice between A and B and choose A, then with a choice between B and C and choose B, and finally with a choice between A and C and choose C does not prove that preferences are intransitive, because the experiments are temporally separate. Tastes may change; constancy should not be confused with rationality.[50]

Economics is forward-looking, but should be viewed as calculation of how to obtain ends rather than as prediction.[51] For calculations or logical deductions to be useful, they must both be valid and start from true premises. The truth of the assumptions of an economic theory is therefore critical in Austrian eyes.[52] Contrary to Lucas (and Friedman), for the Austrians, a theory's lack of realism can only be a vice.

The Cournot Problem Once More

According to Lucas's exposition, the mistake in treating estimated econometric relations as invariant to shifts in policy regimes arises from attributing constancy to coefficients that are actually the complex outcomes of economic decisions. The new classical answer to the Lucas critique is to return to microeconomics, to attempt to model the economic decisions of individual agents in the context of a general equilibrium of all agents.

In the last chapter, we saw that Friedman rejects this Walrasian solution partly on the grounds that it is practically impossible to implement. It suffers from what we called there 'the Cournot problem'. The Austrians too are aware of the Cournot problem. Hayek cites the very passage from Cournot quoted in the last chapter, and quotes a similar one from Pareto.[53] But the Austrians reject Friedman's conclusion that the Cournot problem argues for applying Marshallian methods to empirical aggregate data. The lesson that they draw from Cournot and Pareto is instead that economic phenomena are irreducibly complex – no one can account for all the relevant factors. A move such as Friedman's is bound to fail because the necessary *ceteris paribus* assumptions do not hold and because controlled experiments are impossible.[54]

The Austrians agree with the new classicals that the aim is to see the individual as part of the whole system of economic relations.[55] Still, they do not conclude that a predictive, closed economics is feasible. The new classicals propose avoiding the Lucas critique by uncovering the bedrock of given tastes and technology. The analysis of human action convinces the Austrians that there is no such bedrock; there are no constants in economics.[56] The Lucas critique, therefore, applies not just to macroeconomic aggregate relations, but to determinate relations at any level. The best we can do is to apply economic reasoning to 'ideal types' rather than to actual individuals.[57] But this is a solution to the Lucas critique in principle only and is a complete capitulation to the Cournot problem. This capitulation is symptomatic of the Austrian's willingness to carry fundamental presuppositions to their logical conclusions.

In empirical practice the new classical response to the Cournot problem is simply to look the other way – treating aggregates and index numbers as if they should obey the principles of microeconomics. Their practical response to the Lucas critique is to use representative-agent models in which one or a few agents (defined by their utility functions) are taken to stand for all agents – ignoring the manifest heterogeneity of economic agents. This is necessary if they are to apply their sophisticated techniques and produce a predictive economics.

In principle, methodological individualism should rule out the use of aggregates or averages in economic explanations for both the Austrians and the new classicals.[58] In practice, most data (even much supposedly microeconomic data) are aggregates or averages. The Austrians object to the use of aggregates on at least three grounds.

First, they imply a commitment to holism which is incompatible with methodological individualism. Wholes are real, but are composed of individuals. Only explanations based on the behaviour of the constituents of an aggregate and the principles upon which they are organized are satisfactory. Explanations based on aggregates falsely suggest that aggregates have a life of their own.[59]

Second, they hide the real action in the economy. Austrian explanations of business cycles (see section 10.3), for example, run in terms of changing relative prices and shifting distributions of income which remain hidden behind concepts such as aggregate income and the general level of prices.

Third, aggregate measures are literally meaningless. 'Nonsensical', 'childish' and 'mystic' are the words Mises uses for such concepts as national income or national wealth, even when measured in nominal or monetary terms. 'The businessman can convert his property into money, but a nation cannot.'[60] Similarly, Lachmann notes that neither capital stocks nor investment flows are measurable.[61] There are no appropriate units of measurement for dissimilar capital goods.

In reply to these objections the new classicals can only plead expediency. Lucas observes that everything we know about the theory of index numbers leads to the conclusion that there is no hope of perfectly aggregating the heterogeneous goods of the economy into the single good used in most new classical models. Yet, he says, experience shows that single-good new classical models will come fairly close to capturing the behaviour of an economy with heterogeneous goods.[62]

Lucas does not say on what measure the closeness of the model to the economy is to be judged. Nor does he cite what experience in particular convinces him that his belief is true. The Austrians understand the conditions needed for perfect aggregation. Mises gave a one-sentence statement of the composite-commodity theorem, usually ascribed to Hicks (1939), in 1912.[63] But the conclusion drawn is that perfect aggregation is impossible and that there are no measures which would justify Lucas's assumption that a model with a single homogeneous good approximates the economy fairly well. The experience that he refers to could not exist in Austrian eyes.

The fact that Austrians reject the use of aggregate data and index numbers raises the question: how are they to proceed with economic analysis in the face of the Cournot problem? The answer is that they analyse the behaviour not of actual individuals but of hypothetical constructs – *ideal types*.[64] The point is to use the method of understanding (*Verstehen*) to isolate important general features of the problem as economic actors see it, and then to apply the axioms of human action and the principles of economics to its solution.

New classicals seem to make an analogous move. Rather than attempt to model every individual, they typically model a single representative agent. A utility function is postulated for this agent, and the usual methods of microeconomics are used to obtain his optimal choices given the constraints he faces.

It is important to recognize that representative agents are very different from ideal types. The Austrians understand that the use of ideal types places a severe, although unavoidable, limit on the relevance of their conclusions. They provide answers in principle and not definite predictions about the actions of particular individuals or segments of the economy. In contrast, the new classicals use representative-agent models in order to derive supposedly theoretically sound restrictions on admissible empirical observations. They use these models for prediction, and not simply for understanding principles. Used this way, the representative agent is simply a backdoor illicit solution to the aggregation problem. The new classicals are critical of other macroeconomists who work with aggregates and without explicit optimization. But to posit a representative agent and then to use aggregates such as consumption in his utility function and national income in his budget constraint is not really to provide microfoundations for macroeconomics and thus to secure macroeconomics from problems such as the Lucas critique. Rather it is to apply the mathematics of microeconomics in a context in which their justification and relevance is tenuous at best.[65]

Praxeology and History

The Austrians divide the sciences of human action into history and praxeology.[66] Praxeology comprises the general principles of human action known *a priori*, while history is the application of praxeology to the interpretation of concrete events. Economics is a branch of praxeology, whereas empirical or descriptive economics and statistics are branches of history.

Praxeology is logically prior to history. Nothing learned from empirical economics (history) can compel us to reconsider the core principles of economics (praxeology). In order to interpret events as intelligible economic phenomena, one must relate them according to the general principles of economics, which must necessarily be presupposed. Experience, then, does not teach us the general rules guiding human action. It may none the less teach us the wise and judicious application of those principles to the particular interpretation of concrete events.

Economic phenomena are necessarily complex and are not subject to controlled experiment. The only way to render them intelligible, then, is to attempt to understand the situation as the individuals involved do and to apply the general principles of economics. Such attempts are not likely to yield unique interpretations. The very complexity of the events means that no interpretation can consider all factors. Some interpretations may perhaps be rejected as conflicting with economic (or praxeological) principles.[67] Other interpretations arise from disagreements over the non-praxeological assumptions to which these principles are to be applied.[68]

The Cournot problem and the intrinsic openness of human action, which the Austrians believe render economic prediction impossible, leave history open to alternative interpretations. Prediction is an attempt to write a history of the future before it occurs. Such an effort is bound to be futile when the history of the past is itself uncertain.

Although empirical evidence cannot overrule judgements of economic principle, it can nevertheless direct our attention to appropriate subjects for economic analysis and it can cause us to question the non-praxeological premises to which economic principles are applied in concrete cases.[69]

In keeping with the recognition that experience can suggest the reconsideration of the non-praxeological assumptions of a theory, Hayek draws a useful distinction between the empirical content of a theory and the pure logic of choice. If it is supposed that all relevant information is known, that preferences are given and that there is complete knowledge of available means, then the application of economic principles in order to discover the best means to one's ends is simply an exercise in logical deduction.[70]

The pure logic of choice is not useless. Hayek distinguishes between explanations of principle and predictive explanations. The Walrasian theory of general equilibrium, which demonstrates the consistency of an equilibrium of self-interested individuals, is an example of the pure logic of choice used as an explanation of principle.[71] Furthermore, Hayek believes that disequilibrium economic relations are inconstant and transitory. The pure logic of choice, which generates descriptions of economic equilibria, is the only available tool to provide insights into more permanent economic relations.[72]

Lachmann writes:

> ... the Pure Logic of Choice with its equations and its indifference curves is [not] altogether useless. On the contrary, it serves a most useful purpose by making economic activity *intelligible* to our problem-solving mind. For it is only by reducing the apparently chaotic World of Action to a mental pattern of relative simplicity that our problem-solving mind can comprehend it. All we have to remember is that to describe an action in terms of a problem is, of course, not to say that it will succeed in solving it.[73]

Hayek agrees with this analysis: the data needed to solve economic problems as pure deductions is not given to a single mind.[74] The empirical content of a theory is economic knowledge, while the pure logic of choice is merely tautology.[75] The manner in which information is dispersed in society is on this view the sort of thing which should count as economic knowledge. In contrast, the description of an economic equilibrium is tautology, while the hypothesis that the economy actually converges to such an equilibrium is the real content of the theory.[76]

For the Austrians, then, the attention which the new classicals and many other economists give to the elaboration of the pure logic of choice – to finding determinate solutions to models – is misplaced.

Lachmann puts the Austrian objection succinctly: 'Determinateness . . . is a possible property of problems; it is not a possible property of human action.'[77] Economics is an open praxeological discipline, not a closed predictive one.

The Illusion of Technique

For Lucas, the history of economic thought is the history of the development of technique. Our advantage over our forerunners in economics arises mostly from our greater technical capacity. He implies that had the techniques been available in the past, earlier economists would surely have used them.

> To ask why the monetary theorists of the 1940's did not make use of the contingent-claims view of equilibrium is . . . like asking why Hannibal did not use tanks against the Romans instead of elephants. There is no reason to view our ability to think as being any less limited by available technology than is our ability to act (if, indeed, this distinction can be defended). The historical reason for modeling price dynamics as responses to static excess demands goes no deeper than the observation that the theorists of that time did not know any other way to do it.[78]

Elsewhere Lucas identifies progress in economics with quantification and formalization of economic models.[79] He justifies his concern for the technical aspects of model building with the remark:

> Working out the predictions of the model is just a matter of technique . . . But technique is interesting to technicians (which is what we are, if we are to be of any use to anyone) . . . [80]

We are now in a position to see why the Austrians reject this emphasis on technique.

Austrians vary in their dislike of mathematics and statistics applied to economics. Mises takes perhaps the strongest stand:

> The mathematical method must be rejected not only on account of its barrenness. It is an entirely vicious method, starting from false assumptions and leading to fallacious inferences.[81]

Hayek argues that the use of mathematics often obscures the real problems.[82] Later he admits that mathematics is not incompatible with subjectivist economics and may even be indispensable in the description of complex social structures. He warns, however, against the attempt to quantify such mathematical models.[83] He reserves his greatest scepticism for statistical measurement as generating attention to irrelevant but measurable aspects of social reality and producing absolutely meaningless measures.[84]

The Austrians' dislike of mathematics and statistics in economics does not arise from lack of technical facility. Rather it reflects a well-articulated belief that such techniques are out of place in economics. To take one example, Lucas advocates business cycle models based on modifications of the Arrow–Debreu general equilibrium model with contingent claims. In this framework, he argues:

> Our task as I see it . . . is to write a FORTRAN program that will accept specific economic policy rules as 'input' and will generate as 'output' statistics describing the operating characteristics of time series we care about, which are predicted to result from these policies.[85]

The Austrians would certainly object to the closed formulation of this problem, to its assumption that prediction is possible in economics. Well before Lucas wrote these words, however, Lachmann expressed a more particular objection to the programme that Lucas endorses:

> . . . assuming all tastes to be 'given', whether in the form of utility functions or of indifference curves, is in fact evading the whole problem of how plans are made, a problem which is of crucial significance to subjectivism. The indifference curves which are imputed to consumers are in reality comprehensive lists of alternative plans to be put into operation if and when opportunity offers. In other words, what is really assumed here is that individuals never need make actual plans, because from the start they are equipped with such a large number of alternative plans that all contingencies are covered! The question of how these lists of alternative plans ever came into existence is then ruled out of order as falling outside the sphere of economic questions! . . . Consumers' preferences, separated from the mental acts which daily shape and modify them, are turned into independent variables of a system in which there is no scope for planning and plan revision. Spontaneous action has been transformed into a response stimulus.[86]

Lucas sometimes characterizes the formulation of economic policy as a problem of choosing paths for policy variables that are among the 'state variables' of a stochastic difference equation which accurately describes the evolution of the economy.[87] Lachmann is explicit in his rejection of this approach:

> But we shall not indulge in building 'dynamic' models based on 'behaviour functions' expressed in terms of 'difference equations'. Our reason for this refusal is that to assume that entrepreneurial conduct in revising plans at the end of successive periods is, in any objective sense, *determined* by past experience and thus *predictable*, would mean falling into a rigid determinism which is quite contrary to everyday experience.[88]

There is no reason to assume that Lachmann would find the slightly less rigid determinism of *stochastic* difference equations any more congenial.

Rational expectations is, for Lucas, just another manifestation of the increasing technical rigour of economics. The same level of technical sophistication that has long characterized static price theory is now applied to the dynamic and probabilistic aspects of economic theory.[89] Once again, however, Lachmann anticipated and contradicted this view. He asks: why should we assume that the correct interpretation of past events can be taken for granted? This of course is what the rational expectations hypothesis does assume up to a serially uncorrelated random error. Again, he sees the assumption that there are given behavioural or reaction functions as equivalent to the assumption that economic agents are incapable of interpreting unique historical experience, as equivalent to the abolition of human mind and treating people as if they were automata.[90] Specifically, he writes:

> A method of dynamic analysis which fails to allow for variable expectations due to subjective interpretation seems bound to degenerate into a series of economically irrelevant mathematical exercises.[91]

The rational expectations hypothesis has no doubt lived up to his expectations.

10.3   Business Cycles and Equilibrium

Both the superficial plausibility of the claim that the new classicals are successors to the Austrians and the deeper essential differences between the two schools can be illustrated by their treatment of business cycles. Austrian models of the cycle, which are no doubt unfamiliar to most readers, come in as many varieties as new classical models, although, as with new classical models, they share a common core with one another. In order to keep the analysis as concrete as possible, we shall compare Hayek's model developed in *Prices and Production* ([1931] 1935), which is perhaps the best articulated Austrian model of the cycle, with the new classical models already discussed in detail in chapter 3.

An Austrian Model of the Business Cycle

Hayek's theory of the business cycle is built on the twin pillars of Böhm-Bawerk's theory of capital and Wicksell's theory of the natural rate of interest. Consumption goods are produced with the aid of capital goods in processes which partly for technological reasons and partly for economic reasons take some definite period of time. The longer is the process needed to produce a given amount of consumer goods, the greater, in some ill-defined sense, is the stock of capital involved in the process and the more productive is the process itself.[92]

This greater productivity must be balanced against the additional time that the investor must wait in order to reap his profits with a longer production process. A rational capitalist would not tie up his resources in the form of capital goods unless he expected them to earn a competitive rate of return. Future returns must then be discounted by the current rate of interest. Böhm-Bawerk concludes that the lower that rate of interest is, i.e. the less the future is discounted, the longer are the production processes that a rational capitalist would adopt.[93]

Wicksell argued that for any economy there was a rate of interest that would keep the general level of prices constant. If market interest rates fell below that rate, borrowing from banks and therefore the stock of deposits would increase, so that prices would be bid up. If market rates rose above the natural rate, prices would fall.

Hayek rejects the notion of a general level of prices. He none the less reformulates Wicksell's idea. The natural rate, for Hayek, is that rate at which the desires of savers to save and of investors to invest exactly balance. If the market rate of interest falls below this natural rate, lending is increased; if it rises above the natural rate, lending is curtailed. From its definition, it is clear that when the market rate is below the natural rate, if the additional loans are spent on investment goods, desired savings must fall short of desired investment. To the extent that investment plans are successfully implemented, the economy must be forced to save more than its members desire. The process of 'forced savings' is possible only because banks create additional deposits (i.e. expand the supply of money) when they make loans without corresponding inflows of savings. This money is spent, bids up prices and reduces the real value of the rest of the public's nominal claims. Resources are transferred to investors, and the economy as a whole is, in this sense, forced to save more than savers had originally intended. In contrast with Wicksell's original theory, the prices that are bid up are not prices in general (or all prices proportionally) but the particular prices of goods upon which capitalists spend the newly borrowed money, which is where Böhm-Bawerk's theory of capital comes in.

Suppose that the central bank lowers the interest rate through open-market operations and discount policy. Banks now find it more desirable to lend and firms find it more desirable to borrow. In particular, since the lower rate of interest lengthens the desirable period of production for any specific consumer good, firms are encouraged to invest the newly available funds in earlier stages of production rather than in stages close to the final consumption good. It is the prices of the capital goods in these earlier stages which are bid up in the first instance. This price signal redirects resources away from consumption goods and later stages of production towards these earlier stages. Output of capital goods rises to meet the increased demand, and, since labour is a complementary factor of production, employment and wages also arise. This is the boom.

Of course the increase in wages increases the funds available for consumption. Coupled with a shortage of consumer and later-stage capital goods (because of the redirection of resources to earlier stages), the prices of these goods in turn rise. This encourages a reversal of the direction of resources back towards later stages of production. Generally expanded levels of investment place upward pressure on interest rates. Unless banks are able to expand credit indefinitely, rates rise. The desirable period of production becomes shorter, and, for this reason also, resources are shifted towards consumption and later stages of production. This is the beginning of the slump.

What makes the slump particularly painful is that some capital goods are highly specific to particular production processes. Thus, in the return to shorter periods of production, many of the capital goods used in longer production processes become completely useless. Since labour is complementary to capital, at least in the short run, workers become unemployed.[94]

Hayek insists that a satisfactory model of business cycles must be a monetary model.[95] This means that monetary factors must in his view be the ultimate causes of cyclical fluctuations. He does, however, recognize the importance of non-monetary factors as proximate causes of fluctuations, i.e. as a propagation mechanism. His position in this respect is quite similar to Lucas's.

Hayek discusses three proximate causes of fluctuations and rejects two of them.[96] The first is changes in the amounts of factors of production. This he rejects as a non-explanation, for the level of use of resources is not exogenous but itself requires an economic explanation. It is unlikely that Hayek would view exogenous shocks to technology, such as drive many new classical real business cycle models, with any more favour.

The second is changes in the willingness of people to work. This is the central element in models such as those of Lucas (1975) or Kydland and Prescott (1982) which rely on the intertemporal substitutability of leisure in order to generate cycles. Hayek argues that whether willingness to work fluctuates in a manner sufficient to generate cycles is not a matter of principle but of empirical fact, and that it is not justified by common experience. It is, he believes, a highly artificial explanation and should probably be adopted only as a last resort.[97]

The third and, as we have already seen, Hayek's favoured explanation of the propagation of fluctuations is the lengthening and shortening of the period of production (i.e. changes in the degree of capitalization). It is in some sense also part of new classical theories in which the capital stock deviates optimally from its trend, although the treatment of capital as homogeneous in those models prevents them from addressing issues such as the complementarity between capital and labour as a source of unemployment, upon which Austrians put great store.

As in new classical models, prices in Austrian models are flexible. Flexible prices, however, present a problem for business cycle theories. Hicks points out that if wages are flexible, then increased investment in Hayek's model, which supposedly shifts resources into longer production processes, would drive wages up immediately. This would generate greater demand and higher prices for consumption goods and would nip in the bud those shifts in relative prices which Hayek believes drive the cycle.[98]

Hicks seems to miss Hayek's references to ' . . . the notorious rigidity of wages . . .' and to long-term contracts.[99] Prices and wages for Hayek are flexible in that they respond over time to altered conditions. He does not agree with Keynes that they can somehow become more or less permanently out of line. They do not, however, respond instantaneously. The lags between prices and wages will finally disappear only when monetary disturbances cease.[100] Prices convey information efficiently, but not with the efficiency of a Walrasian auctioneer. Prices are therefore less flexible for Hayek than for new classical economists.

It is only their informational assumptions that prevent Hicks's objections from applying with full force to new classical models of the business cycle. The inability of producers to separate perfectly transitory fluctuations in relative prices from fluctuations in the general level of prices causes them to choose levels of the capital stock and output that turn out to be unsustainable. Although the initial effects are on interest rates rather than prices, misinformation leading to malinvestment drives Austrian models of the cycle as well.[101] Unlike the new classicals, the Austrians do not find the source of misinformation in randomness in the economy. Misinformation arises instead from the projection of current prices and interest rates into the future in which they turn out to be reversed.

Lachmann observes that the Austrian theory of the cycle requires that expectations of future prices be 'elastic', i.e. if prices rise today they are expected to remain higher or even to rise further tomorrow.[102] If prices were expected to return to their initial levels in fairly short order, firms would not be misled into making investments which could be profitable only at the new prices. Of course, rational expectations would have the same effect, preventing all but random misinformation from generating malinvestment.

In a reply to Lachmann, Mises notes that he and other earlier Austrians were under no illusion about the importance of elastic expectations, and he shows foresight about the effect of the assumption of rational expectations on the Austrian model:

> The economic consequences of credit expansion are due to the fact that it distorts one of the items of the speculator's and investor's calculation, namely, interest rates. He who does not see through this, falls victim to an illusion; his plans turn out wrong because they were based on falsified data. Nothing but a perfect familiarity with economic theory and a careful scrutiny of current monetary and credit phenomena can save a man from being deceived and lured into malinvestments.[103]

Knowledge of the relevant theory and complete information would eliminate business cycles, but the Austrians simply do not believe that economic agents possess this sort of knowledge.[104] Expectations are clearly critical to Austrian models of the business cycle, but they are just as clearly not rational expectations.

An Embarrassment of Detail?

There are similarities between the Austrian and new classical models of the business cycle. But two differences are far more striking. The first, as we have already seen, is the incompatibility of the Austrian model with the key new classical assumptions of rational expectations and perfectly clearing markets. The second is the richness in detail of the Austrian models, sharply contrasting with the sparse, even austere, structure of new classical models. New classical models assume that agents are essentially alike, while Austrian models treat each as unique. Most new classical models assume that capital is homogeneous, while Austrian models treat it as a heterogeneous collection of specific producers' goods. New classical models assume that the economy is always in equilibrium, while Austrian models treat equilibrium as a limiting case at best, permitting a wealth of alternative paths for the economy.

One explanation for the greater richness of Austrian models, which is consistent with Lucas's views, is that their apparent richness is the inverse of their lack of precision.[105] New classical models are simple and rely on representative agents in order to permit exact specification of utility functions and budget constraints, so as to obtain exact predictive solutions. As techniques improve, new classical models will more fully mimic the actual economy and will approach the apparent richness of Austrian models. At the same time, they will not surrender their closed form, which is the key to their predictive ability. By Lucas's standard, the Austrians did not even formulate models, but rather expressed unscientific (though perhaps largely correct) opinions or beliefs. On this view, the Austrians simply lacked the necessary techniques (including the concepts of rational expectations and dynamic equilibrium) to formulate precise models which could be manipulated to provide quantitative analysis of economic problems. They are not to be faulted for this as the techniques had not yet been developed, but their method was surely a cul-de-sac in the history of economic thought.

This view of the Austrians as the benighted forbears of modern (scientific) new classical economics is one which the Austrians would surely reject. What it misses is that Austrian capitulation to the Cournot problem is fundamental and complete. Austrians do not believe that it is possible *in principle* to develop exact closed models of a complex economy composed of rational (i.e. freely choosing) agents. The concepts of rational expectations and the related new classical analysis of economic equilibrium are incompatible with what Austrians believe to be the essential foundations of economics.

Concepts of Equilibrium

While Lucas does not explicitly mention the differences between the two schools' analyses of business cycles in his brief references to the Austrians, it would be surprising if he were not aware of them. His judgement of a fundamental harmony between them must, then, rest on the belief that the differences are superficial and attributable to the unavailability of the requisite concepts or techniques to these earlier theorists.

For Lucas, the problem of business cycles is '[w]hy is it that, in capitalist economies, aggregate variables undergo repeated fluctuations about trend, all of essentially the same character?'[106] Lucas then cites Hayek as a leading example of the view of interwar theorists on how this problem is to be solved:

> The incorporation of cyclical phenomena into the system of economic equilibrium theory, with which they are in apparent contradiction, remains the crucial problem of Trade Cycle Theory.[107]

Equilibrium theory for Hayek is best represented in the Walrasian school's analysis of the general interdependence of economic quantities.[108] Lucas sees new classical theory as a movement away from Keynesian analysis and as a technically superior but natural extension of the interwar views represented by Hayek. It is clear from his description of his own work and the work of other new classical economics that Lucas sees the equilibrium nature of new classical business cycle models as most important and as closely linked to the Austrian analysis.[109]

It is, however, unlikely that any interwar business cycle theorist thought of business cycles as equilibrium phenomena; it is certain that Hayek and the other Austrians did not. The passages that Lucas cites from Hayek's *Monetary Theory and the Trade Cycle* are actually all aimed at showing the inadequacy of equilibrium theory as a basis for the explanation of business cycles. 'We cannot', Hayek writes, 'superimpose upon the system of fundamental propositions comprised in the theory of equilibrium, a Trade Cycle theory resting on unrelated logical foundations.'[110] Trade cycles, he continues,

> ... can be explained only by widening the assumptions on which our deductions are ... based, so that cyclical fluctuations would follow from these as a necessary consequence, just as the general propositions of the theory of price followed from the narrower assumptions of equilibrium theory.[111]

The wider assumption that Hayek argues for is the incorporation of money into the theory of the trade cycle. The importance of money is not in its effect on the general level of prices, which Hayek rejects as a deeply misleading abstraction, but precisely in the fact that it subverts equilibrium relations. Unlike the case of pure barter, when money exists, equilibrium relations may break down; supply need not equal demand; money absorbs the slack. It is only this loosening of the tight links of static equilibrium theory that makes a trade cycle possible at all.[112]

Lucas is always at pains to point out that treating equilibrium as a state of rest is now an avoidable mistake.[113] It might then be tempting to ascribe Hayek's view simply to his lack of the appropriate technical tools – particularly to the lack of a notion of dynamic equilibrium. But this would read too much into the word 'static'. The notion of an intertemporal or moving equilibrium was already an important part of Hayek's theoretical apparatus in the 1920s.[114]

The Austrian and new classical definitions of equilibrium appear on the surface to be similar. 'Equilibrium' for Hayek is the

> ... proposition that, given the particular constellation of ... circumstances that exist, there is only one particular mode of behaviour by an economic subject that corresponds to his interests, and he will continue to change his decisions until he has achieved the most advantageous uses of the resources available to him.[115]

Later he writes

> For a society ... a *state* of equilibrium ... means ... that the different plans which the individuals composing it have made for action in time are mutually compatible.[116]

Similarly, for Lucas equilibrium obtains when

... each agent is doing the best he can in light of the actions taken by others, and ... these actions taken together are technologically feasible.[117]

Despite these superficial similarities, because the new classicals insist on closed predictive models while the Austrians insist on open models aimed at understanding (*verstehen*) the economy, their concepts of equilibrium are fundamentally different.

Rational expectations is essential to the new classical concept of equilibrium. For the Austrians, however, this raises a problem related to the paradoxes of omniscience discussed in section 10.2: who holds the model – the economist (observer) or the economic agents (actors), or does each hold a different model?[118] Rational expectations presupposes that it is the economic agents who all effectively know the same (correct) model of the economy. The Austrians, however, place great emphasis on the dispersion of knowledge within the economy. The importance of the market process is that it permits coordination with *limited* information. Given their recognition of the Cournot problem, the comprehensive knowledge implied by rational expectations is too much to assume even for the professional economist, much less for the general public. It is an evasion of the central problem of economic theory.[119] Lachmann explicitly maintains that different agents hold different theories, which necessarily generate divergent (i.e. non-rational) expectations.[120]

The new classicals use the rational expectations hypothesis as a means of securing closure in their models. The Austrian insistence on divergent expectations, then, is at once an affirmation of their belief in open economics and a challenge to the new classical concept of equilibrium.

Equilibrium for the Austrians is the coincidence of plans with realizations. For an individual, equilibrium is a well-defined notion. It is more problematic for a society composed of numerous individuals: in what sense can they be said to have *a* plan? Hayek suggests that the equilibrium of many individuals together might be rendered either as the mutual compatibility of their plans or as a correspondence between the subjective data and the objective data. This last rendering sounds remarkably like rational expectations, although Hayek is careful to say that such an equilibrium could be judged only retrospectively.[121] Either rendering of social equilibrium must be judged relative to expectations. To be mutually compatible, individual plans must be based on the same correct expectations. Equally, for subjective and objective data to correspond, foresight must be perfect (or rational). Correct foresight is not then, Hayek maintains, a precondition of equilibrium, but the essence of its definition.[122]

Once rational expectations is seen as defining equilibrium, new classical accounts must be seen as completely inadequate by Austrian standards. Hayek writes:

> The situation seems here to be that, before we can explain why people commit mistakes, we must first explain why they should ever be right.[123]

The new classicals simply assume that people are right; the mechanism by which they come to be so remains mysterious. For Hayek, the real substance of economics is found in the tendency toward social equilibrium:

> ... the knowledge and intentions of the different members of society are supposed to come more and more into agreement or, to put the same thing in less general and less exact but more concrete terms, ... the expectation of the people and particularly entrepreneurs will come to be more and more correct.[124]

Whether such a tendency to equilibrium, to rational expectations, actually occurs is, according to Hayek, an empirical proposition. We are in the dark, he believes, about the conditions under which it may occur and about the detailed nature of the process. In contrast, equilibrium for Lucas and Sargent, i.e. rational expectations and cleared markets, is an *a priori*, not an empirical, proposition.[125] If Hayek's views are correct, by assuming equilibrium *a priori*, the new classical economists have gutted the substance of economics and reduced it to an uninformative framework based on the pure logic of choice.

Lachmann goes even further than Hayek. Individual equilibrium makes sense, but the equilibrium of diverse unconnected individuals is too problematic to be a useful notion. Instead of concentrating on the empirical conditions under which a general equilibrium would occur, Lachmann advocates that we attend more closely to the market process – precisely those aspects of the economy about which Hayek believes we are most in the dark.[126] The relations between the many individuals in the market are infinitely complex; there is no well-defined notion of equilibrium or of expectations converging at all, much less on correct foresight or rational expectations.[127] But this is not to say that expectations are a complete jumble. While they are not necessarily – indeed, not even likely – to be interpersonally or intertemporally consistent as rational expectations assumes, success in the market brings some sort of consistency. Such consistency, however, relies heavily on market institutions, e.g. the stock market, which provide public information on what other individuals, taken together, are expecting. Lachmann is particularly impressed with the role of futures markets in this regard.[128] Lachmann's views stand the new classical position on its head: markets are efficient in the new classical view because agents act on rational expectations; expectations approach rationality in Lachmann's view only when market institutions coordinate divergent expectations.

It should now be clear that Austrian business cycle theorists reject the notion of equilibrium business cycles so dear to new classical hearts not because they lack an appropriate concept of intertemporal equilibrium nor because they lack the concept of rational expectations or the appropriate mathematical techniques. Instead their understanding of the nature of rationality and human action rules out the new classicals' conception of a closed economics and their related analyses of rational expectations and equilibrium. The Austrians really do not believe that business cycles can be fruitfully analysed as equilibria.[129]

Notes

Chapter 1

1 Leontief (1936). While in the *General Theory* (chapter 2, especially p. 14) Keynes seems to deny Leontief's assertion, he seems to welcome it in his comment on Leontief (Keynes, 1937, p. 209). This is perhaps simply a tactical move. Chick (1983, chapter 7) argues convincingly that workers in the *General Theory* do not suffer from 'money illusion'.

2 Hicks (1935)

3 Modigliani and Brumberg (1954) and Friedman (1957).

4 Patinkin (1956, 1965).

5 Clower (1965).

6 For example, Barro and Grossman (1971, 1976), Malinvaud (1977) and Muellbauer and Portes (1978).

7 Lucas and Rapping (1969a, b).

8 Friedman (1968a) and Phelps (1967).

9 Lucas (1972a, b) and Sargent (1973).

10 Muth (1961).

11 Sargent and Wallace (1975, 1976).

12 The oldest use of the term I have been able to locate is in the title 'Aspects of the New Classical Macroeconomics' of Chapter XVI of Sargent (1979).

13 Keynes (1936, p. 3, fn 1).

14 For example, we would normally think of the anti-Bolshevik forces in Russia as a *bourgeois* and not a *communist* counter-revolution.

15 Hicks (1937, p. 138).

16 See, for example, Samuelson's famous *Economics*. The term 'neoclassical synthesis' first appears in the 3rd edn (1955), although the idea is readily recognizable in earlier editions.

17 It is useful to recall Leijonhufvud's (1968) distinction between 'Keynesian' economics and the 'Economics of Keynes'.

18 See, for example, Friedman (1956a, b).

19 See Stein (1976), Mayer (1978), Laidler (1981, 1982) and Meade (1981).

20 Friedman (1968b, p. 105).

21 For example, see Friedman and Schwartz (1982, chapter 2) and Dornbusch (1976).
22 Friedman (1974a). Even Brunner and Meltzer (1976), who vehemently reject the IS–LM framework, use a model which is but a specialization of Tobin's (1969) portfolio balance model, which is usually regarded as a 'Keynesian' construct. Dornbusch (1976) shows how many of Brunner and Meltzer's results can be teased out of the standard IS–LM framework properly interpreted.
23 See, for example, Lucas (1976), Lucas and Sargent (1979) and Sargent (1982).
24 Lucas (1977, p. 232) believes that long-run neutrality is the best-supported empirical proposition in economics. See also Lucas (1980b, 1986).
25 See chapter 6, Section 6.3.
26 For example, King and Plosser (1984).
27 See Sheffrin (1983) and Begg (1982).
28 Muth (1961, pp. 4, 5)
29 Lucas (1987, p. 13, fn 4).
30 Lucas (1987, p. 13, fn 4).
31 Friedman (1953).
32 See Blaug (1980, chapter 4), Boland (1979) and Hoover (1984a).
33 Hahn (1986, p. 281).
34 See, for example, Chow (1986) and Lovell (1986). Lovell compares the empirical successes of a number of competing hypotheses about the formation of expectations. He is unable to declare a clear winner. He makes the interesting observation that recent empirical work by Muth, the father of rational expectations, rejects the rational expectations hypothesis in favour of an alternative concept – 'implicit expectations'.
35 Sargent (1982).
36 For example, Fischer (1977), Phelps and Taylor (1977) and Tobin (1980).
37 See chapter 4, section 4.1.
38 Lucas (1981b).

Chapter 2

1 Keynes (1940) warned of the dangers of inflation in the fully employed wartime economy.
2 Phillips was not the first to notice the inverse relation between wage inflation and unemployment. See, for example, Brown (1955, chapter 4, especially pp. 99–101).
3 Desai (1975, 1984) offers a persuasive case for this interpretation of Phillip's work.
4 For reasons peculiar to the United Kingdom Phillips's measure of inflation is the change of import prices.
5 Phelps (1967, 1968) arrived independently at similar conclusions to Friedman.

6 Friedman's attacks on Phillips became less charitable with time: a measured reproof ('...an important and original contribution. But, unfortunately, it contains a basic defect'(1968a, p. 8)) becomes an unqualified assertion of professional incompetence ('...utterly fallacious ...no economic theorist has ever asserted that the demand and supply of labour were functions of the *nominal* wage rate' (1975, p. 15)). As should now be clear, the lapse is in Friedman's scholarship, for his attack is more accurately directed at the standard interpretation rather than at Phillips's own work.

7 Friedman (1968a, p. 8)

8 Friedman attributed the inflation in this period to the monetization of debt issued in the United States in order to finance the Vietnam War. The system of fixed exchange rates ensured that American inflation would be transmitted to other countries. The early 1970s witnessed a boom in the prices of internationally traded commodities, culminating in the steep rise in oil prices following the OPEC oil embargo in late 1973. This is, of course, just the situation in which Phillips himself had expected the Phillips curve for the United Kingdom to break down.

9 Friedman (1968a, p. 9) was careful to point out that his analysis implied only that macroeconomic or monetary policy was impotent in the long run. Microeconomic policy (particularly the structure of taxes and labour laws) might profoundly affect the natural rate.

10 Lucas and Rapping (1969b) directly address the application of their analysis to the Phillips curve.

11 Lucas and Rapping (1969a, pp. 30,31) write: 'The [United States] government generates an unemployment series based on the number of persons who answer "yes" to the question: "Are you actively seeking work?" There is a strong temptation to assume that respondents to this survey take the question to mean, "Are you seeking work at the current wage rate?" – but it is important to recognize that this assumption is simply a hypothesis, the truth of which is far from obvious. In our model it has been implicitly assumed that this interpretation is *not* correct, since the wage is assumed to equate quantity demanded and quantity supplied exactly each period.'

Other countries generate their unemployment statistics by other means. In the United Kingdom only those who register with the state as unemployed are counted. The same ambiguity nonetheless still arises in this context.

12 See, for example, the determination of permanent income in Friedman (1957).

13 Lucas (1972b, p. 93).

14 Of course if λ were close to unity, the gain to output would quickly become miniscule.

15 See chapter 1, section 1.1.

16 Altonji (1982) tested the Lucas–Rapping model with rational expectations and found that their initial assumption of intertemporal substitutability was not supported empirically.

17 To make these assumptions more concrete Lucas borrows a simile from Phelps (1970). It is as if people were dispersed on separate islands, so that they know the price of goods produced on their own island, but in order to learn the prices of goods on other islands, and from these the general price level, they must spend time and resources travelling from one island to another.

18 Phillips (1958, pp. 283, 284)

19 The exposition here follows Lucas (1973).

20 See Mood, Graybill and Boes (1974, pp. 158, 159, 167–9).

21 Figure 2.1 is similar to figures 1 and 2 of Taylor (1983, p. 12).

22 Empirical tests based on this result are discussed in chapter 8, section 8.2.

23 Patinkin (1956, 1965), Gurley and Shaw (1960), Mundell (1971) and Tobin (1965) are the classic works on non-neutrality due to portfolio substitution, while Sidrauski (1967) is perhaps the best-known model embodying superneutrality.

24 Cf. LeRoy and Raymon (1984), who refer to the older literature on non-neutrality as 'inflation-tax' models and the newer literature as 'signal-extraction' models.

25 See particularly the work of Sargent and Barro discussed in chapter 8, section 8.2.

26 The category 'frictional' is problematic. Keynes (1936, pp. 15, 16) clearly treats it as unemployment that is not permanently desired at the current real wage, yet is unavoidable given the institutional structure of the economy. It cannot be reduced through macroeconomic policy. One might be laid-off and apparently 'involuntarily' frictionally unemployed if it is only a matter of finding a job that is in fact available. One might be 'voluntarily' frictionally unemployed if one quits in order to engage in such search. Neither case poses the policy concern of involuntary unemployment, viz. the unemployed are not offered jobs for which they are qualified and would accept at the current wage.

27 Lucas (1978, p. 241).

28 For a further discussion of these issues, see chapter 3, section 3.4.

Chapter 3

1 See Lucas (1973, p. 134) for this particular variation.

2 Sargent (1979, p. 256), for example, defines the business cycle as ' . . .the phenomenon of a number of important economic aggregates . . .being characterized by high pairwise coherences at the low business cycle frequencies . . .' (i.e. with periodicities of two to four years or eight years in United States data).

3 Lucas (1975, p. 208).

4 Lucas (1975, p. 185) abstracts from possible effects of inflation on real rates of return that might induce non-neutralities in response to antici-pated changes in the stock of money.

5 The distinction between monetary and real models of the cycle based on sources of fluctuations rather than propagation mechanisms is already found in Hayek (1933a. pp. 51–6). See chapter 10, section 10.3.

6 McCallum (1986, p. 398).

7 Prescott (1986b, p. 29) and Eichenbaum and Singleton (1986, p. 92).

8 New classical monetary models generally ascribe monetary fluctuations to the monetary authorities. Earlier monetary models often treated the banking system as an independent source of fluctuations, so that even benign policy might not eliminate cycles. See, for example, Hayek (1933a, pp. 148ff and 189–92) and chapter 10, section 10.3. Although he identifies the monetary authorities as the source of cyclical fluctuations, Lucas (1987, pp. 20–31) argues that the welfare loss from such fluctuations is actually very small.

9 This is a point of elementary logic (cf. Summers, 1986, p. 24).

10 Sims (1972); see also chapter 8.

11 See Sims (1980b) and Eichenbaum and Singleton (1986) for American data, and Litterman and Weiss (1985) for American, French, German and British data.

12 Sims (1980b), Litterman and Weiss (1985) and Eichenbaum and Singleton (1986).

13 McCallum (1986, p. 401). He argues that even during the United States Federal Reserve's 'monetarist experiment' an interest rate target was technically still in operation.

14 See chapter 4, section 4.1, for further details.

15 Cf. Grossman (1980, p. 14, 1983, pp. 231–3).

16 Nelson and Plosser (1982); see also Stulz and Wasserfallen (1985) and Campbell and Mankiw (1987).

17 Cf. McCallum (1986, pp. 404–7).

18 Mishkin (1983, pp. 110–29).

19 Cf. Zarnowitz (1985, pp. 569–71).

20 Kydland and Prescott (1982); a valuable summary, extension and discussion of related literature is found in Prescott (1986a). See also Summers's (1986) criticism of Kydland and Prescott's paradigm and Prescott's (1986b) rejoinder.

21 Altug (1985). McCallum (1986, p. 400) also questions Kydland and Prescott's failure to test their model against an alternative that includes money as an explanatory variable.

22 Prescott (1986a, p. 10). Prescott (p. 21) also suggests that the failure of real business cycle models to agree with the data may be the fault of the data not of the model; see Summers's (1986, p. 23) scathing remarks on this tack.

23 Cf. Lucas (1987, pp. 43–5).

24 Prescott (1986a, p. 15). This method is due to Solow (1957).

25 Robinson (1953–4) and Wallis (1980, pp. 61–3).

26 Prescott (1986b, p. 29).

27 Mining and construction in the United States from 1973 to 1977 for instance; see Summers (1986, p. 25).

28 Summers (1986, pp. 24, 25); see Prescott (1986b, pp. 31, 32) for a rejoinder.

29 Kydland and Prescott (1982, p. 1345).
30 Kydland and Prescott (1982, pp. 1348, 1361).
31 Lucas and Rapping (1969a); see also Lucas (1977, p. 225).
32 Rogerson and Wright (1986) explores various models with indivisible labour and lotteries in which unemployment is not preferred.
33 Long and Plosser (1983, p. 55).
34 'Inside' because the public's assets and the banks' liabilities in the form of deposits cancel when the private sector is aggregated, so that the debt is entirely inside the public sector. Outside money would be the debt of the government or foreigners.
35 Friedman and Schwartz (1963a, b).
36 Key assumptions of King and Plosser's model stand or fall with the success or failure of Fama's argument. This is considered in detail in chapter 5.
37 Walsh (1987).
38 This is a distillation of Keynes's various formulations of the definition of involuntary unemployment. See Keynes (1963, especially pp. 15, 26); cf. Smithin (1985).
39 Monetary models are not strictly speaking Pareto efficient, since everyone can be made better off if the monetary authorities lower the variance of the money stock. None of this inefficiency arises in the private sector, and so the central point remains valid. The authorities are charged by the new classicals with a sin of commission, which suggests that they do not interfere in the economy, and by the Keynesians with a sin of omission, which suggests that they ought to take actions to correct the faults of the private sector.
40 Lucas (1978, p. 241).
41 Lucas (1978, p. 242).
42 Lucas (1977, p. 226).
43 See Yellen (1984) for a survey of efficiency-wage models.
44 Hansen's model in which workers must either work the standard number of hours or not at all would be of this type, except that workers choose lotteries rather than hours.
45 Lucas (1978, p. 243).

Chapter 4

1 A more complicated aggregate demand side, say one based on the IS–LM model as in Sargent and Wallace (1975), could be used without changing the essential point, as long as money is the only nominal asset counted as net wealth.
2 Note: $\log (1 + \lambda) \approx \lambda$ for small λ.
3 Sargent and Wallace (1976, p. 199); see chapter 8, section 8.3, for evidence that serious debate persists, this quotation to the contrary notwithstanding.
4 Buiter (1981) would not deny that this result follows in the simple model developed here, but he gives a comprehensive account of why contingent rules are to be preferred in nearly every more realistic model.

5 Friedman (1969b) himself does argue that perfectly anticipated inflation is bad; a low, even negative, rate of inflation is needed if people are to choose to hold the socially optimal stock of real balances.
6 Barro (1976, pp. 252, 253).
7 Fischer (1977), Phelps and Taylor (1977), Taylor (1979) and Gordon (1982).
8 Sargent and Wallace (1975, pp. 216–18).
9 Sargent (1986, pp. 15–17).
10 See Christ (1968) and Blinder and Solow (1974).
11 This is actually true only asymptotically. As interest payments on the existing debt gradually come to overwhelm the new contributions of each period's deficits to the debt, the total stock of debt, which lies above B_0B_1, gradually approaches it.
12 See Cagan (1956) and Friedman (1969b).
13 Mayer (1984) calls the first fiscal policy the *expenditure* budget and the second the *outlay* budget.
14 The United States budget would have been just about in balance in 1985 if interest payments had been excluded, i.e. service of the debt was almost equal to the reported deficit.
15 See the discussion of the Lucas critique in chapter 8, sections 8.3 and 8.4.
16 Aiyagari (1985) shows that real rates need not rise as more debt is sold in Sargent and Wallace's underlying model, as long as taxes are adjusted to eliminate distribution effects. While this result highlights the role of distribution effects in supporting Sargent and Wallace's result, it is of little practical significance as policies to adjust the incidence of taxation as a function of the level of sales of bonds are not politically feasible.
17 A limit to the debt-to-income ratio seems to follow naturally from the micromodel that Sargent and Wallace (1981, Appendices A–C) offer to support their argument. Their model is an overlapping-generations model with legal restrictions, like that discussed in chapter 6, section 6.1 and chapter 7, section 7.3 in which the rich hold only bonds and the poor hold only money. They derive demand functions for each asset (their equation (A.2)), simplified here as

$$\frac{M_t}{P_t} = \frac{\alpha_1^P + \alpha_2^P (P_t/P_{t+1})}{2} \tag{a}$$

$$\frac{B_t}{P_t} = \frac{\alpha_1^R + \alpha_2^R (1 + r_t)}{2} \tag{b}$$

where (α_1^P, α_2^P) and (α_1^R, α_2^R) are the endowments of the poor and the rich in the first and second periods of their lives. In order to derive version 1 of their model, Sargent and Wallace set $\alpha_2^P = \alpha_2^R = 0$; (a) then becomes a simple quantity equation and (b) sets the real demand for bonds to a constant $\alpha_1^R/2$, which is what generates the limit $\bar{b}$. To derive version 2, they set only $\alpha_2^R = 0$, so that (a) becomes a Cagan demand-for-money function. Miller and Sargent's assumption that the rate of interest is positively related to the level of the stock of bonds would follow in a third version in which $\alpha_2^R > 0$. But then *any* volume of bonds can be accommodated at some rate of interest; $\bar{b}$ is no longer generated in the model. Miller and Sargent do show that it is unlikely that a purely bond-financed *steady state* policy is feasible when r_t rises with B_t; but that does not say that a *non-steady state* bond-financed policy is not feasible.

18 See note 17 for details.

19 There is a substantial older literature on the limits to debt finance. The question was much discussed during and just after the Second World War. See, for example, Ratchford (1942), Domar (1944) and Harris (1947, especially part V).

20 This is a counter-example to Aiyagari (1985, p. 5), who seems to imply that debt cannot exceed income:

> ...if the real interest rate on bonds ...exceeds the growth rate ...[and] if the sum of direct taxes and the inflation tax on money falls short of government consumption, then the level of bonds per unit of output will grow without limit and will *exceed the disposable income of savers.* Consequently, the only choice for monetary policy is when to monetize the debt rather than whether. (*italics added*)

21 Following Friedman (1968a), Barro and Gordon (1983a, p. 593) see the natural rate of unemployment as an equilibrium rate given market imperfections. It is, then, not necessarily the optimal rate. A macroeconomic policy that lowers the actual rate of unemployment to some extent below the natural rate would be a substitute for removing market imperfections.

22 The form of the π line – linear with a slope less than unity – conforms to Barro and Gordon's (1983a, b) actual models.

23 Figure 4.3 (b) reproduces the diagram of Barro and Gordon (1983b, p. 112).

24 But see Backus and Driffill (1985a, b) for extensions and modifications to Barro and Gordon's models.

25 Barro and Gordon (1983a, p. 600).

26 Like Milton they seek to '...assert Eternal Providence, and justify the ways of God to men.' Lucas (1986, p. 8, fn. 1) calls the view, which he nonetheless adopts, that economists can give useful advice 'schizophrenic' because it does not apply the same standard of rationality to the policy maker as to the public. See chapter 8, section 8.4.

27 Barro and Gordon (1983a, pp. 608, 609).

28 Barro and Gordon (1983a, p. 609).

29 Barro (1986, p. 37) senses the difficulty: '...it is unclear why the advice of economists is more pertinent at the level of institutional choice than it is at the level of day-to-day operations.' He goes on to say that economists giving advice should be thought of as another factor of production – inside not outside the economic system. This point of view is echoed in Sims's analysis of econometric policy advice. See chapter 8, section 8.4.

30 Sargent and Wallace (1976, p. 211).

Chapter 5

1   Sargent (1982).
2   Although Keynes (1936, p. 293) clearly draws the distinction he does not use the terminology.
3   The titles of Wallace (1977) and Bryant and Wallace (1980) echo that of Hicks.
4   Hicks (1935, p. 63).
5   Hicks (1935, p. 66).
6   The frictions metaphor is an old one in monetary theory, e.g. Hume (1741/42): 'Money is . . .none of the wheels of trade: it is the oil which renders the motions more smooth and easy.'
7   The term 'new monetary economics' seems to be due to Hall (1982).
8   For example, cf. Cournot ([1838] 1927, p. 127); also see chapter 9, section 9.2.
9   Technically, their utility functions are identical and homothetic or, equivalently, agents' Engel curves are parallel straight lines through the origin (see Gorman, 1953).
10 Patinkin (1961, p. 112).
11 Tobin (1963) seems to have initiated the term 'new view'. Also see Tobin (1961).
12 Gurley and Shaw (1960, p. 87).
13 Patinkin (1956, 1965, part 2). The accusation is by implication only as Gurley and Shaw give no references to the literature (see Gurley and Shaw, 1960, Author's Preface, p. x).
14 Hall (1982, p. 1553). Other recent contributions to this literature include Greenfield and Yeager (1983) and Lucas (1984). White (1984) and McCallum (1985) provide useful critical reviews of the literature.
15 See also King and Plosser (1986).
16 Peter Oppenheimer suggested the term 'separation theorem'.
17 The original statement is by Modigliani and Miller (1958); the most influential restatement is by Stiglitz (1969).
18 For the 'strong/weak' terminology, see Fama (1980, p. 45). For the assumptions, see Fama (1978).
19 Although Fama seems to support the new view of Gurley and Shaw (1960) and Tobin (1961, 1963), he insists, at the same time, on currency's distinctiveness in the manner of Pesek and Saving (1967). Both Fama and Pesek and Saving agree that money is not debt but real wealth. He differs from them primarily in that he places current accounts (checking accounts) with the debt of financial intermediaries in the category of 'financial assets' and therefore excludes them from net wealth rather than placing them, as Pesek and Saving do, with currency in the category of 'money'.
20 Contrast Fama's position with that of Friedman (1951), who makes storability and portability the prime requirements for a successful commodity standard.
21 Cf. Fama. (1982, pp. 6, 7).

22 Compare Pesek and Saving (1967, p. 58) and Black (1970, p. 13).
23 Patinkin (1956, 1961).
24 Fama ignores the difficulties – well known since Hahn (1965) – of demonstrating the existence of a Walrasian equilibrium in which the transactions role of money is left implicit (see section 5.1).
25 Impracticality is a legitimate criticism as Fama's analysis is not meant to be purely hypothetical (see Fama, 1983).
26 Fama (1980, pp. 46, 47).
27 Financial assets will be similarly characterized in a sequence of markets with perfect foresight or rational expectations.
28 This may not be strictly true if the power enjoyed by having a controlling shareholding in a company is considered to be of value even without a direct share of the profits. I owe this point to Lawrence White.
29 Hicks (1982).
30 Fama (1982); cf. Klein (1974).
31 A £10 note is of course convertible by right into ten £1 coins. Such conversions are restricted to a tight circle of related assets and therefore hardly alter the point.
32 Fama (1982, pp. 23–6).
33 Robertson (1948, p. 45) makes this point in a whimsical dialogue between the economist and a paper bank-note. The economist begins:

> You are a fine looking fellow, but are you not a little flimsy and anaemic. If you were to give up working as money do you think you could earn a living?

The bank-note responds:

> . . . No, of course I should be no more use at house decoration or dentistry or other honest work than . . . you would yourself. And it is not only we paper pieces of whom that's true. There is my friend the rupee for instance: . . . if you took his lettering off him his carcase would come tumbling down in value. For it isn't his flesh that gives him the value he has got, it's the writing on him.

34 Vickrey (1964, p. 76). Compare Robertson (1948, p. 46); the bank-note speaks of gold coins:

> They think men run after them because they're strong and handsome, and so it was when men were savages. But the chief reason men run after them now is because they're *money.*

35 Vickrey (1964, p. 82).
36 The point here recalls the debate over whether money is essentially the creature of the state or not: in favour, see Knapp (1924) and Keynes ([1930] 1971, pp. 3–5); in opposition see Mises ([1951] 1981, pp. 83–94); compare Frankel (1977). Legal enforcement of money's status as legal tender itself provides sporadic but inessential support to its value; see also Robertson (1948, pp. 42, 43).
37 This example closely follows from Sinclair (1983, pp. 84–6).
38 The assumptions needed to prove the Modigliani–Miller theorem are listed in Section 5.1.

39 Like Polonius he prefers both himself and the firm to 'Neither a borrower nor a lender be.'

Chapter 6

1 For example, Cass and Yaari (1966), Lucas (1972a) and Martins (1980). Wallace (1980) gives the most general discussion of this model as a basis for new classical monetary theory.
2 Fisher (1930, pp. 41, 67) used the perhaps more felicitous illustration of strawberries for a similar purpose.
3 Cf. Vickrey (1964, p. 76) and Robertson (1948, pp. 45, 46).
4 Abstracting from the possibility of non-stationary equilibria. See the discussion below.
5 Hahn (1982, chapter 1) treats the overlapping-generations model as a monetarist model and then cites the implication of the model that increases in money are not necessary for inflation as an internal contradiction of the monetarist view that inflation is always and everywhere a monetary phenomenon. Hahn's belief that the overlapping-generations model is monetarist is surely wrong. On the one hand, Sargent and Wallace (1982) use it to attack the quantity theory. On the other hand, Friedman and Schwartz (1982, p. 37), the high priest and priestess of monetarism, explicitly disavow it.
6 Farmer (1984).
7 McCallum (1983a).
8 Hahn (1965). See chapter 5, section 5.1.
9 Bryant and Wallace (1979).
10 Bryant and Wallace (1984) and Wallace (1983).
11 Lucas (1980a, 1984).
12 Clower (1967). Clower is by no means a new classical economist (see Clower (1984, pp. 270, 271), and the finance constraint is widely used by economists outside the new classical school. See Kohn (1981, 1984) for references and for the history of its use before Clower.
13 Clower (1967, p. 5); cf. the first sentence of Patinkin (1956, 1965): 'Money buys goods, and goods do not buy money.' If not, how is money obtained?
14 For example Lucas (1984).
15 Lucas (1980a).
16 It is worthwhile recalling that the model is easily extendable to lives with many periods. The unrealistic assumption that pay periods are equal to the agent's whole working life is easily dispensed with.
17 Rogers (1984, p. 76), argues ' . . .that the quantity theory acted as a technological restriction on the rate at which trade could occur with the help of a monetary medium' (i.e. through a finance constraint). Patinkin's attempts to reformulate it using real-balance effects, he believes, obscure this point. Cf. Valavanis (1955) and Hickman (1950).
18 See note 5.
19 Bryant and Wallace (1980, p. 8) assert the advantages most clearly.

20 Bryant and Wallace (1980).
21 Bryant (1980).
22 McCallum (1983b).
23 For example Bryant and Wallace (1980). Hands (1986) argues that there are several types of *ad hoc*ness, and, despite *ad hoc* being a favourite slur cast on the work of economists who assume what others wish to prove, not all forms of *ad hoc*ness are invidious.

Chapter 7

1 See chapter 5, section 5.2 and appendix.
2 Ricardo (1821, chapter 17, 1951).
3 Barro does not refer to Ricardo. The term 'Ricardian equivalence' came into common use after Buchanan (1976) chided Barro for ignoring earlier literature on the subject. Buchanan (1958) himself had raised the issue of Ricardian equivalence before Barro, although his efforts were largely ignored. That Ricardo did not actually believe that the equivalence held in practice is obvious to anyone who bothers to read him – a point made forcefully by O'Driscoll (1977).
4 Neglecting money might appear to be a mere convenient simplification. None the less, to include it would raise all the issues of rate-of-return dominance discussed in chapter 6.
5 The novelist Samuel Butler (1903, chapter 18), seems not only to anticipate but also to recommend this simplification of Barro's model:

> Why should the generations overlap one another at all? Why cannot we be buried as eggs in neat little cells with ten or twenty thousands pounds each wrapped round us in Bank of England notes, and wake up, as the sphex wasp does, to find that its papa and mama not only left ample provision at its elbow, but have been eaten by sparrows some weeks before it began to live consciously on its own account?

6 For convenience the vertical axis shows the children's consumption rather than their utility; these are equivalent representations.
7 It has been suggested to me that it would not be rational for parents to be concerned about the absolute size of bequests rather than the utility children gain from them. Normally in economics 'rational' refers to the properties of preferences (e.g. transitivity) and not to their domain. Economists are in no position to dictate what things people should treat as goods.
8 Cf. Feldstein (1976).
9 Hayashi (1985) argues that kinked budget constraints may arise when credit is rationed optimally. For example, when a lender cannot distinguish between borrowers but they in fact pose different risks, rationing is optimal. In such cases he shows that Ricardian equivalence may still hold.
10 Barsky et al. (1986) explain the argument in detail and show exactly what tastes must be to secure the result. They also give reasons to believe that the magnitudes of the effects may be large.

11 Evidence in support is reviewed by Seater (1985); an example of evidence against is Boskin and Kotlikoff (1985).
12 Barro (1979).
13 See, for example, Barro (1980) for, Kremers (1985) against and Barro (1987b) conceding the difficulty posed by the current United States debt.
14 Cf. Buiter (1981, p. 662).
15 One suspects that Wallace does not use a nominal financial asset as that would more readily expose the essential triviality of his result.
16 The fact that private holdings of real assets cannot be negative puts a downward limit on the adjustability of private portfolios and may cause the Modigliani–Miller theorem to fail in some cases.
17 Wallace (1981, p. 274).
18 See Wallace (1985, especially p. 10).
19 Barro (1987a, p. 396).
20 Smith and Sargent (1987) and Sargent and Smith (1986).
21 For this reason Wallace (1985) concludes that Ricardian equivalence is not generally compatible with money dominated in rate of return.
22 Laidler (1984) rightly objects to Sargent and Wallace's associating their analysis, which is based on the desirability of fluctuations in the price level, with the classic real bills doctrine, which shared with the quantity theorists the goal of a stable price level, differing only over what policy would achieve that end. The doctrinal association is, however, merely an ornament in Sargent and Wallace's argument. Laidler's discussion and references are a good source for the history of the real bills doctrine.
23 See chapter 5, section 5.1, especially note 9, for a discussion of the importance of this assumption.
24 See note 23.
25 After all, Friedman believes that banks are about the only industry the government should regulate.

Chapter 8

1 There is a certain irony in criticizing any econometrics as 'Keynesian' given Keynes's own well-known scepticism of econometrics – see his review of Tinbergen (Keynes, 1939). What is of course true is that most builders of large-scale macroeconometric models classified themselves as 'Keynesians'.
2 Granger (1980, p. 330). The formal statement of this definition, which is more general than that in the original paper is

Y_n is said to cause X if
Prob $(X_{n+1} \in A \,|\, \Omega_n) \neq$ Prob $(X_{n+1} \in A \,|\, \Omega_n - Y_n)$
for some A.

X_n and Y_n are time-ordered sets of variables defined for time $t = -\infty, \ldots, 0, 1, \ldots, n$, A is a set of variables of which X_{n+1} is a member and Ω_n is the set of non-redundant information available at time n. Granger (1980) also contains his reflections on the meaning and use of his definition after a decade of criticism.

3 Cf. Granger (1980, section 3). For a discussion of optimal linear predictors, see Sargent (1979, pp. 203–14).

4 Granger's general definition suggests that the number of lags should be infinite, which is impossible in practical application. It usually turns out that long lags reduce the variance very little so that they can be omitted. How many lags to include varies considerably in practice.

5 Heuristically, a times series is stationary if its statistical properties are independent of time. For a more precise definition, see Harvey (1981, p. 25).

6 The notation here is taken from Jacobs et al. (1979).

7 See the references cited by Granger (1980) for a sample.

8 Sims (1972, p. 393).

9 Sims (1972, p. 389).

10 Engle et al. (1983, p. 297) and Cooley and LeRoy (1985, p. 298), for example, define 'strict exogeneity' in such a way that Granger-causality is a necessary but not sufficient condition for it, while Leamer (1985, p. 283) prefers to replace the term 'Granger-causality' with 'precedence'.

11 Engle et al. (1983, pp. 281–3) gives an exact definition.

12 See Engle et al. (1983, p. 280); cf. Cooley and LeRoy (1985, pp. 297–310).

13 Sims (1972, p. 391). It has been suggested that the logical error is so egregious that Sims must have his tongue in his cheek. It may be so. But it cannot pass as so many economists have made practical application of the fallacy.

14 Sims (1977, p. 29, 1986, p. 2).

15 Sims (1980a, pp. 20–32, 1980b, 1982, pp. 134, 135).

16 Sims (1977, p. 23, 1979, p. 103).

17 Sims (1977, p. 26–31, 1980a, p. 12), Simon (1953) and Hurwicz (1962).

18 This example follows Jacobs et al. (1979, p. 404); cf. Sims (1972, p. 390).

19 Cf. Leamer (1985, pp. 283–7) and Cooley and LeRoy (1985, pp. 297–301, 306, 307). The term 'incremental predictability' is due to Schwert (1979).

20 Engle et al. (1983, p. 282).

21 Eichenbaum (1985, p. 309).

22 To see more precisely what is at stake consider equations (8.3) and (8.4). Multiply (8.4) through by $\mu = \text{cov}(u_{1t}u_{2t})/\text{var}(u_{2t})$ and subtract from (8.3) to yield

$$Y_t = \mu X_t + \phi_1 X_{t-1} + \phi_2 Y_{t-1} + \omega_t \tag{i}$$

where $\phi_1 = \Pi_{11} - \mu\Pi_{21}$, $\phi_2 = \Pi_{12} - \mu\Pi_{22}$ and $\omega_t = u_{1t} - \mu u_{2t}$ (cf. the derivation of equation (8.37), section 8.4). Observe that ω_t and u_{2t} are not correlated:

$$\begin{aligned}
\text{cov}(u_{2t}\omega_t) &= \text{E}(u_{2t}\omega_t) \\
&= \text{E}\left\{ u_{2t}\left[u_{1t} - \frac{\text{cov}(u_{1t}u_{2t})}{\text{var}(u_{2t})} u_2 t \right] \right\} \\
&= \text{cov}(u_{1t}u_{2t}) - \frac{\text{cov}(u_{1t}u_{2t})}{\text{var}(u_{2t})} \text{var}(u_2 t) \\
&= 0 \qquad\qquad\qquad\qquad\qquad\qquad\text{(cf. n. 73).}
\end{aligned}$$

Lag (i) one period and substitute back into itself to eliminate Y_{t-1}:

$$Y_t = \mu X_t + \phi_1 X_{t-1} + \phi_2 \mu X_{t-1} + \phi_2 \phi_1 X_{t-2} + \phi_2^2 Y_{t-2}$$
$$+ \omega_t + \phi_2 \omega_{t-1}. \tag{ii}$$

Repeating this process indefinitely (as long as $|\phi_2| < 0$) yields

$$Y_t = \mu X_t + \sum_{j=0}^{\infty} (\phi_1 \phi_2^j + \phi_2^{j+1} \mu) X_{t-j-1} + \Omega_t, \tag{iii}$$

where

$$\Omega_t = \sum_{k=0}^{\infty} \phi_2^k \omega_{t-k}.$$

Lagging (iii) one period and substituting into (8.4) yields

$$X_t = \Pi_{21} \mu X_{t-1} + \Pi_{21} \sum_{j=0}^{\infty} (\phi_1 \phi_2^j + \phi_2^{j+1} \mu) X_{t-j-2} + \Pi_{22} X_{t-1} + U_t, \tag{iv}$$

where $U_t = u_{2t} + \Pi_{21} \Omega_{t-1}$. Since X_t is determined by (iv) and since Ω_{t-1} and Ω_t share many of the error terms, ω_{t-k} between them, X_t is in general correlated with Ω_t in (iii). But note that, if X_t does not Granger-cause Y_t, $\Pi_{21} = 0$. Then Y_{t-1} drops out of equation (8.4) and Ω_{t-1} out of (iv). Since u_{2t} and ω_t are not correlated, the X_t in (iii) will not be correlated with Ω_t. This is the sufficient condition in Sims's theorem: if X does not Granger-cause Y, then Y can be expressed as an equation dependent on the current and an infinite number of lagged Xs and the Xs will be uncorrelated with the error term. Note, however, that the coefficients on the Xs in (iii) (viz. μ and the $(\phi_1 \phi_2^j + \phi_2^{j+1}\mu)$s) do not correspond to our original parameters of interest in (8.1) and (8.2) (viz. θ, γ and the β_{ij}), and these parameters cannot be recovered from the coefficients of (iii). Sims's result therefore shows, at best, that it is possible to write down a certain sort of predictive equation but gives no aid in recovering structural parameters.

23 If all the countries in this sample except Argentina and Paraguay (Lucas, 1973, pp. 138, 139) are ranked from low to high on their slope coefficient (ϕ in his table 2) and from high to low on their variance of inflation (his table 1), the resulting rank correlation coefficient $r = 0 \cdot 687$ rejects the null of no correlation at the 1 per cent significance level (critical value, $0 \cdot 601$). Nevertheless, Froyen and Waud (1980), in an investigation along the same lines as Lucas's, found only a weak correlation between measures of the volatility of aggregate demand and the slope of the aggregate supply curve.

24 Lucas (1973) suggest a test of cross-equations restrictions as well. He acknowledges, however, that his model does not actually imply the supposed restriction. See his note on the reprinted version of this paper (Lucas 1981a, pp. 144, 145).

25 See chapter 2, section 2.2. Muth (1960) demonstrates circumstances in which autoregressive expectations are rational.

26 The mechanism is similar to Sargent and Wallace's unpleasant monetarist arithmetic (see chapter 4, section 4.2). Webb (1985) provides detailed historical and institutional evidence that the supply of money during the German hyperinflation of 1923–4 was endogenous in this sense.

27 Sargent (1977) is, nevertheless, unhappy with Cagan's actual estimates of the demand for money in hyperinflations because they seem to imply that the monetary authorities typically choose suboptimal rates of money creation. He re-estimates the money demand functions using advanced econometric techniques, but with mixed results.

28 Sargent (1976a, p. 547).

29 The notation here is different from that of Barro (1977).

30 By distinguishing between permanent and transitory income in the derivation of the price equation, Barro was able to modify the model in such a way that the cross-equation restrictions were not rejected. As he notes, however, his modification was only one of the many possible, and its validity was not independently checked.

31 Sargent (1976a, p. 527).

32 For those familiar with the algebra of lag operators, equation (8.25′) is derived much more simply: equation (8.19) can be written $(1 - \gamma L)y_t = (\alpha - \beta L)m_t + \eta_t$ and equation (8.20) can be written $(1 - \delta L)m_t = e_t$. Substituting (8.20) into (8.19) yields $(1 - \gamma L)y_t = (\alpha - \beta L)(1 - \delta L)^{-1}e_t + \eta_t$ or, using (8.20) once more, $(1 - \gamma L)y_t = (\alpha - \beta L)(1 - \delta L)^{-1}(m_t - {}_{t-1}m_t^e) + \eta_t$, which is the same as (8.25′).

33 See Mishkin (1983, pp. 13–16).

34 See Small (1979), Gordon (1982) and, particularly, Mishkin (1983), who performs econometric tests along the same lines as Barro and confirms that people make full use of available information (i.e. have rational expectations) but finds that perfectly anticipated growth in the money stock affects real variables.

35 Lucas (1976, pp. 111–15).

36 Lucas (1976, p. 112) and Muth (1960).

37 Lucas (1981a, pp. 11, 12) and Lucas and Sargent (1979).

38 The example is fairly common. See particularly Turner and Whiteman (1981, p. 7).

39 Cf. Buiter (1980) and Sims (1982, p. 112).

40 Haavelmo (1944, p. 28); cf. Sims (1982, p. 122, 1986b, p. 7).

41 Simon (1953, pp. 25–7).

42 For example, Sargent (1981) and Hansen and Sargent (1980).

43 Sims (1982, p. 108). It is sometimes questioned whether Sims is really a new classical economist. As far as I know he does not dissent from the fundamental tenets of new classicism. This and the close working relation he has had with Sargent (especially co-authored papers) and the influence of his techniques in new classical circles (see for example Sargent (1979, part II)) all argue that the classification is correct.

44 Unless of course the advice was to do nothing new.

45 See, for example, Taylor (1975) and Bray (1982, 1983).

46 Lucas (1977, p. 15, 1986).

47 The empirical results in this paper are borrowed from Lucas (1980b).
48 See Phillips (1958).
49 Lucas (1986, p. S404). See chapter 2, section 2.1, for a discussion of Phillips's own interpretation of the Phillips curve.
50 Cooley et al.'s view is compatible with policy's being characterized by parameters when cross-country rather than intertemporal differences in regime are being considered; the policies of France and Britain are simply different; one did not turn into the other.
51 Cooley et al. (1984b, p. 5).
52 Cooley et al. (1984a, p. 468).
53 This interpretation was suggested by Stephen LeRoy in a private letter. LeRoy finds my criticisms of Cooley et al. incoherent. Despite assiduous efforts, we were not able to resolve our disagreements.
54 Sims (1986a, p. 299) observes that the source of the randomness in Cooley et al.'s (1984b) model illustrating their view of policy is not explained.
55 Again by LeRoy privately.
56 Sims (1986a, p. 297); cf. Sims (1980a, p. 12).
57 Sims (1982, pp. 119–20); cf. Cooley et al. (1984a, pp. 468, 469).
58 Sims (1982, especially p. 118, 1986a); cf. Litterman (1984, p. 38).
59 Sims (1982, pp. 108, 112, 1986a, p. 9).
60 Blinder (1984) provides a light-hearted analysis of the issues of free will raised by the debate between Sargent and Sims. Also see Gardner's (1973, chapter 5) discussion between Grendl and the dragon.
61 Sims (1980a, section 1).
62 Lucas (1981a, p. 10).
63 Sims (1982, pp. 118–20).
64 Sims (1980a, p.14, 1982, pp. 122, 123).
65 Sims (1980a, p. 31, especially fn. 29).
66 Sims (1986a, p. 298).
67 For a formal model of such a process, see Roberds (1986).
68 Estimates of (8.36′) are consistent only if x_t and e_t are not correlated, i.e. v_t and e_t are not correlated.
69 Sims (1980a, p. 14, 1982, p. 108, 1986a, p. 298).
70 Barro and Gordon (1983a, pp. 608, 609).
71 Sims (1986a, p. 306).
72 See for example Wold (1954, 1956, 1960). For criticism of the significance of Wold's idea, see for example Theil (1971, pp. 461–2).
73 $$\begin{aligned} \text{cov}(u_{1t}\eta_t) &= \text{E}(u_{1t}\eta_t) \\ &= \text{E}\left\{ u_{1t}\left[u_{2t} - \frac{\text{cov}(u_{1t}u_{2t})}{\text{var}(u_{1t})}u_{1t} \right] \right\} \\ &= \text{cov}(u_{1t}u_{2t}) - \frac{\text{cov}(u_{1t}u_{2t})}{\text{var}(u_{1t})}\text{var}(u_{1t}) \\ &= 0. \end{aligned}$$

74 Sims (1986b, pp. 9, 10).
75 Block recursion corresponds to Simon's (1953) notion of causal ordering.
76 Simon (1953, pp. 24–6), Basmann (1965) and Granger (1969, p. 374); cf. Sims (1977, pp. 27–9).

77 Cooley and LeRoy (1985, p. 301) offer several examples of these equivocations.
78 For a standard treatment of identification, see Johnston (1972, sections 12.2–12.4). The source for most textbook treatments is Koopmans (1950).
79 For example, Lucas and Sargent (1979), Lucas (1981a, Introduction) and Cooley and LeRoy (1985). Cooley et al. (1984b, p. 1) define 'economics' as optimization.
80 Sargent (1978, p. 479).
81 Haavelmo (1944, p. 29).
82 Sims (1986b, p. 15).
83 Sims (1980a, p. 30).
84 Miller (1983) and Blanchard (1984) have conducted such tests, although with slightly different ends in view.
85 This idea is developed more fully by Hoover (1985).

Chapter 9

1   See also Kantor (1979).
2   Friedman (1956b, 1959b, 1968a).
3   Lucas (1977, 1981a, 1981b).
4   Although see the earlier Friedman (1977, 1978).
5   Friedman (1956b, 1969b, 1974a) and Friedman and Schwartz (1982).
6   It is the shared presupposition of the natural rate as the outcome of a Walrasian system that suggests to Hahn (1980, 1982) that Friedman and the new classicals should be grouped together under the title 'monetarists'.
7   Friedman (1974a) and Friedman and Schwartz (1982). Gordon (1981) ascribes the aggregate supply explanation to Friedman, failing to distinguish between Friedman (1968a) and (1974a). Laidler (1981, 1982) correctly notes the shift. Friedman does not, however, adopt an aggregate supply version to the exclusion of his earlier explanation.
8   Friedman (1974a) and Friedman and Schwartz (1982, chapter 2).
9   Friedman and Schwartz (1982, chapter 10).
10 Simons (1936) and Friedman (1948, 1959a, 1974b). 'Discretion' is now the more usual term, but 'authorities' is the more venerable, having been coined by Simons.
11 Friedman (1961, 1977).
12 Lucas (1980d, 1981b).
13 Sargent and Wallace (1976, p. 199). For a contrary view, see Buiter (1980) and Goldfeld (1982). Sargent and Wallace (1981) note a circumstance under which Friedman's rule may not be an appropriate policy for securing a lower rate of inflation. Nevertheless, this possible objection does not alter the new classicals' support for rules over discretion in general.
14 Lucas (1980d).
15 Friedman (1974a). His view of the matter is controversial. For supporters, see, for example, Mayer (1978); for an opponent see, for example, Hahn (1971).

16 Friedman and Schwartz (1982, chapter 9).
17 Friedman and Schwartz (1982, p. 630).
18 Friedman (1949, p. 490).
19 Friedman does not seem to perceive the implicit contradiction between a theory's being completely general and photographically exact. Generality permits numerous possibilities; a photograph presents just one of them.
    There is another sense of 'general' – namely, when one theory is a special case of, or is nested in, another (e.g. Einstein's theory is general with respect to Newton's) – and the more general may be photographically exact. Nevertheless, I believe that, taken in context, Friedman uses 'general' in the first sense of open to various instantiations.
20 Cournot ([1838] 1927, p. 127).
21 Friedman (1955, p. 904).
22 Friedman (1959b, 1974a).
23 Friedman (1956b, 1957, 1959b).
24 Friedman (1957), for the example of the consumption function.
25 On Friedman's positivism and the F-twist see Boland (1979, 1982).
26 For example Lucas (1977, 1981b) and Muth (1961).
27 Lucas (1977).
28 Lucas (1980c).
29 Friedman (1949, p. 480).
30 Lucas (1980c).
31 Friedman (1955, p. 905).
32 There is a third sense of 'Walrasian' which *cannot* be ascribed to the new classicals. This is perhaps the most common, but not the most useful, sense – indicating those who pursue *purely mathematical* general equilibrium theory. Weintraub (1983, p. 37) concludes his historical review of the literature on the existence of equilibrium: 'The [Walrasian] "equilibrium" story is one in which empirical work, ideas of facts and falsifications, played no role at all.' The Austrian precursors of the new classicals were sceptical of empirical economics (see chapter 10). The new classicals themselves are sceptical of empirical economics that does not pay heed to general equilibrium, but not of empirical economics in general (Lucas 1976, Sargent 1982). The acceptance of the importance of empirical economics is one thing that distinguishes the new classicals most clearly from the Austrians.
33 Buiter (1980) correctly observes that all that is needed for the 'Lucas critique' to go through is a direct effect of government policy on private expectations. Rational expectations is but one way of getting it.
34 Friedman and Schwartz (1982, chapter 2).
35 Lucas (1981a, Introduction) qualifies his position somewhat. How far back one must go to secure invariance depends in part on the particular problem at hand. Nevertheless, he would generally prefer to take only tastes and technology as given.
36 Lucas and Sargent (1979) and Lucas (1981b).
37 See Reder (1982).
38 For example, see Sargent (1982) and Lucas (1977).
39 Friedman (1976, p. 19).

40 Lucas (1977).
41 Friedman (1982).
42 Friedman and Schwartz (1982, chapter 2).
43 Marshall (1930, book 5).
44 Friedman (1974a) and Friedman and Schwartz (1963b).
45 Lucas (1977, p. 15).
46 Friedman (1976, pp. 82, 282). I am grateful to Gianluigi Pelloni for pointing out my error in attributing approval of the risk–uncertainty distinction to Friedman in the earlier version of this chapter (Hoover, 1984b). See Pelloni (1986) for a discussion of Friedman's Bayesian interpretation of probability.
47 Friedman and Schwartz (1982, chapter 12).
48 Lucas (1975, p. 180).
49 Lucas (1975, p. 180).
50 Lucas (1977, p. 215) and Hayek (1933a, p. 42).
51 Lucas (1981a, Introduction).
52 Lucas (1977, p. 234).
53 Lucas (1980c, p. 287).
54 'Secular' here is used in the usual modern sense, which differs from Marshall's usage in which the secular is a longer horizon than the long run (Marshall, 1930, book 5, chapter 5).

Chapter 10

1 Hicks (1967b).
2 Lucas (1987, p. 108).
3 Lucas (1977, pp. 215, 217, 1980c, 1987, p. 47). The word 'casually' indicates that Lucas reflects the lack of *systematic* interest, common among new classical economists, in locating their doctrine within the history of economic thought. He remarks that, while viewing doctrine in terms of 'schools' and historical development may be interesting and illuminating and perhaps even particularly appropriate to debates over public policy, it is unlikely to be informative about the issues which are critical to the substantive development of macroeconomics and the theory of business cycles (see Lucas, 1981a, pp. 1, 2, 1987, p. 1). He has not hesitated, however, to take up rhetorical cudgels in order to do a little school-bashing himself; see particularly Lucas and Sargent's (1979) attack on 'Keynesian' economics.
4 For example, Kantor (1979), Laidler (1981, 1982, 1986) and Moss and Vaughn (1986, pp. 546, 547).
5 This assessment of Mises' monetary theory is due to Rothbard (1976, p. 160), who provides an excellent summary of its main points.
6 In particular, the economics departments of New York University and George Mason University, Virginia, are hotbeds of Austrian thinking. Good accounts of the main lines of modern Austrian thought as well as some indication of the significant differences between Austrian economists are found in Shand (1984) and O'Driscoll and Rizzo (1985).

7   Mises ([1949] 1966, p. 10 and chapter 4).

8   Mises ([1949] 1966, chapter 4) and Hayek (1945b, 1979, chapter 4).

9   See, for example, Sargent and Wallace's analysis of the real bills doctrine in chapter 7, section 7.3.

10 Mises ([1949] 1966, p. 2).

11 Mises ([1949] 1966, pp. 2, 42).

12 While no Austrian believes that social entities are not real, there appears to be a disagreement between Hayek and Mises over the epistemological status of the assertion that any collective entity is real. Collectivism, according to Hayek (1979, p. 93), treats wholes (e.g. society, economy or class) as objects subject to laws. This is, he claims, an example of Whitehead's 'fallacy of misplaced concreteness' (or, as he often writes, of 'conceptual realism') (p. 95ff.). Only the individuals, which constitute the whole, are truly concrete. He writes: 'What make [*sic*] a number of individual phenomena facts of one kind are the attributes which we select in order to treat them as members of one class' (p. 80). And later, ' ... the wholes about which we speak exist only if, and to the extent to which, the theory is correct which we have formed about the connection of the parts which they imply, and which we can explicitly state only in the form of a model built from those relationships' (p. 98). These statements seem to support the philosophical position of nominalism: the view that the general does not exist independently of our explicit or implicit theorizing; the view that such theorizing is constitutive of the reality of non-individuals. Mises ([1949] 1966, p. 42), however, argues that nominalism versus realism is not an issue for methodological individualism. He says flatly: 'It is uncontested that in the sphere of human action social entities have real existence.' He goes on to say, ' ... a social collective has no existence and reality outside the individual members' actions.' But he never endorses the position that the reality of social entities depends on our own theorizing about them. His position is not, however, completely unambiguous (see p. 124, fn. 3). Hayek's position seems to square well with Lucas's (1987, p. 2) stipulation that theory is a 'synonym' for 'model', as well as with his view that phenomena such as involuntary unemployment do not exist outside models which find them to be helpful constructs (see chapter 3, section 3.4, and Lucas (1987, pp. 48–54, especially p. 52, fn. 3)).

13 Hayek (1979, p. 67).

14 Mises ([1949] 1966, pp. 31ff.) and Hayek (1979, pp. 72, 73).

15 Mises ([1949] 1966, pp. 51–8) and Lachmann (1943, p. 20). The Austrian term 'understanding' is a translation of Max Weber's German *Verstehen* and should be read as a technical term describing this imaginative transposition – the attempt to see another's actions from the inside as it were.

16 Lucas (1987, p. 57).

17 For example Hayek (1979, pp. 104, 105). Lachmann alone among the Austrians seems to be less than wholehearted in his condemnation of macroeconomics (see Lachmann 1956, p. 14).

18 Lucas (1987, pp. 107, 108). Lucas promotes a solecism. Marshall virtually

invented the term 'economics'; Smith and Ricardo certainly knew the subject only as 'political economy' (see Schumpeter, 1954, p. 21).

19 Of course, particular new classical models may start at a less fundamental level, so that profits rather than utility or, perhaps, no functions at all are maximized. New classicals must suppose, however, that a well-defined exercise in utility maximization lies behind every such simplified problem.

20 Mises ([1949] 1966, p. 10).

21 Mises ([1949] 1966, pp. 19–22).

22 Mises does not deny that humans often behave reactively, e.g. involuntary twitches and perhaps even flashes of anger. He does deny that much behaviour which outside observers might call 'irrational' is not, because even if it does not represent an objectively best or even feasible means of attaining the actor's ends as seen by the observer, it nonetheless represents the actor's own adaptation of his behaviour to his ends.

23 For example Mises ([1949] 1966, p. 582), Hayek (1937, pp. 40, 52) and Lachmann (1956, p. 25).

24 Mises ([1949] 1966, part 3, [1951] 1981, chapters 5 and 6 and appendix) and Hayek (1935a, b, 1940).

25 It is difficult to find a single sentence or paragraph in which Mises makes this point explicit. It is, however, the essence of much of his writing on economic calculation. The argument can be reconstructed from Mises ([1949] 1966): economic calculation is impossible without money prices, which carry relative price information (pp. 201, 208, 209, 214); inflation is defined to be expansion of the supply of money (p. 414) and leads to widespread, but not proportional, price increases (pp. 202, 412 *passim*) (see also Mises, [1912] 1981, p. 163 ff.); such disproportional fluctuations disturb accurate economic calculation (p. 424), and if they are sufficiently large, as in hyperinflation, people seek to avoid money altogether, which would render calculation impossible, except that the avoidance of money produces a self-destruction of the inflation (pp. 427, 428), so that, finally, the policy implication is not to stabilize the price level, which is a chimerical goal because the general price level is an ill-defined concept, but to control the stock of money (pp. 219–24).

26 Lachmann (1956, p. 22).

27 Lachmann (1956, pp. 23, 24).

28 Lachmann (1956, p. 30).

29 Lucas (1980c, 1987).

30 This is an interpretation of Lucas's general views applied to the specific case of the Austrians. Modern Keynesians usually bear the brunt of his direct criticism.

31 See, for example, chapter 9, section 9.2 and Lucas (1987, pp. 46, 47).

32 Lucas (1987, p. 108).

33 Lucas (1980c, pp. 271, 272). Lucas's point is not at all obviously correct. The reason a model answers simple questions well may have as much to do with the questions as with the model. Harder questions may be so far outside the range of the model's applicability that no matter how well it answers simple questions we would not or should not trust it.

34 Lucas (1987, p. 451).
35 Lucas (1977, especially pp. 218–22, 1980c, pp. 287–91, 1987).
36 Lucas (1977, p. 218).
37 Lucas (1986) provides the justification for this procedure, while Lucas (1973, 1980b, 1986, pp. S403–8) are examples of its application.
38 Mises ([1949] 1966, pp. 2, 3, 39) and Friedman (1953).
39 Mises ([1949] 1966, p. 10 *passim*) and Hayek (1979, p. 42ff.).
40 Mises ([1949] 1966, p. 105).
41 Mises ([1949] 1966, p. 105). That Mises accepts Knight's risk–uncertainty distinction is clear from his discussion of insurance (e.g. pp. 289–94).
42 See chapter 4, section 4.3, and chapter 8, section 8.4.
43 Lucas (1987, p. 8, fn. 1).
44 Mises ([1949] 1966, pp. 32–6).
45 Mises ([1949] 1966, pp. 38–40).
46 How many economists would agree with the following statement? 'In the concept of money all the theorems of monetary theory are already implied. The quantity theory of money does not add anything to our knowledge which is not virtually contained in the concept of money' (Mises, [1949] 1966, p. 38).
47 For example compare Lucas (1977, pp. 223, 224) with Mises ([1949] 1966, pp. 11, 12).
48 For example see Lucas (1986, pp. S405–S406). Rationality, he asserts, implies that people 'ought' not to care about pure changes in units. He and other new classical economists stand Hume's dictum on his head by deriving 'is' from 'ought'.
49 Lucas (1987, p. 15) observes that the general solutions to the particular intertemporal maximization problems which he believes should be used to characterize policy are not known: 'This is a mathematical frontier on which there is much to be done.' Given that agents within the model are supposed to have rational expectations, this is an extraordinary testament to the seductive power of Friedman's 'as-if' methodology.
50 Mises ([1949] 1966, p. 103).
51 Mises ([1949] 1966, p. 199).
52 Mises ([1949] 1966, p. 237).
53 Hayek (1979, p. 75, fn. 8).
54 Hayek (1979, p. 72 ff.) and Mises ([1949] 1966, pp. 31, 41, 351 *passim*).
55 Mises ([1949] 1966, p. 69).
56 Mises ([1949] 1966, pp. 55, 103, 354).
57 Hayek (1979, pp. 72, 73) and Mises ([1949] 1966, 59–64).
58 Levy (1985), although sympathetic to methodological individualism, argues that aggregates may play a legitimate irreducible role in *individual* decision problems when information is imperfect. The general level of prices plays such a role in new classical models of aggregate supply.
59 Hayek (1979, pp. 93ff, 124) and Lachmann (1976, p. 152).
60 Mises ([1949] 1966, p. 217).
61 Lachmann (1976, p. 153).
62 Lucas (1987, p. 96).

63 Mises ([1912] 1981, p. 217).
64 Hayek (1979, p. 73) and Mises ([1949] 1966, pp. 59–64).
65 See the similar observations of Laidler (1986, p. 36).
66 Mises ([1949] 1966, p. 30ff).
67 Mises ([1949] 1966, p. 41).
68 Mises ([1949] 1966, p.52) observes that historians often disagree about the teachings of the non-historical sciences.
69 Mises ([1949] 1966, pp. 65, 66).
70 Hayek (1945a, p. 77).
71 Hayek (1979, p. 74); cf. Lachmann (1969, p. 89).
72 Hayek (1933a, p. 197).
73 Lachmann (1943, p. 17).
74 Hayek (1945a, p. 77).
75 Hayek (1937, p. 33).
76 Hayek (1937, p. 44).
77 Lachmann (1943, pp. 16, 17).
78 Lucas (1980c, p. 286).
79 Lucas (1987, pp. 46, 47).
80 Lucas (1987, p. 35).
81 Mises ([1949] 1966, p. 350). Mises (pp. 350–5) then proceeds to a detailed condemnation of the various species of mathematical economics: econometrics, production theory and the theory of general equilibrium.
82 Hayek (1945a, p. 78); cf. Hayek (1933a, p. 55).
83 Hayek (1979, p. 89).
84 Hayek (1979, p. 90; cf. p. 108). Hayek's views on mathematics and statistics are perhaps ambivalent and may have changed over time. He is probably the first, and maybe the only, important Austrian ever to include an integral in a footnote (Hayek, [1931] 1935, p. 41, fn. 1). He once headed a statistical institute (Hayek, 1984, p. 3). He also once thought that better statistical understanding of business cycles would lead, not to predictive models, but to a 'symptomology' which would provide some basis for stabilization (Hayek, 1925, p. 6).
85 Lucas (1980c, p. 288).
86 Lachmann (1969, p. 96).
87 Lucas (1987, pp. 7–11).
88 Lachmann (1956, p. 14).
89 Lucas (1986, p. 2).
90 Lachmann (1956, pp. 14, 15). Historically, Lachmann is reacting to expectations schemes such as adaptive or extrapolative expectations rather than to rational expectations. Rational expectations are not the product of *simple* reaction functions; they are nonetheless a species of reaction function, which eliminates the need for subjective interpretation.
91 Lachmann (1956, p. 15).
92 The Austrians argue that a longer or 'more roundabout' method of production is necessarily more productive. For if the same volume of consumption goods could be produced with the same commitment of

resources but in a shorter time, the longer process would simply not be used. There must be a trade-off between the length of the efficient production process and the ratio of output to resources expended. 'Efficiency' must be stressed, because less productive longer processes are possible but would never be chosen. See Mises ([1949] 1966, chapter 18).

93 The 'reswitching' debate of the late 1950s and early 1960s demonstrated that the length of the most economically efficient process (the one with the greatest net present value) need not be monotonically related to the interest rate (see Hicks, 1973, chapter 4).

94 This explanation of unemployment comes closer to Lilien (1982) than to any new classical model.

95 Of all the Austrians, Lachmann (1956) seems to be the most sympathetic to real business cycle models.

96 Hayek ([1931] 1935, pp. 32–5).

97 Lucas and Rapping use intertemporal substitutability of leisure, as we saw in chapter 2, to explain unemployment as a voluntary response to price signals. Hayek clearly disagrees. Unemployment, he believes, is the unfortunate consequence of the rearrangement of the structure of capital. Mises ([1949] 1966, pp. 577, 598, 599) is closer to the new classicals: unemployment, he argues, is always the result of too high a price for labour.

98 Hicks (1967b, pp. 207–9).

99 Hayek ([1931] 1935, pp. 106, 160); see also Hayek (1933b, p. 161).

100 Hayek (1933a, pp. 124, 125).

101 This is true in Hayek's model, but is also explicit in Mises ([1949] 1966, pp. 553ff.).

102 Lachmann (1943, p. 23). The term 'elasticity of expectations' is due to Hicks (1939, p. 205).

103 Mises (1943, p. 252).

104 Mises (1943, p. 251) does not rule out the possibility that expectations might become more rational in the future: 'The teachings of the monetary theory of the trade cycle are to-day so well known even outside of the circle of economists, that the naive optimism which inspired the entrepreneurs in the boom periods has given way to a greater scepticism. It may be that business men will in future react to credit expansion in another manner than they did in the past. It may be that they will avoid using for an expansion of their operation the easy money available, because they will keep in mind the inevitable end of the boom. Some signs forebode such a change. But it is too early to make a positive statement.'

105 Lucas (1980c, 1987).

106 Lucas (1977, p. 213).

107 Lucas (1977, p. 213) and Hayek (1933a, p. 33 fn.).

108 Lucas (1977, p. 213) and Hayek (1933a, p. 42 fn.); see also chapter 9, section 9.2.

109 Lucas (1975, pp. 179, 180, 1977, p. 214).

110 Hayek (1933a, p. 28).

111   Hayek (1933a, p. 30).
112   Hayek (1933a, p. 42ff. especially p. 44).
113   Lucas (1980c, p. 278, 1987, p. 15).
114   Hayek (1928, especially p. 101); cf. Hayek (1937, pp. 36, 37, 41).
115   Hayek (1928, p. 75). Lachmann (1969, p. 89) argues that the notion of equilibrium growth is absurd. But this reflects his belief that growth involves structural change rather than the idea that equilibrium is necessarily a state of rest.
116   Hayek (1937, p. 41).
117   Lucas (1987, p. 16).
118   Hayek (1937, p. 39) asks to whom the data of the economy are given. In the context of rational expectations, the model itself is a datum of the economy.
119   Hayek (1937, p. 51).
120   Lachmann (1945, p. 252). Mises (1943, p. 252) implies the same thing. Many commentators have observed that the assumption of rational expectations conflates the modeller with the agent modelled and does not allow sufficiently for the variety of views that economic agents, like economists themselves, hold about how the economy functions; see, for example, Kantor (1979, p. 1424) and O'Driscoll and Rizzo (1985, pp. 43, 216ff.). Laidler (1986, p. 45) finds it slightly silly for Barro to assume, in his empirical test of the Lucas supply function (see chapter 8, section 8.2), that agents held rational expectations as early as 1945 and yet to believe that there has been a 'rational expectations revolution'. Economists are sometimes thought to know no more about the economy than the public; they are not usually thought to know less. For empirical evidence that this may in fact be wrong, see Bryan and Gavin (1986).
121   Hayek (1937, p 40)
122   Hayek (1937, pp. 38, pp. 40–2).
123   Hayek (1937, p. 34).
124   Hayek (1937, p. 45).
125   Lucas and Sargent (1979, p. 311).
126   Lachmann (1969, p. 89, 1976, p. 126, 1956, pp. 13, 14).
127   Lachmann (1976, p. 130).
128   Lachmann (1956, pp. 25, 50).
129   See Lachmann (1956, p. 113), O'Driscoll and Rizzo (1985, pp. 75, 199) and O'Driscoll (1979, p. 166).

References

Aiyagari, S. Rao (1985) 'Deficits, interest rates and the tax distribution,' *Federal Reserve Bank of Minneapolis Quarterly Review* **9**(1), Winter, 5–14.

Altonji, Joseph G. (1982) 'The intertemporal substitution model of labour market fluctuations: an empirical analysis', *Review of Economic Studies* **49**(5), special issue, 783–824.

Altug, Sumru (1985) 'Gestation lags and the business cycle', unpublished working paper, University of Minnesota, Minneapolis, MN.

Ashenfelter, Orley (1984) 'Macroeconomic analyses and microeconomic analyses of labor supply', in Karl Brunner and Allan H. Meltzer (eds) *Essays on Macroeconomic Implication of Financial and Labor Markets and Political Processes*. Carnegie–Rochester Conference Series on Public Policy, Vol. 21, Autumn. Amsterdam: North-Holland, 117–56.

Backus, David, and John Driffill (1985a) 'Inflation and reputation', *American Economic Review* **75**(3), 530–8.

——and—— (1985b) 'Rational expectation and policy credibility following a change in regime', *Review of Economic Studies* **52**(2), 211–21.

Barro, Robert J. (1974) 'Are government bonds net wealth?' *Journal of Political Economy* **59**(2), 93–116.

——(1976) 'Rational expectation and the role of monetary policy', in Lucas and Sargent (1981, pp. 229–59). Reprinted from *Journal of Monetary Economics* **2**(1), 1–32.

——(1977) 'Unanticipated money growth and unemployment in the United States', in Lucas and Sargent (1981, pp. 563–84). Reprinted from *American Economic Review* **67**(2).

——(1978) 'Unanticipated money, output, and the price level in the United States', in Lucas and Sargent (1981, pp. 585–616). Reprinted from *Journal of Political Economy* **86**(4).

——(1979) 'On the determination of public debt', *Journal of Political Economy* **87**(5, part 1), 940–71.

——(1980) 'Federal deficit policy and the effects of public debt shocks', *Journal of Money, Credit and Banking* **12** (4, part II), 747–61.

——(1986) 'Recent developments in the theory of rules versus discretion',

Conference Papers: Selected Papers from the Annual Conference of the Royal Economic Society and the Association of University Teachers of Economics, Keble College, Oxford, 1985. Supplement to *Economic Journal* **96**, 23–37.

——(1987a) *Macroeconomics*, 2nd edn. New York: Wiley.

——(1987b) 'Budget deficit: only a minor crisis', *Wall Street Journal*, 16 January, p. 22, col. 3.

Barro, Robert J., and David B. Gordon (1983a) 'A positive theory of monetary policy in a natural rate model', *Journal of Political Economy* **91**(4), 589–610.

——and—— (1983b) 'Rules, discretion and reputation in a model of monetary policy, *Journal of Monetary Economics* **12**(2), 101–21.

Barro, Robert J., and Herschel Grossman (1971) 'A general disequilibrium model of income and employment', *American Economic Review* **61**(1), 82–93.

——and——(1976) *Money, Employment and Inflation.* Cambridge: Cambridge University Press.

Barro, Robert J., and Zvi Hercowitz (1980) 'Money stock revisions and unanticipated money growth', *Journal of Monetary Economics* **6**(2), 257–67.

Barsky, Robert B., N. Gregory Mankiw and Stephen P. Zeldes (1986) 'Ricardian consumers with Keynesian propensities', *American Economic Review* **76**(4), 676–91.

Basmann, R. L. (1965) 'A note on the statistical testability of "explicit causal chains" against the class of "interdependent" models', *Journal of the American Statistical Society* **60**(312), 1080–93.

Begg, David K. H. (1982) *The Rational Expectations Revolution in Macroeconomics: Theories and Evidence.* Deddington, Oxford: Philip Allan.

Black, Fischer (1970) 'Banking and interest rates in a world without money', *Journal of Bank Research* Autumn, 9–20.

Blanchard, Oliver J. (1984) 'The Lucas critique and the Volcker deflation', *American Economic Review* **74**(2), 211–15.

Blaug, Mark (1980) *The Methodology of Economics: or How Economists Explain.* Cambridge: Cambridge University Press.

Blinder, Alan S. (1984) 'Discussion' [of Sargent (1984)], *American Economic Review* **74**(2), 417–19.

Blinder, Alan S., and Robert M. Solow (1974) 'Analytical foundations of fiscal policy', in Alan S. Blinder et al., *The Economics of Public Finance.* Washington, DC: Brookings Institution, 3–115.

Boland, Lawrence A. (1979) 'A critique of Friedman's critics', *Journal of Economic Literature* **17**(2), 503–22.

——(1982) *The Foundation of Economic Method.* London: Allen & Unwin.

Boskin Michael J., and Laurence J. Kotlikoff (1985) 'Public debt and US savings: a new test of the neutrality hypothesis', National Bureau of Economic Research Working Paper no. 1646, June.

Bray, Margaret (1982) 'Learning, estimation and the stability of rational expectations', *Journal of Economic Theory* **26**(3), 318–39.

——(1983) 'Convergence to rational expectations equilibrium', in Roman Frydman and Edmund S. Phelps (eds) *Individual Forecasting and Aggregate Outcomes.* Cambridge: Cambridge University Press, 123–32.

Brown, A. J. (1955) *The Great Inflation: 1939–1951*. London: Oxford University Press.

Bryan, Michael F., and William T. Gavin (1986) 'Comparing inflation expectations of households and economists: is a little knowledge a dangerous thing?', *Federal Reserve Bank of Cleveland Economic Review* Quarter 3, 14–19.

Bryant, John (1980) 'Transactions demand for money and moral hazard', in Kareken and Wallace (1980, pp. 233–42).

Bryant, John, and Neil Wallace (1979) 'The inefficiency of interest-bearing national debt', *Journal of Political Economy* **87**(2), 365–81.

——and——(1980) 'A suggestion for further simplifying the theory of money', *Federal Reserve Bank of Minneapolis Staff Report* no. 62.

——and——(1984) 'A price discrimination analysis of monetary policy', *Review of Economic Studies* **51**(2), 279–88.

Brunner, Karl, and Allan H. Meltzer (1976) 'An aggregative theory for a closed economy', in Stein (1976, pp. 69–103).

Buchanan, James M. (1958) *Public Principles of Public Debt*. Homewood, IL: Irwin.

——(1976) 'Barro on the Ricardian equivalence theorem', *Journal of Political Economy* **84**(2), 337–42.

Buiter William H. (1980) 'The macroeconomics of Dr. Pangloss: a critical survey of the new classical macroeconomics', *Economic Journal* **90**(357), 34–50.

——(1981) 'The superiority of contingent over fixed rules in models with rational expectations', *Economic Journal* **91**(363), 647–70.

Butler, Samuel (1903) *The Way of All Flesh*.

Cagan, Philip (1956) 'The monetary dynamics of hyperinflation', in Friedman (1956a, pp. 25–120).

Campbell, John Y., and N. Gregory Mankiw (1987) 'Permanent and transitory components in macroeconomic fluctuations', *American Economic Review* **77**(2), 111–17.

Cass, David, and Menahem Yaari (1966) 'A re-examination of the pure consumption loans model', *Journal of Political Economy* **74**(4), 353–67.

Chick, Victoria (1983) *Macroeconomics after Keynes: A Reconsideration of the General Theory*. Deddington, Oxford: Philip Allan.

Chow, Gregory C. (1986) 'Are expectations rational in present value models?', Princeton Econometric Research Program, Research Memorandum no. 328, October.

Christ Carl A., (1968) 'A simple macroeconomic model with a government budget constraint', *Journal of Political Economy* **76**(1), 53–67.

Clower, Robert (1965) 'The Keynesian counter-revolution: a theoretical appraisal', in Hahn and Brechling (1965, pp. 103–25). Reprinted in Clower (1984, pp. 34–58).

——(1967) 'A reconsideration of the microfoundations of monetary theory', *Western Economic Journal* **6**(1), 1–8.

——(1984) *Money and Markets: Essays by Robert W. Clower* (ed. Donald A. Walker). Cambridge: Cambridge University Press.

Cooley, Thomas F., and Stephen F. LeRoy (1985) 'Atheoretical macroeconometrics: a critique', *Journal of Monetary Economics* **16**(3).

Cooley, Thomas F., Stephen F. LeRoy and Neil Raymon (1984a) 'Economet-ric policy evaluation: note', *American Economic Review* **74**(3), 467–70.

——,—— and—— (1984b) 'Modeling policy interventions', unpublished typescript University of California, Santa Barbara, CA, and University of Missouri, Columbia, MO.

Cournot, Augustin ([1838] 1927) *Researches into the Mathematical Principles of the Theory of Wealth* (trans. Nathaniel T. Bacon). New York: Macmillan.

Craine, Roger, and Gikas Hardouvelis (1983) 'Are rational expectations for real?', *Greek Economic Review* **5**(1), 5–32.

Darby, Michael (1984) 'Some pleasant monetarist arithmetic', *Federal Reserve Bank of Minneapolis Quarterly Review* **8**(2), Spring, 15–20.

Desai, Meghnad (1975) 'The Phillips curve: a revisionist interpretation', *Economica* NS **42**(1), 1–19.

——(1984) 'Wages, prices and unemployment a quarter century after the Phillips curve', in David F. Hendry and Kenneth F. Wallis (eds) *Econometrics and Quantitative Economics*. Oxford: Basil Blackwell.

Dolan, Edwin G. (1976) *The Foundations of Austrian Economics*. Kansas City, MO: Sheed and Ward.

Domar, Evsey S. (1944) 'The "burden of the debt" and the national income', *American Economic Review* **34**(4), 798–827.

Dornbusch, Rudiger (1976) 'Comments', in Stein (1976, pp. 104–25).

Eichenbaum, Martin (1985) 'Vector autoregressions for causal inference?: a comment', in Karl Brunner and Allan H. Meltzer (eds) *Understanding Monetary Regimes*. Carnegie–Rochester Conference Series on Public Policy, Vol. 22, Spring. Amsterdam: North-Holland, 305–18.

Eichenbaum, Martin, and Kenneth J. Singleton (1986) 'Do equilibrium real business cycle theories explain postwar U.S. business cycles?', in Stanley Fischer (ed.) *NBER Macroeconomics Annual 1986*. Cambridge, MA: MIT Press.

Engle, Robert E., David F. Hendry and Jean-Francois Richard (1983) 'Exogeneity', *Econometrica* **51**(2), 277–304.

Fama, Eugene (1978) 'The effects of a firm's investment and financing decisions on the welfare of its security holders', *American Economic Review* **68**(3), 272–84.

——(1980) 'Banking in the theory of finance', *Journal of Monetary Economics* **6**(1), 39–57.

——(1982) 'Fiduciary currency and commodity standards', unpublished typescript, January.

——(1983) 'Financial intermediation and price level control', *Journal of Monetary Economics* **12**(1), 7–28.

Farmer, Roger E. A. (1984) 'Bursting bubbles: on the rationality of hyperinflations in optimizing models', *Journal of Monetary Economics* **14**(1), 29–36.

Feldstein, Martin (1976) 'Perceived wealth in bonds and social security: a comment', *Journal of Political Economy* **84**(2), 331–6.

Fischer, Stanley. (1977) 'Long-term contracts, rational expectations, and the optimal money supply rule', in Lucas and Sargent (1981, pp. 261–84). Reprinted from *Journal of Political Economy* **85**(1), 191–206.

Fisher, Irving (1930) *The Theory of Interest*. New York: Macmillan.

Frankel, S. Herbert (1977) *Money: Two Philosophies: The Conflict of Trust and Authority*. Oxford: Basil Blackwell.

Friedman, Milton (1948) 'A monetary and fiscal framework for economic stability', *American Economic Review* **38**(3), 245–64.

——(1949) 'The Marshallian demand curve', *Journal of Political Economy* **37**(6), 463–95.

——(1951) 'Commodity-reserve currency', *Journal of Political Economy* **59**(3), 203–32.

——(1953) 'The methodology of positive economics', *Essays in Positive Economics*. Chicago: University of Chicago Press.

——(1955) 'Leon Walras and his economic system: a review article', *American Economic Review* **45**(5), 900–9.

——(ed.) (1956a) *Studies in the Quantity Theory of Money*. Chicago: University of Chicago Press.

——(1956b) 'The quantity theory of money: a restatement', in Friedman (1956a).

——(1957) *A Theory of the Consumption Function*. Princeton, NJ: Princeton University Press.

——(1959a) *A Program for Monetary Stability*. New York: Fordham University Press.

——(1959b) 'The demand for money: some theoretical and empirical results', *Journal of Political Economy* **67**(3), 327–51.

——(1961) 'The lag in the effect of monetary policy', in Friedman (1969a, pp. 237–60).

——(1968a) 'The role of monetary policy', *American Economic Review* **58**(1), 1–17.

——(1968b) *Dollars and Deficits: Inflation, Monetary Policy and the Balance of Payments*. Englewood Cliffs, NJ: Prentice-Hall.

——(1969a) *The Optimal Quantity of Money and Other Essays*. London: Macmillan.

——(1969b) 'The optimal quantity of money', in Friedman (1969a).

——(1974a) 'A theoretical framework for monetary analysis', in Robert J. Gordon (ed.) *Milton Friedman's Monetary Framework*. Chicago: University of Chicago Press.

——(1974b) 'Monetary correction', IEA Occasional Paper no. 41. London: Institute for Economic Affairs.

——(1975) 'Unemployment versus inflation: an evaluation of the Phillips curve', IEA Occasional Paper no. 44. London: Institute for Economic Affairs.

——(1976) *Price Theory*. Chicago: Aldine.

——(1977) 'Nobel lecture: Inflation and unemployment', *Journal of Political Economy* **85**(3), 451–72.

——(1978) 'How stands the theory and practice of monetary policy', unpublished paper presented to the Mount Pelerin Society Conference on Monetary Problems and Policy, Hong Kong.

——(1982) Personal communication, 8 July.

Friedman, Milton, and Anna J. Schwartz (1963a) *A Monetary History of the United States*. Princeton, NJ: Princeton University Press.

——and—— (1963b) 'Money and business cycles', in Friedman (1969a).

——and—— (1982) *Monetary Trends in the United States and United Kingdom: Their Relation to Income, Prices and Interest Rates 1867–1975.* Chicago: University of Chicago Press.

Froyen R. T., and R. N. Waud (1980) 'International evidence on output–inflation tradeoffs', *American Economic Review* **63**(3), 326–34.

Gardner, John (1973) *Grendl.* London: Picador.

Goldfeld, Stephen (1982) 'Rules, discretion and reality', *American Economic Review* **72**(2), 361–6.

Gordon, Robert J. (1981) 'Output fluctuations and gradual price adjustment', *Journal of Economic Literature* **19**(2), 493–530.

——(1982) 'Price inertia and policy ineffectiveness in the United States, 1890–1980', *Journal of Political Economy* **90**(6), 1087–117.

Gorman, W. M. (1953) 'Community preference fields', *Econometrica* **21**(1), 63–80.

Granger, C. W. J. (1969) 'Investigating causal relations by econometric models and cross-spectral methods', in Lucas and Sargent (1981, pp. 371–86). Reprinted from *Econometrica* **37**(3).

——(1980) 'Testing for causality: a personal viewpoint', *Journal of Economic Dynamics and Control* **2**(4), 329–52.

Greenfield, R. L., and L. B. Yeager (1983) A *laissez faire* approach to monetary stability, *Journal of Money, Credit and Banking* **15**(3), 302–15.

Grossman, Herschel I. (1980) 'Rational Expectations, business cycles, and government behavior', in Stanley Fischer (ed.) *Rational Expectations and Economic Policy.* Chicago: University of Chicago Press.

Gurley, John, and Edwin Shaw (1960) *Money in a Theory of Finance.* Washington, DC: Brookings Institution.

Haavelmo, Trgyve (1944) 'The probability approach in econometrics', *Econometrica* **12**, supplement, July.

Hahn, F. H. (1965) 'On some problems of proving the existence of equilibrium in a monetary economy', in Hahn and Brechling (1965, pp. 126–35).

——(1971) 'Professor Friedman's views on money: a review article', *Economica* NS **38**(149), 61–80.

——(1980) 'Monetarism and economic theory', *Economica* **47**(185), 1–17.

——(1982) *Money and Inflation.* Oxford: Basil Blackwell.

——(1986) 'Review of Arjo Klamer, *Conversations with Economists: New Classical Economists and Opponents Speak Out on the Current Controversy in Macroeconomics', Economics and Philosophy* **2**(2), 275–82.

Hahn, F. H., and F. P. R. Brechling (eds) (1965) *The Theory of Interest Rates.* London: Macmillan.

Hall, Robert E. (1982) *'Monetary Trends in the United States and the United Kingdom*: a review from the perspective of new developments in monetary economics', *Journal of Economic Literature* **20**(4), 1552–6.

Hands, D. Wade (1986) '*Ad hoc*ness in economics and the Popperian tradition', unpublished typescript, University of Puget Sound, Tacoma, WA.

Hansen, Gary D. (1985) 'Indivisible labor and the business cycle', *Journal of Monetary Economics* **16**(3), 309–28.

Hansen Lars Peter, and Thomas J. Sargent (1980), 'Estimating and formulating dynamic linear rational expectations models', in Lucas and Sargent (1981, pp. 91–125). Reprinted from *Journal of Economic Dynamics and Control* 2(1).

Harris, Seymour E. (1947) *National Debt and the New Economics*. New York: McGraw-Hill.

Harvey, A. C. (1981) *The Econometric Analysis of Time Series*. Deddington, Oxford: Philip Allan.

Hayashi, Fumio (1985) 'Tests for liquidity constraints: a critical survey', unpublished paper, August.

Hayek, Friedrich A. von (1925) 'The monetary policy of the United States after the recovery from the 1920 crisis', trans. from the German in Hayek (1984, pp. 5–23).

——(1928) 'Intertemporal price equilibrium and movements in the value of money', trans. from the German in Hayek (1984, pp. 71–117).

——([1931] 1935) *Prices and Production,* 2nd edn. London: Routlege & Kegan Paul.

——(1933a) *Monetary Theory and the Trade Cycle* (trans. N. Kaldor and H. M. Croome). London: Jonathan Cape.

——(1933b) 'On "neutral" money', trans. from the German in Hayek (1984, pp. 159–62).

——(1935a) 'Socialist calculation I: *The Nature and History of the Problem*', in Hayek (1948, pp. 119–47). Reprinted from Hayek (ed.) *Collectivist Economic Planning*. London: Routledge.

——(1935b) 'Socialist calculation II: *The State of the Debate (1935)*', in Hayek (1948, pp. 148–80). Reprinted from Hayek (ed.) *Collectivist Economic Planning*. London: Routledge.

——(1937) 'Economics and knowledge', in Hayek (1948, pp. 119–47). Reprinted from *Economica* NS 4(1), 33–54.

——(1940) 'Socialist calculation III: *The Competitive "Solution"*', in Hayek (1948, pp. 181–208). Reprinted from *Economica* NS 7(26).

——(1945a) 'The use of knowledge in society', in Hayek (1948, pp. 77–91). Reprinted from *American Economic Review* 35(4), 519–30.

——(1945b) 'Individualism: true and false'. Reprinted in Hayek (1948, pp. 1–32).

——(1948) *Individualism and the Economic Order*. Chicago: University of Chicago Press.

——(1979) *The Counter-Revolution in Sciences: Studies in the Abuse of Reason*, 2nd edn. Indianapolis: Liberty Press.

——(1984) *Money, Capital and Fluctuations: Early Essays*. London: Routledge & Kegan Paul.

Hickman, W. B. (1950) 'The determinacy of absolute prices in classical economic theory', *Econometrica* 18(1), 9–20.

Hicks, John R. (1935) 'A suggestion for simplifying the theory of money'. Reprinted in Hicks (1967a, pp. 61–82).

——(1937) 'Mr. Keynes and the Classics', in Hicks (1967a, pp. 126–42). Reprinted from *Econometrica* 5(2).

——(1939) *Value and Capital: An Inquiry into Some Fundamental Principles of Economic Theory*, 2nd edn 1946. Oxford: Clarendon Press.

——(1967a) *Critical Essays in Monetary Theory*. Oxford: Clarendon Press.

——(1967b) 'The Hayek story', in Hicks (1967a, pp. 203–15).

——(1973) *Capital and Time: A Neo-Austrian Theory*. Oxford: Clarendon Press.

——(1982) 'The foundation of monetary theory', *Money, Interest and Wages*. Oxford: Basil Blackwell, chapter 19.

Hoover, Kevin D. (1984a) 'Methodology: a comment on Frazer and Boland, II', *American Economic Review* **74**(4), 789–92.

——(1984b) 'Two types of monetarism', *Journal of Economic Literature*, **22**(1), 58–76.

——(1985) 'Econometrics as observation: an investigation of the logic of causal inference', University of California, Davis, Working Papers in Applied Macroeconomics and Macro Policy no. 33.

Hume, David (1741/42) 'Of money', *Essays: Literature, Moral and Political*, no. 25.

Hurwicz, Leonid (1962) 'On the structural form of interdependent systems', in Ernst Nagel et al. (eds) *Logic, Methodology and the Philosophy of Science*. Stanford, CA: Stanford University Press.

Jacobs, Rodney L., Edward E. Leamer and Michael P. Ward (1979) 'Difficulties with testing for causation', *Economic Inquiry* **17**(3), 401–13.

Johnston, J. (1972) *Econometric Methods*, 2nd edn. New York: McGraw-Hill.

Kantor, Brian (1979) 'Rational expectations and economic thought', *Journal of Economic Literature* **17**(4), 1422–41.

Kareken, John H., and Neil Wallace (eds) (1980) *Models of Monetary Economics*. Minneapolis, MN: Federal Reserve Bank of Minneapolis.

Keynes, John Maynard ([1930] 1971) *A Treatise on Money*, Vol. 1. London: Macmillan.

——(1936) *The General Theory of Employment, Interest and Money*. London: Macmillan.

——(1937) 'The general theory of employment', *Quarterly Journal of Economics* **51**(2), 209–23.

——(1939) 'Professor Tinbergen's method', *Economic Journal* **49**(3), 558–68.

——(1940) *How to Pay for the War: A Radical Plan for the Chancellor of the Exchequer*. New York: Harcourt, Brace.

King, Robert G., and Charles I. Plosser (1984) 'Money, credit and prices in a real business cycle', *American Economic Review* **74**(3), 363–80.

——and——(1986) 'Money as the mechanism of exchange', *Journal of Monetary Economics* **17**(1), 93–116.

Klein, Benjamin (1974) 'The competitive supply of money', *Journal of Money, Credit and Banking* **6**(4), 421–5.

Knapp, George Friedrich (1924) *The State Theory of Money* (trans. H. M. Lucas and James Bonar), abridged. London: Macmillan.

Knight, Frank (1937) *Risk, Uncertainty and Profit*. London: London School of Economics and Political Science.

Kohn, Meir (1981) 'In defense of the finance constraint', *Economic Inquiry* **19**(2), 177–95.

——(1984) 'The finance (cash-in-advance) constraint comes of age: a survey of some recent developments in the theory of money', Dartmouth College Working Paper Series.

Koopmans, Tjalling C. (1947) 'Measurement without theory', *Review of Economics and Statistics* **29**(2), 161–72.

——(1950) 'When is an equation complete for statistical purposes', in Koopmans (ed.) *Statistical Inference in Dynamic Economic Models.* New York: Wiley; London: Chapman and Hall, 393–409.

Kremers, Jeroen J. M. (1985) 'On the stability of the U.S. Federal debt', unpublished paper, Nuffield College, June.

Kydland, Finn E. (1984) 'Labor-force heterogeneity and the business cycle', in Karl Brunner and Allan H. Meltzer (eds) *Essays on Macroeconomic Implication of Financial and Labor Markets and Political Processes.* Carnegie–Rochester Conference Series on Public Policy, Vol. 21, Autumn. Amsterdam: North-Holland.

Kydland, Finn E., and Edward C. Prescott (1977) 'Rules rather than discretion: the inconsistency of optimal plans', in Lucas and Sargent (1981, pp. 619–37). Reprinted from *Journal of Political Economy* **85**(3).

——and——(1982) 'Time to build and aggregate fluctuations', *Econometrica* **50**(6), 1345–69.

Lachmann, Ludwig A. (1943) 'The role of expectations in economics as a social science', *Economica* NS **10**(1), 12–23.

——(1945) 'A note on the elasticity of expectations', *Economica* NS **12**(4), 248–53.

——(1956) *Capital and its Structure.* London: London School of Economics and Political Science; London: Bell.

——(1969) 'Methodological individualism and the market economy', in Erich Streissler et al. (eds) *Roads to Freedom: Essays in Honour of Friedrich A. von Hayek.* New York: Kelley, 89–103.

——(1976) 'On the central concept of Austrian economics: Market Process,' in Dolan (1976, pp. 126–32).

Laidler, David (1981) 'Monetarism: an interpretation and an assessment', *Economic Journal* **91**(361), 49–55.

——(1982) *Monetarist Perspectives.* Deddington, Oxford: Philip Allan.

——(1984) 'Misconceptions about the real bills doctrine: a comment on Sargent and Wallace', *Journal of Political Economy* **92**(1), 149–55.

——(1986) 'The new classical contribution to macroeconomics', Banca Nazionale del Lavoro, Rome, *Quarterly Review* (156), 27–55.

Leamer, Edward E. (1985) 'Vector autoregressions for causal inference?', in Karl Brunner and Allan H. Meltzer (eds) *Understanding Monetary Regimes.* Carnegie–Rochester Conference Series on Public Policy, Vol. 22, Spring Amsterdam: North-Holland, 225–304.

Leijonhufvud, Axel (1968) *On Keynesian Economics and the Economics of Keynes: A Study in Monetary Theory.* New York: Oxford University Press.

Leontief, Wassily (1936) 'The fundamental assumption of Mr. Keynes's monetary theory of unemployment', *Quarterly Journal of Economics* **51** (1) 92–197.

LeRoy, Stephen F., and Neil Raymon (1984) 'A monetarist model of inflation', University of California, Santa Barbara, CA, Working Paper in Economics no. 240.

Levy, David M. (1985) 'The impossibility of a complete methodological individualist: reduction when knowledge is imperfect', *Economics and Philosophy* **1** (1), 101–8.

Lilien, David M. (1982) 'Sectoral shifts and cyclical unemployment', *Journal of Political Economy* **90** (4), 777–93.

Litterman, Robert B. (1984) 'Forecasting and policy analysis with Bayesian vector autoregression models', *Federal Reserve Bank of Minneapolis Quarterly Review* **8** (4), Fall, 30–41.

Litterman, Robert B. and Laurence Weiss (1985) 'Money real interest rates, and output: a reinterpretation of postwar U.S. data', *Econometrica* **53** (1), 129–55.

Liviatan, Nissan (1984) 'Tight money and inflation', *Journal of Monetary Economics* **13** (1), 5–16.

Long, John B., Jr, and Charles I. Plosser (1983) 'Real business cycles', *Journal of Political Economy* **91** (1), 39–69.

Lovell, Michael C. (1986) 'Tests of the rational expectations hypothesis', *American Economic Review*, **76**(1), 110–124.

Lucas, Robert E., Jr. (1972a) 'Expectations and the neutrality of money'. Reprinted in Lucas (1981a, pp. 66–89).

——(1972b) 'Econometric testing of the natural rate hypothesis', in Lucas (1981a, pp. 90–103). Reprinted from Otto Eckstein (ed.) *The Econometrics of Price Determination Conference*. Washington, DC: Board of Governors of the Federal Reserve System, 50–9.

——(1973) 'Some International Evidence on Output-Inflation Tradeoffs', in Lucas (1981a, pp. 131–45). Reprinted from *American Economic Review* **63** (3), 326–34.

——(1975) 'An equilibrium model of the business cycle', in Lucas (1981a, pp. 179–214). Reprinted from *Journal of Political Economy* **83** (6), 1113–44.

——(1976) 'Econometric policy evaluation: a critique', in Lucas (1981a, pp. 104–30). Reprinted from Karl Brunner and Allan H. Meltzer (eds) *The Phillips Curve and Labor Markets*. Carnegie–Rochester Conference Series on Public Policy, Vol. 1. Amsterdam: North Holland, 19–46.

——(1977) 'Understanding business cycles', in Lucas (1981a. pp. 215–39). Reprinted from Karl Brunner and Allan H. Meltzer (eds.) *Stabilization of the Domestic and International Economy*. Carnegie–Rochester Conference Series on Public Policy, Vol. 5, Spring. Amsterdam: North Holland.

——(1978) 'Unemployment policy', in Lucas (1981a, pp. 240–7). Reprinted from *American Economic Review* **68** (2), 353–57.

——(1980a) 'Equilibrium in a pure currency economy', in Kareken and Wallace (1980, pp. 131–46).

——(1980b) 'Two illustrations of the quantity theory of money', *American Economic Review* **74** (3), 467–70.

——(1980c) 'Methods and problems in business cycle theory', in Lucas (1981a, pp. 271–96). Reprinted from *Journal of Money, Credit and Banking* **12** (4, part 2).

——(1980d) 'Rules, discretion and the role of the economic policy advisor', in Stanley Fischer (ed.) *Rational Expectations and Economic Policy*. Chicago: University of Chicago Press, 199–210. Reprinted in Lucas (1981a, pp. 248–61).

——(1981a) *Studies in Business Cycle Theory*. Oxford: Basil Blackwell.

——(1981b) 'Tobin and monetarism: a review article', *Journal of Economic Literature*, **19** (2), 558–67.

——(1984) 'Money in a theory of finance', in Karl Brunner and Allan H. Meltzer (eds) *Essays on Macroeconomic Implications of Financial and Labor Markets and the Political Process*. Carnegie–Rochester Conference Series on Public Policy, Vol. 21, Amsterdam: North-Holland, 9–46.

——(1986) 'Adaptive behavior and economic theory', *Journal of Business* **59** (4, part 2), pp. S401–426.

——(1987) *Models of Business Cycles*. Oxford: Basil Blackwell.

Lucas, Robert E. Jr, and Leonard A. Rapping (1969a) 'Real wages, employment and inflation', in Lucas (1981a, pp. 19–58). Reprinted from *Journal of Political Economy* **77** (5), 721–54.

——and——(1969b) 'Price expectation and the Phillips curve', *American Economic Review* **59** (3), 342–50.

Lucas, Robert E., Jr, and Thomas J. Sargent (1979) 'After Keynesian macroeconomics'. Reprinted in Lucas and Sargent (1981, pp. 295–320).

——and——(eds) (1981) *Rational Expectations and Econometric Practice*. London: Allen & Unwin.

Malinvaud, Edmund (1977) *The Theory of Unemployment Reconsidered*. Oxford: Basil Blackwell.

Mankiw, N. Gregory, Julio J. Rotemberg and Lawrence H. Summers (1985) 'Intertemporal substitution in macroeconomics', *Quarterly Journal of Economics* **100** (1), 225–51.

Marshall, Alfred (1930) *Principles of Economics*, 8th edn. London: Macmillan.

Martins, Marco Antonio Campus (1980) 'A nominal theory of the nominal rate of interest and the price level', Journal of Political Economy **88** (1), 174–85.

Mayer, Thomas (ed.) (1978) *The Structure of Monetarism*. New York: W. W. Norton.

——(1984) 'The government budget constraint and standard macrotheory', *Journal of Monetary Economics* **13** (3), 371–80.

McCallum, Bennett T. (1983a) 'On non-uniqueness in rational expectations models: an attempt at perspective', *Journal of Monetary Economics* **11** (2), 139–68.

——(1983b) 'The role of overlapping-generations models in monetary economics', in Karl Brunner and Allan H. Meltzer (eds) *Money, Monetary Policy and Financial Institutions*. Carnegie–Rochester Policy Series on Public Policy, Vol. 18. Amsterdam: North-Holland, 9–44.

——(1985) 'Bank deregulation, accounting systems of exchange, and the unit of account: a critical review', in Karl Brunner and Allan H. Meltzer (eds) *The 'New Monetary Economics', Fiscal Issues and Unemployment*. Carnegie–Rochester Conference Series on Public Policy, Vol. 23. Amsterdam: North-Holland, 13–46.

——(1986) 'On 'real' and 'sticky-price' theories of the business cycle', *Journal of Money, Credit and Banking* **18** (4), 397–414.

Meade, James (1981) 'Comments on the papers by Laidler and Tobin', *Economic Journal* **91** (361), 49–55.

Metzler, Lloyd (1951) 'Wealth, savings and the role of interest', *Journal of Political Economy* **59** (2), 93–116.

Miller, Preston J. (1983) 'Higher deficit policies lead to inflation', *Federal Reserve Bank of Minneapolis Quarterly Review,* **7** (1), Winter, 8–19.

Mises, Ludwig von ([1912] 1981) *Theory of Money and Credit.* Indianapolis: Liberty Classics.

——(1943) 'Elastic expectations' and the Austrian theory of the trade cycle', *Economica* NS **10** (3), 251–2.

——([1949] 1966) *Human Action: A Treatise on Economics,* 3rd edn. Chicago: Henry Regnery.

——([1951] 1981) *Socialism: An Economic and Sociological Analysis* (trans. J. Kahane). Indianapolis: Liberty Classics.

Mishkin, Frederic S. (1983) *A Rational Expectations Approach to Macroeconomics: Testing Policy Effectiveness and Efficient Market Models.* Chicago: University of Chicago Press.

Modigliani, Franco, and R. Brumberg (1954) 'Utility analysis and the consumption function: an interpretation of cross-section data', in K. Kurihara (ed.) *Post-Keynesian Economics.* New Brunswick, NJ: Rutgers University Press.

Modigliani, Franco, and Merton H. Miller (1958) 'The cost of capital corporation finance and the theory of investment', *American Economic Review* **48** (3), 261–97.

Mood, Alexander M., Franklin A. Graybill and Duane C. Boes (1974) *Introduction to the Theory of Statistics,* 3rd edn. London: Macmillan.

Moss, Laurence S., and Karen I. Vaughn (1986) 'Hayek's Ricardo effect: a second look', *History of Political Economy* **18** (4), 543–66.

Muellbauer, John, and Richard Portes (1978) 'Macroeconomics with quantity rationing', *Economic Journal* **88** (352), 788–812.

Mundell, Robert A. (1971) *Monetary Theory: Inflation and Growth in the World Economy.* Pacific Palisades, CA: Goodyear.

Muth, John F. (1960) 'Optimal properties of exponentially weighted forecasts', in Lucas and Sargent (1981, pp. 23–32). Reprinted from *Journal of the American Statistical Association* **29** (290), 299–306.

——(1961) 'Rational expectations and the theory of price movements'. Reprinted in Lucas and Sargent (1981, pp. 3–22).

Neftci, Salih, and Thomas J. Sargent (1978) 'A little bit of evidence on the natural rate hypothesis from the U.S.', *Journal of Monetary Economics* **4** (2), 315–20.

Nelson, Charles R., and Charles I. Plosser (1982) 'Trends and random walks in economic time series: some evidence and implications', *Journal of Monetary Economics* **10** (2), 139–62.

O'Driscoll, Gerald (1977) 'The Ricardian nonequivalence theorem', *Journal of Political Economy* **85** (1), 207–10.

——(1979) 'Rational expectations, politics and stagflation', in Mario J. Rizzo (ed.) *Time, Uncertainty and Disequilibrium: An Explanation of Austrian Themes.* Lexington, MA: D.C. Health, 153–76.

O'Driscoll, Gerald, and Mario J. Rizzo (1985) *The Economics of Time and Ignorance.* Oxford: Basil Blackwell.

Patinkin, Don (1956, 1965) *Money, Interest and Prices*, 1st edn 1956, 2nd edn 1965. New York: Harper and Row.

——(1961) 'Financial intermediaries and the logical structure of monetary theory: a review article', *American Economic Review* **51** (1), 93–116.

Pelloni, Gianluigi (1986) 'A note on Friedman and the neo-Bayesian approach', University of Hull Economic Research Papers no. 143, revised May.

Pesek, Boris, and Thomas Saving (1967) *Money, Wealth and Economic Theory*. New York: Macmillan.

Phelps, Edmund S. (1967) 'Phillips curves, expectations of inflation and optimal unemployment over time', *Economica* NS, **34** (3), 254–81.

——(1968) 'Money wage dynamics and labor market equilibrium', *Journal of Political Economy* **76** (4), 678–711.

——(1970) 'Introduction: The new microeconomics in employment and inflation theory', in E.S. Phelps (ed.) *Microeconomic Foundation of Employment and Inflation Theory*. New York: W. W. Norton.

Phelps, Edmund S., and John B. Taylor (1977) 'Stabilizing powers of monetary policy under rational expectations', *Journal of Political Economy* **85** (1), 163–90.

Phillips, A. W. (1958) 'The relation between unemployment and the rate of change of money wage rates in the United Kingdom, 1861–1957', *Economica* NS **25**(2), 283–99.

Poterba, James M., and Lawrence H. Summers (1986) 'The irrelevance of finite lives', unpublished typescript, MIT, Harvard and NBER, March.

Prescott, Edward C. (1986a) 'Theory ahead of business cycle measurement', in Karl Brunner and Allan H. Meltzer (eds) *Real Business Cycles, Real Exchange Rates and Actual Policies*. Carnegie–Rochester Conference Series on Public Policy, Vol. 25, Autumn. Amsterdam: North-Holland. Reprinted in *Federal Reserve Bank of Minneapolis Quarterly Review* **10** (4), Fall, 9–22.

——(1986b) 'Response to a skeptic', *Federal Reserve Bank of Minneapolis Quarterly Review* **10** (4), Fall, 28–33.

Ratchford, B. V. (1942) 'The burden of a domestic debt', *American Economic Review* **32** (3), 451–67.

Reder, Melvin W. (1982) 'Chicago economics: permanence and change', *Journal of Economic Literature* **20** (1), 1–38.

Ricardo, David (1821) *Principles of Political Economy and Taxation*, 3rd edn.

——(1951) 'Funding System', *The Works and Correspondence of David Ricardo* Vol. 5 (ed. Piero Sraffa). Cambridge: Cambridge University Press, 143–201.

Roberds, William (1986) 'Models of policy under stochastic replanning', *Federal Reserve Bank of Minneapolis Staff Report* no. 104, March.

Robertson, D.H. (1948) *Money*. London: James Nisbet; Cambridge: Cambridge University Press.

Robinson, Joan (1953–4) 'The production function and the theory of capital'. Reprinted in *Contributions to Modern Economics*. Oxford: Basil Blackwell, 1978.

Rogers, Colin (1984) 'A study in the foundations of monetary theory', Doctor of Commerce Thesis, University of South Africa.

Rogerson, Richard, and Randall Wright (1986) 'On the nature of unemployment in economies with efficient risk sharing', Rochester Center for Economic Research Working Paper no. 58, September.

Rothbard, Murray N. (1976) 'The Austrian theory of money', in Dolan (1976, pp. 160–84).

Samuelson, Paul A. (1955) *Economics*, 3rd edn. New York: McGraw-Hill.

——(1958) 'An exact consumption-loan model of interest with or without the social contrivance of money', *Journal of Political Economy* **56** (6), 467–82.

Samuelson, Paul A. and Robert M. Solow (1960) 'Analytical aspects of anti-inflation policy,' *American Economic Review* **50** (2), 177–94.

Sargent, Thomas J. (1973) 'Rational expectations, the real rate of interest and the natural rate of unemployment', *Brookings Papers on Economic Activity* no. 2, pp. 429–72.

——(1976a) 'A classical macroeconometric model for the United States', in Lucas and Sargent (1981, pp. 521–2). Reprinted from *Journal of Political Economy* **84** (2).

——(1976b) 'The observational equivalence of natural and unnatural rate theories of macroeconomics', in Lucas and Sargent (1981, pp. 553–62). Reprinted from *Journal of Political Economy* **84** (3).

——(1977) 'The demand for money during hyperinflations under rational expectations'. in Lucas and Sargent (1981, pp. 429–52). Reprinted from *International Economic Review* **18** (1).

——(1978) 'Estimation of dynamic labour demand schedules under rational expectations', in Lucas and Sargent (1981, pp. 463–500). Reprinted from *Journal of Political Economy* **86** (6).

——(1979) *Macroeconomic Theory*. New York: Academic Press.

——(1981) 'Interpreting economic time series', *Journal of Political Economy* **89** (2), 213–48.

——(1982) 'Beyond demand and supply curves in macroeconomics', *American Economic Review* **72** (2), 382–9.

——(1984) 'Autoregressions, expectations and advice', *American Economic Review* **74** (2), 408–15.

——(1986) *Rational Expectations and Inflation*. New York: Harper and Row.

Sargent, Thomas J., and Preston J. Miller (1984) 'A reply to Darby', *Federal Reserve Bank of Minneapolis Quarterly Review* **8** (2), Spring, 21–6.

Sargent, Thomas J., and Christopher A. Sims (1977) 'Business cycle modeling without pretending to have too much *a priori* economic theory', *New Methods in Business Cycle Research: Proceedings from a Conference*. Minneapolis, MN: Federal Reserve Bank of Minneapolis.

Sargent, Thomas, J., and Bruce D. Smith (1986) 'The irrelevance of government foreign exchange operations', unpublished paper, May.

Sargent, Thomas, J., and Neil Wallace (1973) 'Rational expectations and the dynamics of hyperinflation', in Lucas and Sargent (1981). Reprinted from *International Economic Review* **14** (2).

——and——(1975) "Rational expectations", the optimal monetary instrument and the optimal money supply rule', in Lucas and Sargent (1981, pp. 215–28). Reprinted from *Journal of Political Economy* **83** (2), 241–54.

——and——(1976) 'Rational expectations and the theory of economic policy', in Lucas and Sargent (1981, pp. 199–213). Reprinted from *Journal of Monetary Economics* **2** (2), 169–83.

——and——(1981) 'Some unpleasant monetarist arithmetic', *Federal Reserve Bank of Minneapolis Quarterly Review* **5** (3), Fall, 1–17. Reprinted in Sargent (1986, pp. 158–90).

——and——(1982) 'The real-bills doctrine versus the quantity theory: a reconsideration', *Journal of Political Economy* **90** (6), 1212–36.

Schumpeter, Joseph A. (1954) *History of Economic Analysis*. London: Allen & Unwin.

Schwert, G. William (1979) 'Tests of causality: the message in the innovations', in Karl Brunner and Allan H. Meltzer (eds) *Three Aspects of Policy Making: Knowledge, Data and Institutions*. Carnegie–Rochester Conference Series on Public Policy, Vol. 10. Amsterdam: North-Holland, 55–96.

Seater, John J. (1985) 'Does government debt matter? A review', *Journal of Monetary Economics* **16** (1), 121–32.

Shand, Alexander H. (1984) *The Capitalist Alternative: An Introduction to Neo-Austrian Economics*. Brighton, Sussex: Wheatsheaf Books.

Sheffrin, Steven M. (1983) *Rational Expectations*. Cambridge: Cambridge University Press.

Sidrauski, M. (1967) 'Rational choice and patterns of growth in a monetary economy', *American Economic Review* **57** (2), 534–44.

Simon, Herbert A. (1953) 'Causal ordering and identifiability', in *Models of Man*. New York: Wiley, 1957, chapter 1.

Simons, Henry C. (1936) 'Rules versus authorities in monetary policy', *Journal of Political Economy* **44** (1), 1–30.

Sims, Christopher A. (1972) 'Money, income and causality', in Lucas and Sargent (1981, pp. 387–403). Reprinted from *American Economic Review* **62** (4), 540–52.

——(1977) 'Exogeneity and causal ordering in macroeconomic models', *New Methods in Business Cycle Research: Proceedings from a Conference*. Minneapolis, MN: Federal Reserve Bank of Minneapolis.

——(1979) 'Comment on Zellner', in Karl Brunner and Allan H. Meltzer (eds) *Three Aspects of Policy Making: Knowledge, Data and Institutions*. Carnegie–Rochester Conference Series on Public Policy, Vol. 10. Amsterdam: North-Holland, 104–8.

——(1980a) 'Macroeconomic and reality', *Econometrica* **48** (1), 1–48.

——(1980b) 'Comparison of interwar and postwar business cycles: monetarism reconsidered', *American Economic Review* **70** (1), 250–9.

——(1982) 'Policy analysis with econometric models', *Brookings Papers on Economic Activity* (1), 107–152.

——(1986a) 'A rational expectations framework for short run policy analysis', Center for Economic Research, in William A. Barnett and Kenneth J. Singleton (eds) *New Approaches to Monetary Economics: Proceedings of the Second International Symposium in Economic Theory and Econometrics*. Cambridge: Cambridge University Press, 293–310.

——(1986b) 'Are forecasting models usable for policy analysis?', *Federal Reserve Bank of Minneapolis Quarterly Review* **10** (1), Winter, 2–15.

Sinclair, P J N. (1983) *The Foundations of Macroeconomic and Monetary Theory.* Oxford: Oxford University Press.

Small, David A. (1979) 'Unanticipated money growth and unemployment in the United States: Comment', *American Economic Review* 69 (4), 996–1003

Smith, Bruce D., and Thomas J. Sargent (1987) 'Irrelevance of open-market operations in some economies with government currency being dominated in rate of return', *American Economic Review* 77 (1), 78–92.

Smithin, John Nicholas (1985) 'The definition of involuntary unemployment in Keynes' *General Theory*: a note', *History of Political Economy* 17 (2), 219–22.

Solow, Robert M. (1957) 'Technical change and the aggregate production function', *Review of Economics and Statistics* 39 (3), 312–20.

Stein, Jerome (ed.) (1976) *Monetarism.* Amsterdam: North-Holland.

Stiglitz, Joseph E. (1969) 'A re-examination of the Modigliani–Miller theorem', *American Economic Review* 59 (4), 748–93.

Stulz, René M., and Walter Wasserfallen (1985) 'Macroeconomic time-series, business cycles, and macroeconomic policies', in Karl Brunner and Allan H. Meltzer (eds) *Understanding Monetary Regimes.* Carnegie–Rochester Conference Series on Public Policy, Vol. 22, Spring. Amsterdam: North-Holland, 9–54.

Summers, Lawrence H. (1986) 'Some skeptical observations on real business cycle theory', *Federal Reserve Bank of Minneapolis Quarterly Review* 10 (4), Fall, 23–7.

Taylor, John B. (1975) 'Monetary policy during a transition to rational expectations', *Journal of Political Economy* 83 (6), 1009–21.

——(1979) 'Staggered wage setting in a macro model', *American Economic Review* 69 (2), 108–13.

——(1983) 'Rational expectations models in macroeconomics', National Bureau of Economic Research Working Paper no. 1224.

Theil, Henri (1971) *Principles of Econometrics.* New York: Wiley.

Tobin, James (1961) 'Money, capital and other stores of value', *American Economic Review* 59 (4), 26–37.

——(1963) 'Commercial banks as creations of "money"', in Deane Carson (ed.) *Banking and Monetary Studies.* Homewood, Il. Irwin, 408–19.

——(1965) 'Money and economic growth', *Econometrica* 33 (4), 671–84.

——(1969) 'A general equilibrium approach to monetary theory', *Journal of Money, Credit and Banking* 1 (1), 15–29.

——(1980) *Asset Accumulation and Economic Activity.* Oxford: Basil Blackwell.

——(1981) 'The monetarist counter-revolution today – an appraisal', *Economic Journal* 91 (361), 29–42.

Turner, Thomas H., and Charles H. Whiteman (1981) 'Econometric policy evaluation under rational expectations', *Federal Reserve Bank of Minneapolis Quarterly Review* 5, Spring/Summer, 6–15.

Valavanis, S. (1955) 'A denial of Patinkin's contradiction', *Kyklos* 8, 351–68.

Vickrey, William S. (1964) *Metastatics and Microeconomics.* New York: Harcourt, Brace and World.

Wallace, Neil (1977) 'On simplifying the theory of money', *Federal Reserve Bank of Minneapolis Research Department Staff Report* no. 22, June.

——(1980) 'The overlapping generations model of fiat money', in Kareken and Wallace (1980).

——(1981) 'A Modigliani–Miller theorem for open-market operations', *American Economic Review* **71** (3), 267–74.

——(1983) 'A legal restrictions theory of the demand for "money" and the role of monetary policy', *Federal Reserve Bank of Minneapolis Quarterly Review* **7** (1), Winter 1–7.

——(1985) 'Ricardian equivalence and money dominated in rate of return: are they mutually consistent generally?', *Federal Reserve Bank of Minneapolis Research Department Staff Report* no. 99. May.

Wallis, Kenneth (1980) *Topics in Applied Econometrics,* 2nd edn. Minneapolis, MN: University of Minnesota Press.

Walsh, Carl E. (1987) ' "Real" business cycles', *Federal Reserve Bank of San Francisco Weekly Letter*, 30 January.

Webb, Stephen B. (1985) 'Government debt and inflationary expectations as determinants of the money supply in Germany: 1919–23, *Journal of Money, Credit and Banking* **17** (4, part I), 479–92.

Weintraub E. Roy (1983) 'On the existence of a competitive equilibrium: 1930–1954', *Journal of Economic Literature* **21** (1), 1–39.

White, Lawrence H. (1984) 'Competitive payments systems and the unit of account', *American Economic Review* **74** (4), 699–712.

Wold, Herman (1954) 'Causality and econometrics', *Econometrica* **22** (2). 162–77.

——(1956) 'Causal inference from observational data: a review of ends and means', *Journal of the Royal Statistical Society*, Series A **119** (1), 28–50.

——(1960) 'A generalization of causal chain models', *Econometrica* **28** (4), 443–63.

Yellen, Janet L. (1984) 'Efficiency wage models of unemployment', *American Economic Review* **74** (2), 200–5.

Zarnowitz, Victor (1985) 'Recent work on business cycles in historical perspective', *Journal of Economic Literature* **23** (2), 523–80.

Index